ROME AND CHINA

OXFORD STUDIES IN EARLY EMPIRES

Series Editors
Nicola Di Cosmo, Mark Edward Lewis, and Walter Scheidel

The Dynamics of Ancient Empires: State Power from Assyria to Byzantium
Edited by Ian Morris and Walter Scheidel

Rome and China: Comparative Perspectives on Ancient World Empires
Edited by Walter Scheidel

Rome and China

*Comparative Perspectives on
Ancient World Empires*

Edited by
Walter Scheidel

OXFORD
UNIVERSITY PRESS

OXFORD
UNIVERSITY PRESS

Oxford University Press, Inc., publishes works that further
Oxford University's objective of excellence
in research, scholarship, and education.

Oxford   New York
Auckland   Cape Town   Dar es Salaam   Hong Kong   Karachi
Kuala Lumpur   Madrid   Melbourne   Mexico City   Nairobi
New Delhi   Shanghai   Taipei   Toronto

With offices in
Argentina   Austria   Brazil   Chile   Czech Republic   France   Greece
Guatemala   Hungary   Italy   Japan   Poland   Portugal   Singapore
South Korea   Switzerland   Thailand   Turkey   Ukraine   Vietnam

Copyright © 2009 by Oxford University Press, Inc.

Published by Oxford University Press, Inc.
198 Madison Avenue, New York, New York 10016

www.oup.com

First issued as an Oxford University Press paperback, 2010

Oxford is a registered trademark of Oxford University Press

Library of Congress Cataloging-in-Publication Data
Rome and China : comparative perspectives on ancient world empires /
edited by Walter Scheidel.
p.   cm.—(Oxford studies in early empires)
Includes bibliographical references and index.
ISBN 978-0-19-975835-7
1. History, Ancient—Historiography.   2. History—Methodology.   3. Rome—History—
Republic, 265–30 B.C.   4. Rome—History—Empire, 30 B.C.–284 A.D.   5. China—History—
Han dynasty, 202 B.C.–220 A.D.   6. Imperialism—History   I. Scheidel, Walter, 1966–
D56.R65 2009
931'.04—dc22   2008020445

Printed in the United States of America
on acid-free paper

Acknowledgments

F IVE of the seven chapters in this volume grew out of contributions to the international conference "Institutions of Empire: Comparative Perspectives on Ancient Chinese and Mediterranean History" that was held at Stanford University on May 13–14, 2005, under the auspices of the "Stanford Ancient Chinese and Mediterranean Empires Comparative History Project." It is a great pleasure to thank our generous Stanford sponsors, above all the Social Science History Institute and its director, Steve Haber, as well as the Department of Classics and the Freeman Spogli Institute for International Studies. I would also like to acknowledge the support of my co-organizers Mark Lewis and Joe Manning. Lai Ming-Chiu, Luuk de Ligt, Joe Manning, David Schaberg, Robin Yates, and Zhao Dingxin presented papers that are not included in this collection but greatly enriched our discussion. Finally, thanks are due to Stefan Vranka of Oxford University Press for his interest in this project, to Brian Hurley for his assistance, and to Gwen Colvin for her work on this volume.

Contents

Contributors

PETER FIBIGER BANG is Associate Professor of History at the University of Copenhagen. His research focuses on the comparative economic history and political economy of early empires. He is the author of *Roman Bazaar: A Comparative Study of Trade and Markets in a Tributary Empire* (2008) and is working on a comparative study of the Roman state and patrimonial government. He has also published a number of articles on the comparative history of early empires and is the coeditor of the forthcoming *Empires in Contention* (with Chris Bayly) and *The Oxford Handbook of the Ancient State* (with Walter Scheidel). He chairs the management committee of the European research network "Tributary Empires Compared" that coordinates comparative study of the Roman, Mughal, and Ottoman empires.

MARIA H. DETTENHOFER is Professor of Ancient History at the University of Munich. Her research focuses on Roman political and court history, gender, and the comparative history of Rome and Han China. She is the author of *Perdita Iuventus: Zwischen den Generationen von Caesar und Augustus* (1992) and *Herrschaft und Widerstand im augusteischen Principat: Die Konkurrenz zwischen res publica und domus Augusta* (2000) and the editor of *Reine Männersache: Frauen in Männerdomänen der antiken Welt* (1994).

MARK EDWARD LEWIS is Kwoh-Ting Li Professor in Chinese Culture at Stanford University. He specializes in the history of ancient China and is the author of *Sanctioned Violence in Early China* (1990), *Writing and Authority in Early China* (1999), *The Construction of Space in Early China* (2006), and *The Flood Myths of Early China* (2006). He has recently completed a series of three books on the history of early Chinese empires, *The Early Chinese Empires: Qin and Han* (2007), *Between Empires: The Northern and Southern Dynasties* (in press), and a forthcoming sequel on the Tang period.

NATHAN ROSENSTEIN is Professor of History at Ohio State University. He specializes in Roman military, political, and social history, and is the author of *Imperatores Victi: Military Defeat and Aristocratic Competition in the Middle and*

Late Republic (1990) and *Rome at War: Farms, Families, and Death in the Middle Republic* (2004), and coeditor of *War and Society in the Ancient and Medieval Worlds* (1999, with Kurt Raaflaub) and *A Companion to the Roman Republic* (2006, with Robert Morstein-Marx).

WALTER SCHEIDEL is Professor of Classics and, by courtesy, History at Stanford University. His research focuses on ancient social and economic history, premodern historical demography, and comparative and transdisciplinary world history. He has authored or (co)edited nine other books, including *Measuring Sex, Age, and Death in the Roman Empire* (1996), *Death on the Nile: Disease and the Demography of Roman Egypt* (2001), *Debating Roman Demography* (2001), *The Cambridge Economic History of the Greco-Roman World* (2007, with Ian Morris and Richard Saller), and *The Dynamics of Ancient Empires: State Power from Assyria to Byzantium* (2008, with Ian Morris). He is currently editing *The Cambridge Companion to the Roman Economy*, *The Oxford Handbook of Roman Studies* (with Alessandro Barchiesi), and *The Oxford Handbook of the Ancient State* (with Peter Bang), and working on monographs on ancient empires and ancient demography.

KAREN TURNER is the Rev. John Brooks Chair in the Humanities and Professor of History at the College of the Holy Cross. Her work focuses on comparative law, Chinese legal history, Vietnamese history, law and human rights in Asia, and women and war. Her publications include *Even the Women Must Fight: Memories of War from North Vietnam* (1998) and *The Limits of the Rule of Law in China* (2000), as well as numerous articles on comparative legal history, women and war, and women veterans in Vietnam. She produced and directed the documentary film *Hidden Warriors: Voices from the Ho Chi Minh Trail* and is currently working on a book on the origins of law in China.

Chronology

618–907 C.E.	Tang Dynasty
907–960 C.E.	Five Kingdoms Period
960–1276 C.E.	Song Dynasty
960–1126 C.E.	Northern Song Period
1127–1276 C.E.	Southern Song Period
1271–1368 C.E.	Yuan Dynasty (Mongols)
1368–1644 C.E.	Ming Dynasty
1644–1911 C.E.	Qing Dynasty (Manchu)

ROME

753 B.C.E.	Foundation of Rome (conventional date)
753–510 B.C.E.	Roman regal period (conventional dates)
c.650–600 B.C.E.	Emergence of Latin city-state culture
509–27 B.C.E.	Roman Republic (conventional dates)
396 B.C.E.	Conquest of Veii (conventional date)
338 B.C.E.	Full control over Latium
326–272 B.C.E.	Wars of conquest in peninsular Italy
264–146 B.C.E.	Wars against Carthage
215–168 B.C.E.	Wars against Macedon
192–188 B.C.E.	War against the Seleucid Empire
206–133 B.C.E.	Conquest of Iberian Peninsula
133–30 B.C.E.	Period of civil wars
91–89 B.C.E.	Social War against Italian allies
88–64 C.E.	Wars against Pontus and Armenia
58–51 B.C.E.	Conquest of Gaul
48–44 B.C.E.	Dictatorship of Julius Caesar
43–32 B.C.E.	Second Triumvirate
27 B.C.E.	Formal restoration of the Republic
27 B.C.E.–235 C.E.	Principate (early imperial monarchy)
27 B.C.E.–14 C.E.	Reign of Augustus
235–284 C.E.	Period of the Soldier Emperors
284–305 C.E.	Reign of Diocletian
284–602/641 C.E.	Later Roman Empire
306–337 C.E.	Reign of Constantine
313 C.E.	Formal toleration and beginning of state support for Christianity
325 C.E.	Council of Nicaea
330 C.E.	Establishment of Constantinople
391 C.E.	Ban of pagan temples and sacrifices
395 C.E.	Final separation of the eastern and western halves of the empire

410 c.e.	Sack of Rome by the Goths
476/480 c.e.	Termination of the Western Roman Empire
527–565 c.e.	Reign of Justinian
534–554 c.e.	East Roman wars of reconquest in the western Mediterranean
602–628 c.e.	War against the Sasanid Empire (Persia)
634–718 c.e.	Arab invasions
800 c.e.	Charlemagne crowned Roman Emperor
962 c.e.	Otto I crowned Roman Emperor
1204 c.e.	Crusader conquest of Constantinople
1453 c.e.	Turkish conquest of Constantinople
1806 c.e.	Dissolution of the Holy Roman Empire of German Nation
1870 c.e.	End of the Papal State

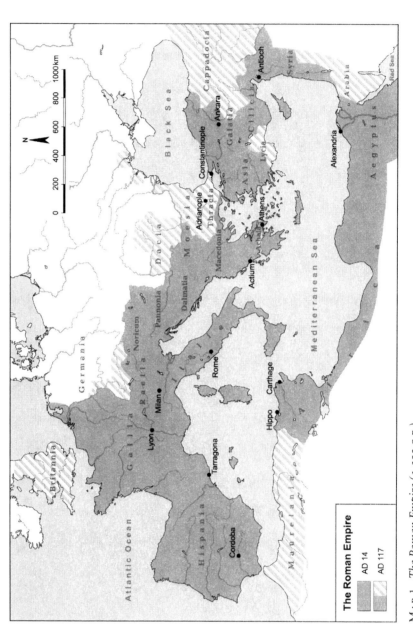

MAP 1. *The Roman Empire (c. 200 C.E.)*

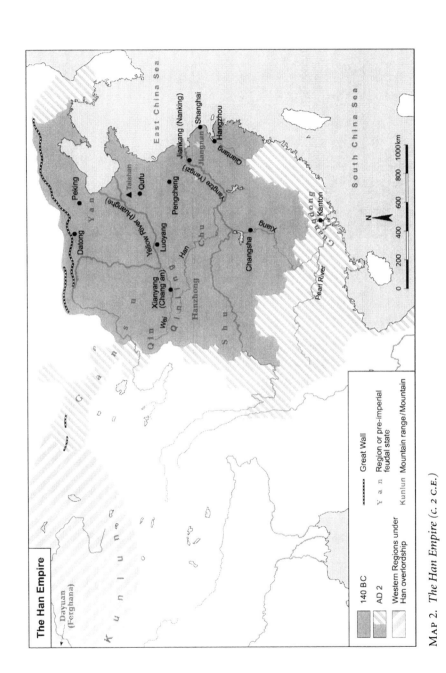

MAP 2. *The Han Empire* (*c. 2 C.E.*)

The Han Empire

140 BC

AD 2

Western Regions under Han overlordship

----- Great Wall

Y a n   Region or pre-imperial feudal state

Kunlun   Mountain range/Mountain

Dayuan (Ferghana)

Kunlun

Gansu

Qin   Wei   Xianyang (Chang'an)   Qinling   Hanzhong   Shu

Datong   Yellow River (Huanghe)   Luoyang   Han   Chu

Peking   Yan   Taishan   Qufu   Pengcheng

Jiankang (Nanking)   Shanghai   Jiangnan   Hangzhou   Qiantang

Yangtze (Yangzi)

Xiang   Changsha

Lingnan   Kanton   Pearl River

East China Sea

South China Sea

N

0   200   400   600   800   1000km

ROME AND CHINA

Introduction

Walter Scheidel

T HE "History of the Later Han Dynasty" reports the customs of Da Qin, or "Greater China," a distant realm near the western ends of the earth. Its inhabitants were tall and shaved their heads, wore embroidered clothes, and planted silkworm mulberry trees. Their ruler occupied five palaces whose columns were made of crystal glass. Wary of natural disasters that would require him to step down and be replaced by someone else, he was known to honor this convention without complaint. That these features bear no discernible resemblance to the Roman Empire as we know it may well have something to do with the fact that access to this remote place was inconveniently blocked by "many lions and ferocious tigers which intercept and harm travelers: if the party does not include over a hundred men furnished with arms, they are invariably devoured."[1] Roman observers faced a similar predicament: for them, the easternmost reaches of Asia were "not easy of access; few men come from there, and seldom." This made it difficult to visit the Seres or "Silk-People," atheists who lived for more than two hundred years, occupied themselves with scraping silk from trees, were fierce and warlike as well as gentle and peaceful, sported blue eyes and flaxen hair, and never talked to strangers.[2]

---

1. *Hou Hanshu* 88d, translated by Leslie and Gardiner 1996: 47–52. (The work itself dates from the fifth century C.E. but processes information from the first three centuries C.E.) The final observation seems to pertain to the route to Da Qin rather than the country itself: ibid. 52, n.89. For the probable meaning of the term "Da Qin," see ibid. 232. Leslie and Gardiner 1996 is now the most comprehensive collection and detailed discussion of the relevant sources, superseding Hirth 1885.

2. Difficult access: *Circumnavigation of the Erythrean Sea* 64 (first century C.E.); atheists: Kelsos in Origenes, *Against Kelsos* 7.62–3 (second century C.E.); longevity: Strabo, *Geography* 15.37 (first century C.E.); silk trees: Pliny the Elder, *Natural History* 6.53 (first century C.E.; Pausanias, *Description of Greece* 6.26.6–9, from the second century C.E., is the earliest extant source to ascribe silk production to an animal source, a "silk insect"); fierce and warlike: Avienus, *Description of the World* 935 (fourth century C.E.); gentle and peaceful: Pliny 6.54; physical appearance (for which cf. Liebermann 1957) and silence: ibid. 6.88. For collections of relevant references, see esp. Coedès 1910; Dihle 1984; Leslie and Gardiner 1996: 121–27. Dihle 203–4 rightly stresses the topical nature of many of these alleged attributes. Faint traces of factual information about the Chinese state may not have become available in the west until the seventh century C.E.: see Theophylactus Simocatta, *Histories* 7.9.2–11, with Boodberg 1938: 223–43.

This was unfortunate: had communication been less arduous, contemporary observers could hardly have failed to notice numerous similarities between their two mighty empires. Indeed, conditions in the Han state would have seemed less remarkable to a Roman observer than the sheer scale and order of Kublai Khan's China were bound to appear to visitors from medieval Europe such as Marco Polo and their audience.[3] Under even more auspicious circumstances, centuries of sustained contact might have allowed historians and political philosophers on both sides to track convergent trends over time: shifts from city-states to territorial polities and from military mass mobilization for interstate warfare to professional armies for border control; the growth of a protobureaucratic civil service accompanied by functional differentiation of power; formal dichotomies in provincial organization eclipsed by centralization of governmental control; the settlement and military use of peripheral groups in frontier zones; massive expansion of the money supply through standardized state-controlled minting; state intervention in manufacturing and trade; census registration and formal status ranking of the general population; codification of law; the growth of markets in land and the gradual concentration of wealth among elites; the transformation of smallholders into tenants, coupled with the growing strength of private patronage ties encroaching on state authority; unsuccessful attempts at land reform and eventual rural unrest; ideological unification through monumental construction, religious rituals, and elite education; the creation of a homogeneous elite culture and of corpora of classics; the emergence of court-centered historiography; ideologies of normative empire sustained by transcendent powers; and, later on, religious change leading to the formation of autonomous church systems and a philosophical and religious shift in emphasis from community values to ethical conduct and individual salvation. They might also have pondered the significance of conspicuous differences, such as the Republican background of the Roman state; the relative weight of local landowners and salaried officials in imperial government; the scale and functions of slave labor; the degree of autonomy of military power; the other party's lack of a close equivalent to Rome's civil law tradition or its emperor cult and to China's dynastic stability or its Confucian-Legalist philosophy that underpinned state authority and legitimacy.

But distances were too great to permit these kinds of comparisons: the overland route from Chang'an to the Mediterranean coast wound its way across 4,500 miles (7,000 km) of steppe and mountains while even the most direct sea route from Egypt to northern Vietnam measures almost 6,500 nautical miles (12,000 km). For each side, empirical knowledge of its counterpart remained confined to the goods that had been hauled across this forbidding expanse by

---

3. It does not matter here whether Marco Polo actually went to China: cf. Wood 1995 (no) vs. De Rachewiltz 1997, Jensen 1997, and Haw 2005 (yes): Ibn Battuta was also impressed.

intrepid intermediaries: silk, jade, and iron objects from China, linen, glass, and gypsum from the Mediterranean.[4]

Modern students of ancient history have no such excuse. While linguistic requirements and academic conventions continue to impede cross-cultural research, a vast amount of readily accessible information invites a comparative approach.[5] Yet even today, scholarly interest in contact and exchange, in the objects and mechanisms of the transcontinental luxury trade, and in the concurrent transmission of supernatural beliefs and technical skills dramatically outweighs the amount of attention paid to the potential benefits of comparative analysis. The growing popularity of "Silk Road Studies" is emblematic of this imbalance, which, for all its persistence, has always been hard to justify.

It is hard to justify because only comparisons with other civilizations make it possible to distinguish common features from culturally specific or unique characteristics and developments, help us identify variables that were critical to particular historical outcomes, and allow us to assess the nature of any given ancient state or society within the wider context of premodern world history. Comparative history can take many forms. For instance, social scientists have distinguished between "analytical comparisons" between equivalent units for the purpose of identifying independent variables that help explain common or contrasting patterns or occurrences, and "illustrative comparisons" between equivalent units and a theory or concept that evaluate evidence in relation to predictive theory rather than particular units in relation to one another. Others think in terms of "parallel demonstration of theory" (equivalent to "illustrative comparison") that aims for the empirical verification of theory, "contrast of contexts" that shows how the unique features of particular cases affect the unfolding of common social processes, and "macrocausal analysis" that employs comparisons in order to draw causal inferences about macrohistorical processes and structures and, ideally, to generate new theory. Others still advocate "universalizing," "encompassing," and "variation-finding" techniques.[6] Most actual work in this area has followed a "case-oriented" rather than a "variable-oriented" approach that views historical cases as configurations of characteristics that are to be related to particular outcomes.[7] Comparative history, by its very nature,

4. Adshead 2000: 37–9 gives a concise summary. Raschke 1978 is the most detailed study. For the pivotal role of India, see esp. Liu 1988 and Ray 2003.

5. In August 2007, Paul Goldin's "Ancient Chinese Civilization: Bibliography of Materials in Western Languages" (http://lucian.uchicago.edu/blogs/earlychina/research-and-resources/bibliographies/) contained about 6,700 entries. Compare the estimate by Cheng 2007: 300, n. 11 that at least 600 monographs and 13,000 articles on the Qin and Han periods have been published "in modern times," primarily in Chinese and Japanese. Meanwhile, published scholarship on Greco-Roman civilization has reached one million titles (cf. Scheidel 1997).

6. For these concepts, see Bonnell 1980; Skocpol and Somers 1980; Tilly 1984.

7. See esp. Ragin 1987: ch. 1–4 for the difference between "case-oriented" and "variable-oriented" comparisons. The latter typically seeks "to produce generalizations about relationships among variables" (ibid. 17), preferably through multivariate statistical analysis.

is not about "laws" but about the search for what has been called "robust processes," defined as combinations of characteristic initial conditions that produce a particular outcome. The main questions are which factors were crucial rather than incidental to observed developments and how different contexts could produce similar outcomes, or vice versa. In other words, comparative history uses case-based comparisons to investigate historical variation, to offer causal explanations of particular outcomes by identifying critical differences between similar situations and/or by identifying robust processes that occur in different settings.[8] These are the main goals of the following chapters.

Comparative research is necessarily sensitive to sample size. In principle, consideration of a large number of cases makes it easier to identify significant variables or conjunctures and to support generalizations. In the present case, however, the absolute scarcity of what world-systems theorists would call "corewide empires" imposes severe constraints on the range of comparative analysis.[9] Our focus on two very large and durable states that were created through the absorption of all or almost all state-level polities in their respective ecologically bounded macroregions ensures direct comparability in terms of observation as well as analysis: both proceed at the (very) macrosocial level of the emerging or mature near-monopolistic super-state.[10]

As I have already noted, this approach has seldom been adopted in modern scholarship. Moreover, although some explicitly comparative work on China and the Mediterranean in antiquity has appeared in recent years, it is very heavily weighted in favor of intellectual history. These studies tend to focus on the nature of ethical, historical, and scientific thought in ancient Greece and early China. The most prominent and prolific proponent of this line of inquiry has been Geoffrey Lloyd, who has published no fewer than six books on science, medicine, and ways of understanding the world in these two environments.[11] A small number of other scholars have produced comparative work in related areas.[12] Fritz-Heiner Mutschler has shown particular interest in the historiographical traditions of imperial Rome and Han China.[13]

8. See Goldstone 1991: 50–62.

9. For the concept of "world state" or "corewide empire," see Chase-Dunn and Hall 1997: 209–10. I will elaborate on this in Scheidel in progress b. These are ideal types that do not occur in pure form: other candidates include the Inca Empire and to a lesser degree the Achaemenid and Mughal empires. Parthia/Persia represented the principal exception to Roman dominance.

10. Ragin 1987: 7–9 (who distinguishes between "observational" and "explanatory" units) stresses the importance of clarity about the nature of units of analysis.

11. Lloyd 1996; Lloyd and Sivin 2002; Lloyd 2003, 2004, 2005, 2006.

12. Raphals 1992, 1994, 2002; Hall and Ames 1995, 1998; Lu 1998; Kuriyama 1999; Schaberg 1999; Shankman and Durrant 2000, 2002; Reding 2004; Sim 2007. On Greek and Chinese education and sociability, see now Wooyeal and Bell 2004; Zhou 2004; Bell 2006: 121–51. Cross-cultural work on the so-called "Axial Age" also belongs in this category: see, e.g., Eisenstadt, ed. 1986; Breuer 1994; Arnason, Eisenstadt, and Wittrock, eds. 2005; Bellah 2005.

13. Mutschler 1997, 2003, 2006, 2007. See also Konrad 1967 and the recent dissertation by Kim 2007 (forthcoming), as well as Stuurman 2008. Cf. furthermore Poo 2005, a study of attitudes toward foreigners in the ancient Near East and China.

At the same time, comparative studies of political, military, social, economic, or legal institutions have remained extremely rare.[14] The comparativist interests of Max Weber, Karl Wittfogel, Shmuel Eisenstadt, and Samuel Finer have had little impact on the research agenda of specialist historians in either field.[15] Recent historico-sociological studies of imperialism and social power that deal with ancient Greece and Rome comparatively and within a broader context do not normally pay much attention to conditions in China.[16] Concrete case studies by professional historians are almost impossible to find: Hsing I-Tien's unpublished dissertation on the political role of the Roman and Han military is the only book-length study that comes to mind. More general but shorter comparative surveys by Günther Lorenz, Christian Gizewski, and Samuel Adshead have recently been joined by a similar contribution by Maria Dettenhofer but have thus far generally failed to generate further debate.[17] It is emblematic of the ideational focus of existing research that the most ambitious project to date, a substantial collection of papers prepared for an international conference on "Conceiving the 'Empire': Ancient China and Rome—An Intercultural Comparison in Dialogue" held in Germany in 2005, deals exclusively with textual and artistic representations and reflections of large-scale state formation.[18] Victoria Tin-bor Hui's recent political science analysis of balancing mechanisms in Warring States China and early modern Europe provides an attractive model for the comparative study of Rome and China but eschews a synchronic approach.[19]

The present volume is the first in a series of works to engage in the comparative institutional study of ancient Rome and early China. A few years ago,

14. It is only fair to say that this has been true of ancient history in general. The study of ancient city-states and warfare has produced some ostensibly cross-cultural work that has, however, largely been limited to the juxtaposition of conventional "single-case" essays: see esp. Molho, Raaflaub, and Emlen, eds. 1991; Hansen, ed. 2000 and 2002; Raaflaub and Rosenstein, eds. 1999; and Raaflaub 2007 (the first volume of a new series on "The Ancient World: Comparative Histories;" cf. also Raaflaub and Talbert, eds. forthcoming). Genuinely comparative efforts are even rarer. Peter Bang's ongoing studies of the comparative history of the Roman and Mughal empires hold particularly great promise: see Bang 2002, 2003, forthcoming, and in progress; and cf. also De Ligt 2003. DeMarrais 2005 compares Romans and Inka. My own more modest efforts include Scheidel 2008a and 2008c. See also Bang and Scheidel, eds. forthcoming.

15. Weber 1980, 1991; Wittfogel 1957; Eisenstadt 1963; Finer 1997. The "Warring States Project" at the University of Massachusetts (http://www.umass.edu/wsp), while interested in comparative perspectives, primarily focuses on the Chinese literary tradition and is exclusively concerned with preimperial China. An explicitly comparativist online discussion list set up by this body in the late 1990s proved to be short-lived.

16. E.g., Doyle 1986; Mann 1986 (with a brief excursus on early China). Kautsky 1982 largely excludes post-Western Zhou China.

17. Hsing 1980; Lorenz 1990; Gizewski 1994; Adshead 2000: 4–21; Lieven 2000: 27–34; Adshead 2004: 20–9; Dettenhofer 2006. See also Motomura 1991. Graff in progress will compare Tang and Byzantine military history. More idiosyncratic forays into comparative history have likewise elicited little response: see Teggart 1939, on putative historical correlations between Chinese and Roman history mediated by steppe populations, and Quaritch Wales 1965, on the Roman and Angkorian empires.

18. Mutschler and Mittag 2005, to be published as Mutschler and Mittag, eds., forthcoming. The presenters at the "Third International Conference on Ancient History" at Fudan University in Shanghai in August 2005 showed only modest interest in comparative approaches: see Scheidel forthcoming c.

19. Hui 2005. Cf. now Eckstein 2007 and Hui 2007.

I launched an international collaborative research initiative called the "Stanford Ancient Chinese and Mediterranean Empires Comparative History Project." It has three principal objectives:

> To contribute to our understanding of state formation in the ancient Mediterranean (with particular emphasis on the Roman empire) and in China (with particular emphasis on the Warring States and Qin-Han periods). Two conferences have been devoted to this goal.[20]
>
> To study the character and causes of the long-term divergence between periodic imperial reunification in China and the absence of core-wide empire from western Eurasia following the fall of the Han and Roman empires. A separate workshop has focused on this phenomenon.[21]
>
> To ask whether ancient and/or early medieval state patterns of formation and associated developments in eastern and western Eurasia were instrumental in determining the nature of what has been called the "Great Divergence" of the last two centuries that witnessed a dramatic acceleration of technological progress and increases in consumption and well-being in the modern "West." This is the subject of a fourth meeting.[22]

The first of these issues calls for case studies of different aspects of state-society relations in these two historical environments. The chapters in this volume cannot be more than a modest first step in this direction. The opening chapter proposes a preliminary interpretative framework for more detailed work by highlighting the scale and limits of convergent trends in ancient imperial state formation. Nathan Rosenstein's contribution elaborates on a key element of this perspective in his comparative analysis of the relationship between interstate conflict and the development of state institutions. His focus on systemic forces is complemented by Karen Turner's study of internal coercion as embodied by penal law. Maria Dettenhofer considers the location of women and eunuchs in the emerging power centers of the Han and Roman imperial courts. The remaining chapters deal with the social and political contexts of economic issues. Peter Bang offers a wide-ranging survey of imperial styles of surplus extraction and consumption. Mark Lewis deals more specifically with traditions of euergetism and seeks to account for the different mechanisms of welfare provision in Han and Roman society. My own final chapter surveys the divergent evolution of coinage in these two systems and explores its underlying causes and economic consequences.

In their own ways, all of these contributions share the goal of identifying and explaining specific features with reference to particular contextual variables.

---

20. Stanford 2005, 2008a.
21. Stanford 2008b. For a brief preliminary survey, see Scheidel forthcoming a.
22. Stanford 2009. The term was coined by Pomeranz 2000.

Their comparative perspective heightens our appreciation of similarities as well as differences between the Roman and Chinese experiences that is crucial to this endeavor: without it, causal analysis lacks vital controls. At the same time, these contributions show how much work remains to be done. The sequel to this volume will return to some of these issues while introducing additional themes: the character and functioning of different levels of imperial rule from the monarchs to state officials and local elites; the accommodation and instrumentalization of religious beliefs by the state; the political and economic dimension of urbanism; and the relations between self-proclaimed "universal empires" and their peripheries.[23] In a forthcoming monograph on state-society relations in ancient Rome and China and their immediate successor states, I will develop a more synthetic account of many of these features by assessing the changing configurations of political, military, economic, and ideological power.[24] In addition, my colleague Ian Morris and I are planning to publish the results of two separate meetings that deal with divergent trends in eastern and western Eurasian state formation since late antiquity and their long-term consequences.[25] Early periods of history also occupy a prominent position in Morris's comparative study of social development in western Eurasia and China.[26]

Together with the present volume, these forthcoming studies are meant to contribute to the creation of a broader framework for the study of particular regions, periods, and processes that transcends the historical specifics of those regions, periods, and processes. They are also meant to link up to the efforts of other cross-culturally oriented collaborative initiatives such as the European research network "Tributary Empires Compared," which juxtaposes developments in the Roman, Mughal, and Ottoman empires, and the United Kingdom–based "Network on Ancient and Modern Imperialisms."[27] All these efforts are necessary for creating a basis for multicase comparisons: larger samples make it easier to design and test causal hypotheses and, in time, may even allow us to complement case-oriented comparisons with variable-oriented analysis of premodern historical societies. A generation ago, Moses Finley mused that "[i]deally, we should create a third discipline"—in addition to anthropology and sociology—"the comparative study of literate, ... pre-industrial, historical societies," and suggested "pre-Maoist China, pre-colonial India, medieval Europe, pre-revolutionary Russia,

23. Scheidel, ed. forthcoming, based on Stanford 2008b.
24. Scheidel in progress a. For this quartet of factors, see Mann 1986: 22–32. Dingxin Zhao's forthcoming study of the Warring States period and its aftermath adopts a similar approach.
25. Stanford 2008c. This part of the project is linked to a year-long Mellon-Sawyer Seminar on the "First Great Divergence" (2007/8) funded by the Andrew W. Mellon Foundation.
26. Morris forthcoming.
27. COST Action 36A "Tributary Empires Compared: Romans, Mughals and Ottomans in the Pre-Industrial World from Antiquity till the Transition to Modernity," 2005–2009, initiated by Peter Bang and funded by the European Union. See http://tec.saxo.ku.dk/home. "Network on Ancient and Modern Imperialisms," 2007–, organized by Phiroze Vasunia.

medieval Islam" as appropriate comparanda for students of the Greco-Roman world.[28] But what the (academic) world needs is not yet another discipline that would inevitably end up policing its very own boundaries: what we need instead is the specialists' willingness to overcome existing compartmentalization and contribute their expertise to collaborative efforts that address bigger questions. The study of ancient civilizations, all too often weighed down by the need to accumulate recondite yet indispensable technical knowledge, has much to gain and nothing to lose from broader perspectives.

---

28. Finley 1986: 119 (from "Anthropology and the Classics," the publication of his Jane Harrison Memorial Lecture of 1972).

From the "Great Convergence" to the "First Great Divergence"

Roman and Qin-Han State Formation and Its Aftermath

Walter Scheidel

1. TWIN EMPIRES?

Two thousand years ago, perhaps half of the entire human species had come under the control of just two powers, the Roman and Han empires, at opposite ends of Eurasia. Both entities were broadly similar in terms of size.[1] Both of them were run by god-like emperors residing in the largest cities the world had seen so far, were made up of some 1,500 to 2,000 administrative districts, and, at least at times, employed hundreds of thousands of soldiers. Both states laid claim to ruling the whole world, *orbis terrarum* and *tianxia*, while both encountered similar competition for surplus between central government and local elites and similar pressures generated by secondary state formation beyond their frontiers and subsequent "barbarian" infiltration. Both of them even ended in similar ways: one half, the original political core—the west in Europe, the north in China—was first weakened by warlordism and then taken over by "barbarian" successor states, whereas the other half was preserved by a traditionalist regime. It was only from the late sixth century C.E. onward that the two trajectories of state formation began to diverge, slowly at first but more dramatically over time, between the cyclical restoration of a China-wide empire in the East and the decline of empire and central government in the West, followed by the slow creation of a polycentric state system that proved resistant to any attempts to impose hegemony, let alone unification, and ultimately evolved into the now-familiar cluster of modern nation states. In terms

---

1. Both empires controlled approximately 4 million square kilometers of territory. The Han census of 2 C.E. recorded 59.6 million individuals. Lower census tallies of between 47.6 and 56.5 million during the second century C.E. are probably marred by higher levels of underregistration (Bielenstein 1987: 12). The Roman imperial population may have grown to around 65 to 75 million by the mid-second century C.E. (Scheidel 2007: 48), but this is just a rough estimate, and an even larger total cannot be ruled out. Recent guesses concerning the total number of humans in the first two centuries C.E. range from 170 to 330 million (Cohen 1995: 400).

of state size, state capacity, and state institutions, we observe a prolonged process of gradual convergence that lasted for many centuries but was eventually replaced by a process of increasing divergence that continued into the early twentieth century. I argue that this allows us to speak of a "Great Convergence" that spanned the entire first millennium B.C.E. and the first half of the first millennium C.E., until a "(First) Great Divergence" began to unfold from about the sixth century C.E. onward.[2]

2. ENVIRONMENT

As far as the ecological context is concerned, both imperial entities shared the fundamental requirement of being located within the temperate zone of Eurasia, which thanks to its climate, flora, and fauna had long favored the development of social complexity and large polities.[3] The two empires also had in common a division into two different ecological spheres: in the case of Rome, a Mediterranean core and a continental European northern periphery, and, in China, a loess and river plain core and a hotter and wetter southern periphery. In both cases, albeit well after the end of antiquity, the locus of development eventually shifted into these former peripheries. However, the environment also accounted for substantial differences, most notably the fact that the Roman Empire centered on a temperate sea core that was highly conducive to communication, the transfer of goods and people, and the projection of power, whereas China consists of river valleys that are separated by mountain ranges and, at least prior to the creation of ambitious canal systems from the sixth century C.E. onward, posed far greater physical obstacles to integration. Moreover, whereas the main western rivers such as the Rhône, Danube, and Nile converge upon the inner sea core, Chinese rivers all flow eastward, thereby reinforcing regional separation. In view of these differences, one might suspect that *ceteris paribus*, western Eurasia was more likely to end up politically united than its eastern counterpart. On the other hand, China is more compact (in terms of the ratio of surface area to border length) and self-contained, well shielded by mountains and sea on three sides, and open only to the arid Central Asian steppe. By contrast, the temperate ecumene in western Eurasia extends twice as far west-east from the Atlantic into eastern Iran and is endowed with a much more permeable frontier to the northeast that used to facilitate movement by agriculturalists and nomads alike. We must ask whether and to what extent these contrasting features help account for the fact that while the Chinese "core" (conservatively defined as the region controlled by the Qin Empire at the time of its maximum extension in 214 B.C.E.) was united for 936 of

---

2. I refer to this process as the "*First* Great Divergence" in order to distinguish it from the better-established (second) "Great Divergence," a moniker that Pomeranz 2000 applied to the technological and economic expansion of the "West" during the last two centuries.

3. Diamond 2005.

the past 2,220 years, or 42 percent of the time, the corresponding tally for the section of the western ecumene that was under Roman rule at the death of Augustus in 14 C.E. is perhaps three and a half centuries, or merely 18 percent of the past 1,998 years.[4] More importantly, for the past sixteen centuries, the latter score has been exactly zero. Only the Umayyad Empire ever managed to stretch all the way from the Atlantic to the Indus, and that only for some forty years.

3. PARALLELS

Both the Roman and Qin-Han empires were built on templates provided by antecedent states and expanded into a widening ecumene: in the West, from the river cultures of the Middle East into the Mediterranean and on to continental Europe, in the East from the Wei and middle Yellow River valleys into the Central Plain and then on to the south. In the East, the basic context had been created by the Shang-Western Zhou polities (*c.* 1600–771 B.C.E.) and their dominant elite culture and the spread of the Western Zhou garrison cities across the Central Plain region. In the Mediterranean, this role had been performed by the dissemination of Greek settlements across the Mediterranean littoral (from the eighth century B.C.E) and the cultural Hellenization of autonomous local elites.

Back in 1994, Christian Gizewski proposed a useful nine-phase parallel model of the development of the Qin-Han and the Roman states, which, in somewhat modified form, can be used to illustrate the striking degree of parallel movements at the most basic level of state formation.[5] The first stage (down to about 500 B.C.E.) witnessed the creation of polities at the western margins of a much wider ecumene, a positioning that favored a focus on military capability, in both Rome and Qin. The main difference was that whereas Qin was already tied into a wider state system, the feudal network of Western Zhou, Rome, farther removed from the "Great Powers" of the Levant, was autonomous and embedded only in regional city state clusters (Latins and Etruscans). At the second stage, in the fifth and into the fourth centuries B.C.E., both entities grew into autonomous middling powers and experienced conflict with comparable competitors: within central Italy in the case of Rome, and in the "land within the passes" (*Guanzhong*) in the case of Qin. Both polities continued to retain their independence because they were physically shielded from "Great Power" conflicts in more developed regions farther east. Making the most of their "marcher state advantage," this allowed them to accumulate military capabilities without encountering the superior absorptive capacity of more powerful states. The third phase resulted in hegemonic power over a large sector of the ecumene in the

---

4. For the first estimate, see Hui forthcoming. This supersedes her earlier calculations in Hui 2005: 257–8. Owing to frequent usurpations in the third and fourth centuries C.E., Roman unity is more difficult to measure.

5. Gizewski 1994, with my own revisions.

fourth and early third centuries B.C.E., all over Italy for Rome and expansion into Sichuan in the case of Qin. Once again, this growth occurred without triggering major conflict with the leading powers of their respective *koine* but nevertheless brought it closer, driven by Rome's encroachment on the Greeks in Italy and Qin pressure on the kingdom of Wei in China. Both Rome and Qin benefited from low protection costs thanks to strong natural borders, the sea and Alps in Italy and mountain ranges in Qin and Sichuan. Successful expansion strengthened Rome's aristocratic collective leadership and Qin's monarchy (this difference in regime type will be considered below). The fourth step brought hegemony over the entire core ecumene in a series of high-stakes wars, in the third through first centuries B.C.E. in Rome and in a more compressed format in the third century B.C.E. in China. In both cases, hegemony preceded direct rule, although the pro-tobureaucratization of Qin facilitated more rapid outright annexation than the much more limited administrative capabilities of the oligarchic regime in Rome. Also in both cases, large-scale conquest triggered violent adjustment processes: in the East, a shift from the "war-machine" state of Qin to the less overtly central-ized regime of the early Han, and in the West a more protracted transition that replaced the established oligarchy with a military monarchy. Owing to the more profound character of this latter shift, conflict in Rome was more sustained, but in both cases the result was the same: a monarchy with, at least at first, strong aristocratic participation.

The fifth stage, in the first two centuries C.E. in Rome and from the second century B.C.E. to the second century C.E. in Han, was characterized by slowing expansion and increasing internal homogenization. In both cases, we witness the strengthening of powerful local elites who cooperated with the state but also constrained its range of action. This process was interrupted in phase 6 by war-lordism and temporary fragmentation in the third century C.E., a crisis that was more readily contained by the professional military of the Roman Empire than by the warlords of Three Kingdoms China. The seventh phase of attempted res-toration was much more prolonged and at least temporarily successful in Rome than in the internally riven state of Jin but in both cases ended in barbarian conquest, from the early fourth century C.E. in northern China and from the early fifth century C.E. in the western Roman Empire. The subsequent phase 8 saw the already-mentioned division into rump states in the Roman East and the Chinese South and "barbarian" successor states closer to the northern frontiers. In both cases, conquerors increasingly merged with local elites, and transcendent religions that claimed autonomy from the state—Christianity and Buddhism—made considerable progress. Sixth century C.E. attempts at reunification were more successful in China than in the Mediterranean. However, it was only after-ward, in phase 9, that developments finally diverged sharply, between the Tang consolidation in the East and the near-destruction of the East Roman or "Byzan-tine" state by Persians and Arabs and the subsequent political fragmentation of both the Islamic and the Frankish successor states, a process that was particularly prolonged and intense in western Europe. These developments mark the onset of the "First Great Divergence" that led to the creation of the Song, Yuan, Ming, and Qing empires in China, culminating in the current People's Republic, and to the gradual entrenchment of state polycentrism in Europe.

4. CONVERGENCE

Convergent trends in state formation were not lastingly impeded by substantial initial differences in regime type and state organization. The most obvious difference between Rome and China lay in the increasing centralization of the Warring States period that created stronger state structures than anywhere in Europe prior to the modern period.[6] Put in the most general terms, the Warring States of China implemented parallel self-strengthening reforms designed to increase their military competitiveness vis-à-vis their rivals. In the fourth and third centuries B.C.E., the state of Qin went the farthest by breaking the power of hereditary nobles, reorganizing its entire territory into thirty-one uniform conscription districts (*xian*), creating a pathway grid across the country, ranking the entire population in eighteen grades and dividing it into groups of five and ten for collective surveillance and liability, instituting rewards for military prowess, imposing codified penal law, and standardizing currency, weights, and measures. These reforms, however imperfectly they may have been implemented in practice, went some way in creating a homogeneous territorial state, sought to extend state control across all levels of society, concentrated power in the hands of the king, raised both the power of the state and the autonomy of the central government to unprecedented levels, and reputedly enabled Qin to mobilize and deploy military and corvée work forces numbering in the hundreds of thousands. In forthcoming work, Dingxin Zhao argues that this development was ultimately a function of prolonged inconclusive warfare between fairly evenly matched competitors, an environment in which only intensification could produce decisive outcomes.[7] When the state of Qin finally absorbed its six rivals in the 230s and 220s B.C.E., the regime of the First Emperor attempted to impose and perpetuate this system across China. In the novel absence of the centripetal force of interstate competition, this endeavor triggered resistance that rapidly overthrew the Qin regime and led to a reassertion of regional forces that underwrote the establishment of the Han monarchy. It took the new dynasty at least half a century to curtail regional and aristocratic autonomy, a process that was aided by conflict with the Xiongnu, confirming the principle that war making precipitates state

---

6. Li 1977; Lewis 1990: 54–67; Kiser and Cai 2003. See also Nathan Rosenstein's discussion in chapter 2. For comparisons with Europe, see Hui 2005.
7. Zhao 2006 and forthcoming.

making. After the temporary displacement of the Han dynasty during the Wang Mang usurpation in the early first century C.E. and ensuing civil war, the clock was once again set back 200 years, restoring much power to regional cliques and magnates. In the end, the growing power of provincial gentry and command-ers-turned-warlords conspired to undermine and finally eliminate the central government in the late second and early third centuries C.E.[8]

In the last three centuries B.C.E., Rome accomplished conquests on the same scale as Qin that were not accompanied by comparable intensification of govern-ment. In both cases, however, successful expansion was made possible by mass conscription of peasants. In the fourth century B.C.E., when Rome faced com-petitors of comparable strength and military organization within the Italian pen-insula, it introduced a series of self-strengthening reforms that echoed many of Qin's reforms in the same period, albeit usually in a more muted fashion: the introduction of direct taxation to fund war making (*tributum*); the strengthen-ing of the peasantry by abolishing debt-bondage; the expansion of conscription across the entire citizenry; periodic registration of adult men; the creation of thirty-five conscription districts (*tribus*), functionally at least in some ways com-parable to the thirty-one *xian* of Qin; land grants to soldiers drawing on annexed territories; and political reform to accommodate social mobility at the elite level.[9] Beginning in 295 B.C.E., and certainly after 202 B.C.E, Rome did not normally face state-level competitors with matching mobilization potentials. This, and the con-sequent absence of prolonged inconclusive warfare against other states, obviated the need for farther-reaching domestic reforms promoting centralization and bureaucratization. In other words, the benefits of asymmetric warfare (against states that relied more on mercenaries in the eastern and southern Mediterra-nean and against less complex chiefdoms and tribes in the northern and western periphery) enabled Rome to succeed with less domestic restructuring than was required in the intensely competitive environment of Warring States China.[10]

Moreover, protobureaucratization was logically incompatible with the gov-ernmental arrangements of the Roman Republic, which was controlled by a small number of aristocratic lineages that relied on social capital, patronage rela-tionships, and the manipulation of ritual performances to maintain power, and more mundanely drew on their own friends, clients, slaves, and freedmen to ful-fill key administrative tasks.[11] Tightly regimented popular political participation

8. See chapters 1–5 in Twitchett and Loewe 1986, and Lewis 2007: 253–64.

9. E.g., Cornell 1995: chapters 12–15, as well as the reforms conventionally ascribed to "king Servius Tullius" discussed in his chapter 7.

10. For Rome's eastern competitors, see, e.g., Aperghis 2004: 189–205; Chaniotis 2005. In the second century B.C.E., the bulk of Roman military manpower was directed against "barbarians": Brunt 1987: 422–34; and for much of the first century B.C.E., war against other Romans or Italians required the largest commitments: ibid. 435–512. When Eckstein 2006 claims that Republican Rome found itself in an unusually competitive anarchic environment, he fails to appreciate the more severe nature of conflict in Warring States China.

11. Schulz 1997 and Eich 2005: 48–66 are the best analytical accounts.

provided a benign arbitration device equivalent to the services that in more conventionally organized states would have been furnished by a weak monarch. Financial management, which required a greater concentration of human capital, was largely farmed out to private contractors. In this context, the army was the only institution that attained a certain level of professionalization. This, in turn, laid the groundwork for the increasing autonomy of military power near the end of the Republic, which facilitated warlordism and the creation of a military monarchy.

In terms of Michael Mann's distinction of the four main sources of social power,[12] the oligarchic regime of the Roman conquest state was maintained as long as political, military, and ideological power were closely tied together and controlled by the same aristocratic collective. Once military power broke free from political and ideological constraints, the rule of the collective was replaced by warlords and monarchs, who came to rely on a fully professionalized army and managed political power through the traditional mechanisms of patronage and patrimonialism. The main difference to China is that in China, military power was mostly (though by no means always) successfully contained and for long periods even marginalized by political-ideological power. The near-perfect Han fusion of political and ideological power was a function of the centralizing reforms of the Warring States period and the subsequent adoption of a hybrid Confucian-Legalist belief system that reinforced state authority.[13] Except in the early city-state phase of the Roman polity, Roman regimes never benefited from a comparably close linkage of political and ideological power. Economic power was arguably less constrained in the West than in China, which allowed the Qin and Han states to aim for greater interference in economic affairs, an approach that the Roman state only belatedly adopted from the late third century C.E. onward.

Over time, both systems experienced what one might call a "normalization" of the degree of state control, in the sense of a regression to the mean, the mean being defined as the range of conditions observed in most premodern imperial states. In a manner of speaking, Warring States Qin and Republican Rome started out at opposite ends of the spectrum: Qin was unusually centralized and bureaucratized, whereas Rome was run by a collective and greatly depended on private administrative resources. These dramatic differences may have affected the differential pace of conquest but did not impact ultimate outcomes, that is, eventual domination of the entire ecumene. Over time, both political systems converged, a process that began around 200 B.C.E. in China and in the late first century B.C.E. in Rome. It is the mature Roman Empire of the fourth century

12. For the concept, see Mann 1986: 22–32. Cf. now chapters 6–9 in Hall and Schroeder, eds. 2006.
13. See now especially Zhao's work referred to above (n. 7). For legalism, see Fu 1996; on the legalist permeation of Han-period state Confucianism, see Lewis 2007.

c.e. that most resembles the Han Empire in institutional as well as practical terms.[14] Both empires were divided into around 100 provinces with separate civilian and military leadership that were in turn supervised by about a dozen inspectors ("vicars" and "shepherds," respectively); the central administration was organized around a number of ministries (the *praefectus praetorio, magister officiorum, praepositus sacri cubiculi*, and *magister militum* in Rome, the "Three Excellencies" and "Nine Ministers" in China); the "inner" court and its agents, including eunuchs, had gradually gained influence relative to formal state institutions, while the emperors became increasingly sequestered. Even child emperors managed by powerful regents, who had long been common in China but rare in Rome, eventually appeared in the later Roman Empire.

In the final analysis, the major differences in political and administrative organization between Rome and China can be explained by initial differences in regime type. In the case of Rome, collective aristocratic rule accounted for an early reluctance to annex, for the lack of bureaucracy not just during the Republic but also during the first three centuries of the monarchy, and for the continuing use of aristocrats as delegates of the ruler and as his military commanders for the same three-hundred-year period. In China, by contrast, centralization, the creation of territorial states, and the disempowerment of aristocrats facilitated rapid annexation and bureaucratic expansion. A second variable, the nature of interstate conflict, mediated political structure, as the shift to "asymmetric" conflict may have helped extend the shelf-life of Roman oligarchy, whereas prolonged inconclusive "symmetric" warfare in China rewarded centralization and concentration of power.[15] But this is not to say that oligarchic traditions continued to constrain Roman state formation indefinitely. As soon as an impetus for reform had been provided by the military and political crisis of the mid-third century c.e., Roman state institutions rapidly converged with those of the Han state: a strong numerical expansion of the bureaucracy, homogenization of registration and taxation, the separation of military and civilian administration, the creation of formal hierarchies and spheres of competence in administration, and the severing of traditional ties between the ruler and his court on the one hand and the capital and its hinterland on the other.[16]

The common notion that early imperial China was considerably more "bureaucratized" than the Roman Empire inflates actual differences. First of all, the number of senior positions was essentially the same in both states, a few hundred in

    14. Compare Bielenstein 1980 and chapters 7–8 in Twitchett and Loewe, eds. 1986 with Demandt 1989: 211–72 or Kelly 2004.
    15. In the case of Rome, the main counterfactual outcomes would have been a shift to monocracy in response to greater-than-historical interstate competition (a scenario made plausible by the well-attested tendency to prolong and expand individual commands in times of crisis) or state failure if oligarchic institutions had proven too resilient. Real-life analogies to the latter outcome are furnished by preimperial Chinese states that failed to curtail aristocratic power.
    16. See now esp. Eich 2005: 338–90.

each case. Second, even before the reforms in late antiquity did Roman governors draw on the services of thousands of seconded soldiers as well as their own slaves and freedmen while the *familia Caesaris*, the patrimonial staff of the emperors, must have contained thousands of slaves and ex-slaves. By 400 C.E., the Roman state employed over 30,000 civilian officials, compared to around four times as many in Western Han China.[17] The principal shift between the early and the later monarchical state in Rome was from the ad hoc use of soldiers and the intense patrimonialism of relying on slaves and ex-slaves to the use of a salaried civilian workforce. The most significant differences between Rome and China were retained at the city level. For one, Han cities did not feature self-governing city councils or elections. For another, a recently discovered provincial archive from the end of the Western Han period indicates that just as in later and better documented periods of Chinese history, even low-level government officials were recruited from outside the province they served in.[18] Thus, while many of the one hundred thousand-odd provincial administrators and clerks on the Han government payroll may well have come from a similar (local elite or "gentry") background as the more than one hundred thousand men who populated the city councils of the Roman Empire, the two groups operated in rather different social contexts, as leaders of their own communities in the latter case and as more detached state agents in the former. Moreover, Roman cities relied more heavily on public slaves than on salaried officials.[19] Only very late were Roman cities assigned an external *curator rei publicae* or *defensor civitatis*.[20] Even so, we may wonder if ultimate outcomes differed greatly: shielding of resources by local elites in the Roman Empire and rent seeking by imported Han officials would both have interfered with revenue collection on behalf of the state. It would be unwise to overestimate the meritocratic dimension of early Chinese officialdom: many Han state agents obtained office via recommendation, that is, through straightforward patronage, just as in Rome; others bought offices, as in the later Roman Empire.[21] In quantitative terms, instruction at the imperial academy was a fringe phenomenon, producing only a relatively small number of graduates each year, and even in Rome, where formal credentialing remained unknown, certain kinds of officials came to benefit from having studied law.[22]

---

17. Kelly 2004: 111 and 268, n. 9; Loewe 1986: 466.

18. See now Loewe 2004: 38–88, on the Yinwan documents from *c*.10 B.C.E.

19. Wei 2004. For Han city-level officials, see Bielenstein 1980: 99–104.

20. Langhammer 1973: 165–75.

21. Compare Bielenstein 1980: 132–42 to Saller 1982. By the late imperial period, the Roman state had created elite echelons that depended to a large degree on office holding, while the Han state, notwithstanding pretensions to meritocracy, also favored recruitment of the propertied for governmental service. This suggests that the distinction between Rome as an empire run by an elite of property owners and China as an empire of office holders (Wood 2003: 26–32) is overdrawn.

22. Bielenstein 1980: 138–41; Ausbüttel 1998: 178–9. Although statutes found in an early Han tomb at Zhangjiashan (Hubei province) indicate that entry examinations appear to have been more widespread than one might previously have thought (*Zhangjiashan* 2001: 46–7, 203–4), it is nevertheless likely that qualified clerks remained scarce. (I owe this reference to Enno Giele.)

In the end, even the vaunted separation of military and civilian administration in China and the containment of military power by political-ideological power failed quite spectacularly. It is true that in Rome, military power had long been more autonomous than in China; yet by the late second century c.e., China was rapidly catching up with and soon surpassing corrosive Roman habits and likewise began to suffer at the hands of military pretenders and usurpers. In both cases, moreover, we observe infiltration by "barbarian" settlers, Xiongnu, Xianbei, and Qian in China, Goths, Burgundians, and others in the West, groups that nominally accepted imperial rule but increasingly exercised political autonomy.[23] In both cases, the introduction of this element perturbed the extractive-coercive equilibrium between local elites and the central government, eroded the state's monopoly on the sale of protection, interfered with revenue collection, and ultimately prompted bargains between local elites and outsiders that undermined central government. In the ensuing successor states in both East and West, foreign conquerors and indigenes were initially kept apart and subject to separate registration procedures, the former as warriors, the latter as producers of extractable surplus. In both cases, these barriers eroded over time, and we witness a synthesis of foreign and local elites.[24]

5. DIVERGENCE

Trajectories of state formation signally diverged from the sixth century c.e. onward.[25] At that time, Justinian's attempted reunification of the original Roman Empire was only partially successful, and the following century witnessed the diminution of the East Roman state at the hands of Persians, Avars, and most importantly Arabs. Hamstrung by the autonomy of their regional armies, the Arab conquerors were unable to establish a durable ecumenical empire.[26] After the failure of Charlemagne's imperial revival, political fragmentation throughout western Eurasia intensified during the late first millennium c.e., most notably in Christian Europe, where states lost the ability to control and tax populations and sovereignty de facto came to be shared among monarchs, lords, local strongmen, semi-independent towns, and clergy. The (re-)creation of centralized states was a drawn-out process that primarily unfolded during the first half of the second millennium c.e. but in some cases took even longer, resulting in a cluster of polities in which balancing mechanisms prevented the creation of a core-wide empire.[27] Instead, intense interstate competition,

23. De Crespigny 1984; Wolfram 1997; Heather 2006; Goffart 2006.
24. Most concisely, Wickham 2001; Graff 2002: chapters 3 and 5.
25. For more detailed discussion, see Scheidel forthcoming b.
26. Kennedy 2001: chapters 1–3.
27. For this process, see esp. Tilly 1992; Spruyt 1994; Ertman 1997. See Hui 2005 for an innovative comparative analysis of balancing in early modern Europe and its eventual failure in Warring States China.

internal social and intellectual upheavals, the creation of new kinds of maritime empire, and (eventually) technological progress gave rise to the modern nation state in the eighteenth (or perhaps only nineteenth) century. In sixth century C.E. China, by contrast, imperial reunification restored the bureaucratic state that largely succeeded, albeit with substantial interruptions, in maintaining a core-wide empire under Chinese or foreign leadership until 1911 and, in effect, up to the present day.

Why did this happen? In principle, a whole variety of factors may have been relevant. For instance, the larger size of the western ecumene was more conducive to fragmentation: China lacked state-level competitors of the caliber of the Persians and Arabs. Climatic change in the second half of the first millennium C.E. may have benefited northern China more than Europe. The Sino-"barbarian" successor states were more adept at containing movement in the steppe, whereas European regimes were vulnerable to Avars, Slavs, Bulgarians, Magyars, and Vikings. China was spared the two hundred years of recurrent plague that ravaged the early medieval West.[28] The contribution of ideological power also requires consideration. The Sinological tradition habitually emphasized the long-term impact of Confucian elite traditions (or rather of the Confucian-Legalist version that had been created in the Western Han period), which favored the notion of a well-ordered unified state managed by scholarly civilian bureaucrats. However, the significance of ideational forces needs to be evaluated in a comparative context: in this case, we must give due weight to the comparative lack of substantive political impact of ideological commitments to Christian unity in the post-Roman West, of attempts to harness the notion of "eternal Rome" for empire building (as in the case of Charlemagne and the Ottonians), and of the Islamic ideal of the unity of the *umma*. Moreover, the post-Han period in China was characterized by increased competition from rival belief systems, such as Daoism and Buddhism. The temporary efflorescence of Buddhist monasteries in the Northern Wei period even suggests a measure of convergence between developments in early medieval China and late Roman and post-Roman Europe, where the clerical establishment accumulated vast resources, eclipsed the state in its access to human capital, and eventually came to share in its sovereignty.[29] Nevertheless, it is true that Confucian scholars provided a suitable instrument of state management, whereas the absence of an equivalent group in the Christian West may have made it more difficult for post-Roman regimes to maintain or restore a "strong" state: the intrinsically autonomous and schismatically riven Christian churches that had evolved outside and in some sense in opposition to the imperial state could not offer comparable services. Abiding frictions between

28. For discussion, see Adshead 2000: 58–64. For the putative impact of the plague, see now Little 2007 and more sweepingly Rosen 2007.
29. On the early Buddhist expansion, see Demiéville 1986: 846–72.

political and ideological power in the post-Roman world may have impeded the strengthening of state capacity and thus successful empire building.

However, while state capabilities would necessarily have been influenced by these and other contextual features, causal analysis ought to focus more narrowly on the ways in which differences in state-society relations shaped trends in overall state formation. Chris Wickham has proposed an explanatory model of proximate causation for large parts of postancient western Eurasia that can also be used to shed light on contrasting developments in East Asia.[30] In brief, the "strong" Roman state (which counted and taxed a demilitarized population in order to support a large standing army) was succeeded in part by states that maintained systems of taxation and salaried military forces (the East Roman and Arab states) and in part by weak or weakening states whose rulers gradually lost the ability to count and tax their subjects (the Germanic successor states in the west), while in some marginal areas, state institutions collapsed altogether (such as in Britain). In "strong" states with registration, taxation, and centrally controlled military forces, rulers enjoyed greater autonomy from elite interests, and elites depended to a significant degree on the state (for offices, salaries, and other perquisites) to maintain their status. In "weak" states, elites relied more on the resources they themselves controlled and enjoyed greater autonomy from rulers. In the absence of centralized tax collection and coercive capabilities, the power of rulers largely depended on elite cooperation secured through bargaining processes. From the perspective of the general population, local elites rather than state rulers and their agents dominated, and feudal relationships were a likely outcome. At the same time, in the absence of the kind of transregional integration that is characteristic of "strong" states, elites tended to be less disproportionately wealthy. These conditions had profound consequences for economic performance, eroding interregional exchange in and among "weak" states. Over time, even the relatively "strong" post-Roman successor states experienced a decline of state taxation and salaried military forces, most notably in seventh- and eight-century Byzantium. The Umayyad Empire also suffered from the regionalization of revenue collection and military power.[31] In this context of fiscal decline and decentralization of political and military power, it became more difficult to maintain state capabilities (especially in the military sphere), and the prospects for the creation of very large stable empires were poor.

In terms of state capacity, developments in early medieval China differed quite dramatically from conditions in much of western Eurasia. The late fifth and sixth centuries c.e. in particular witnessed the gradual restoration of Han-style governmental institutions that enabled rulers to count and tax a growing proportion of their subjects, curb elite autonomy, and mobilize ever larger resources

---

30. Wickham 2005. I also draw here on the review by Sarris 2006b for a convenient summary.
31. For the East Roman state, see esp. Haldon 1997.

for military efforts that eventually resulted in imperial reunification.[32] Serious challenges to recentralization, such as intense conflict between rival nomadic groups and the emergence of large numbers of fortified settlements that were organized around clans and village units and designed to protect (and hence secure local control over) the agricultural population, were eventually contained: in consequence, radically different outcomes were avoided, such as feudalization and long-term fragmentation across China—a real-life counterfactual that had indeed already materialized on a previous occasion, back in the early Spring and Autumn period in the eighth century B.C.E.[33] This raises the question of why the foreign conquest elites succeeded in shoring up state capabilities where their western counterparts failed. The nature of antecedent governmental institutions and differences in the compensation of military forces (most notably between the state-managed allocation of goods in the East versus the assignation of land in parts of the West) and their organization (a predominance of cavalry or infantry) may all have played a critical role. All these issues call for further investigation. A comparative perspective will be essential in identifying factors that precipitated dramatically different long-term outcomes in East and West: the famous "dynastic cycle(s)" in China and the resilient polycentrism of the medieval and modern European state system.

32. See esp. Eberhard 1965; Pearce 1987; Lewis forthcoming. For evidence of continuing taxation in the "Period of Disunion," see Yang 1961: 140–8; for an example of continuity in bureaucratic practice, see Dien 2001.
33. Cf. Tang 1990: 123–4; Huang 1997: 77.

2

War, State Formation, and the Evolution of Military Institutions in Ancient China and Rome

Nathan Rosenstein

1. WAR AND SATE FORMATION I

Warfare in Bronze Age China during the Xia, Shang, and Western Zhou periods (c.2000–770 B.C.E.) constituted one of the two great affairs of the state—the other being the sacrifice of animals and humans.[1] These "affairs" were the exclusive prerogative of the aristocracy and formed the basis for legitimating its rule as well as its self-definition. Consequently, war was central to state formation in this era.[2]

The aristocracy at this date formed a segmentary lineage system, that is, a group of clans and households that organized and ranked itself according to their genealogical proximity to the ruling lineage.[3] Monarchs enjoyed primacy in honor but a rough degree of social parity with their aristocratic peers. The members of this class thought of themselves as sharing a common nobility but jealously guarded the honor to which each believed his rank entitled him. It is not surprising, therefore, that the personal slights, real or imagined, formed an endless source of feuding or that such feuds regularly issued in violence among members of a class that defined itself in large part through war. Monarchs became progressively less able to control these conflicts owing to the inherent weakness of the governments they headed. The segmentary lineage system not only shaped the social hierarchy of the aristocracy but the political landscape of Bronze Age kingdoms. Lineages' rankings within the system determined which of the various ministries at court and territories of the realm a clan controlled. These positions were the hereditary possessions of the lineages and replicated the institutions of

---

1. Lewis 1990: 17; Yates 1999: 12; Chung 2007: 46.
2. On war and state formation in early modern Europe, see the classic account of Tilly 1992, esp. 14–15; on ancient China, Hui 2005: 54–108; for Republican Rome from a somewhat different perspective, Eich and Eich 2005.
3. Lewis 1990: 28–29; on the development of the Shang and Zhou empires, see now Chung 2007: 15–40.

the monarchy on a smaller scale. Clans possessed their own temples and sacrifices and networks of aristocratic dependents and retainers who could be mobilized for war. They constituted, in fact, fully autonomous states in their own right since they were fully capable of carrying out independently the "great affairs of the state." Thus, the structure of what passed for the state in the Bronze Age can best be described as feudal because the "state" as such was nothing more than an aggregate of "mini-states"—including the monarchy itself—on whose collective military resources the power of the kingdom depended. It is scarcely surprising, then, that the ministerial and territorial lineages gradually grew to rival the power of the monarch himself or that the vendettas and wars spawned by aristocrats' extreme sensitivity to slights to their honor led finally to centuries of internecine bloodshed that the monarchy was powerless to check. The Spring and Autumn period that followed (722–481 B.C.E.; note that the Eastern Zhou dynasty [770–256 B.C.E.] overlaps with this and the following period, the Warring States [453–221 B.C.E.]) witnessed a long era of violence through which the Zhou aristocracy not only largely destroyed itself and more than 100 ministates but the greater political order that they had constituted.

Out of this carnage a very different form of state emerged as the intense conflict among the lineages led them to social and administrative innovations aimed at securing a military advantage against their rivals.[4] The first steps were taken in the mid-seventh century, when the state of Qi abandoned the aristocratic monopoly on warfare in order to enlarge its armed forces. Other states were forced to follow suit. At first, only the nonaristocratic portions of the capital populations were enrolled in the army, but over time as conflicts intensified and demanded ever larger armies, the state of Jin in the mid-sixth century extended conscription to subject peoples and the rural population of its agricultural hinterland. This development was at first only a temporary expedient, but the pressures of war forced Jin and other, competing states to make such measures permanent until by the third century they were fielding armies of enormous size numbering in the hundreds of thousands of men (if the sources are to be believed). Finally, the state of Qin under the guidance of the legalist thinker and general Shang Yang in the mid-fourth century established what would become the paradigmatic structure of the "warring state." It is not clear that every state subsequently conformed completely to the administrative pattern that Qin created, but the various reforms it undertook were to one degree or another replicated among its rivals. Central to the Qin reforms was the grouping of the population into units of five households that were each responsible not only for providing the squads of five recruits that formed the building blocks of Qin armies but also for

---

4. On the following paragraphs, see generally Lewis 1990: 96; Hui 2005: 64–87; Lewis 1999: 603–16; Chang 2007: 40–64.

mutual surveillance. Members of the households who did not report the crimes of another member were held jointly liable for his or her transgressions. Second, because Qin's rulers viewed agricultural productivity as crucial to a strong military, the government systematically discouraged other forms of economic activity, for example by imposing various penalties on merchants and craftsmen. To ensure that the maximum amount of land was brought under cultivation, Qin also penalized households with adult sons living at home. These penalties forced sons to establish independent households and to cultivate their own allotments of land in order to support them. In tandem with this step, Qin also divided its territory into a grid of blocks, each of which was sufficient to support a family from the food produced on it. This reshaping of the countryside in order to ensure the maximum extraction of the resources for war was given physical expression through a system of paths forming a rectangular grid over the crop lands of the state. Finally, the government financed its war making through a head-tax imposed on the population.

Qin carried out this vast effort at social and economic engineering through the creation of an equally extensive administrative apparatus. The entire territory was divided into administrative districts, the *xian*, which were identical with the units of military administration and recruitment. The subunits of the *xian*, the *jin*, became the basis for local government. To control this system, Qin established a bureaucracy capable of extending the central government's reach down to the local level. Unlike civil administration under the Bronze Age monarchies, officeholders were not nobles and did not enjoy hereditary tenure of their posts. They were commoners, professionals who earned their positions through specialized skills and abilities and served at the pleasure of the monarch. These administrators collected taxes and conducted levies for military service and corveé labor, and to facilitate these tasks, they carried out detailed censuses of the population. They also enforced a severe but apparently relatively impartial system of justice among the subjects. Finally, the taxes extracted from the peasantry paid not only for the bureaucracy that governed them but for a standing corps of professional soldiers that formed not only the core of the Qin military but in addition gave rulers a ready and reliable source of coercive force for use against recalcitrant subjects. These innovations created "warring states," as Mark Lewis puts it, "states built through the institutions of military recruitment and control. In these states warfare was no longer the means by which an aristocracy defined its authority, but rather the primary institution used by the rulers of states to organize, rank, and control their subjects."[5] Military necessity, in other words, brought about the militarization of these states.

5. Lewis 1990: 67.

In this climate of endemic warfare, mass armies were essential to the survival of any warring state, and to mobilize them their governments relied not simply on the coercive power that their bureaucratic apparatus provided but also on the tangible incentives that they offered to peasants for their compliance with demands for taxes and service and for zeal in battle when conscripted. In this light, the governments' concern to maximize their populations' agricultural productivity and the concrete measures that they undertook to do so can be seen, from a different angle, as efforts to secure the welfare of their subjects. If subjects were to pay taxes, it was in their rulers' interest to ensure that they did not lack the wherewithal to do so. In addition, because land was apparently plentiful in this period, rulers could not afford to be too harsh in their demands on their subjects, for subjects who felt themselves oppressed in one kingdom could easily migrate to another where conditions were better. The system of highly competitive states each eager to attract additional subjects created a kind of "'right of exit' which could serve as an implicit rein on arbitrary power."[6] Moreover, because justice came through salaried local officials appointed by the central government rather than at the hands of some local potentate, the laws, if severe, were at least applied even-handedly. But the most important incentive that these governments held out was the prospect of bettering one's economic and social position through success in war. The warring states established elaborate hierarchies of ranks or titles that rewarded meritorious service to the state, particularly in war. Once again, Qin is paradigmatic. Lewis describes its system of seventeen ranks in this way:

> Military success measured by the number of heads of slain enemies was rewarded with promotion in rank. For individual squad members or the chiefs of a squad of five, rewards were given for heads of enemies actually killed by the individual. For the commander of a unit of a hundred men or more, rewards were given for the total number of enemy killed by his troops. Those killed in battle could have their merits transferred to their descendants. Reaching certain ranks entitled the bearer to the possession of specified quantities of land, houses, and slaves. Those of the eighth rank or above also obtained the tax income of a specified number of villages…and the highest four ranks in Qin's hierarchy of military merit were the lords (*jun*…) and *hou*…found elsewhere. Lower titles matched with ranks in the army and government administration, with the lowest four ranks corresponding to the soldiery, and ranks five and above serving as officers in the army and officials in the administration. The ranks likewise entailed certain legal and religious privileges. In the legal realm,

---

6. Hui 2005: 177.

the surrender of titles could be used to remit certain punishments, so they provided a degree of protection against severe penalties. In the religious realm, they entitled the holder to privileges in burial, including the right to a higher tomb mound and the planting of more trees on the tomb.[7]

The subjects of Qin and the other warring states therefore appear to have been willing and perhaps even happy to go to war because they perceived it to be in their material self-interest to do so and because their rulers looked after their general economic welfare and offered them access to impartial justice.

The formation of the Roman imperial state was strikingly different, despite its origins in a similar pattern of constant, intense warfare.[8] Italy in the sixth, fifth, and fourth centuries B.C.E. was a region of small city-states and loose tribal confederations, of which the centrally located Roman Republic was one of the stronger. Gradually, Rome extended its hegemony over most of Italy during the fourth and third centuries and over the whole of the Mediterranean in the second and first. Yet although Rome went to war almost every year during these four centuries and mobilized Italy's population in proportional terms on a scale comparable to China's warring states, it never developed the sorts of administrative structures that in China were a concomitant and prerequisite for the full mobilization of state resources for war. Indeed, the institutions of government during Rome's greatest period of military mobilization, in the late third, second, and first centuries B.C., were minimal compared to those of Qin and the other warring states. Until 49 B.C.E., an aristocracy controlled public affairs through a council (the senate), which had little formal legal power but enormous informal authority. Its members also staffed all magistracies, which were filled through a system of competitive elections in which all Roman citizens were theoretically entitled to vote (although the organization of the voting assemblies and other circumstances made these elections far from democratic). These magistrates conducted all the business of state, but because the magistracies were few, the business they conducted was quite limited. A quinquennial census of the Republic's citizens was taken for the purposes of establishing liability to military service and taxation. However, despite draconian penalties for evasion, the census basically depended on the voluntary cooperation of registrants for its success. No bureaucracy was in place to enforce compliance. Similarly, to administer its towns and rural areas the Republic relied on the cooperation of local elites whose power bases were independent of the central administration. Conscription, too, was predicated on the willingness of recruits to come forward in the absence of an extensive bureaucracy or police force to enforce compliance. Beginning in the fourth century, taxes of a sort (the *tributum*) were collected to fund the

---

7. Lewis 1999: 612–13.
8. See, conveniently, Cornell 1995: 186–90, 226–30, 293–326, 345–98; Forsythe 2005: 150–54, 234–358.

Republic's military endeavors, but these were technically loans from the citizens to the Republic that might, at least on occasion, be repaid at the end of a victorious campaign. In 167 B.C.E., following the conquest of Macedon, the senate abolished their collection altogether, and thereafter Roman citizens enjoyed immunity from direct taxation for several centuries (although they were subject to a number of indirect taxes).

The divergence in the trajectory of state-formation in Republican Rome and the warring states of China may be attributable, in part, to significant differences in the nature of the military challenges each faced. Warfare among the warring states of China was nearly continuous. One calculation puts the number of wars between the major states between 656 and 221 B.C.E. at 256.[9] Alliances among the several major states that competed for power in this period were impermanent and frequently shifting, and for over four centuries no one of them was able to gain a position of such unchallenged superiority that it could either conquer its rivals or force them to accept its hegemony. These wars moreover often lasted several years and could result in the complete annihilation of the losing dynasty, the destruction of its alters and temples, and the absorption of its domains into the victor's kingdom. In a context of such existential danger to the states and their inability to depend on resources beyond their own frontiers for the means to defend themselves, it is not surprising that rulers adopted a strategy of maximizing the extraction of money and manpower from their own territories through the establishment of strong controls at the center, an effective administrative apparatus, and the extensive regimentation of their subjects. The pattern of Roman warfare was quite different. Rome began as the dominant city-state in Latium, and its path to dominion in Italy was largely uninterrupted despite major military challenges and occasional serious setbacks. Beginning in the later fifth century, it overcame one rival after another in the peninsula, and when it faced war on more than one front, it was generally able to prevent its enemies from combining effectively against it. After *c*.275 B.C.E., its existence as a state was threatened only once, by Hannibal, and for a comparatively brief period, from 218 to 207 B.C.E. (Although Hannibal did not leave Italy until 203 B.C.E., the Roman defeat of reinforcements from Spain led by his brother in 207 B.C.E. effectively ended any threat he posed to Rome.) It did not face the sorts of long-term challenges that threatened states in China, and this fact may to some extent account for the failure of the Republic's leaders to make the sorts of extensive alterations in the institutional structure of the Republic that Chinese rulers resorted to in order to survive.

It would be wrong, however, to downplay too much the military dangers that the Republic did face. During the fifth and fourth centuries, Rome confronted

9. Hui 2005: 242–48.

powerful enemies, any one of which could have destroyed it, and the consequences of defeat in the major wars it waged in the third century could have led to the unraveling of its hegemony in Italy and quite possibly the annihilation of the Republic and the death or enslavement of its citizens. Military pressures were at times unquestionably severe and the challenges often daunting, and in response Rome's leaders naturally sought to increase the Republic's military resources. However, instead of expanding the apparatus of government and enhancing its effectiveness in extracting the resources for war from its citizens, Rome's leaders turned to alliance building and the enlargement of the citizen body itself in order to build up their city's military capabilities. These measures in effect substituted for the more intensive control of state territory that furnished China's warring states with their strength. Initially Rome and its closest neighbors, the Latins, formed a league for mutual defense as early as the regal period, and this alliance furnished much of the bedrock of its military power in the fifth and fourth centuries following the fall of the monarchy and the establishment of the Republic (trad. 509 B.C.E.). In this era and continuing on into the third century, as Rome subdued various Italian states and others sought its protection, it struck treaties with them. These imposed no money tax on the Republic's Italian allies (the *socii*); instead the treaties required them to furnish contingents for the Republic's armies and "to have the same friends and enemies as Rome," that is, to cede control of their foreign affairs to the Republic. These alliances, which gradually grew to encompass the whole of Italy south of the Po river, proved to be far more dependable than was the case among the warring states of China. There the existence of several relatively evenly matched competing states created endless possibilities for realignment as each sought to maximize its power or to counter perceived threats. Rome's allies had no alternative but to acquiesce because no other Italian state could rival Rome's power. Consequently, Rome could bring overwhelming military force to bear in putting down attempted revolts. Only with the aid of a potent, external source of military strength, such as Pyrrhus in 281–279 B.C.E. or Hannibal in 218–207 B.C.E., could the allies hope to break free of Roman dominance, and a number of them did desert. Yet even during these relatively brief episodes, enough allies remained loyal to enable Rome ultimately to turn back the challenge and restore its hegemony. However, Roman hegemony, if distasteful and not to be preferred to freedom if the opportunity presented itself, was nevertheless in general not oppressive. In return for placing their military forces at Rome's disposal, the allies were left almost entirely autonomous in their local affairs, which their local elites continued to control, and their soldiers and citizens were entitled to share in the fruits of Roman victories.

In view of the Republic's success in enlarging the number of allies from which it could extract the wherewithal for war, intensification of extraction through an enlarged state apparatus was unnecessary. Rome's rulers took a similarly quantitative rather than qualitative approach within the Republic itself. Beginning in 338 B.C.E., following the suppression of a serious revolt among its allies in Latium and Campania, Rome used the extension of its citizenship to ensure the loyalty and support of various groups of non-Romans in Italy. New tribes were created in which to accommodate these newly enfranchised Romans and merge them into the civic and political structure of the Republic. Citizenship was not an unmixed blessing: it meant obligations for military service and taxes, while benefits such as the right to vote or hold public office were largely beyond the reach of most new citizens. Yet new citizens during the later fourth, third, and second centuries were integrated on terms of complete equality with the old, and there is no evidence of resistance or rebellion among them. Rome steadily enlarged its territory (the *ager Romanus*) until by the late third century it encompassed much of the best land in central Italy. At that date, the citizen body probably numbered around 300,000 adult males out of a total of perhaps 970,000 in the peninsula south of the Po Valley. Romans therefore constituted somewhat less than a third of the Italian population at this date, making them the largest of Italy's ethnic groups and so able to overwhelm any single group, much less any individual state, that might challenge their suzerainty.[10]

The ability of the citizen body as well as of the Italian allies to bear the burdens of warfare was enhanced by the one form of social engineering that the Republic regularly undertook, the dispatch of colonies to occupy conquered lands.[11] The primary purpose of such foundations was military—the colonies were located at strategic points in recently conquered areas to serve as de facto garrisons and staging areas. Down to the early second century, their participants, Roman citizens and members of allied communities, acquired Latin rights, modeled on those possessed by members of Rome's former Latin neighbors (who had become citizens following the suppression of their revolt). After the Hannibalic War, however, new colonists retained or were granted Roman citizenship. Citizens of the earlier Latin colonies enjoyed a privileged status vis-à-vis ordinary *socii*, which linked them closely to Rome and made them among the Republic's most dependable allies. They enhanced Rome's military potential by perhaps somewhat fewer than 150,000 men. Those who elected to participate in any of these colonial foundations were men who lacked adequate farms on which to support themselves and their families. Colonies thus to some extent prevented the creation of a class of landless citizens and allies who were unable to pay taxes or serve in the army (since at Rome as in the classical Greek poleis a minimum amount of wealth was required to qualify for infantry or cavalry service), while those who remained behind were spared the need to divide their holdings among too many heirs. As the result of these policies of colonization, alliance building,

---

10. Brunt 1987: 44–60; however, Lo Cascio 1999: 166–71. I would put the figure much higher.
11. Salmon 1969.

and the extension of citizenship, when Rome finally did face a comparatively prolonged military crisis during the early and middle years of the Hannibalic War, it was able to muster the overwhelming numbers of soldiers from among its citizens and its Latin allies as well as other allies that it needed to suppress revolts, prevent more, and gradually wear Hannibal down by attrition.

Rome's hegemony in Italy as well as its large citizenry also supplied much of financing for war.[12] Rome's allies paid the troops they contributed to the Republic's armies (although Rome provided grain rations for these troops at no charge), while the size of the Republic's citizen body meant that the financial burdens Rome's wars imposed on its own population were also widely distributed. More importantly, as Rome began to acquire control of territories outside of the Italian peninsula, first the islands of Sardinia and Sicily, later in Spain, southern France, North Africa, and large parts of the Greek East, it imposed a tax in money or grain on the provincials but did not require soldiers from them on a regular basis as it did from the Latin and Italian *socii*. These areas contributed substantial sums to the Roman treasury both in the short run, as war reparations following their initial subjugation, and over the long term as Rome gradually imposed regular taxation, which further eased the financial burdens that were imposed on Roman citizens. However, the Republic depended on the cooperation of local figures or institutions or on private companies of Romans and Italians for provincial tax collection. And as in Italy, provincial administration was minimal. Although powerful ruling dynasties were eliminated, the cities of their former kingdoms largely governed themselves and administered their own hinterlands. The governors dispatched from Rome exercised only a very general supervision, serving as judges in certain court cases, ensuring that the cities adhered to the terms of their treaties, and maintaining order in their provinces.

The Republic, like the warring states of China, was able to mobilize the mass armies that fought its battles by offering incentives to those it conscripted in order to secure their willing compliance and their enthusiastic participation in combat. Initially, these incentives seem to have taken the form of political rights. Even before the establishment of the Republic, when Rome was still governed by a monarchy, King Servius Tullius's creation of the *comitia centuriata* in the mid-sixth century in connection with the establishment of a new type of army based on an enlarged body of citizens gave all those whom he expected to participate in future wars a voice in decisions about whether to go to war and when to make peace. With the establishment of the Republic, the *comitia centuriata* also acquired the right to select those who would lead Rome's armies. And according to many, although not all, scholars of the early Republic, the plebeians' threat to refuse military service at times when the city was in grave danger from its

12. Nicolet 1980: 115–17, 149–206.

neighbors forced a variety of concessions from Rome's patrician rulers.[13] These included the fundamental citizen right of *provocatio*, that is, appeal to the judgment of the people from a magistrate's capital sentence; recognition of the power of the tribunes of the plebs to offer protection against arbitrary arrest and punishment by magistrates; a voice in the conduct of the *res publica* via an assembly known as the *concilium plebis*; the abolition of enslavement for debt; and a major alteration in the composition of the ruling class itself as a consequence of the opening up of the chief magistracies and priesthoods to wealthy men of plebeian stock. After the first quarter of the third century, however, political concessions to the citizens by the Republic's rulers grew much less frequent. Such concessions, one may suppose, were always distasteful to the aristocracy since they limited in one way or another their power in the state and over its citizens, but Rome's rulers had little choice since the military situation made granting them imperative. A change in the military situation, however, made possible a shift in the kinds of concessions Rome's rulers were prepared to grant in exchange for ordinary citizens' military service.

The Republic's great victory at Sentinum in 295 B.C.E. broke the back of a grand coalition of its principal enemies in Italy, the Samnites, Etruscans, and Gauls, and a rising of the former in connection with Pyrrhus's victories in 280–279 B.C.E. was brutally suppressed following Rome's defeat of the Epriot king in 275 B.C.E. Thereafter, no Italian opponent ever again posed a serious threat to the Republic, and it is possible that this far less threatening situation in the peninsula made aristocrats much less ready to grant political rights and powers to ordinary Roman citizens. However, it may also be true that for the latter the prospect of a greater voice in the community's decision-making processes or increasingly well-defined civil rights grew less attractive to them, since the territorial expansion of the Republic and the attendant dispersal of the citizen body over an increasingly wide area made civic and political rights, which for the most part could only be exercised at Rome itself, of little immediate value. Instead, what may have come to matter far more to ordinary Romans were opportunities for personal advancement through warfare. After battles generals regularly paraded their legions and presented decorations to foot-soldiers and cavalrymen who had displayed exceptional gallantry by risking their lives above and beyond the call of duty. These awards, like the ranks of Chinese warring states, enhanced the social and particularly the religious status of those who won them. As Polybius reports, only these sorts of decorations were permitted to be worn in religious processions. Spoils taken from an enemy killed in man-to-man combat were hung up outside the victors' houses. They served as permanent markers in

---

13. On the plebeians' threat of a military strike (*secessio plebis*), see, recently, Raaflaub 2005. On the concessions and the political struggles in this period generally, see Cornell 1995: 242–92, 327–68; Forsythe 2005: 234–67.

civilian life of the prestige a soldier had won at war, for the spoils remained in place even after a house changed owners.[14] But an even more powerful incentive was the prospect of loot. As early as 264 B.C.E., the consuls could incite voters in the *comitia centuriata* to approve the dispatch of forces to relieve the Mamertines in Sicily by pointing out "the great benefit in the way of plunder which each and every one would evidently derive" from the war, as Polybius puts it, undoubtedly drawing on the early Roman historian Fabius Pictor.[15] And nearly a century later, volunteers flocked to Rome when the consuls were levying an army for the war against Perseus because they had seen that those who had served in the previous two wars in the East had come back rich.[16] When after the defeat of Perseus at Pydna the Roman general Aemilius Paullus disappointed them in their hopes of rich plunder from the Macedonian royal treasury, these soldiers came very close to denying him a triumph.[17] By contrast, thirty years later, when Rome was waging difficult wars in Spain that offered little prospect for booty, recruits were notoriously reluctant to come forward.[18] In addition, some, though by no means all, veterans could expect to receive allotments in the colonies that the senate from time to time founded in Italy to secure Rome's hegemony. In the distribution of these material rewards, the troops of Rome's Italian allies apparently shared on equal terms with the Republic's citizens.

Because Rome was able to marshal the money and manpower it needed to meet the military challenges it faced in establishing its empire without having to create an extensive state apparatus in order to extract the resources required, other factors were able to play the decisive role in determining how the Republic's administrative institutions developed—or rather failed to. Chief among these were the needs of Rome's ruling aristocracy to protect its corporate interest in preserving its supremacy in the state and in ensuring its cohesion. The most striking difference between the governments of China's warring states and the Roman Republic is of course the absence of a monarchy in the latter. The importance of a monarch for Roman state formation is clear in the role that is attributed to King Servius Tullius in creating several of the key institutions of the Republic during the mid-sixth century B.C.E.: a new type of army, an enlarged citizen body, and the assembly of the centuries.[19] Once the monarchy fell around 509 B.C.E., the aristocracy that took power sought to ensure that no one of their number ever gained similar monarchic power again. Collegiality in office and one-year terms were the most important checks on individual magistrates' ability to accumulate and exercise power, but the senate's refusal to countenance the

14. Polybius 6.39.1–11; Gellius, *Attic Nights* 2.11.3.
15. Polybius 2.11.2. (tran. Patton).
16. Livy 42.32.6.
17. Livy 45.35.5–36.10; Plutarch, *Aemilius* 30.2–32.1.
18. Polybius 35.4.1–7; Appian, *Iberian Wars* 49; Livy, *Periocha* 45.
19. Cornell 1995: 173–97.

creation of any sort of professional bureaucracy, although justified ideologically by the aristocratic ethos of public service, also in effect worked to preclude the establishment of an institution that could rival its authority in the state and serve as an instrument of domination by a would-be monarch.

Yet the tension between the senate's practice of collective leadership of the state and the exigent demands that war could impose was never resolved. It was reflected structurally in the institution of the dictatorship. During the fourth and third centuries, military emergencies often led to the appointment of a dictator, who had full and unconstrained power in order to deal with the crisis. However, dictators served only for six months, not the year that other magistrates normally held office, and this limitation reflected the deep suspicion within the aristocracy of concentrating too much power in the hands of any one of its members. Ideologically, the need to keep such power within bounds was expressed in legends of idealized heroes like Cincinnatus, who was summoned from his farm and appointed dictator to save a Roman army that the enemy had trapped. Once he had accomplished his mission, however, Cincinnatus laid down his office and returned to his plow a mere fifteen days after leaving it.[20] For most of the Republic's history, the tension between the need for effective military leadership in a crisis and the danger this could pose to the aristocracy's collective rule was obviated by the deep reserves of military power that Rome could bring to bear along with a highly effective tactical system of infantry combat (on which, see below). Together, these factors secured victory regularly enough to permit the practice of placing command in the hands of politically successful members of the aristocracy, even if they had evinced little prior aptitude for generalship or had even led Roman armies to defeat. Military efficiency, in other words, yielded to the need to distribute high public offices and bestow honor widely among the aristocracy in order to foster cohesion among its members and prevent one or a few individuals from dominating public life at Rome by virtue of their repeated success on the battlefield.[21]

The primacy of politics over war in Roman state formation continued when a monarchy was reestablished in the late first century b.c.e.[22] Civil war had engulfed most of the Roman world between 49 and 31 b.c.e., although fighting was not continuous. These wars were ended by Rome's first emperor, Augustus, who subsequently established a long-lasting rule in 27 b.c.e. that became the basis for imperial government over the ensuing centuries. In doing so, Augustus created the germ of the administrative and financial bureaucracy that would form the institutional backbone of that government. He also altered the Roman military,

---

20. Livy 3.26.7–29.7.
21. Rosenstein 1990.
22. See generally the chapters in Bowman et al., eds. 1996: 1–197.

substituting long-service professionals for the conscripted citizen-soldiers of the Republic. His aim in undertaking this latter reform was not to increase military effectiveness but to secure his own hold on power. Augustus had come to dominate Rome by gaining the loyalty of armies nominally under the authority of the senate or his rivals, and these had enabled him not only to survive the deadly struggles of the period but eventually overcome all opposition. By substituting professional soldiers for conscripts, he sought to secure the loyalty of these troops to himself and his family in order to ensure that no potential challenger to his rule would be able to gain control of military forces sufficient to overthrow him. Augustus therefore took responsibility for paying each legionary a substantial bonus upon his discharge, and he retained nominal command of nearly all legions, exercising day-to-day authority through lieutenants. Soldiers therefore took an annual oath of allegiance to him personally, and in his name decorations and money donatives were awarded after successful campaigns. These practices were continued by all subsequent emperors.[23]

Yet these changes came at a time when the external military dangers threatening Rome's empire were virtually nil. Augustus's reign did witness a continuation of the regular, large-scale warfare that had characterized the Republic as Augustus sought to enlarge his empire, but thereafter down to the later second century C.E., Rome was at war much less frequently and, except for relatively brief periods, on a far less extensive scale. Yet despite this slackening in the pace and intensity of warfare, the imperial bureaucracy at this time enjoyed a long period of sustained development and growth. Augustus's aim in his administrative measures was simply to increase his ability to control the vast empire he had won without having to depend too heavily on an aristocracy of whose loyalty he could not be certain. Politically, his position was somewhat fragile, despite his success in destroying his military rivals, for he could not rule effectively without at least the tacit support of a senatorial aristocracy that had a visceral hatred of monarchy and of whom at least some considered themselves as worthy of supremacy as Augustus. Consequently, he went to great lengths to mask the reality of his monarchy behind a façade of claims to have "restored the Republic." Rather than create an obvious administrative apparatus staffed with his appointees, which would have smacked of royalty, he instead turned to his personal household slaves and freedmen to help him manage the vast quantity of administrative and financial business that now came within his purview. He also began to use men from the wealthy but nonsenatorial equestrian class as his agents in the provinces. Subsequently, as the position of emperor came to be accepted as permanent, emperors expanded these practices, eventually creating a formal structure of administrative departments in the palace with fixed responsibilities. Over time, emperors

23. Campbell 1984.

were able to draw the upper classes increasingly into collaboration in imperial rule, and consequently the social status of those who filled the positions within the palace bureaucracy as well as the provincial administration rose dramatically, until they comprised those from the top of the social hierarchy rather than the bottom.[24] The needs of war were responsible for very little of this.

However, these administrative reforms were by no means as thoroughgoing as those in the Chinese warring states, as the ad hoc nature of imperial provincial administration demonstrates.[25] Some provinces were technically under the control of the senate, an institution that emperors preserved from the Republican era although remade so that it was completely subservient to the emperors' wishes. Members of the senate governed these provinces, yet these governors were in effect imperial appointees because of the emperors' ability to control the decisions of the senate. Other provinces the emperors governed directly through lieutenants (*legati* or *procuratores*), while increasingly large portions of the empire came to be owned by the office of the emperor. These areas, too, were controlled by imperial appointees (also termed procurators). Where China, under the constant stress of war, developed a cadre of professional civil servants who were eventually appointed through a rigorous examination system and were quite distinct from the old Zhou nobility, Rome's civil administration remained socially much like the Republic's. The senatorial class filled the top positions in the imperial bureaucracy (although nearly all of the leading families during the Republic had disappeared from the senate's ranks by the end of the first century C.E., and new families had risen to prominence) and holders of lesser posts were drawn from the wealthy equestrian class. No objective system of evaluation of an individual senator's or equestrian's qualifications for a post existed; rather birth and patronage were the keys to securing both the magistracies that were prerequisite to appointment to the top positions within the imperial administration and those positions themselves as well as any other.[26] Likewise, there is no evidence of the kind of far-reaching social and economic engineering that Qin put in place. At most, one can point to a limited number of colonial foundations under the empire that imposed uniform survey grids on the countryside surrounding them according to which allotments were apportioned among the settlers. For the most part the administration's reach did not extend to the local level, but, as under the Republic, the central government depended on the cooperation of local elites to collect taxes and execute its directives. Under Rome's first emperor, the census was extended to his provincial subjects along with Roman citizens in order to establish the liability of the former to taxation. However,

24. Wallace-Hadrill 1996: 296–306; Eck 2000a.
25. Eck 2000b.
26. Saller 1982.

there was no attempt at this stage to impose a uniform system of laws or governmental institutions throughout the empire. Those who lived under Roman rule
enjoyed a wide variety of legal statuses and institutional arrangements (although
this was more pronounced in the eastern half of the empire than in the west,
where the imperial government founded a number of cities and so was able to
impose much more institutional uniformity on their internal arrangements).

2. WAR AND THE RULING CLASS

War was as integral to the identity and legitimacy of the Roman aristocracy
under the Republic as it was for the Zhou nobility before and during the Spring
and Autumn era. Down to the early first century b.c.e., no Roman aristocrat
could run for political office until he had completed ten years of military service,
and a reputation for courage and the glory obtained from extraordinary feats of
arms represented a strong commendation in the eyes of the voters for election
to magistracies.[27] This link between military and political success arose from two
factors. The first was an aristocratic ideology that elevated service to the state
above all else and made it the paramount source of personal prestige; the second
was simply the fact that during most of the Republic's history the most critical
issue confronting the state was war. Naturally, therefore, leadership in war and
the victories Rome's generals won came to constitute far and away the greatest
services to the state and so the richest source of glory and renown. Those who
had bestowed such benefits upon the Republic enjoyed enormous authority in
the conduct of public business by virtue of them. This nexus between war, personal prestige, and political influence is often thought to have been a critical
element in the Republic's bellicosity between the fourth and the first centuries
b.c.e., although the matter is controversial.[28] Yet even in the first century, when
other sources of personal prestige were increasing in importance, the cachet of
military glory remained strong, and the Republic's armies continued to be led by
members of the senatorial class. The closest thing to a class of military experts
at Rome in this period was the *viri militares* ("military men"), aristocrats who
served frequently in positions of subordinate command. But they were in no
sense professional soldiers; they were merely members of the political class who
competed for the same high public offices and political influence that other senators did. Their strategy was simply to focus their efforts primarily on military
achievement, the traditional source of glory at Rome, rather than the kinds of
endeavors like forensic oratory or expertise in the law that had recently come to
take their places alongside a military reputation as sources of prestige at Rome.

---

27. Rosenstein 2007.
28. Harris 1979: 17–41, *contra* Eckstein 2006: 194–200.

The primacy of political over strictly military needs manifested itself on a tactical level as well.[29] The system of rotational command of armies has been alluded to above: the Republic's chief magistrates, the two consuls, were selected by the Roman voters and served only for a single year. Reelection became progressively rarer between 300 and *c.*151 B.C.E., when it was outlawed altogether (although exceptions were occasionally made). This system meant that generals who had demonstrated real aptitude for command only rarely got the chance to lead armies a second time. The men who succeeded them might have had considerable experience as soldiers during their twenties, but thereafter the offices they held were mainly civilian in character. They came to the task of leading their armies untested in the exercise of overall command. It is not surprising, therefore, that Roman infantry tactics, based on legions arrayed in maniples, remained largely unchanged during the Republic. Even the shift from legions organized by maniples to one drawn up by cohorts represented mainly a refinement of the earlier technique. The Roman tactical system had to be straightforward enough to be mastered by a general who had never exercised overall command of an army before (even though previous experience might have shown him how the system worked.) The manipular legions were highly effective in combat, as the Republic's many victories attest, and the legions organized into cohorts that succeeded them were even more so, so there was little incentive to change. As a consequence, the expectation of success in battle on the basis of a proven tactical system simply reinforced the tendency to give priority to the political needs of the aristocracy rather than emphasize experience and demonstrated success in selecting generals at Rome.

This republican integration of civilian and military leadership within its aristocracy carried over into the empire, in keeping with the claim of Augustus to have "restored the Republic." Because emperors determined who held the highest public offices, aristocrats who sought them were forced to become their collaborators in order to obtain these honors, which they needed in order to validate the elite social status they had inherited or to which they aspired. Although overall command of Rome's armies was now vested in the emperor himself, in practice day-to-day command of the legions was in the hands of imperial appointees, also termed *legati*, who were drawn from the ranks of those senators who had been allowed to hold the higher public magistracies. These men were no more military specialists than their Republican predecessors had been. They had typically held a variety of lower civilian and military posts prior to appointment as a legate of a single legion or a group of two or three legions. What secured these positions was, first, loyalty to the reigning emperor and, second, the patronage of those with influence with the emperor or the personal friendship of the emperor himself

---

29. Rosenstein 2007.

(although obvious incompetence would not have been tolerated). Behind this, however, lay an aristocratic ideology carried over from the Republic that held that an aristocrat's innate personal qualities, especially his individual excellence or *virtus*, were what enabled him to lead in either a civilian or a military capacity, not any special training or talent.[30]

The integration of civil and military administration at Rome was reflected in the position of the emperor himself. Roman emperors were commanders in chief of all military forces—not simply in name but often in fact. When major wars had to be fought, emperors frequently took the field at the head of their forces, even if they did not usually lead troops into battle and relied on others to handle the strategic, tactical, and logistical details of their campaigns. When emperors were not present in person, overall command in such cases rested with close relatives, usually sons and successors. Victories were ascribed to an emperor's personal divine spirit or *genius*, and all were celebrated in his name, even if he had not been present. Indeed, the title of emperor derives from *imperator*, an accolade bestowed upon a victorious general by his troops under the Republic. The difference with the advent of the monarchy was that now there was only one *imperator* in place of the several aristocrats who might previously have laid claim to that title. Military prestige was in turn crucial in constructing the ideological foundations of imperial rule. The republican notion that service to the state was the basis for political authority and leadership was made to serve the ends of monarchy through the emperors' monopoly over such benefits. And since victory in war still represented, as it had under the Republic, the paramount service to Rome, each victory an emperor's armies won became a further confirmation of the legitimacy of his rule.[31]

Relations between the civilian elite and military leaders in Warring States China stand in sharp contrast to the situation at Rome.[32] There the destruction of the Zhou nobility during the wars of the Spring and Autumn period and the rise of warfare involving mass armies that required a very different set of skills than individual fighting prowess opened the way for the creation of a class of military specialists. These men were commoners and professionals, like their counterparts in the bureaucracy. And like them, military commanders owed their positions to training and demonstrated competence. They not only commanded the armies of the warring states but were often the authors of theoretical works on warfare, such as Sunzi's *The Art of War*. Indeed, the ability to command successfully came to be associated with mastery of a body of such texts rather than a general's innate personal capabilities. This literature stressed not only discipline in managing mass armies but trickery and deceit in the conduct of military operations,

30. Campbell 1984: 325–62.
31. Campbell 1984.
32. Lewis 1990: 97–135.

the ability to penetrate an enemy's stratagems and to mask one's own. Whereas at Rome the ability to win military victories formed the basis for authority in the civilian sphere, in China this approach to strategy and tactics put warfare at odds with the basis of a ruler's legitimacy. As Lewis puts it, "The prince, whether as the moral exemplar of the Confucians or the distributor of rewards and punishments of the Legalists, could only rule if his commands were trustworthy, so the deceit and trickery that defined the Way of the commanders undercut the foundations of the Way of the ruler."[33] To resolve this dilemma, some Chinese philosophers argued that war and the military constituted a realm separate and distinct from the civilian world, so that what was acceptable and necessary there did not impinge upon the ruler. Consequently, they argued, commanders in the field could not be controlled by rulers and to attempt to do so would lead to disaster. The ruler, when he formally invested a general with his command by ceremoniously handing him an ax in the ruler's ancestral temple, at the same time granted him absolute and autonomous authority during his conduct of the campaign. To further underscore that separation, the army itself used clothing, language, and rituals that were distinct from the civilian world.

However, this position was strongly opposed by scholars of both the Legalist and Confucian schools, who insisted on "the unquestioned supremacy of a ruler who upheld the social order through proper laws or appropriate rituals."[34] This premise led each school, for different reasons, to deny the propriety of and need for a separate military sphere governed by its own distinct sorts of rules. Their arguments in either case began with the assertion that a virtuous ruler at the head of a properly constituted state had no need of the clever stratagems and trickery that military writers insisted that war required. For the Confucians and the Legalists alike, the conduct of war was merely an aspect of social relations: "A properly governed people was the basis of military power...the virtues of the ruler manifested in governmental policies led to success on the battlefield just as they did within the walls of the capital."[35] For the Confucians, that meant a state characterized by harmony between the ruler and his subjects and one in which a proper hierarchy existed among them. Since the army was identical with the people, the proper hierarchy and formations within the army would arise naturally out of a properly ordered society. Soldiers would be linked by the same ties of obedience and affection that united families. For the Legalists, on the other hand, "the army was the primary form of organizing the people, so the techniques that preserved social order also maintained discipline in the army, and no separate military arts were needed."[36] The consequence of this line of thought

33. Lewis 1990: 125.
34. Lewis 1990: 127.
35. Lewis 1990: 129.
36. Lewis 1990: 131.

was to deemphasize the role of the military specialists who had emerged during the Warring States period, to identify the military with civil society, and—as at Rome—to characterize the ruler as the natural leader of both. This line of thinking gradually prevailed and ultimately profoundly affected military command during the Han and later dynasties.

> [F]or the philosophers who asserted that the social order depended on the trustworthiness of the ruler in his rituals or punishments, the claims to autonomy of an art [i.e., of command] based on manipulation and deceit were clearly unacceptable. This tension is reflected in the history of the Han officer corps, where powerful, semi-independent commanders of the military elite of the civil war and early decades were gradually supplanted by agents of the court with no military experience, and military command ultimately became the province of imperial affines and courtiers chosen for their obedience rather than their skill. The triumph of apologists for autocracy over the claims of expertise initiated both the long-term devaluation of military command in China and the emergent ideal of the literary man who was able when necessary to bring his general skills to bear on military command.[37]

This culture of antimilitarism was made possible to a considerable degree because for several centuries following the foundation of the empire by Qin in 221 B.C.E. and then, after a period of civil war, the establishment of the Han dynasty, China did not face a military challenge on its borders that seriously threatened its existence. At this time, the empire's most potent opponents were the Xiongnu, nomadic horse-archers living on the steppe north of China.[38] Their mobility and fire-power presented an insurmountable tactical challenge to the Qin and early Han empires' slow moving infantry armies, and the fact that the livelihood of the Xiongnu depended exclusively on flocks that could be easily and quickly moved when danger threatened made them economically invulnerable to any military campaign that China could mount. Because the steppe was too arid to support the agriculture that was the essential economic basis for Chinese society, the empire could not hold captured territory by establishing colonies of peasants to support garrisons of soldiers, while the cost of transporting food and other necessities from the center to large concentrations of troops on the periphery proved to be prohibitively expensive. However, despite the military strength of the Xiongnu, they never represented a serious threat to the imperial government's existence. China's much larger population dwarfed their numbers,

---

37. Lewis 1990: 132–33. On officers during the Western Han era, some of whom were quite able and successful commanders, see now Chung 2007: 271–92.
    38. Barfield 2001.

but more importantly, the central aim of the Xiongnu rulers' strategy was not to conquer Chinese territory—for the Xiongnu had no desire to become farmers—but to extract tribute from the empire. The position of the Xiongnu rulers depended upon their ability to redistribute the luxury goods they received from the Chinese emperors to their elite supporters and to force the emperors to open Chinese markets to ordinary Xiongnu in the frontier regions, where they could exchange their pastoral products for the grain and other goods from China that they could not grow or manufacture themselves. The Xiongnu state in effect was parasitic on its Chinese counterpart, for without a steady supply of luxury goods to pass along and the ability to provide access to the markets that supplied everyday items in demand among ordinary Xiongnu, a ruler would lose his support and his "empire" would fall apart. And despite the fact that buying peace from the Xiongnu was deeply distasteful to the imperial court and, during the reign of the Emperor Wudi (or Wu, r. 140–87 B.C.E.), despite a huge effort to defeat the Xiongnu through massive military campaigns and extensive colonization, in the end the cost and ultimate futility of attacking them made paying the Xiongnu not to raid Chinese territory the only acceptable option during the Former or Western Han era (206 B.C.E.–9 C.E.).[39] Thus, a philosophical aversion to war and the military among Confucian and Legalist thinkers could flourish in China in large part because the situation on the empire's northern frontier made a strong and effective military response there both unnecessary and ineffective.

Imperial China, therefore, like Rome during the Republic and under the first and second centuries of imperial rule, came to vest command in an elite whose entitlement to those positions arose from their personal qualities, cultural attainments, and relationship to the emperor rather than technical expertise or demonstrated talent for the conduct of war. Although the paths each took to reach this state of affairs were quite different in detail, they were to some extent similar in origin. In either case, the result arose from the demands of political power: in China, that meant upholding absolute supremacy of the ruler at the expense of military expertise, while at Rome a Republican form of government militated strongly against anything that could lead to the elevation of one aristocrat to a commanding position within the state, such as the ability to monopolize the personal glory that accrued from victory because of a superior aptitude for leadership in war. At Rome, too, any aristocrat who had demonstrated the requisite personal qualities was considered fit to lead an army, a presumption that was carried through into the empire by emperors who ruled through the active collaboration of a tame senatorial class that still sought honor through service to the state. However, in each case objective conditions made this development possible, especially the situation on the frontiers. Neither the Han rulers

---

39. On the Emperor Wudi's efforts to crush the Xiongnu, see now Chung 2007.

nor Rome's emperors for most of the first two centuries of their rule faced dire military threats from beyond their borders. Hence, each could assign command on the basis of criteria other than training, skill, and experience at little cost to the empire's military position.

3. WAR AND STATE FORMATION II

The changed nature of the military threat facing the Qin dynasty and its successor, the Han, also culminated in the abolition of mass armies and the system of universal male conscription upon which they depended under the Eastern Han dynasty (23–220 C.E.) in 30–31 C.E.[40] The large infantry armies of the Warring States era had been developed to combat similar armies fielded by the various Chinese states contending for power during that period. Once Qin had overcome its rivals and established China's first universal empire, the need for warfare against other Chinese armies vanished, save for periods of civil war like those that brought about the fall of Qin in 206 and the establishment of the Han dynasty in its place in 202. But these outbreaks were rare thereafter, and consequently the need for mass armies and universal military service disappeared. Instead, the military focus under the Han shifted to the northern frontier and the Xiongnu, against whom, as noted above, mass infantry armies were largely ineffective. Defense against this sort of highly mobile enemy required long-service garrisons to protect distant frontiers and, ideally, armies of mounted archers that could meet the Xiongnu on their own terms. In his efforts to conquer them, the Emperor Wudi began to remake the imperial army, employing large corps of mounted troops as well as professional soldiers during his campaigns.[41] However, since horses cannot easily be raised in the great river valleys that formed the Chinese heartland owing to unsuitable environmental conditions, emperors had to seek horses and horsemen in the north, and this meant that the best soldiers with which to combat the Xiongnu were other Xiongnu. Eastern Han emperors began therefore to employ tribes of southern Xiongnu, who had lost out in a civil war against their northern cousins and who subsequently surrendered to the emperor to oppose the latter. To man the garrisons that guarded the frontier and also watched over the empire's barbarian allies, volunteers and convicts reprieved from death sentences proved much more suitable than peasants conscripted for only a year or two at a time. These forces and small garrisons of elite troops in the center to protect the emperor formed the Eastern Han military for much of that dynasty's history. This reorganization offered the additional advantages of, first, security, since—as at Rome under the empire—these sorts of soldiers obviated

---

40. Lewis 2000.
41. Chung 2007: 161–87.

the danger that a commander would win the loyalty of his army of peasant conscripts and lead them in an attempt to overthrow the reigning emperor and, second, economy, since these smaller forces were much cheaper to run. In its former aspect, China's shift to professional soldiers parallels the similar innovation by Rome's first emperor: his goal, too, was political security for his regime more than military effectiveness.

This system was largely successful at defeating the threat of the northern Xiongnu by the end of the first century c.e., but that very success proved disastrous to the Eastern Han.[42] Unlike the legionaries of imperial Rome, armies of barbarians and convicts evinced little loyalty to the state, while the empire's barbarian allies, once the northern Xiongnu had been defeated, lost their importance to the court and hence the subsidies that had been the price of their cooperation. Consequently, they turned to plunder, and because so many of them had been brought into the empire, the garrisons proved incapable of deterring their attacks. More serious was the fact that the main threat to China's borders in the second century came now from the west in the persons of the Qiang. The elaborate border fortifications, especially the Great Wall, developed to defend against the northern nomads, were of no use against a threat emanating from the west. Further complicating the problem of defense was the fact that the Qiang had no overarching political order and did not form large confederacies as had the Xiongnu. These facts made negotiation difficult, while the effects of military victories were limited only to the specific tribes conquered. The solution of establishing colonies of Chinese peasants in the border regions in order to protect the conquered tribes and bring the Qiang into the Han economic and political system foundered on the difficulties of maintaining agricultural communities in the arid west in the face of the constant depredations of the Qiang and on the expense of supporting them when they could not feed themselves. Finally, the decision to move the capital to Luoyang in the eastern part of the empire in the early first century c.e. led to the ascendancy of easterners at court, whose interest in western matters was very limited. Ultimately, as the Han government lost control of the western frontier, provincial governors began to take the initiative in defense. The forces they led began to develop into private armies under the control of great families whose loyalty was to their commanders. The result was the breakup of the Han military system and a loss of control of warfare by the court that ultimately contributed to the collapse of the dynasty.

The Han's failure to control its western frontiers therefore led to serious military problems, which in turn brought with them significant threats to the ruling dynasty, although not to the empire itself. Similar problems at Rome would prove even more dire. Major military threats on its northern frontiers had arisen

42. Lewis 2000.

during the latter decades of the second century, and a full-blown crisis developed toward the middle of the third.[43] As on China's western borders, Rome did not confront a single adversary whose authority could control Rome's enemies and who could either be appeased by gifts or markets or whose defeat would entail the termination of the threat its people posed. Instead, Rome faced raids on multiple fronts as a variety of tribes and protostates took advantage of the empire's distractions to go on the attack. In addition, the Persian Empire, created by a new and energetic dynasty in the East, the Sasanids, undertook an aggressive policy of territorial expansion in Syria that demanded a strong and effective military response. The military situation, which would have been difficult enough to resolve by itself, became critical owing to the political turmoil that arose at the same time. Throughout the first and second centuries, emperors had managed to pass power on to their successors for the most part peacefully. However, beginning in the late second century, civil war came to displace peaceful transfers of power. A multitude of emperors, rebels, and pretenders competed for the throne during the third century, and their wars with one another gravely weakened the empire's frontier defenses at a time when these were coming under the most serious military threats they had sustained in centuries. The result was fifty years of political turmoil at Rome and collapse on the frontiers punctuated by a succession of military disasters. The empire had never before come under such long-lasting, severe, and widespread military pressure, and its response was to undertake major changes not only in its armed forces but in its government and society as well.

The seriousness of the crisis demanded competent generals in command, and competence lay not among the senatorial elite, who had long supplied the empire's military leaders, but among the commoners, who by this point made up the middle and lower ranks of the officer corps.[44] The military was a great reservoir of talent, and it supplied the commanders who brought the empire back from the brink of disaster. Even emperors themselves in the third century often came from humble backgrounds and had risen to prominence in the army through their military talents, which the military crisis had afforded them ample scope to display. These developments inaugurated a lasting split within the empire between the holders of social and cultural power, that is, members of the senatorial class, on the one hand and the military leadership on the other. Under these new leaders, military efforts increased dramatically. During the later third century, when invaders had breached the frontiers at many points to attack the empire's undefended core, cities there began to be heavily fortified. Once the crisis had passed, the frontier defenses, too, were greatly augmented. At the

---

43. Birley 2000: 160–85; Drinkwater 2005.
44. Campbell 2005: 110–20.

same time, mobile field armies, which constituted strategic reserves, were created to rush to trouble spots and strike at attacking forces.[45] Even more important was the decision of the emperor Diocletian (r. 284–305 C.E.) in 286 C.E. to create a second, coemperor to govern the western half of the empire and then to supply both himself and his coregent with seconds-in-command and eventual successors, styled Caesars.[46] This division of responsibility among four rulers, which is termed the tetrarchy, permitted a much closer monitoring of the frontiers than had been possible under a single emperor; and because each tetrarch commanded his own field army, a military emergency on any frontier could be met much more swiftly and effectively. However, this regime not only allowed for a much better defense against external threats but, equally important, simultaneously was able to put an end to civil war for many years because a potential usurper now faced the challenge of overthrowing not one ruler but his three colleagues as well in order to secure power. In addition, the position of the emperor himself changed in response to the military and political crisis of the third century. Under Augustus and most of his successors, the distance between emperors and their subjects, particularly at the highest social levels, had not been great—successful emperors presented an image of comity with members of the senatorial class while all emperors claimed to be "fellow-soldiers" of the legionaries. Diocletian, however, inaugurated a much different stance of emperors toward their subjects. Emperors now began to live in deep seclusion. Access to them was highly restricted and surrounded by elaborate ceremony and protocol intended to evoke awe and reverence in their subjects high and low. The aim was to elevate the person of the emperor to a status beyond merely human and so in this way to ward off attempts to overthrow him on the presumption that no mere mortal could take his place. Diocletian's solution of the political crisis in turn enabled the tetrarchs to concentrate their energies on the empire's foreign foes, which finally brought the military crisis to an end. Even though the tetrarchy did not long survive its founder and civil war once again led to the establishment of a single emperor, the changes in the military and government that Diocletian put into place brought the empire a century of protection.

However, the resolution of the empire's third century crisis did not come without significant costs.[47] Military expenses had risen dramatically during the crisis of the third century, for in addition to the mobile field armies to combat major invasions, frontier garrisons were still in place to deal with minor incursions as well. The empire's military establishment doubled in size, and this enlargement necessitated a dramatic increase in taxation to pay for it. And the elevation of the

---

45. How to understand these events is controversial: Luttwak 1976: 127–90 argues for the adoption of a new defensive "grand strategy" while Whittaker 1994: 206–9 sees instead only a series of *ad hoc* measures.

46. Bowman 2005: 67–89; Campbell 2005: 12–30; Lo Cascio 2005: 170–81.

47. Jones 1964.

imperial person to his new, exalted status meant an enlarged court to undertake the elaborate round of ritual that now surrounded him, all of which also cost money and required additional revenue. In order to ensure the full collection of the taxes due, the civil administration had to expand as well. The empire's former administrative units were subdivided again and again to ensure closer supervision of the populace. More administrators further exacerbated the tax burden, and as the government met increasing resistance to its payment, it took steps to impose even greater control on civilian society. Diocletian not only undertook a vast census of his empire's population to further the effectiveness of tax collection, but under his direction the basis of taxation itself was now rationalized and made uniform. Standard units of agricultural production were established, and farmland throughout the empire was categorized in accordance with these units so that in theory every unit, although differing in size, was capable of the same output in crops. Similarly, standard units of manpower were established so that each adult male farmer counted as one unit while women's agricultural value could vary. All of this enabled the government through its census to know how much agricultural production could be expected in each region on the basis of the number of farmland and manpower units it contained, making income from the taxes levied on agriculture predictable and reliable. And the government could easily increase the amount it collected simply by increasing the levy on each unit, which the government did repeatedly during the fourth century. As the tax burdens grew heavier and less avoidable, peasants sought to escape them by fleeing, which brought forth from the government various measures tying them to the lands they worked. Similarly in the case of the empire's nonagricultural population, sons were required to follow their fathers in their professions and trades in order to ensure that the taxes the latter had paid would continue after their retirement or death. Members of the provincial upper classes, who had long had the task of supervising tax collection in their locales, were now made personally liable for the taxes themselves in the event of nonpayment by the peasants. In addition, to combat the inflation that had resulted when earlier emperors, to meet their military and other expenses, had diminished the precious metal content of their coinage, Diocletian promulgated an edict that attempted to set maximum prices for all goods and services throughout the empire. In sum, from the third century onward, Rome's imperial government increasingly penetrated the society it ruled to an unprecedented extent in an effort to secure the resources it needed to support its vast military endeavors and the civil administrative apparatus this entailed, much as Qin and the other warring states of China had done centuries before.

In the end, however, these measures proved insufficient. When the Roman Empire once again came under severe military pressure in the fifth century from tribes beyond its frontiers seeking to migrate into imperial territory, the western half of the empire proved unable to muster the military resources necessary either to resist or at least control these incursions, for reasons that go well beyond the scope of this chapter. As in Han China, however, part of the problem lay in the decision of western emperors to employ troops drawn from some of the recent barbarian immigrants who served in their native formations under their own rulers. Emperors had recourse to them because plague and other factors had caused the empire's population to decline, making recruits difficult to find but unoccupied farmland plentiful. Hence, the decision to allow barbarian migrants to settle in Roman territory in exchange for military service seemed like a solution to two problems at once. However, the loyalty of these troops, like the Han dynasty's barbarian allies, was difficult to depend on, and their military effectiveness was often questionable. Ultimately, emperors in the west simply grew less and less able to govern the provinces they nominally ruled, even Italy itself, until finally a new emperor simply failed to be nominated when his predecessor fell. Instead, in a constellation of successor states in the West, non-Roman, immigrant dynasties ruled that eventually forged ties with the old Roman ruling classes in their territories. In the East, however, imperial government proved much more resilient, even endeavoring to reconquer much of the West in the seventh century, until the emergence and conquests of Islam deprived it of much of its territory. Imperial government in China, by contrast, survived because its most powerful external military challenge came from opponents who were ecologically quite different and who, consequently, sought not to invade and occupy its territories but only extract material benefits from it, which ironically gave them a powerful stake in ensuring the empire's survival.

4. Conclusion

Clearly, war profoundly affected the trajectories of state-formation in China and Rome. Just as clearly, however, the severity of the threats each confronted strongly influenced those trajectories. In Spring and Autumn and Warring States China, a multistate system in which each component enjoyed a rough parity of strength failed to reach a stable balance of power.[48] The uncertainty of alliances and the existential threat that each state faced forced them all to develop in ways that maximized their ability to extract from their own subjects the financial and manpower resources they needed to defend themselves and overcome their opponents. The process imposed highly bureaucratized central administrations upon their societies capable of extending the government's reach down to the level of five household units. Although Latium during the early Republic represented a similar multistate system, the states it comprised all faced the additional challenge of a common external threat that forced them to find ways of cooperating

---

48. Hui 2005: 67–79.

in order to survive. Coalition building at Rome substituted for increasing the government's ability to squeeze more men and money out of its citizen population. Crucially, too, Rome had overthrown its monarchy (trad. 509 B.C.E.), while in China that form of government remained unquestioned. Thus, Rome lacked a central authority around which a bureaucratic administration could coalesce. In the absence of a military threat that would have compelled Rome to develop in the ways that China did and because coalition building and, after 338 B.C.E., the incorporation of many non-Romans into the Republic's citizen body enabled it to meet successfully the threats it did face, the aristocracy's self-interests could determine how the Roman state evolved. These interests entailed, first, preventing any single aristocrat or small faction from gaining control of the Republic and, second, preserving a system of aristocratic control over the citizenry based on personal prestige and patronage. Each militated strongly against the establishment of a bureaucratic administration that could displace the vertical links of patronage that tied ordinary Romans to those in power or challenge aristocratic consensus in the senate as the dominant organ controlling public affairs. Only after aristocratic power was overthrown could the first emperor begin to establish just such a system to control his empire. Yet Roman imperial administration during its first two centuries never progressed as far down that road as Warring States China had, in large part because patronage and ideology along with a limited bureaucracy were adequate to the task of governing the empire. Not until the military and political crisis of the third century did the exigencies of war once again become the dominant force shaping state formation, forcing the creation of the sort of extensive and intrusive bureaucracy that China had developed centuries earlier.

The nature of the threats that each empire faced, their severity, and political factors also affected who was mobilized for war as well as how they were mobilized and led. The danger of utter annihilation forced the governments of Spring and Autumn and Warring States China to move from warfare as an elite monopoly to a system of mass conscription and to offer substantial material rewards (as well as penalties) in exchange for the participation of ordinary subjects in their kingdoms' wars. A class of military experts developed at the same time to lead these new types of campaigns, men whose origins and training paralleled the cadres of administrative bureaucrats that were being formed at the same time. Once the armies of Qin had vanquished its rivals, however, mass levies were gradually abandoned. Because the military challenges confronting early imperial China proved to be both intractable and yet not serious enough to threaten the existence of its government, the mass armies that its bureaucracy had been created to mobilize could be dispensed with. Professional soldiers drawn from lowest strata of the Chinese population and cavalry hired from the steppe tribes were more effective against the empire's opponents, less of a burden on the treasury, and less of a threat to the regime. Similarly, the men charged with leading these armies could be selected on criteria other than military expertise and competence since the consequences of failure were no longer dire. The elite monopoly on war ended early at Rome as well, for reasons that are not well understood. The mass conscription that replaced it, however, took place in the context of a struggle over political rights within the community, and consequently the incentives offered in exchange for participation in war were political as well as material. The end of that struggle coincided with the end of the most serious long-term military challenges to Roman hegemony within the peninsula, and for that reason, as well as the changing nature of the citizen body, the aristocracy's political concessions to the citizens who composed the Republic's armies subsequently grew much less frequent. Professionalization only occurred once the political landscape had drastically changed and the need of the newly established monarchy for security against potential challengers made it imperative to create a military loyal to the ruling dynasty. This change only pertained to the rank and file, however. Aristocratic nonspecialists commanded Rome's armies throughout the Republic and during the first two centuries of the empire. Only the rise of a much graver threat than the empire had confronted up to that point forced the character of the officer class to change in the third century, inaugurating a lasting split between the civilian and military elite that in important ways hastened the fall of the western empire two centuries later.

3

Law and Punishment in the Formation of Empire

Karen Turner

> ...law is so inextricably entwined in culture that, for all its
> specialized capabilities, it may, indeed, best be seen not simply as
> a mechanism for attending to disputes or enforcing decisions, not
> solely as articulated rules or as evidence of differential power...but
> as a framework for ordered relationships.
>
> — Lawrence Rosen, *Law as Culture*

A commitment to civil law stands as one of Rome's enduring legacies, the basis for the rule of law in the countries that preserved Roman legal ideals and practices long after the empire disappeared. But, as Bauman has noted in his study of crime and punishment in ancient Rome, the criminal law always operated as the "poor relation on the Roman legal scene."[1] Indeed, many textbook surveys of Roman law devote little attention to penal philosophies and practices.[2] By contrast, observers of Chinese history who argue that imperial China's preoccupation with criminal law continues to hinder legal reform point to the political system that emerged in Qin and Han times as the source of harsh penal laws designed to guard the resources of the state rather than the rights of subjects.[3] True, by the time of the Qin unification in China, as Mark Lewis has shown, a body of mythology, political theory, and historical anecdote legitimated the state's right to monopolize and manage coercion.[4] But the "grand theory" based on the Confucian ideal of the "rule of man" that has dominated narratives about the nature of political authority in China obscures the attention that Warring States and Han writers paid to law as a measure to legitimate institutionalized violence.

In this chapter, I want to focus on one of the most sensitive matters faced by any expanding polity: how to justify the state's right to punish elites whose support was necessary for political survival and commoners whose compliance and labor

1. Bauman 1996: 3.
2. See, for example, a classic, Wolff 1951.
3. See, for example, Liang 1989. Shen 2000 discusses debates in China about the rule of law.
4. Lewis 1990.

sustained the institutional apparatus. Judging from the wealth of writing on the topic from observers in both empires, no other area of statecraft generated more unease among elites who witnessed the emergence of universal rulership than ceding to the emperor and his courts the authority to determine categories of deviance and the level of punitive action necessary to maintain order and deter further violence. Shauel Eisenstadt's contention that traditional bureaucratic empires dealt with the common predicament of balancing the desires of rulers and elites—committed to traditional, ascriptive modes of power—with the ambitions of "new men" dependent on bureaucratic positions and values provides a useful starting point. No imperial polity could survive by coercive methods alone, he argues, but his scheme places undue weight on the actions of rulers to manage state violence.[5] More useful is Danielle Allen's study of punishments in ancient Greece, which shows how individual actors at many levels of the state apparatus influenced penal policies. As she observes, informal bodies, such as clans and guilds, do not have to rationalize their decisions to touch the bodies of their members. "In contrast, legitimate punishments based on state authority must be justifiable at large within the political community. Punishments that make use of state power (or the power of the *polis* in the ancient Greek case) must be defensible according to definitions of fairness and justice that prevail throughout the polity." Allen finds more value in Bourdieu's theory of practice, which argues that individuals can exert agency and manipulate rules even in situations of relative powerlessness, than in Foucault's model of political theater, governmentality, and scripted dramas of violence. As Allen observes, "Some rules are less flexible than others or require greater effort to manipulate, but strategic actors may sometimes be willing to take on that work."[6]

It is important to note at the outset that no institutional checks existed to curb the sovereign's absolute power over matters of life and death in either empire. In a deadly game in which the emperors held the highest cards, persuasion remained the only avenue for curbing the discretionary power of rulers. As well, I am not suggesting in this chapter that in the case of China, patterns from the past have not affected attempts to foster legal reform in modern times, as I note in the conclusion. But in the spirit of this project, I want to redirect attention from the problems in the present to suggest how conceptions of law that emerged in the early empires contributed to the longevity of the imperial system. In other words, I acknowledge that what was healthy for the body politic might not have favored the individuals who supported it. But I also want to argue that critics fearful of the consequences of rule by personality in early Han China drew from a particular blend of cultural and historical "bricolage" that gave teeth to their attempts to temper the arbitrary use of imperial power. Indeed, from a

5. Eisenstadt 1963.
6. Allen 1999: 17.

comparative vantage, Roman elites seemed less prepared than their Chinese counterparts to contend with the legal implications of universal rulership. Some scholars attribute this reluctance to formulate rules for imperial behavior to the persistence of republican interests embodied in the Senate;[7] but in any case, as Jill Harries concludes in her study of Roman law in late antiquity, an institutional relationship between law and monarchy came about slowly in the process of adjusting republican ideals to the realities of empire.[8]

1. PATTERNS OF HISTORY

Chinese political theory from its inception centered around a conflict between state builders bent on controlling human and material resources and local elites who understood the dangers of the interventionist state. As the warring territorial kingdoms encapsulated new populations after the fourth century B.C.E., general laws that transcended local custom became necessary as a standard for maintaining order and adjudicating disputes. The legalists' argument for clear, public laws and consistent punishments did not aim to protect subjects from state power but to deter dissent and create an efficient machinery to mobilize the population for military and labor service. The Warring States legalists did not view the state as an arena for moral teaching as did Aristotle and the Chinese Confucians, for example, but rather as a mechanism for exerting control through carefully calculated rewards and harsh punishments. Few arguments surface in any of the texts in favor of popular opinion as a source of law or motive for legal reform. As the third century eclectic manual of political theory *Guanzi* declared, law existed to mobilize the common people to perform duties for the state contrary to their inclinations: "The laws are more important than the people. Therefore the wise ruler should not alter laws out of affection for the people. The people must be esteemed less than the laws."[9] The treatise on "Conforming to the Law" in this remarkable text expands on the legalist notion that the human factor must be muted, allowing laws to serve as the "marking line" for all state affairs: "Statutes, regulations, and procedures must be patterned on the *dao* . . . and must be public and clear. . . . Rewards and punishments

---

7. For a useful analysis of how changing contemporary concerns about the state and autocratic leadership have influenced perceptions of Augustus, and how the classic works of Mommsen and Syme interpreted the transition to empire in Rome, see Raaflaub and Tober, eds. 1990; and the introduction to Mommsen 1996.

8. Harries 1999.

9. Si bu bei yao [hereafter SBBY] edition, Shanghai 1927–1937, 16.6.5a–b. For a translation and analysis of selected chapters, see Rickett 1985. See especially "Fa Fa" for the text's conception of law and punishments. I have left the term "dao" untranslated because I believe it is not easily rendered into English. Here it refers to the natural and consistent order of things. As well, debate in the field continues about the proper rendering of "fa," which I translate as "law," for I believe that especially when *fa* is linked with punishments, the laws of the state are what is meant. And just as "law" in English can extend from the rules of the road to the law of God, so too in Chinese *fa* can encompass all of these conceptions, sometimes at once. See my discussion in Turner 1992.

must be predictable and certain."[10] The text repeats the legalist dictum that pardons must never be granted. The Confucian pragmatist Xunzi (fl. 238 B.C.E.), who witnessed the costs of the more violent wars that preceded the unification, assessed the state's oppressive demands for labor and military service: "The state is the most powerful instrument for benefit in the world . . . and it is the heaviest burden."[11] Early Confucian critics correctly identified law as a tool that legalistic bureaucrats could utilize to order human affairs at the expense of their own privileges as educators and ceremonial masters. But though they longed for a sage ruler in a spirit akin to Plato's benevolent despot, who could recreate the hallowed old Zhou Empire and administer justice without the hindrance of law, Confucian writers famously defined rules based on the activities of legendary sage kings for judging the behavior of the kings of their own day.[12] Indeed, Mencius's (d. 389 B.C.E.) declaration that a king whose actions contradicted his responsibilities no longer deserved the respect of his office echoes Aristotle's justification for tyrannicide.

The Qin Empire should have represented the culmination of legalist efforts to create a bureaucratic state ruled by a political machine that tempered the whims of rulers. And in fact, as we know from the legal materials buried with a low-level Qin official discovered at Shuihudi in 1975, at the local levels of governance, a very rigid system of controlling official discretion did exist on the books. Even the First Emperor of China, the ultimate despot in standard versions of Chinese imperial history, promised to clarify the laws, as stele inscriptions from his reign attest.[13] It was at the level of court politics that the Qin regime failed to meet the challenge of institutionalizing its power: a succession crisis encouraged a revolt by lowly commoners attempting to escape corvée labor service. The Qin example provided Han Empire builders with several advantages. The empire had engendered a respite, albeit short-lived, from constant warfare and had created a model for expanding institutional structures suitable for governing a centralized state.

Han narratives of the fall of Qin, whose emperors and officials were charged with making laws and implementing punishments "according to their own wanton lights,"[14] also provided critics with a rich rhetorical fund for censuring contemporary rulers and their henchmen. When the Han elder statesman Lu Jia reminded the Han founder that he might have won the empire on horseback but could not govern it by force, the emperor understood the message; before he entered the rebellion against Qin, he had served as a low-level bureaucrat in the

10. *Guanzi* 16.6.4b.

11. *Xunzi* 11.1a (SBBY edition). For a translation, see Knoblock 1988–1990.

12. See my article comparing late classical Chinese and Greek notions of kingship and law in Turner 1990.

13. See Kern 2000. Kern rightly critiques the use of terms such as "Legalist" and "Confucian," but I cannot come up with better general terms for the very real opposing positions these thinkers took, and I use these categories here with caution.

14. This statement is from Chao Cuo in *Hanshu* 49. 2296. Throughout I have used the Zhonghua edition, Beijing 1962.

Qin system. His roots in the state of Chu, which rivaled Qin for a well-developed legal system down to the local level as we know from recently excavated materials, must have also contributed to his concern with legal matters. Despite his promise to simplify the laws of Qin at a critical moment in his bid for the empire, Gaozu ordered his officials to collect and preserve the Qin laws and to build on its ritual liturgy and court ceremonials to enhance his own position. And so Han rulers and reformers went about the business of centralizing power—adopting the Qin laws and employing some of its officials—even while decrying the onerous demands made by the defeated regime. But there were disagreements about how to integrate holdovers from the earlier empire at the time and disagreements among sinologists about how much dissent from subaltern actors went on during the Han. I agree with Mark Lewis that a commitment to unity and wholeness emerged out of the constant warfare that troubled the preimperial era and with Nathan Sivin that few voices surfaced in favor of restoring a fragmented political system.[15] Sivin contends that as the Han Empire developed in the first century, "intellectuals bound the structure of Heaven and earth, and that of the human body to that of the state," and transformed the image of the conqueror from a warrior to a dispenser of benefactions and life.[16] But Sivin overlooks how theories based on resonance with the monarch at the center also created a discursive space in which clever intellectuals could place at the feet of the emperor blame for improper decisions and their consequent manifestations in the natural world. Moreover, the Han emperors could not simply act as benefactors but had to take a role in legislation and execution. As Puett argues, the tension that surfaced in the early Han writings centered around the suspicion that the empire, while necessary, had been founded by force and sustained by principles of governance alien to the sage kings, who supposedly maintained unity by virtuous rule. Nostalgia reached far back, to the golden age of the unified Western Zhou Empire. The "traditions" supposedly embodied in this distant utopia were reinvented and manipulated over the course of the Han, for the political contours of this ancient empire remained conveniently malleable to fit current concerns.[17] Thus, the early Han is marked by a struggle between emperors claiming their right to manage "All under Heaven" and bureaucrats reminding them that the lessons of history taught that the Liu family's mandate to rule was conditional.

There was no articulated doubt by Han times, however, that a unified polity under a single ruler, "The One Man," offered the only viable system to put an end to chaos. Threats in the form of ambitious kin and officials did endanger the Han emperors, and resentment toward cultural and political centralization did surface. But there is little evidence that any of these ambitious rebels envisioned a

15. See Lewis 2006: ch. 5.
16. Sivin 1995: 7.
17. See, for example, Puett 2001.

truly pluralistic polity. The universal emperorship was the prize, and as later history has shown, rebels manipulated Han symbols and institutions to legitimate their own conquests. No alternative political forms emerged out of China's classical era as had happened in Greece, and by the republican era in Rome, monarchy was tolerated as a temporary expedient in response to a period of internal conflict that threatened the very existence of the Republic. It is interesting for the historian of China to note that some contemporaries regarded Julius Caesar's attempt to extend his dictatorship beyond the crisis that justified it with the same mix of awe and hatred that greeted the undeniable accomplishments of China's First Emperor. In his study of Roman legal and constitutional history, Kunkel outlines the problems faced by Caesar's successors:

> The creator of the Roman monarchy was faced with the grave task of reconciling his situation in some more or less satisfactory way with the traditions of the republican period and with the republican outlook of, at any rate, the leading sections of the Roman citizen body. It was in dealing with these impalpable things that Caesar had failed when, with his usual consistency, he entered upon a course of action which...must have led forthwith to an unambiguously monarchical order. Warned by the failure of his adoptive father, Augustus now sought and found the solution of his problem in a peculiar compromise.... Seen from the standpoint of formal constitutional law, the new order (28–27 B.C.) seemed expressly and ceremoniously to restore the Republic which had been shaken to its foundations in the turbulence of the last century B.C.... The newly organized republican constitution bestowed indeed upon the bearer of the monarchical power a whole series of functions of the greatest political significance.... Augustus's creation can be understood, therefore, only as a force standing outside the republican order, whose vocation of trust was to support and supplement it.[18]

Kunkel points out that Roman emperors were charged with maintaining order but hindered by a legal and constitutional legacy that was in fact not suitable for the task of governing an empire.

Despite the continuing existence of republican institutions and values, Augustus's gradual assumption of control over all aspects of civil and military matters is regarded in Roman historiography as a revolutionary departure from the ideals of the Republic. How much the Roman principate truly marked a new form of government continues to be debated, just as historians of China disagree about the extent of the difference between the late Warring States kingdoms and the Qin and Han imperial systems. But from a comparative look, it seems that

18. Kunkel 1966: 47.

the shift in Rome, from an oligarchic government based on the rights of elites to decide and dole out punishments to a monarchy intent on asserting its right to define crime and assign remedies either personally or through state controlled courts, constituted a far more serious psychological break with the past than the Qin centralization. Under the Republic, except for heinous crimes such as parricide or acts that harmed the public welfare, citizens could decide when to invoke the law and were expected to use private means to enforce decisions. Bauman assesses the shift in his study of criminal law, "When Augustus founded the Principate in 27 B.C. he created the conditions for as profound a change in criminal justice as in any other sphere of government and society."[19] Borkowski in a textbook on Roman law defines clearly why this change mattered, although it is important to remember that only gradually was the formulary system replaced: "Virtually all aspects of civil procedure were now firmly in the hands of the State, and subject to increasingly detailed regulation, as has tended to occur in modern legal systems. . . . The old system, comprising a preliminary hearing and full trial, was abandoned. The case now consisted of a cognition—an investigation by the magistrate, who conducted the whole trial and made the decision himself."[20]

This reference to modern systems and the reach of the state must be qualified. Both civil and criminal processes in Roman imperial courts were initiated by the citizen, although the duty of the provincial governor to keep order and hunt down serious criminals also enabled prosecution—or rather the infliction of summary justice—by the state. Cognition, which originated as the process of adjudication conducted by provincial governors, was gradually extended to the city of Rome itself. There republican trials by jury ceased to function (adultery was probably the last to go, early in the third century C.E.) and jurisdiction by cognition was concentrated in the office of the urban prefect of the city of Rome. While statutory guidance was provided on penalties and punishments, this was gradually subverted over time by imperial modifications of the system, which were themselves responses to court decisions, made in line with changed conventions on punishment.[21] The increased "judicial savagery" of the Roman Empire in late antiquity should therefore be seen as caused not only by imperial fiat, but also by decisions of local judges and courts in line with social expectations.[22]

2. LAW AND DISCRETION

Tacitus, prominent statesman and staunch believer in the spartan values of the early Republic, regarded Augustus as a shrewd politician who ended dissention

19. Bauman 1996: 50.
20. See Borkowski 1997: 81.
21. Harries 2007: 35–8.
22. MacMullen 1990: 204–24.

but at a high price. Whether his cynical accounts of interactions between the clever emperor and cowed senators, when "the protection of laws was unavailing," belie his own promise to write "without bitterness or partiality" continues to confound assessments of the early emperors.[23] In general, however, while historians of Roman law disagree about the role of Augustus vis-à-vis the Senate, the early Roman Empire is not generally castigated as a despotic regime.[24] In fact, ancient and modern writers, in Asia as well as the West, have pointed to "Oriental" legal systems as tools of "sultanism,"[25] which relied on personal rather than lawful rule. Oriental despotism was associated with eastern regimes closer to home in ancient Greece and Rome, but for later observers, imperial China has served as the premier example of a system ruled by men rather than law. But one writer's despotism is another's utopia. Ambivalence about law and litigation that colors debates about the value of the rule of law in the West has led some legal thinkers to admire China for its cynical approach to law. For example, the legal realist Jerome Frank praised China for its disdain of litigation and commitment to the discretion of the good judge rather than black letter law.[26] For premodern state builders, the realities were more complex because they did not enjoy the luxury of a sturdy legal system in the first place.[27] No modern thinker has stated the dilemma more eloquently than Xunzi: "Laws cannot stand alone . . . for when they are implemented by the right person they survive but if neglected they disappear. . . . Law is the basis for good government but the superior man is the basis for law. So when there is a superior man, the law even if sparse, will cover any situation, but when there is no superior man, even if the laws are all-embracing, they will neither apply to all situations nor be flexible enough to respond to change."[28]

Plutarch's description of the activities of the ideal lawmaker, Solon, modifies Aristotle's famous dictum that the laws must govern the magistrates. Of Solon he writes approvingly: "It is said that he was obscure and ambiguous in the wording of his laws, on purpose to increase the honor of his courts; for since their differences could not be adjusted by the letter, they would have to bring all their causes to the judge, who thus were in a manner masters of the laws."[29] Chinese Confucians would have agreed with this portrait of the ideal lawgiver, but with the provision that the judge be trained to act as a virtuous guardian of the general welfare without personal interests at stake. Other texts from the Warring States and early Han era declare that rulers and their delegates must distinguish

23. *Annals* 1.1 (trans. A. Church and W. Brodribb). See Raaflaub and Toher, eds. 1990 for the historiography of the reign of Augustus.

24. See the discussion in Raaflaub and Tober, eds. 1990.

25. See, for example, MacMullen 1990: 214.

26. Frank 1973.

27. See Dworkin 1986 for an argument about the importance of judicial attitude rather than rules; H. L. A. Hart's classic definition of law as rules, uniformly applied, is in Hart 1961.

28. *Xunzi* 8.1.

29. Plutarch, *Solon* 18 (trans. J. Dryden).

between personal agendas and the public good when calling on the force of the state to wage war or punish deviance: "Eliminate selfish interests and act only for public concerns,"[30] for the "world is not the world of any one man."[31]

Even the legalists who argued for strong monarchy placed the health of the state above the whims of individual monarchs. Shang Yang (d. 338 B.C.E.), the early legalist reformer credited with giving the state of Qin an edge in the competition for dominance among the contending states, defined the enlightened ruler as one who heeds laws in all matters of government.[32] He accorded institutional continuity more weight than talented kings: "Sages cannot transfer to others their personal and natural characteristics. Only through law can this be accomplished." Disagreement centered on the appropriate foundation for law. R. P. Peerenboom has argued that Huang Lao philosophy, a pragmatic Daoism that prevailed in the early Han as a corrective to the meddling policies attributed to the Qin regime, represented a theoretical constraint on the ruler by binding him to a predetermined moral order.[33] I agree that the conception of *dao* in the Huang Lao texts represented a timeless, universal standard for law but view the text's purpose as oriented far more toward pragmatic rather than moralistic concerns. As the *Jingfa* begins: "The *dao* gives birth to the law and law is what marks success and failure.... Laws and regulations are of the utmost importance in governing because there is no confusion in the government that uses them and no disorder once the laws and regulations are produced. If you are public-spirited and without private bias, and your rewards and punishments are trusted, you will have good government."[34] This theory that subordinated positive law to a higher law based on a standard as immutable as the rotation of the seasons clearly aimed to mute the personal influence of rulers. But the case for natural law as a check on power was rarely made in recorded debates in the Han sources. In light of how often the decisions of sage kings were used to critique the current state of affairs, much more deeply ingrained was the belief that there was no escaping the fact that human actions did, in fact, affect the workings of the natural world.[35] One of the most important manuals for managing the universal empire, written under the direction of the Chancellor of the Qin state around 239 B.C.E., delineates the ruler's obligations but also his overarching power: "A command issues from the ruler's mouth. Those in official positions receive it and carry it out.... It moves unimpeded all the way down and it permeates the people's hearts and propagates to the four quarters of [the realm]."[36]

30. *Jingfa* 1980.
31. *Lushi chunqiu* 1.8b (SBBY). For a translation and study of this text, see Knoblock and Riegel 2000.
32. See *Shangjunshu jiegu* 4.9a–5.7b (Chengdu 1935). Duyvendak 1928: 243. See Turner 1990.
33. See Peerenboom 1993.
34. From "Daofa" in the *Jingfa*. For a more complete discussion of this conception as one possible component of the rule of law, see Turner 1992.
35. Durrant 1995 discusses Sima Qian's ambivalence about human power.
36. *Lushi chunqiu* 3.3.5. See Sivin 1995: 22.

Chinese thinkers never distinguished a law of the metropole from the laws of outsiders as did republican jurists, who refrained on principle from extracting general principles from specific cases and distinguished the *ius civile*, the law of Roman citizens, from the laws of other peoples. It seems that a larger conception of law emerged under the later empire in Rome. Writers such as Ammianus and Symmachus demonstrated their understanding that emperors should not stand above the laws, as their critiques of individual emperors reveal.[37] But others described the law in larger terms. Law served justice, ensured a balanced function of the state as a whole, and applied to everyone, even the emperor, according to Priscus in the fifth century, for example.[38] In terms that would have sounded familiar to Han thinkers who embraced a pragmatic, syncretic political theory, the famous jurist Ulpian argued in the third century C.E. that established laws should not be altered without good reason and defined the burden of empire for men like himself: "For we serve the needs of justice and advance knowledge of the good and the just, distinguishing the just from the unjust, separating the legal from the illegal, seeking to make men good not only through fear of punishment but through the incentive of rewards...."[39] According to Harries, Ulpian conceived of a law that extended to all living creatures, as did the Chinese thinkers who linked law with the natural world. In practical terms, as the Roman emperorship became more institutionalized and a bureaucracy beholden to the state developed, lawmaking became more routinized and codified. What Ulpian tried to do, she writes, "was to limit the impact of the emperor's activities as part of the operation of general law, by which the empire was governed." By the late empire, she concludes, "The emperor was not the only constitution the empire had."[40]

3. THE EMPEROR AND THE LAW

Textbook accounts of Roman and Chinese imperial law point to the emperor as the supreme legislator. It is true that the final decision about making and changing law rested with the emperors, but the histories reveal a much more complex situation at work, one that often involved a multitude of actors and agendas. The personalities of emperors loom large in Tacitus, and later in Ammianus, because they were public figures who operated in a vast, urban political theater. In the early empire, according to Tacitus, the emperors personally directed the legal system but at least paid lip service to the Senate. The Han emperors, more sequestered within the palace walls as the dynasty matured, appear in the histories most often to delegate the dangerous business of controlling the imperial relatives, clarifying

---

37. See Seager 1986: 40.
38. See Harries 1999: 6.
39. Harries 1999: 7.
40. Harries 1999: 20 and 26.

laws, and adjudicating difficult cases to the bureaucrats, leaving to themselves the right to pontificate about the need to ameliorate the harsh punishments in their fiduciary role as guardians of the people's welfare. This lack of attention to the direct intervention of Han rulers in actual cases might have stemmed in part from the historians' fear of the consequences of pinning blame for misgovernment squarely on the rulers under whom they composed their work. But in general, a deep-seated wariness of direct, personal involvement in legal change seems to have characterized Han imperial attitudes toward legislation.

Han emperors advocated that laws be clarified to eliminate confusion and sponsored court debates about the harshest punishments, but they are not identified with particular laws (such as Augustus's law on adultery); the regulations and statutes Han historians and officials mention when appealing to precedent appear to be timeless, universal products without reference to human authorship. And yet, as we know from the histories and the discovery of fragments of the Han code at Zhangjiashan in 1983, the Han dynasty preserved and amplified the Qin laws. While a coherent code did not appear until the Tang Dynasty, laws proliferated over the course of the Han. We learn about legislation and reform mostly from negative portraits of bureaucrats at work. Du Zhou (d. 95 B.C.E.), placed by Sima Qian among the harsh officials in Wudi's reign for his sycophantic attitude, declared pragmatically: "Whatever the earlier rulers thought was right they made into statutes and what later rulers thought right they added as orders. So how can the old laws be appropriate for the times?"[41] Zhang Tang (d. 116 B.C.E.), one of Wudi's most active legislators in his position as Commandant of Justice, defined statutes and ordinances and added treasonous thoughts to crimes punished by death. He was castigated by his contemporaries for tampering with the old laws, hated by the imperial princes for impinging on their privileges, and eventually forced to commit suicide. These officials were not simple technocrats for the most part but had either studied with or patronized erudites who could deduce legal principles from the most sacred texts. Chao Cuo (d. 154 B.C.E.), for example, enjoyed imperial patronage for his loyalty to the Liu clan and knowledge of the canonical *Book of Documents* but eventually earned the hatred of rival officials and the territorial kings after submitting thirty new statutes to the laws and was ordered to be executed in his court robes in the marketplace.[42] His fate was not unusual: from the time of Shang Yang through the Han, the act of tampering with the laws often brought a violent end to the men who dared undertake the task.

This conservative stance toward altering the law reflects what Puett calls the "ambivalence of creation" that characterized late classical thinking.[43] Change, as

---

41. *Shiji* 122: 3153 (Zhonghua edition, Beijing 1959).
42. *Shiji* 101: 2746. See the discussion by Puett 2001 of Chao Cuo and other reformers.
43. *Shiji* 101: 2746.

the eclectic texts with a Daoist slant contended, always carried unforeseen dangers. Laws were changed of course, but a deep attachment to "the laws of old" and reluctance to link rulers with legislation masks the records of the actual process of reform. We do know that Zhang Tang collected Wudi's decisions to be used as precedents in later cases but have no evidence of how particular statutes affected decisions. At work is what Henry Maine called the "legal fiction," in which new laws were constructed according to the myth that they simply reinforced traditional values.[44] Ban Gu, in his treatise on punishments in the *Hanshu*, neatly outlined how the need to formulate workable laws while remaining true to tradition worked out: "I will present what has happened since the Han arose—to show how the laws and regulations have been fixed to conform with antiquity even though changed to suit the present age."[45] In early imperial China, where public law never completely replaced clan law and military law, so too in the transition to empire in Rome, the process of institutionalizing the magistrate's courts and the role of the emperor in legislative and judicial affairs proceeded slowly. By the reign of Theodosius (379–455 C.E.), especially in the eastern half of the empire, law became more bureaucratized and less dependent on the emperors' direct involvement in the day-to-day business of deciding laws and punishments. In Rome as in China, massive and organized codification of the laws began only after a period of crisis: division between the eastern and western empires in Rome, and the fall of Han and ensuing period of disunion in China.

The history of the reign of the third Han emperor, Wendi (r. 180–157 B.C.E.), is particularly rich with accounts about wrangling between the emperor and court officials over fundamental issues of governance, from how to balance the interests of the imperial family against the needs of the state to defining the role of the emperor in religious rites and legal decisions.[46] Wendi had no need to justify his attention to law, since the founder's promise to mitigate the harsh laws of Qin provided a mandate that later emperors were required to honor. But law was not his only concern: tension within the imperial clan for favors and territory, succession problems, an unstable frontier, and the need to establish a viable institutional and ritual apparatus consonant with his position as head of state all demanded attention.

What is interesting in the Chinese case is just how many men of ability believed that the good of the state must take precedence over the interest of rulers and their kin and who then rose to the dangerous challenge. In one famous passage included in the histories, Wendi's intrepid *tingwei* [Commandant of Justice], the highest law officer in the realm, articulated his vision of the relation between the

---

44. Maine 1888: 20–28.
45. *Hanshu* 23: 1102.
46. Wendi is known as a sage king, but I have called him a "studied sage" in earlier work since I believe that he was far more cynically disposed to centralize power in his own person than has been recognized. See Turner Gottschang 1983.

emperor and the law when forced by the emperor to justify his decision to fine a commoner, who had ignored an order to clear the way for the imperial entourage. When the irate emperor protested the light sentence, Zhang Shizhi set forth his own responsibilities: "The *tingwei* is the one who maintains balance in the world. To allow even one deviation in the laws would cause them to no longer be taken seriously. And then how would the people know how to behave?" He went on to clarify the ruler's position within the legal system: "The law must be upheld by the Son of Heaven and his people alike and this is the penalty prescribed by law." Zhang admitted that if the emperor had ordered the man executed on the spot, that would have been the end of it. But once the business of assigning the correct punishment entered his purview, he was bound to uphold his duty to maintain impartiality. Moreover, he threatened: "If [the punishment] were made heavier in this case, the people would no longer trust the laws. May I ask the Emperor to consider these consequences?" Wendi conceded: "The sentence you decided matches [the crime]."[47]

4. The Critics

The most obvious critics in the early Roman Empire were associated with the Stoic school. When Nero attempted to deflect a move to resurrect *maiestas* (treason) as a punishable offense, the Stoic, Thrasea, opposed the death penalty, not on grounds of clemency, but to guard legality. The emperor's motive seemed to have been to gain credit for himself; of the resistance of Thrasea, Bauman writes: "It was also a reaction against the idea that clemency was the special prerogative of the hereditary monarchy that the Julio-Claudian dynasty had become. To those Stoics who disliked that sort of ruler in principle, the *leges* were the one sure shield against tyranny."[48] Veyne has claimed that the Stoics served as Rome's protobureaucrats because of their disdain for the cult of personality and commitment to a rule-bound legal system.[49] But while individual figures associated with the Stoic school did, at times, challenge imperial power, unlike Han bureaucrats, their authority was often personal rather than institutional, and they were more devoted to republican values than the security of the imperial apparatus.

It is only later, as a bureaucracy began to develop, that an instance similar on the surface to Zhang Shizhi's showdown with Wendi appears, in the writing of the fourth century Roman historian Ammianus Marcellinus. When the Emperor Valentinian I—who was well known for his apoplectic fits when crossed—

---

47. *Shiji* 102: 2754. See his translated biography in Watson 1993: 466–72. For negative views of Zhang's admission that the emperor had the right to execute a criminal without an investigation, see MacCormack 2001: 108; for implications for the rule of law, see Turner 1992.

48. Bauman 1996: 85.

49. Veyne 1976.

learned that certain Roman senators had resorted to magic and religious invocation potentially harmful to his position, he ordered the harshest punishments applied under a general ruling that all such crimes be classified as treason, with serious consequences, as Ammianus records: "All whom the justice of the ancient law and the decisions of previous emperors had exempted from interrogation under torture, should, if the investigation demanded, be liable to torments."[50] After a series of trials and executions, a delegation of three high-ranking senators approached the angry ruler to make their case that "punishments should not be out of proportion to the offense and that no senator should be subjected to torture, a proceeding which was neither customary nor legal." Valentinian denied that he had authorized the decree in the first place and complained that such a charge amounted to slander. But Eupraxius tactfully contradicted him, and Ammianus reports that "his frankness brought about the repeal of the cruel edict which was of unexampled frightfulness."

As Harries observes, while the delegation gained an audience because of their privilege as senators, the aversion of violence in the end depended on the courage and verbal adroitness of the quaestor. But it was the senators and not the official who clearly stated the role of law in their plea for the freedom from bodily harm they had once enjoyed under the Republic.[51] On another occasion, Eupraxius intervened when the emperor ordered local elites from three towns put to death: "Show more restraint, your highness. These men who are to be executed as criminals on your orders will be honored by the Christians as martyrs." These direct confrontations are as rare in Ammianus's history as in the Han histories, but it is interesting that Eupraxius's advice seems directed more toward strategic than legal concerns. Before the reign of Wudi, who tolerated little interference from any high official, the Commandant of Justice enjoyed a higher standing than the quaestor, whose role in Ammianus's time was still limited to polishing and dictating the emperor's legal pronouncements and who depended on literary talent in some cases more than knowledge of the law.[52] As the Roman bureaucracy developed in the east under Theodosius, the quaestors began to take charge of regularizing the laws.[53] As the Han Empire wore on, legal power became less regulated in one office. Wudi instituted a practice in which special commissioners were sent out to punish "wicked and troublesome persons and to take charge of important law cases."[54] These commissioners had the power to apply military law and carried axes to symbolize their power over life and death—an image that conjures up the *fasces* borne by the lictors who accompanied Roman magistrates vested with imperium.

50. Ammianus Marcellinus 28.1.10.
51. Harries 1999: 40–41.
52. See Honoré 1993.
53. Honoré 1998: 12. See also Harries 1988.
54. *Hanshu* 19: 3–4.

The excavated materials from the Qin and Han periods confirm that the historians' preoccupation with the relation between monarchy and law was matched by the government's attention to administering the empire according to law. In the final analysis, however, the codes reveal the worries of the state rather than how the laws were actually implemented, and the historians' narratives of events offer our best guide for viewing how ideals meshed with realities—if only from a limited vantage. As O. F. Robinson has noted in her study of penal policies in ancient Rome, "Our sources are too limited, too partial, for any objective, statistically valid, recognition of attitudes. Perhaps, however, this is a positive feature. We have snapshots of attitudes to specific events.... By definition, our recorded cases are unusual in themselves otherwise they would not have been recorded.... They do not paint a uniform picture, but they are striking because they represent something of great importance to their recorders."[55] Even the Han historians, who worked under the direct gaze of autocratic rulers, betray quite well their attitudes toward law and power. Sima Qian and his father created a fragmented narrative about the fall of Qin and the rise of Han, but the history is constructed in part as a message that the failed policies of the Qin regime should serve as a warning to Han emperors who planned to follow in its path. Sima Qian's doubts about the legitimacy of the dynasty he served, mutilation on Wudi's orders, terrible experiences in prison, and resentment that a man of his position be subjected to bodily harm account for some of the ambivalence about the role of law that surfaces throughout the text. His biographies of the "harsh officials" who served Wudi reiterate the Confucian conviction that men of sound moral conduct will never go wrong no matter what their position and that laws and punishments only encourage litigiousness among the common people. Some sections decry the harsh application of law, but other passages admit that officials faced a hard task in administering laws to keep the common people in line and acknowledge the need for law: "Laws are made to guide the people and punishments are implemented to prevent evil. If the martial and civil elements are not in balance, even law abiding people will be nervous about remaining steadfast."[56] The *Hanshu*, composed nearly two centuries later, when the dynasty had survived an interregnum, the threat of large landholding families loomed to challenge the center and its bureaucrats, and economic and social divisions widened, was no less preoccupied with law, and, in fact, Ban Gu (32–92 C.E.) added a treatise on the development of law from ancient times to his history. But in line with the times, the later historian displays a far more tolerant stance toward harsh punishments than the Sima family, despite his Confucian leanings. In Ban Gu's version of the origins of state violence, the sage kings made good use of laws and punishments, rather than virtue and exemplary conduct, to ensure order.

55. Robinson 2007: 5.
56. *Shiji* 119: 3099.

The life and times of Ammianus Marcellinus are better documented than the early Han. A Greek from the city of Antioch, a military staff officer, a first-hand witness to war and persecution, Ammianus adopted the perspective of someone outside the inner circles of court politics but with sufficient experience to harbor little hope that rules could curb the ambitions of the powerful. His debt to Tacitus is not clear,[57] but he seems less concerned with liberty as a general principle and more preoccupied with modes of behavior. As Seager concludes in a study of the language of Ammianus, for him a civilized man must know his place in the world and must refrain from giving way to anger. The emperor's supreme power made his anger particularly dangerous.[58] Ammianus did not dispute the need for punishments or a ruler's right to protect himself from threats to his well-being. It was abuse of violence that troubled him: "It is not decent to give way to unbridled joy at such unhappy events; it makes men seem the subjects of despotism rather than of lawful authority."[59] He contrasts practices in his own day with the late Republic and calls for emulating Cicero, who appears in the memory of Ammianus as one who "said himself that when it was in his power to spare or to harm he looked for an excuse to pardon rather than punish; that is the mark of a dispassionate and prudent judge." Of his own time, he compared swift and honorable death in battle favorably to unjust death under the cover of laws.

5. DEADLY CONSEQUENCES

In imperial Rome as in China, most writers accepted the need for the death penalty. In the Roman case, one of the hallmarks of the virtue of *humanitas* in action during the Republic was the practice of allowing citizens of sufficient status who were sentenced for capital crimes to escape punishment through voluntary exile. But the death penalty itself was never rejected outright under the Republic. Under the empire, debates, according to Bauman, centered on methods of execution and elite worries that status would no longer serve as a protection from dishonorable punishment.[60] Seneca, Nero's tutor in his earlier years, took a milder approach than other Stoic thinkers of his day but did oppose granting a pardon for anyone already deemed guilty on grounds that a deserved punishment must be carried out. Discretion should be exercised, he argued, before the sentence, with external factors, such as the circumstances of the crime and the state of mind of the accused, weighed carefully. But he was ambivalent about sanctioning too much latitude for the judge even if equity might be better served than under the letter of the law.[61]

57. See Matthews 1989: 470–71.
58. Seager 1986: 133.
59. See *Ammianus Marcellinus*, 183.
60. Bauman 1996: ch. 12 discusses the ongoing debates about punishment from the late Republic through the early empire.
61. Bauman 1996: 78–81.

Seneca's writings distinguish between severity, which could be justified if it safe-guarded the public interest, from cruelty, which he viewed as immoderate violence meted out in anger. It seems that his concern rested not so much on the treatment of the victims of violence as on the character of the men who decided when to use force. In the final analysis, maintaining elite values mattered more than protect-ing vulnerable individuals. According to Bauman, "Roman society confronted a dilemma. Equity could be absorbed into the private law without much discomfort but at the criminal level it threatened the very foundations."[62]

In China, those Warring States manuals identified with Legalist writers express strong disapproval of mitigating the harsh punishments. Other realist texts strongly encouraged that pubishments be implemented consistently in order to discourage deviant behavior. The author of the *Guanzi*, for example, declares that a ruler who adheres to law should never grant pardons: "When the people know that the death penalty is inevitable, only then will they fear it" (7.8a). The most important thinker of Han times, Dong Zhongshu (*c.*195–115 B.C.E.), adopted the Confucian position that education must outweigh the use of force in government but agreed that the death penalty must never be remit-ted once a sentence was determined and criticized the Qin Empire not so much for harsh penalties but for a failure to maintain consistency: "Qin rulers and officials neglected to convince the good that they would be safe from violence and the evil that they would face certain punishment."[63] Indeed, the genius of Han thinkers, especially Dong Zhongshu, rested in a formulation that linked the conviction that the state is best served by consistent, appropriate punishments with the argument that imperial mismanagement of coercion would result in further chaos. In a cosmological scheme based on what Yates calls an "isometric fit" between language and the cosmos, in which determining the correct category for punishment erased the pollution of deviance, officials and emperors bore the responsibility for maintaining harmony between the human and natural worlds. According to Yates, the early Chinese conviction that only by honoring boundar-ies could order be ensured meant in turn that transgressing them disrupted the normal rhythm of human and cosmic patterns: "Heaven, Earth and Man were intimately connected and considered to be homologies of one another: they were similarly constituted and mirrored each other. It was essential that each element in the three different spheres should keep to its own designated function, within its own boundary, for if it did not the entire system was adversely affected."[64] Dong Zhongshu has been described as a servant of the imperial power, but in fact his organismic scheme correlated relations between the human and natural worlds, placing the ruler as the people's heart and the people as the ruler's body.

62. Bauman 1996: 161–62.
63. *Hanshu* 56: 2510.
64. Yates 1994: 69.

He warned rulers that their moods and actions reverberated through the universe and so they must align themselves with the predictable cycles of the natural world when they decided matters of life and death.[65]

The notion that punishments must match crimes rings through the texts at every level. Wendi himself declared that, "Only when laws are just and punishments appropriate will the people follow them."[66] Chao Cuo (d. 154 B.C.E.) castigated the Qin regime for allowing petty laws to proliferate and for failing to control the magistrates, who "took advantage of the numerous, confusing laws...to make life and death decisions according to their own wanton lights."[67] Qin and Han emperors confronted a dangerous dilemma: on the one hand they aspired to centralize all religious activities in their own office in order to prevent competing local cults from challenging their dominance; but on the other they took upon themselves the sole blame when imbalances resulted in signs of Heavenly disapproval. Jia Yi (201–169 B.C.E.) warned the ruler who used his power to punish to satisfy personal grudges that he would in turn become the object of vengeance: "If the punishment is appropriate for the crime, you can punish many people without being at fault. If the punishment is not right and you kill one person [not liable for crime] your crime will be reported to highest Heaven." And Heaven would respond with signs that everyone in the empire could read: "Oppressive laws and ordinances stimulate plagues of insects and furthermore if the innocent are put to death, the country will dry up in drought."[68]

One of the Roman cases involving punishment on a large scale that seems to have created unease in Nero's reign revolved around the murder, by a household slave, of the Urban Prefect, Pedanius Secundus. The trial involved all four hundred members of his household, including his slaves, who could be tortured and put to death as accomplices, no matter what their individual role in the crime. Cassius, a "hard-line" Stoic, according to Bauman, agreed that some slaves might be loyal but argued that only fear could keep them in line: "No doubt innocent people will die....There is an element of injustice in every precedent. But the public interest outweighs that of individuals."[69] Tacitus describes the scene: "No one indeed dared singly to oppose the opinion of Cassius, but clamorous voices rose in reply from all who pitied the number, age, or sex, as well as the undoubted innocence of the great majority. Still, the party which voted for their execution prevailed." Not only many senators but the public who lined the route to the execution according to the

---

65. Early in my study of the Han, I argued the point that Dong Zhongshu was in fact drawing from a vast tradition to both legitimate the empire and limit the ruler's power based on information in his biography in Hanshu 56 (see Turner Gottschang 1983: pt. 3: "Dong Zhongshu's Theory of Monarchy.") Arbuckle 1995 has presented an interesting argument that Dong was actually attempting to subvert the Liu Dynasty and gain the throne for himself.

66. *Shiji* 10: 418–19.

67. *Hanshu* 49: 2216.

68. *Xinshu* 7.4b.

69. Bauman 1996: 82.

account opposed the decision, and in the end the uneasy Emperor Nero showed clemency—to the freedmen in the group. But the law itself was not debated or changed, and Seneca, who had advised the young Nero earlier to favor humane decisions, remained silent. Surprisingly, given the presence of the emperor, and the distaste raised by this mass punishment, Tacitus does not mention fear of odium. As Bauman contends, it was not so much pity or dread of odium at work as special economic interests.[70] Mention of odium does appear in the treason case against the urban praetor Antistius Sosianus, who made the mistake of reading at a banquet satirical verses at the expense of the emperor. According to Tacitus, the Senate stood firm in its decision to exile rather than execute the culprit because "some were afraid to expose the emperor to odium."[71] Other tantalizing references to linking responsibility for unjust punishment to odium surface; the prefect Burrus, for example, insisted that Nero take full responsibility for executions—in order to deflect public opinion and odium from himself.[72] According to Bauman, "The need to deflect the odium of death sentences is a pointer to public dislike of capital punishment as such, but in the end it must be seen as a minority view; Seneca's attack on nasty modes of execution failed to lessen the lure of the arena."[73] Thus, connections between odium and the death penalty can be detected in Roman thought, and emperors did attempt to deflect the consequences of sanctioning the death penalty. The scarcity of mention of the fear of odium as a check on unwarranted cruelty implies that, as Robinson observes, no tradition from the republican period attached religious meaning to punishments, and when the emperor became the supreme executioner the link remained weak,[74] at least until the era of the Christian emperors.

6. TREASON

The problem of defining and punishing treason troubled both early empires, for this most terrible of crimes involved competition among rival elites. Harries observes that new, more inclusive treason laws were a consequence of one-man rule: "Unpredictable though it was, lacking in definition, and open to abuse, a treason law was necessary for emperors to justify the measures they took for their own protection against their soldiers, their governing class and even their supposed friends. . . . But the treason law was also a means by which the elite was brought under increasingly strict control by an ever more overt autocracy."[75] In both early empires, emperors adopted a curiously cautious stance toward this

---

70. Bauman 1996: 162–63.
71. *Annals* 14.48–49.
72. Bauman 1996: 86; *Annals*, 14.49.
73. Bauman 1996: 162.
74. See Robinson 2007: 185.
75. Harries 2007: 85.

delicate matter. Wendi in 178 B.C.E. specifically ordered that those caught utter-ing treasonous opinions not be brought to trial on the grounds that such mea-sures would stifle legitimate criticism from below, that the common people were too ignorant to realize the gravity of their actions, and that the officials were not capable of distinguishing false from accurate reports. Even Roman emperors with a reputation for excess, Caligula and Nero, for example, displayed a lenient attitude toward possible cases of treason. More subtle methods conveyed the message that by refraining to order death, the emperor implicitly claimed the right to take life, as Valentinian cleverly reminded the Senate after agreeing to acquittals in treason cases: "A pardon, conscript fathers, brands those persons whom it frees; it does not take away the infamy of crime but grants remission of punishment as a favor. In the case of one or two accused persons, this may be the right course. He who pardons the Senate condemns the Senate."[76]

In the early empire, *perduellio,* the old term that applied to an act that threat-ened the well-being of the community and could include military incompe-tence or treachery as well as official fiscal mismanagement, was merged with the notion that treason could apply to acts that damaged the greatness, *maiestas,* of the Roman people. According to Garnsey, when the welfare and dignity of the emperor mirrored the health of the state, no limits existed to determine how treason might be construed.[77] At the time, Seneca believed it possible to distin-guish between crimes that truly threatened the public interest and crimes against the emperor, which in fact merely offended one man's dignity: "Kings should only put people to death when they are satisfied that it is in the public interest, for brutality is for tyrants."[78] But as Harries points out, the problem rested in defining what constituted the public interest when court politics all too often led to charges made for political gain rather than to protect the emperors and their authority. Harries describes how the ambiguous legacy of the republican notion of treason led to abuse under the empire: "While the security of the empire was not in fact at risk from outside enemies, the application of the *perduellio* inter-pretation of treason mattered less than the emperor's (and his courtiers') obses-sion with his (and their own) security and status."[79]

In China, elites had little to lose in the transition from the Warring States to empire. The early philosophical treatises that called for consistency in punish-ments did little to temper the brutal, nasty, and short lives of anyone who attracted the displeasure of the strongmen who ruled without any need to legitimate their decisions. By Han times, once the Liu dynasty established itself as legitimate, it was its founder, precedents, and temples, as well as reigning emperors, that

76. Robinson 2007: 147.
77. Garnsey 1968: 145.
78. Bauman 1996: 81.
79. Harries 2007: 83.

could never be violated. In common in both empires is that ambiguity plagued interpretations of treason charges. The Han histories provide examples of the kinds of acts that could be punished as treason. A marquis who offended imperial dignity by failing to dismount at the palace gate was accused of disrespect [*da buching*] and demoted. Others of the same rank who sang drunkenly in the ancestral temple (an even more terrible signal of disrespect than Antistius Sosanius's inappropriate song at a banquet), or wore improper clothing or criticized a dead emperor, were punished more harshly. Cursing the emperor constituted the greatest perversion [*da ni*] and was punished in the case of thirteen marquises by slicing in half at the waist.[80] The Han histories' accounts of terms for treason reveal that there is little consistency in how a particular crime was to be categorized, but the idea that a crime against emperor and the symbols of dynastic authority equated a crime against the natural order of things (*bu dao*) is supported in theory by texts such as *Jingfa*, which defines transgressing the boundaries that maintained hierarchical relations within society and state as the most heinous infraction. In practice, as the Han histories show, the link between the emperor, the dynasty, and the institutions that sanctified it was being worked out case by case. In one famous exchange in Wendi's reign, we find the intrepid Commandant of Justice, Zhang Shizhi, again arguing the case. At stake was a crime considered as "unnatural," the theft of a jade ring from the founder's temple—an action equivalent to treason. The emperor demanded the heaviest penalty, the execution of the condemned man and three generations of his family, but Zhang argued that the lighter punishment of execution in the market place should apply only to the responsible person. Finally, the emperor agreed that Zhang was technically correct, but made clear that the light sentence could not erase so egregious an offense against a sacred place. Zhang Shizhi's argument was simple: "The sentence prescribed by law is sufficient."[81] The two faces of the Chinese emperor, the stern father, who advocates for severity to protect dynastic interests, and the moral mother, who pleads for benevolence toward the people, appear in conflict over this touchy issue. Wendi early in his reign debated with his officials about the need to eliminate the practice of punishing the kin of criminals. The familiar counterarguments emanated from officials who defended the execution of innocent victims unlucky enough to be related to the actual criminal on the grounds that it "made the common people weigh the consequences of breaking the law." But these dissenters caved in to the emperor's plea after he threatened that incorrect penal policies would redound to the responsible officials. In the case of the theft of the jade ring, the angry emperor could afford to forgo the collective punishments because there was little to gain in wiping out the family of a commoner who could never muster sufficient resources to

80. See Ch'ü 1972: 69.
81. *Shiji* 102: 2727.

mount a vendetta against the Liu family. Yet despite Wendi's eloquent argument against collective punishments, we know from the Han historical sources that punishing the relatives of the criminal continued. Moreover, the Qin and Han passion for standardization did not apply to collective punishments; as Lewis shows, the members of the descent group implicated in such punishment varied.[82] It is possible that Wendi's very studied attempts to use his authority for seemingly benign reasons when he advocated eliminating the collective punishments constituted "euergetism," as Paul Veyne has described the freely offered benefactions that only a leader with excess power can offer.[83] But as the many accounts of punishment applied sometimes without trial in the histories and heavy penalty for a commoner's theft of a jade ring attest, when the imperial authority was threatened, the emperor became a ruthless advocate of the harshest penalty. The case of the major Han thinker Dong Zhongshu is instructive, for he experienced life under a tyrant who both feared and needed the support of intellectuals like himself; and he operated on both sides of the law, giving advice about doubtful legal cases when called upon and suffering imprisonment when the emperor suspected him of using his knowledge about the connections between the physical and natural world to start a fire in the ancestral temple. And if Gary Arbuckle's argument that Dong was indeed capable of treason is correct, the emperor had good reason to suspect this man, who manipulated ideas about the cycles of history to place a "cosmological death sentence on the rule of the Liu clan."[84] Arbuckle suggests that Dong had himself in mind as the founder of a new dynasty. Whatever Dong Zhongshu's motives might have been, the most effective means to destroy the dynasty was not to move against the emperor but to demonstrate that the elaborate symbols that supported the dynasty's right to rule no longer remained viable.

7. Bodily Harm

In Warring States China, despite the myth that "the mutilating punishments do not apply to the superior people," in fact, elites enjoyed no legal protection from the harshest punishments. It was not only rulers who acted arbitrarily; many tales in the sources show how men of like status harmed one another with creative methods—boiling alive was one technique that enjoyed a certain popularity.[85] Han emperors did not have to contend with a class of people who expected

---

82. Lewis 1006: 97–100.
83. Veyne 1976.
84. Imperial worries about the use of magic and divination surfaces in both empires and is worthy of more study. Arbuckle's argument is in Arbuckle 1995: 593.
85. Han Gaozu's chief rival in the civil war that preceded the Han, Xiangyu, was particularly fond of this method. Most famously he kidnapped the future Gaozu's father and threatened to boil him alive but is reported to have actually carried out the deed in other cases.

to be exempted from dishonorable punishment as we have seen in the case of the senators who appealed to Valentinian. The problem in imperial China as in Rome was that the state now took upon itself the sole burden and suffered the consequences of defiling the bodies of its subjects. The Han sources reveal how carefully the emperors approached the practice of mutilating the criminal body. An account of Wendi's reign shows that the impetus for reform came not from the emperor or his officers but from a petition from a young woman whose father, an official in charge of a provincial treasury, had been accused of a crime that warranted mutilation. She reminded the sovereign not only that her father had been falsely accused but more generally that the state's right to punish its own people must be used with great care: "Those who are dead cannot again come to life and those who are mutilated cannot regain [wholeness]. Although later they might desire to correct their faults and renew themselves, that road can never be followed." A filial daughter, she offered to become a government slave to redeem her father's sentence, since he had no sons to replace him.[86] After Wendi read the letter, he declared that punishments that severed limbs or pierced human flesh seemed especially unjust and that there were time-honored precedents for marking criminals without permanently disfiguring their bodies—with special clothing, for example. Knowing full well the arguments he would hear against the more benign solution, he assured the bureaucrats that the methods he proposed had not in fact created disorder in the utopian past under the rule of sage kings. He played his top card, reminding the audience that as the "Father and Mother" of the people, responsible for the welfare of the entire world, he held the power to decide matters of life and death and could not allow irrevocable harm to be visited upon his people. Besides, he told them, the recent trend toward harsh punishments had not suppressed crime.

A contradictory "tradition" allowed two known hardliners to argue the opposite point, that even the sage rulers had approved mutilation for certain crimes as one means to preserve order. This was not a new position: Xunzi had rejected the antiquity and efficacy of symbolic punishments on the grounds that defiling the criminal body was necessary to guarantee order and hierarchy.[87] But in the end, the officials at Wendi's court had little choice but to bow to the emperor's desire

---

86. See *Hanshu* 23: 1097 for a more complete account. See Hulsewé 1955 for a translation and discussion of this important treatise. The classic work on slavery in Han times remains that of Wilbur 1943, and much work needs to be done in light of new materials on this issue. From the Qin code we know that slaves were treated as the most lowly humans under the law but were not legally dead and could not be harmed or killed by owners without permission from the local officials. Government slaves were viewed as resources, and therefore, their fate was the business of the state. Moreover, this case of the young woman who would fall from status as the daughter of an official to slavery reveals the fluidity of Han society and reaffirms the notion that slavery could befall anyone caught up in the legal system. The relatives of criminals punished under the penalty of collective punishments were often made government slaves, for example. The Qin and presumably the Han legal systems allowed for redemption, by reduction in rank, or substitution. But the state was careful not to be cheated, and a woman, unless skilled at some work that made her valuable, would not be equal to an able-bodied man in the equation.

87. *Xunzi* 18: 6.

to display his power to grant lenience and counterproposed that the mutilating punishments be abolished and new regulations drawn up to determine how to mark deviant people according to the crime—with shaven heads, iron collars, or beating—without permanently altering their bodies. In fact, however, mutilation was never eliminated, beatings often mangled or killed people, and the debates about changing the laws regarding the harsh punishments continued throughout the early imperial period. Wendi's motives for attempting to end mutilation are a topic of some debate. According to Charles Sanft, it was the scholar official Jia Yi who had argued in a text dated to Wendi's reign that these harsh punishments should not apply to the territorial kings, who constituted the gravest danger to the emperor's power, at the same time that he advocated reducing the size and power of their kingdoms. This very calculated move to appease these troublesome elites was not accompanied by a proposal to eliminate the death penalty—but to allow them the privilege of suicide rather than mutilation or execution.[88] But in fact, as the histories reveal, elites were never protected from the harshest punishments, and some cases show that extraordinary efforts were made to destroy the corpses of powerful enemies in order to destroy their potency. Perhaps one reason the filial daughter's plea did not fall on deaf ears is that her father was an official, and just as in imperial Rome wealth and status offered protection from bodily harm, more often than not, according to Garnsey,[89] so too in China ranked officials and members of the imperial family theoretically could not be punished without per- mission from the emperor, who then usually referred the actual sentencing to the Commandant of Justice.[90] Confucian rhetoric in favor of educating the people before endangering them through war and punishments did not extend to using punishment as a means to reform criminals. Indeed, one of the few arguments for reform through punishment in the ancient world is found in Plato, but the Romans did not adopt his vision. The focus in both empires remained on the body. But as I explain below, the Han beliefs that the boundaries of the individual physical body were permeable, that the material body displayed the inner self, and that humans were malleable creatures all contributed to a heightened sense that any mark that changed a person's outward appearance, even a symbolic one, must be carefully applied.[91]

In China, as in Rome, torture was deemed justifiable in order to secure "truth" by forcing a confession, though in both cases, the unreliablity of coerced

---

88. See Sanft 2005.

89. Garnsey 1970.

90. Hulsewé 1955 observes that determining just which ranks held this privilege is difficult, but we know from the histories that rank protected no one if the emperor decided to punish, especially in cases of treason. Yates 1989 discusses the legal status of commoners under the Qin and notes that during the Han dynasty, the term "*shi wu*" |rank and file| referred to individuals deprived of rank as part of punishment for a crime.

91. For an analysis of changes in ideas about the relation between the inner and physical world of humans and their interactions with the outside world between the time of the Warring States and the early empire in China, see Csikszntmihalyi 2004.

information was recognized. From my reading, it seems that the problem faced under the empire in the Roman case centered on the issue of how far into the upper ranks of society torture could be legitimately applied. In China, preoccupation with standardization dictated that torture be carefully supervised and regulated. A Han text unearthed at Jiangjiashan in 1984 that served as a handbook for reporting and recording appeals from local officials to the Commandant of Justice corroborates historical sources indicating that rules for torture and appeal were in place.[92] A best-case scenario for a commoner convicted and mutilated by mistake is recorded in the *Zhouyanshu*, which Susan Roosevelt Weld translates as "The Book of Hard Cases," a manual designed to guide the submission of difficult decisions to higher authorities—in some cases to the Commandant of Justice himself—and dated to the reign of the Empress Lu, Gaozi's consort, who effectively ruled from 188–180 B.C.E. Many of these cases deal with issues of social control, but others attend to procedures for investigating a crime, questioning witnesses, determining previous liability, motive, and accomplices, and applying torture. In one case, a musician, already sentenced to hard labor and branded as an accomplice to theft, appealed his case and upon reinvestigation was found to have been falsely implicated by the true culprit, who had confessed under excessive torture. The Commandant of Justice's office reversed the sentence as "not warranted" for the crime and ordered that his wife and children, who had been sold, be redeemed. But because he had been mutilated, he was appointed to serve in a job outside the public view.[93] Whether or not these manuals represent reality on the ground rather than the central government's worries about controlling officials and commoners, and how much they reflect conditions in the colonized former state of Chu, the site of the most important legal materials excavated in the past three decades, pose a problem for historians working with scant data.[94] A more cynical view of how a trial worked, one of the few records of any trial in the historical sources, can be found in Sima Qian's colorful account of an encounter between a rat and the young Zhang Tang, destined to become one of Wudi's "harsh officials" in Sima Qian's scheme. As the story goes, after his father beat him for neglecting to watch over a piece of meat that was then stolen by a rat, he exacted vengeance: caught the rat, beat it, and documented its confession, compared the confession with the evidence, proposed a punishment, and executed it on the spot. When the historian has Zhang's father remark that his prodigy carried out the trial like a "seasoned prison official," it is hard to know how much he is exaggerating to make the point that Wudi's officials operated mercilessly and outside the normal procedures or whether this sort of treatment was routine.[95]

92. *Zhangjiashan* 2001. For an overview of the Han legal materials unearthed in the Zhangjiashan cache, see Li and Xing 2001.

93. See also Lau 2002.

94. On Chu law, see Weld 1999.

95. *Shiji* 122: 3139.

8. Economies of Punishment

Economic interests lurked beneath Han emperors' moralistic pronouncements and the bureaucrats' rigid administrative codes. Chinese emperors headed a legal system that, while lacking the level of technology to organize and discipline its population as efficiently as modern states, did in fact pay a great deal of attention to categorizing its legal subjects in terms of their labor potential. Indeed, I would argue that much earlier than in the West, China developed a Foucauldian notion of biopower: the categorizing, standardizing, control, and mobilization of individual bodies to serve the state.[96] The Chinese case challenges Foucault's contention that a passion for organizing bodies for their productive capacities marked a shift in political life from classical to modern systems. In China, patrimonial displays of the ruler's terrible power to punish and bureaucratic imperatives existed in tandem, especially at the lower levels of society. Resources were ultimately at stake. The manuals buried with a low-level Qin official in 217 B.C.E. clearly meant to restrict his decisions about managing and controlling government resources. We can see in these materials that the state's concern for matching crime and punishment played out at the lowest levels of the administration. In a section on answers to questions about the Qin statutes, the state's conception of justice is articulated: "In pronouncing judgment in criminal cases, [what is meant] by 'not straight'? When a crime warrants a heavy [punishment] and purposely to make it light, or when a crime warrants a light [punishment] and purposely to make it heavy, that is the meaning of 'not straight.'"[97]

The fines and labor service spelled out in detail in the Qin administrative manuals describe commoners in terms of precise physical attributes or talents that might be useful for the state. Criminals assigned the heaviest labor could be mutilated, but the sturdiest men, the wall-builders, were usually left intact— marked by shaved heads or beards or special clothing. Strict rules governed the use of resources; food was rationed to provide just enough sustenance to account for the size and jobs of laborers, and officials were harshly punished for neglecting government stores or failing to deliver men for labor service. Mark Lewis concludes that convict labor formed a far more efficient pool than slaves or corvée levies: "With so many types of crime, and the entire empire to draw upon, the convict population provided a bottomless supply of expendable labor." Further evidence that these workers suffered maltreatment and malnourishment surfaces in excavated Qin and Han cemeteries, according to Lewis.[98]

Foucault's model applies to the economic and political realm, but anthropologists have provided useful insights about symbolic connections between the individual body, the social body, and the body politic. As Sivin notes in comparing

96. Foucault 1990.
97. Hulsewé 1985: 144.
98. Lewis 2007: 250–52.

conceptions of the body (*shen*) in China with the Greek term (*soma*), the mind-body duality was alien to early China. "Shen includes the individual personality, and may refer in a general way to the person rather than to the body. It may also refer (and still does) to juridical identity.... [T]he body was defined not by what sets it apart but by its intimate, dynamic relation with the environment."[99] Medical texts from the Han period studied by Kuriyama explain why human bodies and minds had to be anchored within a firm political system: "[The body] was the locus of habitual irregularity.... Human beings required elaborate instructions on what to do and feel at each time of year, precisely because what they did and felt easily diverged from, and even ran counter to, the spirit of the seasonal wind. Individuals thus emerged as individuals in their propensity to slip into idiosyncratic cadences."[100] Moral perfection as well as physical regularity contributed to order. In the larger scheme, as Lewis points out, "Between the mind and the cosmos, the key recurrent unit is the physical body." The boundaries between the human body and the external world were, moreover, considered permeable: the physical self was not separate from the outside environment.[101] Individuals did not own their bodies but were bound by filial duty to maintain physical integrity, to go to death with the same body their parents gave them in life. Just as physical completeness was a necessary condition to carry out their most important duty to society—service to kin both alive and dead—a whole body better served the needs of state and society. On a higher level, amputation of the body politic, in the form of rebellion, for example, threatened the correct order, just as mutilation created a being with no place in the world of the living and the dead, as we saw in the case of the mutilated musician who remained hidden from normal society. Wendi's concern with preventing mutilation might have operated at several levels: concern with the symbolic need for wholeness in the face of possible political dismemberment and with the economic imperative to secure intact bodies for his massive labor projects.[102]

In the Roman Empire, the criminal body served more as a site of symbolic retribution than an economic asset. MacMullen describes the "dramatic appropriateness" of Constantine's punishments: "[T]he person who gives wicked advice is to be choked with molten lead, the seller of false promises, 'smoke,' is to be asphyxiated over a slow fire; and similarly amputation, where the loss of a foot for a deserter...or of sexual organs for the pederast (under Justinian), proclaims symbolically the particular evil being punished." MacMullen points out that as crimes that warranted harsh retribution became more numerous in the later empire, so too did spectacles of death sponsored by emperors become more routine.[103] Economic

---

99. Sivin 1995: 14.
100. Kuriyama 1994: 31.
101. Lewis 1006: 23.
102. Turner 1999.
103. MacMullen 1990: 212. See also Kyle 1998.

imperatives seemed of secondary importance. Fergus Millar, for example, notes that condemnation to the mines did not primarily operate to secure a sturdy labor force and that beatings and lacerations sometimes rendered the condemned criminal less fit for labor. Moreover, labor in the mines was not confined to criminals but reserved for particularly subversive or dangerous groups, including Christians.[104] But even Christian emperors did not exempt fellow believers from assignment to the mines and quarries.[105] If we view punishments as representations and the criminal body as a mirror, or microcosm, of society, displays of cruelty in the arena effectively rendered the deviant as an outsider at a time when the empire incorporated larger numbers of former enemies into its citizen body.[106] Or perhaps in line with Veyne's scheme, the emperor's garnering of large numbers of bodies for his public games satisfied his euergetistic need to display and share the surplus of human resources that only a universal ruler with an empire at his disposal could muster. Donald Kyle's work on spectacles of death in ancient Rome describes the problems created by the sheer numbers of humans and animals cycled in and out of the Roman arena and identifies the source of this human capital: "For Rome noxii [convicted criminals] were a surplus commodity, a leisure resource, a by-product of imperialism."[107]

However we might explain the difference, early imperial Chinese state builders carefully husbanded and managed their convict laborers while later Roman emperors squandered them. In China, public punishment, meted out most often in the market place, did aim to shame the criminal and deter future deviants. But political life in general did not operate on a grand scale with the emperor as a central figure as in imperial Rome. The criminal body in the Chinese case was not viewed as a vehicle to enhance directly the prestige of emperors but as a cog in the vast labor pool needed to create and maintain the important institutional symbols of empire such as massive imperial tombs and great walls.

9. LEGACIES

In the historiography of Roman law, Honoré and Harries argue that by the third century new forces began to limit the power of emperors: legal writings upheld objective standards in private cases that extended to public law and the emperor himself; codification narrowed the scope of imperial discretion; Christian authorities provided a counterweight to imperial power; and a more populist imperial image emerged.[108] But other writers note that despite the impact of Christianity,

---

104. Millar 1984.
105. Gustafson 1994.
106. I have not been able to consult the enormous literature on the body in the Roman Empire but have derived insight from Wyke and Hopkins 2005.
107. Kyle 1998: 92.
108. Honoré 1998.

and despite the fact that emperors endorsed codification and clarification of the laws, penal policies were not humanized in the process. Garnsey argues that the "the increased activity but continued inefficiency of the central administration in the sphere of law enforcement; the removal of limitations within the judicial system through the substitution of flexible for rigid and formalized procedures, and the expansion of criminal law" did not alter the severity of penal policy. Garnsey and MacMullen both attribute a seeming lack of elite sympathy for the suffering of the groups most vulnerable to public degradation to the more rigid social stratification that characterized the later empire.[109]

In the early Han period, the unusually fluid nature of society, in which a lowly official could become emperor and the highest official could fall from grace into servitude or worse, empathy for the suffering of the lower orders might well have accounted for debates about the harsh punishments. As the Han Empire matured, and as divisions between social classes became more rigid, attitudes toward punishments hardened as well, despite the official adoption of Confucianism as the orthodox ideology of the empire. In China after the time of Wudi, emperors continued to portray themselves as guardians of the law on behalf of the people's welfare. Emperor Yuandi, for example, declared in 47 B.C.E. that he intended to clarify the laws because they had become so confused that they could neither be understood clearly nor applied consistently. A generation earlier, Emperor Xuandi had expressed the sentiment that the officials were at fault for abusing the laws and harming the common people and so it was the ruler's duty to reform the laws and manage the officials in the interest of the general welfare.[110] But despite imperial rhetoric in favor of simplifying the laws and standardizing punishments, in fact laws proliferated over the course of the Han; by the Eastern Han period, 610 capital offenses and 1,698 crimes warranting penal servitude appear on the books.[111] Ban Gu's exposition on law and punishment betrays a far more tolerant attitude toward severity than earlier Han writers. His account of a debate about punishment in Jingdi's reign (157–141 B.C.E.) shows the emperor and his officials arguing over the precise number of strokes and where beating should be applied on the criminal body with the emperor concluding: "The bastinado is the means to teach them. Therefore regulate the size of the stick." It is hard to know how much this passage reflects historical reality and how much the sterner attitude taken by the emperor serves Ban Gu's own belief that harsh punishments must be legitimated. But the argument that bodily harm can be rationalized by advocating for carefully measuring its application points to the danger of associating bureaucratization with humane punishments. Values associated with Weberian "rationality," such as uniformity, clarity,

---

109. Garnsey 1968; MacMullen 1990.
110. *Hanshu* 23. See Hulsewé 1955.
111. See MacCormack 2004.

and standardization, did at times provide critics with rhetorical ammunition to challenge the Han emperors' attempts to work around the rules, but also legitimated a pragmatic stance toward the criminal body. Predictability did remove a certain amount of arbitrary interference in the lives of subjects, but the legal machinery aimed to protect resources and order rather than individual rights. And a cadre of bureaucrats who placed the interests of the state above the whims of rulers and their ambitious kin did at times manage to influence decisions, but inevitably, emperors became ensconced in the politics of the "inner court" and centrifugal forces overrode the influence of the bureaucrats.[112]

Yet the blueprint for balancing patrimonial and bureaucratic interests created during the early Han lived on and offered a rich source for later officials and rulers to call upon to support their proposals and decisions. For example, Wendi's famous official, Zhang Shiji, was at times celebrated by later reformers for his ability to withstand imperial pressure and by others castigated for setting a dangerous precedent when in the case of the commoner who startled the emperor's horses he conceded to the emperor the right to have the poor wretch executed on the spot.[113] The script that outlined the ruler's duties to the legal system continued to be drawn upon, and Han actors provided a rich and contradictory fund of precedent. After the demise of the Han, even non-Chinese rulers initiated their reigns by ordering their officials to revise the codes,[114] and worried about their responsibility for capital punishment. Jonathan Spence offers a very accessible portrait of the Manchu Emperor Kangxi (r. 1662–1722) ruminating over the death lists sent up for his ratification: "I...got in the habit of reading through the lists in the palace each year, checking the name and registration and status of each man condemned to death, and the reason for which the death penalty had been given. Then I would check through the list again with the Grand Secretaries and their staff...and we would decide who might be spared."[115] How much the written laws might affect these decisions made at the top depended on the sort of message the emperor wanted to convey and the political implications of the case. Over the course of the two thousand years that the imperial system managed to survive, at the top emperors played their roles out as parental figures, which legitimated severity when necessary and benevolence when expedient.[116] At the lower levels, magistrates, trained in the Confucian classics rather than law, ignored or manipulated the letter of the law as necessary to keep order and maintain their positions. The contemporary legal reformer and scholar He Weifang compares English common law with imperial Chinese law, concluding that the doctrine of *stare decisis* never took hold in China, where the judge "generally preached at the

---

112. Mark Lewis makes this point strongly in Lewis 2007.
113. MacCormack 2001.
114. See MacCormack 2004.
115. Spence 1988: 32–33.
116. See, for example, Bartlett 1994.

parties or reproached them ethically, quoted or did not quote the law articles, and then rendered a judgment to the dispute. He did not attempt to establish any legal principles to be followed by later judges."[117] Confucian-trained judges had little need to challenge the system, which provided them with salaries, benefits, and status. Moreover, after the Han, the Confucian family hierarchy was backed by law—with benefit toward patriarchs and terrible costs for women and youth.

Finally, while Chinese theorists during the Han worked from the assumption that all humans operated within a common moral universe, in fact, their epistemological assumptions about human nature remained narrower than those that prevailed in Greece and Rome. True, Cicero's vision of the "reasonable man" who could participate in political life was confined to a small group of property-owning residents of a small city-state. But over time a more expansive idea of participation developed that formed the basis for an independent judiciary at the higher levels of governance and trial by a jury of peers at the local level. As He Weifang laments, "The English practice of letting illiterate common people take part directly in judiciary activities through the jury system was unthinkable in traditional China."[118] Bauman concludes his study of crime and punishment in Rome by declaring: "It was not by accident that the criminal law missed out on the accolade that greeted its private counterpart over the long centuries following the fall of Rome."[119] And yet, as I see the past and present, the persistence of republican ideals about procedural justice left a positive legacy on which later legal systems would be reconstructed. Even when a "cruel" emperor presided, a common understanding of the rights of the accused remained—a trial to be held in public, with a trusted council to frame the decision, and a chance to mount a defense. In a comparative light, a trial deemed unfair by Roman standards offered far more chance for alternative voices to speak on behalf of the accused person than a magistrate's investigation in China, which presumed guilt from the outset and allowed for no defense. Professor He notes that the Chinese state never promised to maintain a legal system to protect rights or property. Law existed as a means to preserve order and garner the resources needed to maintain the imperial apparatus, and elites, whether Confucian or Communist, have always decided matters of life and death. The system has worked for over two thousand years. But the human costs have been high indeed.

117. He 1990.
118. He 1990: 83.
119. Bauman 1996: 164. I want to express my gratitude to Walter Scheidel and participants in the ACME workshops for useful comparative insights, and to Peter Garnsey, Jill Harries, and Raphael Sealey for commenting on a draft of this paper. Despite their good advice, I take full responsibility for my interpretations.

4

Eunuchs, Women, and Imperial Courts

Maria H. Dettenhofer

EUNUCHS have gained a secure place in ancient Chinese as well as ancient European history. Moreover, they seem to be a phenomenon that is not restricted to the ancient world or, for that matter, to any geographic or cultural region in particular. Many societies knew them and made use of them throughout the centuries. Many examples are to be found in China, India, Persia,[1] Arabian culture, the Roman Empire, the Byzantine Empire, and Russia: eunuchs are a common anthropological feature.

1. EUNUCHS IN THE ANCIENT WORLD

Eunuchs appear in very different contexts. For instance, they are mentioned in the Bible. In Matthew 19.12, we read, "For there are eunuchs who have been so from birth, and there are eunuchs who have been made eunuchs by men, and there are eunuchs who have made themselves eunuchs for the sake of the kingdom of heaven."[2] While a number of religious sects and cults required eunuchs, such as the cult of Cybele in ancient Greece and Rome,[3] the eighteenth-century Christian sect of the Skopzi in Russia,[4] and the Hindu sect of the Hijra in India,[5] the predominant function of a eunuch was to be a servant. As servants, they performed very specific tasks within a household: as women's guardians, bed-attendants, or providers of special erotic services. However, only the courts of centrally organized empires offered an environment where they were able to gain tremendous political influence and legendary wealth. The eunuch system helped

1. Herodotus 8.105–6; Xenophon, *Education of Cyrus* 7.5.62–3. Cf. Llewellyn-Jones 2002.
2. Ringrose 2003: 115.
3. Pindar Fragment 77, ed. Bowra; Aristophanes, *Birds* 877; Catullus 63; Ovid, *Fasti* 4.181ff. Cf. Nock 1988: 58–69.
4. The religious sect of the Skopzi regarded procreation as the greatest evil. It was founded in Russia around 1775 and still existed during the Soviet period. There were various levels of castration. Those of the "small seal" only had their testicles removed while those of the "great seal" had all their sex organs removed. See Wolkow 1995.
5. Nanda 1998.

maintain the mysterious distance between the ruler and his subjects. Well-documented examples in antiquity include the courts of the Eastern Roman emperors from the fourth and fifth centuries C.E.[6] and the Chinese court from the first emperor Qin Shihuangdi until 1912. But what made these castrated men so successful in political systems that also developed elaborate career patterns for the aristocracy to serve in the government? Why did these counterparts to the official and aristocratic male world become the perfect courtiers? And what made them so special that they became a firmly established power at the grandest courts of the ancient world?

1.1. Becoming a Eunuch: Methods and Reasons

The one thing eunuchs all had in common was a deficiency of their genitals, in most cases caused by the irreversible act of castration. Let us first take a closer look at different types of castration. We encounter part-castration, where only the testicles were removed. Total castration was the alternative: it entailed the removal of both the penis (penectomy) and the testicles. Methods varied from a slash of a sword to a clash between two stones.[7] Total castration had a higher mortality rate and seems to have been the norm in China.

The age at which castration took place also played an important role. Most eunuchs seem to have been created before puberty as castration in childhood was less dangerous for the eunuch-to-be: the evidence shows that the mortality rate was higher after puberty. However, there were several reasons for the high number of castrations of adult men. In ancient China, castration was a traditional punishment, for instance, for prisoners of war or traitors.[8] Even high-ranking officials could face this fate.[9] Similarly in the Roman Empire and Byzantium, castration was practiced as a penalty for prisoners of war, political opponents, sexual offenders, and disobedient slaves.[10] It could also be employed as a means of torture.[11]

If the testicles were removed after puberty, the eunuch was still capable of achieving an erection since, although he would be sterile, he continued to receive testosterone through the adrenal glands.[12] Numerous sources show that eunuchs were highly valued sexual partners; moreover, they interacted with both sexes. In Rome, slaves were castrated so that they could be used to satisfy their owners'

---

6. Tougher 1997.
7. For China, see Jugel 1976: 15–17.
8. Mitamura 1970: 55–58.
9. One of the most famous examples for the penalty of castration of a high-ranking man is the case of the historian Sima Qian, who had been the official Director of Records at the court of Wudi before he fell into disgrace. Wudi threw Sima Qian into prison and had him castrated. Rather than commit suicide, as was expected of a scholarly gentleman, Sima Qian chose to live on as a palace eunuch to complete his histories as he had promised his historian father.
10. Guyot 1980: 26–8. See Appian, *Civil Wars* 3.98.
11. Suetonius, *Life of Domitian* 10.5.
12. Bullough 2002: 4.

sexual desires; young men who had already been castrated were likewise regarded as useful additions to the household.[13] They had to play the despised passive role in homosexual relationships and were therefore called *pathici*, meaning "those who give themselves like a woman."[14] In China, too, eunuchs were the submissive sexual partners of most of the emperors. Homosexuality was a normal part of a prince's life. Princes and eunuchs had grown up and been educated together.[15] But eunuchs' erotic services were not limited to homosexual acts, either in the East or in the West.[16] Wealthy women preferred intercourse with castrated slaves for a good reason: there was no risk of pregnancy.[17] In the fourth and fifth centuries c.e., women's intercourse with eunuchs had become a widespread topic of public debate.[18] The women of the emperor's palace in China also seem to have relied on eunuchs to fulfill their sexual desires.[19]

1.2. The Procedure: A Modern Example

Nineteenth-century accounts shed light on how the castration procedure was undertaken in China where total castration was the norm and the "eunuch-maker" was a special occupation. In preparation for surgery, the patient's abdomen and upper thighs were tightly bound with strings or bandages that left the penis and scrotum exposed. These were then washed three times in hot pepper water while the patient sat in a semireclining position on a heated piece of furniture known in Chinese as the *kang*. The "eunuch-maker" repeatedly questioned the patient whether he really wanted to go through with the surgery. If the patient confirmed his commitment, he was firmly held down by assistants while his penis and the scrotum were cut off with one sweep of a razor-sharp sickle-shaped knife. The urethra was plugged and blocked off, and the wound was covered by paper soaked in cold water; tight bandages were applied. The assistant then had to walk the patient around for two or three hours before allowing him to lie down. He was forbidden to take fluids for three days. After this period was over, the urethra plug was removed and if urine gushed out, the operation was regarded as a success. If no urine appeared, the prognosis was that the man would soon die an agonizing death. After castration, the eunuch's genitals were put in a container where they were pickled, after which they were returned to him for safekeeping. The eunuch would have to present them for advancement in rank, and after his death, his genitals would be buried together with the corpse.[20] The wounds usually healed

---

13. Seneca, *Controversies* 10.4.17; Seneca, *On Anger* 1.21.3: "libido...puerorum greges castrat"; Quintilian, *Oratory* 5.12.19; Petronius, *Satyricon* 23.3.

14. Vorberg 1932: 439ff., *s.v.* "pathicus."

15. Jugel 1976: 122ff.; Mitamura 1970: 115.

16. As Guyot 1980: 63 explains.

17. Martial 6.67, 10.91, 12.58; Juvenal 6.366–77; Guyot 1980: 63, 65.

18. See Guyot 1980: 65 and n. 109.

19. Jugel 1976: 122.

20. See Stent 1877: 143–84; and also Bullough 2002: 2.

in about 100 days, whereupon the new eunuch would proceed to the imperial household for instruction. At the end of the first year, the eunuch would be transferred to the Imperial Palace to take up his new occupation.[21]

1.3. Provenance of Eunuchs

Apart from some noble young men from subject tribes who had been taken as hostages and then castrated, eunuchs came from the lowest strata of society. The sources of supply were the same as for slaves. In the Roman Empire, the market for eunuchs prospered because prices for castrates were high, much higher in fact than for normal slaves, which is hardly surprising given that since the end of the first century C.E., castration had been forbidden on Roman soil. The emperor Domitian had passed a law that prohibited castration against somebody's will. Penalties were severe.[22] The poet Martial praised this law that restricted the power of the *pater familias*.[23] Several laws that more or less reiterated this injunction followed during the subsequent centuries. Therefore, most eunuchs apparently came from outside the empire: there was no penalty on owning them.[24] Most of them were slaves or ex-slaves.[25] The provenance of Chinese eunuchs seems to have been mixed. At first, eunuchs were commonly obtained from outside the empire.[26] But toward the end of the Eastern Han Dynasty, there seems to have been a large number of self-castrated men. Voluntary castration was based upon the economic principle of supply and demand. Demand was strong enough to encourage men to accept the risks of castration in the hope of making a career as a eunuch. A cultured man had to study many years to pass the state examinations in order to attain a position as an official. Some lower-class individuals who lacked the means to attend the Confucian schools and master their examination system chose a different road to influence, wealth, and social standing by castrating either themselves or a son. In the latter case, the father was usually responsible for this decision. As a palace eunuch, the son would be expected and able to support his family.[27]

In both cultures, castration was a means of gaining employment in the imperial household. At the Eastern Roman imperial court, a great number of eunuchs were employed in domestic and administrative functions, organized within a separate hierarchy and following their distinct career paths. But religious motivation also played a significant role in the West. In the pre-Christian period, followers of the cult of the ancient mother goddess Cybele sometimes volun-

21. Mitamura 1970: 32–34.
22. Cassius Dio 67.2.3; Ammianus Marcellinus 18.4.5.
23. See, for example, Martial 6.2.2, 6.2.9, 9.7.8.
24. For details, see Guyot 1980: 45–51.
25. Hopkins 1978: 172 and n. 4.
26. Jugel 1976: 31–35.
27. Jugel 1976: 91–120.

tarily castrated themselves; in early Christianity, emasculation was practiced to ensure chastity. The "church father" Origen is the most famous example.[28] Astonishingly, this model turned out to have no future in the Christian church; emasculation was subsequently condemned. It was the sovereign's palace that rapidly became the most promising place for eunuchs, whether in China or in imperial Rome.

In addition to being a form of punishment, castration was also a symbol of conquest as well as of revenge in ancient Europe as well as China. Herodotus gives an example in the vendetta between Periander, the tyrant of Corinth, and the Corinthians: He seized 300 sons of noble families in Corcyra, one of the subjugated cities, and they were sent to Sardis to be castrated.[29] By severing the symbol of manhood from prisoners of war they were to be made completely subservient. A similar pattern can be found in China. We know the sad story of the young prince of Lou Lan, a walled state on the western border. During the reign of Emperor Wudi, he was taken hostage and castrated. Following the death of the king of Lou Lan in 92 B.C.E., the people of the country requested that the prince be returned to take the throne. The ruler of Han rejected the request, however, for it would have been most embarrassing if the prince's countrymen had found him to be a eunuch.[30] In spite of his noble birth, the prince could not return to his homeland because of his shameful deformity, nor could he enter foreign society. Wudi's desire to demonstrate complete conquest is evident. In addition to the political uses of castration, it was also part of early Chinese criminal law: death sentences for capital offences could be commuted to castration.[31] By contrast, castration never became a standard penalty in Roman law.

2. COURT EUNUCHS: AN OLD CHINESE TRADITION

2.1. *Special Skills and Duties*

As Ulrike Jungel has shown, the Chinese language offers a number of very detailed expressions for court eunuchs.[32] Generally speaking, the term *huanguan* may refer to any "castrated man" in general or to one who served in the imperial palace in particular.[33] In fact, *huanguan* is the exact and official term to describe those castrated *and* employed at the imperial court as servants. *Guan* is the general term for "official" in Chinese. Even an emperor's servants were officials and therefore some kind of *guan*. This gives us an indication of their social prestige. Eunuchs were also called *siren*. In *siren*, the *si* means to serve, while *ren* always

28. Stevenson 2002.
29. Herodotus 3.48–49; another example: 6.32.
30. Mitamura 1970: 45–46.
31. Jugel 1976: 57.
32. Jugel 1976: 9–11.
33. Mitamura 1970: 21.

stands for "human being." Generally speaking, *siren* denotes those who serve other people but in our context indicates the eunuch, that is, those who were castrated so that they could serve the households of the emperors. The literal term for eunuch was *yanren*. But *yan*, meaning "castration," was rarely used, except in attempts to slander. For example, officials might use the term *yanzei* (a castrated thief) to scold a eunuch in a dispute. As we can see, the word's modern connotation reflects the subject's history.

One reason for the strong influence of eunuchs on the Son of Heaven was the fact that intimate relations between eunuchs and emperor were established in early childhood. As soon as he was old enough to leave his nurse's side, an imperial prince would be instructed in speech, table manners, deportment, etiquette, and general knowledge by court eunuchs.[34] In addition, eunuchs also took an interest in the natural sciences and technology. It was a eunuch who invented paper in 105 c.e.[35] As well as the prince's teachers, eunuchs were also his companions. Even his first sexual experience was often shared with a eunuch.[36] Palace eunuchs shared the most intimate moments of an emperor's life. The imperial prince (or child emperor) was surrounded by eunuchs and by women, mostly his mother and her kinsfolk, and had hardly any contact with more independent men, especially not with men from outside the court: even executive ministers were excluded from close contact. In theory, the emperor reigned supreme. But in practice, because of his seclusion, the Son of Heaven depended almost entirely on his eunuchs—and on the kinsmen of the empress or more usually those of the regent dowager empress.[37]

Even strong emperors were subject to eunuchs' influence, especially where the sexual aspects to their duties were involved. Like most Chinese emperors, the famous Wudi, who brought the Han Dynasty to its peak of power, was bisexual; and after the death of his favorite concubine, he turned to a handsome eunuch, named Luan Ta, who was familiar with magic practices. After elevating him in rank and conferring upon him unprecedented honors and prestige (which included making him a landed marquis with the right to collect taxes from hundreds of households), he presented him with a palace, a fine carriage, and countless slaves. He even gave him his daughter as a bride and bestowed on him an official jade seal and the title "General of the Heavenly Way." Later, bitterly disappointed, Wudi had this eunuch executed for daring to try to deceive the Son of Heaven.

Most stories about Chinese palace eunuchs come from the 23 standard Dynastic Histories.[38] But historiography was the monopoly of the Confucian scholars that dominated Chinese officialdom. Court eunuchs and Confucian-trained

34. Mitamura 1970: 115.
35. Balazs 1967: 189–91; Jugel 1976: 105–20.
36. Hinsch 1990: 34–54.
37. Chien 1950: 31.
38. Tsai 2002: 221.

officials competed for political influence in the palace. As personal attendants of the sovereign, the eunuchs always had his ear and so were in a better position than even the most powerful minister to curry favor, exercise influence, and accumulate wealth. The view of the historiographers is deeply influenced by the resentments of the office-holding ruling class toward their despised rivals. What is more, the emperor often used eunuchs to balance the power of Confucian civil servants. A generally negative view of eunuchs was the result. A key story, the tale of Zhao Gao, the first genuinely powerful eunuch in Chinese history, provides a perfect example of this slanted vision.

2.2. *The First Famous Eunuch of China: The Tale of Zhao Gao*

During the Qin Dynasty (221–206 B.C.E.), more eunuchs were employed to serve the ambitious empire builder Qin Shihuangdi, who was believed to have kept more than three thousand concubines in his palace and established a new agency called Zhongchangshi for the sole purpose of managing the ever increasing number of court eunuchs. In 210 B.C.E. the emperor died on a routine inspection tour. Immediately, concerns were raised about who should succeed him to the throne, and an attendant eunuch by the name of Zhao Gao suggested that the news of the emperor's death be kept from the public and even from the emperor's eldest son and heir apparent Fu Su, until troops could safely be moved to the capital city Xianyang. Secretly, Zhao Gao, together with the emperor's youngest son Hu Hai, ordered the construction of a special coffin to slow down the decomposition of the emperor's corpse and to conceal its odor. They pitched a tent for the emperor and brought in meals as if the emperor were still alive. In the meantime, the eunuch Zhao Gao, the Prime Minister Li Si, and the emperor's youngest son successfully plotted to kill Fu Su, the heir apparent, and to make Hu Hai the next emperor of the Qin Dynasty. Zhao Gao was promoted to head the eunuch agency Zhongchangshi. On his recommendation, the young emperor ordered all of his father's consorts who had not given birth to sons to follow the dead emperor to the grave; all the artisans who had worked on the terracotta figurines and the tomb went the same way. After winning the young emperor's confidence, Zhao Gao felt that the Prime Minister Li Si knew more than he was supposed to about their secrets and had now become the biggest threat to the new court. With the young emperor on his side, Zhao Gao replaced Li Si while callously but methodically purging Li's associates. However, popular discontent mounted and within only a few months, rebellions broke out all over the empire. During the early autumn of 206 B.C.E., when the rebels began to march into the Wei river valley, Zhao Gao murdered the Second Emperor Hu Hai. But a month later, the army led by Liu Bang, founder of the Han Dynasty, crushed the Qin defenders. Zhao Gao, the first really powerful eunuch in Chinese history, eventually became a casualty of this conflict.[39]

39. *Shiji* 87. Cf. Anderson 1990: 33–41.

A eunuch who installed a puppet emperor must have been a nightmare for all officials. Zhao Gao was forever identified with usurpation, political intrigues, and murders. The story was reported primarily by the Han historians Sima Qian and Jia Yi, both of whom lived in the second century B.C.E. As Confucians, they opposed Legalism, the First Emperor's official philosophy that supported the idea of centralized total power.[40] They consequently portrayed Qin Shihuangdi as a murderer and oppressor who failed to rule with humanity and righteousness. But the vivid rivalry between officials and eunuchs at the palace also shaped the historians' views on Zhao Gao. Their account witnesses the emergence of the stereotypical role that eunuchs came to play in Chinese historiography (as well as in the histories of other empires[41]), that of a scapegoat for an emperor's deeds. The grand eunuch Zhao Gao, who was the shadowy figure behind the emperor, was then singled out to share the blame of the First Emperor's many offensive policies. And forever after, his despised name would be held up to Chinese emperors as a dire warning against granting eunuchs any influence over them.

3. WOMEN AND EUNUCHS: A "NATURAL" ALLIANCE

The evils of the eunuch system have been the subject of much debate in Chinese historiography. The root cause was sought in the extensive system of concubinage in the Imperial Palace. In the case of China, it is easy to see how this conclusion may be reached; nevertheless, a comparative approach to this phenomenon indicates that this need not have been the true reason. Although Europe had abandoned polygamy centuries earlier, eunuchs rose to power at the Eastern Roman court. At the same time, there is no denying that women and eunuchs shared a special connection and common interests in China as well as in Europe.

In all the dynasties succeeding the Qin ruler, court eunuchs continued to grow in number and influence and, ultimately, became an important part of China's apparatus of imperial rule. At first, they suffered a setback under the founder of the Han Dynasty, Gaozu. Fully aware of the damage done by one eunuch in the Qin dynasty, he kept these palace servants under tight control. Eunuchs are seldom mentioned in the histories of his reign. Instead, he gradually developed a bureaucracy based on Confucian principles. The eunuchs' comeback started with Gaozu's wife, empress Lu. After Gaozu was succeeded by his meek, sensitive son Hui in 195 B.C.E., his mother—now empress dowager—came into her own as his regent. Young Huidi was said to sit on the throne "with folded hands and unruffled garments" while his mother ran the government.[42] During daily

---

40. Qin Shihuangdi reportedly buried 460 Confucian scholars alive and burned the Confucian writings. Cf. Eberhard 1971: 76.

41. For the Eastern Roman Empire, see Hopkins 1978: 174ff.

42. Anderson 1990: 45.

audiences with officials, she remained discreetly concealed behind a screen or curtain. She upheld the custom that denied uncastrated men close contact with imperial women. Thus, it was her eunuchs who transmitted state memoranda from the ministers, delivered her imperial decrees, and granted or denied access to her presence; in return, she endowed most of her eunuchs with generous land grants, including tax revenues.[43]

The story of empress dowager Lu's rule should be seen not only as an explanation for the rise of eunuchs at the imperial court, but also as a plea against women in power by the Confucian historiographers. Moreover, they were suspicious of complicity between eunuchs and women. Thus, under her male successor Wendi, matters supposedly took a turn for the better, although the eunuchs did of course remain.[44] It is evident that Confucian Chinese historiographers considered both women and eunuchs to have been an evil influence on the throne.

Traditionally, the number of imperial women was high because every ruler kept a large number of concubines in addition to his empress. As a member of an influential family who had entered the palace as a wife or concubine, a woman faced two crucial duties: apart from giving birth to a son, she was expected to promote the male members of her family to influential positions in the palace. Yet it would have been difficult for a newcomer to gain access to the emperor because even the most intimate aspects of the emperor's life were subject to etiquette and protocol, which were tightly regimented by the eunuchs. They not only organized but also participated in the nocturnal activities of the ruler. There was an office that dealt exclusively with the intimate relations between the emperor and empress and his other wives and concubines. When the emperor engaged in intimate relations with the empress, the date was recorded so as to prove legitimacy in the case of conception. Furthermore, every occasion on which he spent time with one of his concubines was recorded by this office.[45]

Castrated men were considered the perfect servants and guardians for women. According to *Zhouli* ("Book of the Rites of the Zhou Dynasty"), the king invested one queen, three madams, nine concubines, twenty-seven varied ranks of consorts, and eighty-one court ladies for duties in the Inner Court. In conjunction with this system, the Zhou king also employed castrated men to supervise the royal chambers and guard his harem.[46] There was constant competition among the women to give birth to a son and be the emperor's favorite. Eunuchs were always closely in touch with the other informal centers of power in the palace: the emperor's wives, consorts, and concubines.

43. Mitamura 1970: 132.
44. Mitamura 1970: 134–35.
45. Mitamura 1970: 111–13.
46. Tsai 2002: 221; Mitamura 1970: 78.

In the Zhou Dynasty, the number of women around the throne reportedly totaled 120. In the following centuries, the number of concubines seems to have increased steadily. Wudi was said to have acquired several thousands of beautiful women for his harem, which came to be filled to capacity. Following the emperor's example, the custom to have as many concubines as possible soon became widespread among both fiefholders and wealthy officials.[47] And as the number of concubines grew, so did the number of eunuchs.

Organized eunuch power took off under the Eastern Han Dynasty. Again, women's ambitions seem to have been responsible.[48] In this period, the eunuch agency Zhongchangshi was reconstituted, which made it possible for high-ranking castrated courtiers to gain access to the emperor and the empress. Six dowager empresses successively promoted Zhongchangshi eunuchs to powerful positions, unwittingly sowing the seeds for the dynasty's downfall—according to Confucian historiographers, that is. In 135 C.E., the eunuchs were permitted to adopt sons, and their power grew with their wealth as some of them owned large agricultural lands. Early in 189 C.E., emperor Lingdi died at the age of thirty-two, and because his son, the new emperor Shao, was only thirteen years old, the empress dowager—by the name of He—took over the helm of the state. She immediately promoted her older brother He Jin, who had earlier fought the "Yellow Turban" rebels, to be the Grand Commandant and appointed twelve grand eunuchs to manage the Inner Court Zhongchangshi. He Jin, however, sided with the bureaucrats and put his sister, the empress dowager, under pressure to remove the eunuchs, charging them with rampant corruption and abuses of power.[49]

The final showdown came in September of 189 C.E. when the eunuch Qu Mu slew the Grand Commandant He Jin during a court audience. He Jin's deputies in turn brought their troops to the capital Luoyang and killed more than two thousand eunuchs in retribution. The chief eunuch Zhang Rang took the teen-aged Emperor Shao and the Empress Dowager He and fled northward toward the Yellow River. But after being surrounded by his enemies, Zhang Rang jumped into the river and drowned himself, while his patron and protector He was forced to take poison. The Emperor Shao was then deposed and succeeded by his eight-year-old half-brother, the emperor Xiandi. But that was the beginning of the end of the dynasty.[50]

4. WOMEN AND EUNUCHS IN IMPERIAL ROME

It is useful to compare the function of eunuchs in China with practices in ancient Rome, and in particular to try to identify differences and similarities in their

---

47. Polygyny required money and power: the masses practiced monogamy. See Mitamura 1970: 79–80, 82.
48. Eberhard 1971: 117–20.
49. Tsai 2002: 223; Anderson 1990: 83–97.
50. Tsai 2002: 223–24.

alliances with women in the pursuit of influence and power. However, since the development of the role played by Roman eunuchs is slightly different from what we find in Chinese historiography, it is important to start by considering the history and structure of female power in Rome in general, as well as the precursors to the court eunuchs, the freedmen.

4.1. Women and Political Power in Rome

For several reasons, the situation of Roman women differed substantively from that of their Chinese counterparts. Formal monogamy was a principle that had never been seriously questioned in the Greco-Roman world. Indeed, by the end of the Republic, Rome had already developed unusual rights for women. Upon *emancipatio*, a woman was able to live independently from a father or a husband and settle her own affairs.[51] Even so, the right to hold office had never been extended to the female half of the population. A woman seeking influence on politics had to pursue this goal by influencing a man behind the scenes. Our sources seem to become more sensitive to the issue of female political influence with the creation of the Principate. From Augustus's reign onward, the women of the ruling family attracted a great deal of attention from historical writers and were commonly suspected of manipulating their husbands and sons, if necessary through the use of criminal methods. This tradition commences with Augustus's wife and Tiberius's mother Livia and reaches its first peak with Agrippina the Younger. Both women managed to establish their sons (by previous husbands) as heirs to the throne. As emperors, Tiberius and Nero are both portrayed as suffering under their mothers' intrigues.[52]

Agrippina was the sister of the notorious Caligula and the daughter of the consistently popular Germanicus, and hence a direct descendant of the founder of the Principate, Augustus. She already had a son, Lucius Domitius Ahenobarbus Nero, when she became the emperor Claudius's fourth wife in 49 c.e. His decision to marry her was based on dynastic considerations. As Antony Barrett has argued, "Claudius would need a wife, not for sex or companionship,...but because he needed a political ally to help him keep at bay the forces still threatening to topple his principate....He had tried to seek links with the noble houses and they had failed. He must have realized...that the only effective security would come from a union *within* the imperial house."[53] Apart from this, Suetonius claims that Claudius's decision making had always been influenced by his wives and freedmen.[54] What is more, because of her descent, Agrippina might have become a danger to Claudius if she married into another house, an argument ascribed to

---

51. Kaser 2003: 72, 76ff.
52. Suetonius, *Life of Tiberius* 50.2, 51.1; cf. Perkounig 1995: 149–65; Barrett 2002: 146–73. Suetonius, *Life of Nero* 9, 34, 35.3.
53. Barrett 1996: 95; Eck 1995: 38.
54. Suetonius, *Life of Claudius* 25.6. Cf. Friedländer 1922: 41, 46–67.

the influential freedman and confidant Pallas.[55] Family ties were already close: Claudius was Agrippina's uncle. Almost immediately after the marriage, she betrothed her son to Claudius's daughter Octavia and, one year later, in 50 C.E., she received the title of "Augusta." She was the first wife of a living emperor to share in the distinction of this title.[56] Moreover, she received another important distinction, that of participation in the daily *salutatio*. When courtiers and clients paid homage to the emperor, as they did every morning, they would henceforth do the same to her.[57] She even managed to be present during meetings of the Senate, "whose meetings were specially convened in the Palatium, so that she could station herself at a newly-added door in their rear, shut off by a curtain thick enough to conceal her from view but not to debar her from hearing."[58]

As a woman, Agrippina was unable to hold office, but the Roman Principate was never actually an office and not even a clearly defined legal position. The Principate was built on wealth, the *clientelae*, the loyalty of the troops, and the fame of Augustus. Under these circumstances, why was a woman not to play an official role as long as she was legitimated by her Julian background? In any case, Agrippina did not seek to rule by herself; instead, she intended to exercise influence through her son Nero. In February 50 C.E. Claudius adopted Nero, although he did have a younger son of his own, Britannicus. Nero had been built up as heir apparent when in 54 C.E. Claudius seemed to change his mind and put Britannicus in the limelight. Agrippina acted immediately and poisoned her husband. With the help of Agrippina's followers Burrus, Prefect of the Guard, and Seneca, the seventeen-year-old Nero succeeded his adoptive father. In fact, the shadow regiment of Agrippina, Seneca, and Burrus, supported by the influential freedmen who ran the palace's secretariats (they were the heads of the administration of the emperor's household and estates) had taken over. During the following years, Agrippina exercised her ambitions without any attempt to disguise them: her son "allowed his mother the greatest influence over all matters private and public."[59] But the estrangement between mother and son had already begun. Her ally, the freedman Pallas, head of the most important secretariat *a rationibus*, was the first target: he was forced to resign as overseer of the imperial finances very soon after Nero's accession. Finally, in 59 C.E., Nero ordered his mother killed. The reason he gave was that Agrippina had been striving for *consortium imperii*, "participation in government," and that she had hoped that the Praetorian Guard, as well as the people and the Senate, would swear allegiance to a woman, which was considered shameful.[60]

---

55. Oost 1958; Tacitus, *Annals* 12.2.3; Eck 1995: 38.
56. Tacitus, *Annals* 12.26.1; Cassius Dio 60.33.2a; Barrett 1996: 108.
57. Tacitus, *Annals* 13.18.5; Cassius Dio 61.33.1; Barrett 1996: 108.
58. Tacitus, *Annals* 13.5.1 (trans. J. Jackson).
59. Suetonius, *Life of Nero* 9.
60. Suetonius, *Life of Nero* 34; Tacitus, *Annals* 14.11.1. See also Eck 1995: 72–76.

4.2. Forerunners of the Court Eunuchs: Freedmen
in the Roman Palace Administration

It was Claudius who concentrated power among the administrators at his palace to provide a counterweight to his political rivals, the senators. Although the rise of the freedmen had already begun under Augustus,[61] their influence significantly increased under Caligula. Some imperial freedmen were already performing duties of a magistrate and in emergencies were even entrusted with official posts. In 32 C.E. the freedman Hiberius held the Prefecture of Egypt for some months; in 48 C.E. Narcissus was made Prefect of the Guard for one day.[62] When Claudius succeeded Caligula in 41 C.E., he was backed by the Praetorian Guard and the palace freedmen but not by the Senate, which had been debating whether to abolish the Principate altogether.[63] The guardsmen and freedmen depended on this specific form of a monarchy for their livelihood, which turned them into Claudius's allies right from the beginning. The imperial freedmen were foreigners of humble origin but highly educated; most of them were Greek and therefore barred from holding office at that time. Despised by the nobility and entirely dependent on Claudius, their loyalty belonged to him alone. This implied a submissiveness that many aristocrats might still resist. Claudius extended the secretariats in his household, which were already staffed by slaves and ex-slaves, and enhanced the status of the most trusted freedmen. Pallas and Callistus, already influential under Caligula, as well as Polybius and Narcissus were the most important heads of these offices.[64] As head of the secretariat *a rationibus*, the fiscal administration, Pallas occupied a key position. Narcissus, the *proximus ab epistulis*, was responsible for correspondence and served as a private secretary. The department *a libellis* was in charge of petitions, headed by Polybius and then Callistus. *A studiis, a cognitionibus* supported jurisdiction.[65] These Claudian freedmen were notorious for their avarice: they accumulated legendary wealth, which became the most prominent symbol of their influence.[66]

To attain her extraordinary position and establish her son as Claudius's successor, Agrippina also relied on the help of freedmen. Pallas had been Agrippina's ally and later acted in favor of Nero.[67] In 62 C.E., however, Nero ordered his execution in order to seize his wealth.[68] Narcissus had favored a different noblewoman to become Claudius's consort. In October 54 C.E., Agrippina arranged his execution at Messalina's grave.[69] To freedmen, it seems, "senatorial government had

---

61. Boulvert 1970: 55–56.
62. Levick 1990: 47.
63. Dettenhofer 2003.
64. Levick 1990: 57; Suetonius, *Life of Claudius* 25.6, *Life of Nero* 35.4.
65. Suetonius, *Life of Claudius* 28–29.1; cf. Boulvert 1970: 65.
66. Suetonius, *Life of Claudius* 28.1; *Life of Nero* 35.4.
67. Tacitus, *Annals* 13.14.1. See also Suetonius, *Life of Claudius* 28.1; Tacitus, *Annals* 12.1, 12.25.1.
68. Tacitus, *Annals* 14.65.1; Cassius Dio 62.14.3; Suetonius, *Life of Nero* 35.4.
69. Tacitus, *Annals*, 13.1; Cassius Dio 73.16.5.

no more to offer... than it had to women, and this tended to create solidarity among them, for all their natural rivalry."[70] We may conclude that they shared successes and failures on the behind-the-scenes battlefield of dynastic politics. The historian Suetonius repeatedly emphasizes that Claudius depended entirely on his wives and freedmen and therefore considers them as the true architects of most of his policies (*Life of Claudius* 25.6, 29.1).

In the present context, it is essential to note that the high-ranking freedmen of the early emperors were the forerunners of the court eunuchs. When they were replaced by freeborn administrators from the "equestrian" order, they had already paved the way for men with a humble background from outside the empire: eunuchs finally rose to positions of influence in late antiquity and in the Byzantine period. As Barbara Levick notes, "If freedmen were safe to have as confidants, because they were excluded from formal politics, eunuchs were safer still."[71]

4.3. The Power of Eunuchs in Roman Late Antiquity

In Rome, castration was considered something to be an eastern custom that had become a synonym for decadence.[72] Nevertheless, under the new order established by Diocletian and Constantine, eunuchs became a highly influential group at Roman courts in the fourth and fifth centuries c.e., especially in the eastern part of the empire, where elaborate ceremonies governed the emperor's secluded life.[73]

The key characteristics of Roman eunuchs were the same as in China, or at least resembled them closely.[74] Proximity to the emperor and assurance of his favor were the sole firm basis of the court eunuchs' power. As servants of the *cubiculum* (the imperial bed-chamber), they were closely connected with the emperor's intimate sphere. They controlled access to his audiences and derived material gain from this privilege: thus, they exacted fees for audiences and, by the fifth century, took a sizable commission from everyone who was appointed to public office. Much like Claudius's freedmen, court eunuchs were notorious for their greed and wealth. Yet their provenance and physical deficiency ensured that they remained outsiders to Roman society, without a formal base or allies. Rulers viewed this as a decisive benefit. Since they could not be assimilated into the formal aristocracy, they not only acted as a counterweight to aristocracy and magistrates but also, as Keith Hopkins has pointed out, as "lubricants" for

70. Levick 1990: 57.
71. Levick 1990: 57. Suetonius already mentions two eunuchs in Claudius's household: Posides (*Life of Claudius* 28), who enjoyed Claudius's special appreciation, and Halotus (ibid. 44.2), who was Claudius's food taster. Both are counted among the freedmen and had therefore become Roman citizens.
72. Horace, *Epodes* 9.13–14.
73. Guyot 1980: 130; Dunlop 1924: 178–79.
74. Hopkins 1978: 172–96; Guyot 1980: 130–80; and more recently Schlinkert 1994; Scholten 1995; Scholz 2001.

the system.[75] They absorbed criticism that might otherwise have been directed against the emperor. Palace intrigues of malicious eunuchs were conveniently blamed for perceived ills. Despite harsh criticism of the eunuch power system, both emperors who attempted to abolish it, Julian (361–363 C.E.) and Maximus (455 C.E.), failed to establish an effective alternative and the system survived.

One of the empire's most influential positions had become a domain of the eunuchs: the Grand Chamberlain (*praepositus sacri cubiculi*), chief of the chamberlains (*cubicularii*) and, in the course of time, an increasing number of other groups of castrated domestic servants.[76] In the established order of precedence of the Eastern empire, the Grand Chamberlain, a eunuch and ex-slave, held the fourth rank in the realm after Praetorian Prefects, the Prefect of the City, and the Masters of the Soldiers.[77] His tenure continued at the emperor's pleasure and often lasted longer than the three years thought to be normal for Praetorian Prefects. Some of them became famous. Eusebius, a former slave, was *praepositus sacri cubiculi* of the emperor Constantius II (337–361 C.E.) and played an active part in contemporary politics. He was sentenced to death by Constantius's successor, the ascetic emperor Julian (361–363 C.E.).[78] Eutropius, a former slave, probably of Armenian origin, had been made a eunuch in his earliest infancy. He had already won the confidence of the emperor Theodosius and became Grand Chamberlain of Theodosius's son, the emperor Arcadius (395–408 C.E.)—and the rival of empress Aelia Eudoxia. The Grand Chamberlain, who had originally promoted the emperor's marriage with the beautiful Eudoxia, who was herself partly of foreign origin, and the Praetorian Prefect Rufinus can be considered the true rulers during the reign of the child-emperor Arcadius.[79] Finally, Eutropius was sentenced to death. As Chrysaorius exclaimed: "If you have a eunuch, kill him; if you haven't, buy one and kill him!"[80]

The Grand Chamberlain in particular, and the corps of eunuchs in general, expanded their power well beyond the formal confines of palace administration. This had further consequences: eunuchs came to be chosen for special tasks outside the palace. Invested with imperial authority and high rank, eunuchs were sent on special missions. Thus, Eusebius was sent to quell an incipient revolt in the army of Gaul by bribing the rebel leaders.[81] The emperor Theodosius dispatched Eutropius to consult a holy hermit in Egypt about the outcome of his conflict with the usurper Eugenius.[82]

75. Hopkins 1978: 196.
76. Guyot 1980: 24ff.
77. Guyot 1980: 175.
78. Ammianus Marcellinus 14.11, 15.3, 21.15.4; Guyot 1980: 199–201; Dunlop 1924: 260–70; Wiemer 1997: 338.
79. Zosimus 5.24.2; Dunlop 1924: 272–48; Hahn 1997: 374–80.
80. For evidence, see Dunlop 1924: 284.
81. Ammianus Marcellinus 14.10.5.
82. Sozomenus, *History of the Church* 7.22.

Keith Hopkins suggests that the consistent use of eunuchs as court chamberlains and their repeated exercise of power were probably associated with the
elaboration of court ritual, which can approximately be dated to the end of the
third century C.E. The capture of the Persian king's harem by Galerius in 298 C.E.
may also have led to a proliferation of eunuchs at the Roman court.[83] Roman
eunuchs were not linked to women's quarters for the simple reason that they
did not exist in the same form as in China. Nonetheless, the Roman ruling class
seems to have adopted certain habits from the east. Cassius Dio already notes that
a contemporary praetorian prefect under Septimius Severus had a hundred free
Romans castrated so that only eunuchs would wait on his daughter.[84] Emperor
Julian's pretext for the dismissal of the eunuchs was that he was celibate and thus
had no use for eunuchs. However, it is more likely that he abstained from pomp
and luxury to demonstrate that he was not subject to the same influences as his
predecessor Constantius.[85] As servants, eunuchs did manage to obtain access to
the empresses' and other women's quarters.[86] Because they shared the intimate
sphere of the ruler, there seems to have been a latent complicity between the
Grand Chamberlain with his *cubicularii* and the empress. But this, of course,
could just as well result in bitter rivalries.

5. CONCLUSIONS

A comparative approach to the power of eunuchs in Rome and China reveals
a number of structural similarities. Isolation, as a correlate of absolute power,
reinforced by ruler-worship and court ritual, laid the foundations for the political power of eunuchs in both empires. Control over physical access to the ruler
ensured influence. As mediators between the sovereign and his subjects as well as
the females at his court, eunuchs satisfied a divine emperor's need for information and human contact.[87] Although this made them extremely powerful, their
condition lowered their social status to the extent that the ruler would not per-
ceive them as rivals: they would always remain completely dependent upon him.
Eunuchs were unpopular in both societies. They represented a despised group
that was only able to exist inside the court and under the emperor's protection.
Their authority as individuals was a function of the emperor's patronage. In both
empires, they could only exist in the shadow of their ruler.

Eunuchs may not have shared a common interest with any of the emperor's
subjects or any man in particular, but they quite clearly cooperated with another
group that had no presence outside the palace: the emperor's wife, consorts, and

83. Hopkins 1978: 192–93; Klein 1997: 278.
84. Cassius Dio 75.14.
85. Socrates, *History of the Church* 3.1.
86. Ammianus Marcellinus 14.6.17; cf. Guyot 1980: 135.
87. Cf. Hopkins 1978: 187.

concubines. This common interest ultimately seems to have enabled them to gain influence through the bed-chamber, instrumentalizing their intimate relations with the ruler and his dependency on them as a weapon against the officials they were competing against. Both groups had to face and attempt to deal with exclusion from many rights and, at least in China, formal power—and, as a consequence, discrimination. But there is more to the power structures than this.

The phallus has always been seen as symbol—and used as an instrument—of power. This perspective guides us toward an explanation of the phenomenon of eunuchs and their role in power relations in antiquity. What made eunuchs so special? Why did castration change everything for the person affected? Men's identity is primarily based on their genitals, whereas women's identity has traditionally been tied to their fathers or husbands and sons. Valuing men more than women and considering one's own sex inferior has deep roots in women's education. This means that women's ego and self-consciousness were supposed to depend entirely on men, or rather on the family, and on the appreciation they received for giving birth to sons.[88] This encouraged submissiveness and facilitated their integration into the strictly patriarchal structures of Chinese and Roman society. Social background made little difference. In fact, the few women who broke out of anonymity and gained political influence did so as mothers of sons and on their behalf, often acting as their regents.

When a man had lost his genitals he found himself in a similar situation as women did. He still had his birth family but needed a new point of reference for his future life. As he was no longer accepted by other men,[89] the eunuch had become dependent on patriarchal structures similar to those faced by women. By committing themselves entirely to their master—with both body and soul— eunuchs were seen as the perfect servants in both China and Rome.

88. Obedience is one of the three Confucian cardinal virtues of women. A Chinese woman should obey her parents before marriage, her husband after marriage, and her eldest son after her husband's death. Fidelity and sincerity are the other two. Cf. van Gulik 2003: 58–59; Tienchi 1984: 105.

89. The preference for homosexual staff at the British court has a long tradition. It has been observed in the entire royal household. Among men, there seems to be a certain connection between sexual orientation and their utility in certain power structures that goes much deeper than the simple fear of possible political rivals. My special thanks go to Alaric Searle (University of Salford, Manchester), Pei-chuen Kao (University of Beijing) and Uwe Dubielzig, who supported my work with great patience.

5

Commanding and Consuming the World

Empire, Tribute, and Trade in Roman and Chinese History

Peter Fibiger Bang

> Are you aware that all these peoples...exact tribute from us, not
> from our land or from our flocks and herds, but from our folly? For
> if, when by force of arms any people get the upper hand and compel
> the vanquished to pay them silver, this is called tribute, and it is a
> sign that people are not very fortunate or brave if they pay tribute
> to others, then is it not true that if, though no one has attacked or
> compelled them, but because of stupidity and self-indulgence, a
> certain people take that which they prize most highly, silver, and of
> their own volition send it over a long road and across a vast expanse
> of sea to those who cannot easily even set foot upon our soil, such
> conduct is altogether more cowardly and disgraceful?
>
> —Dio Chrysostomus

1. INTRODUCTION

This chapter is about tribute and trade, empire, and markets. This is a set of
issues that Roman and Chinese history not only have in common but also present as one of the great challenges to economic history. The core of the matter
is contained in the excerpt above from a speech by the Greco-Roman orator,
Dio Chrysostomus. There is nothing original or exceptional in his way of reasoning. The contents reflect stock themes of ancient moral and political philosophy. This is precisely why it lays bare what I shall refer to as the "paradox of
agrarian empire" with such particular clarity. In the quotation we encounter Dio
Chrysostomus thundering against the corrupting influences of foreign trade on
the character of the Roman conquerors. Imports of foreign rarities and luxuries
are described as undermining the moral strength of the imperial people. They
place Rome in a position of servile dependence on her inferiors that amounts
to a voluntary submission to the payment of a degrading tribute to barbarian
peoples. If the Roman Empire was not to follow in the footsteps of the Medes,
Persians, and Macedonians, all of them empire builders who had lost their power

as they allowed themselves to become enslaved to their thirst for the "wealth of the wretched and unfortunate," its people had to free themselves of such desires.[1] Yet, as is also clear from the speech, the import of luxuries itself was one of the benefits of empire.

The problem of how to combine a political discourse that was frequently hostile to and always suspicious of trade and merchants with the widespread existence of markets and commercialism constitutes one of the great conundrums in the history of agrarian empires such as Rome and China. It has produced some of the most inspiring scholarship in the field of preindustrial economic history. The year 1973 was to prove one of an exceptionally rich harvest with Moses Finley's *The Ancient Economy* and Mark Elvin's *The Pattern of the Chinese Past*. Both books set out from a similar question, why had Greco-Roman Antiquity and China, despite their brilliant and impressive achievements, not developed modern capitalism? Finley found an explanation in the culture of the Greeks and Romans.[2] Elvin suggested that China had entered a so-called high-level equilibrium trap. Inspired by the comments of Adam Smith on the vast internal market of China, Elvin viewed the "Celestial Empire" as having reached a sort of preindustrial equilibrium state where traditional resources were being exploited in the most efficient way, but where further development, therefore, was also well-nigh impossible.[3] In Finley's scheme it is the cultural and political outlook of the landowning elites and the predatory activities of the state that block development, whereas in Elvin's analysis the politically dominant culture takes a much more marginal position. In spite of intermittent hostility and moral condemnation, the Chinese imperial state effectively had to tolerate, and periodically even promote, the development of commercialism and free market trade. Benign indifference and laissez-faire, sometimes enlightened, sometimes by default, and destructive interventionism mark the two opposite explanatory poles between which modern scholarship has been torn in its debates about the political economy of agrarian empires.

Both kinds of explanation, however, seem in need of modification. Today few students of preindustrial empires would be willing to subscribe to a view of the state as capable of dominating and subjecting the economy to the point of economic retardation. Individual policies could exercise a profound influence on those affected, but their reach would normally have been limited, effects isolated. For the populace at large, the imperial government is bound to have been a fairly distant reality and a relatively light burden to bear; it simply lacked the means to establish a more powerful presence in the daily lives of most people.

1. Dio Chrysostom 79.5 (transl. by H. L. Crosby) 79.6.
2. Finley 1985, esp. chs. 2 and 6.
3. Elvin 1973, and ch. 17 in particular. For Adam Smith on the vast inland market of China and the near stationary state of its economy, see Smith 1976: 111–12, 680–81.

A more restrained view of the role of imperial government might be thought to leave the field to free market explanations. Bin Wong, for instance, has developed Elvin's high-level equilibrium trap into a notion of an economy dominated by Smithian dynamics.[4] Transaction costs, however, seriously weaken the strength of this argument. The vast expanses covered by both the Chinese and Roman empires, slow communications and transport, the absence of a strong state to enforce law and order outside governmental centers, the control of local communities exercised by groups of entrenched gentry—all these and other such factors should caution against overestimating the level of economic integration that could be achieved. Areas of intense commercialization would have alternated with regions almost untouched by the higher levels of trade. Empire-wide, these economies were beset by irregularities, imperfections, and asymmetries. There would still have been plenty of room for optimizing economic performance, in most regions at least, even in densely populated late imperial China.[5]

Oppressive interventionism and relatively free markets, however, need not be treated as mutually exclusive alternatives. Both phenomena seem to have formed part of the same reality. Political coercion and commercialization co-existed and should probably be understood as intimately connected with the process of empire formation. Speaking from a position within the dominant imperial discourse, Dio Chrysostomus insisted that coercion and exchange were inextricably linked. Roman imports of foreign luxuries were derided by him as equal to the payment of a tribute. But it was travelling in the wrong direction. Tribute was something subjects and outlying barbarian peoples were supposed to remit to Rome, not the other way around. From the point of view of empire, relations with the surrounding world presented themselves in terms of submission and tribute. It is an idea that is well known from Chinese history, too, with the establishment of the Han tribute system, which attempted to regulate the sphere of interest of the Chinese Empire in a hierarchy of tributary relations.[6]

Only later was this system to reach its culmination during the Ming and Qing periods with the (ineffective) attempt to achieve a tight regulation of all seaborne foreign trade. In the future, trade was only to be granted as a privilege after foreigners had openly acknowledged their submission by bringing tribute to the Chinese emperor.[7] No less fascinating are the simultaneous grand naval expeditions conducted in the early fifteenth century by the eunuch admiral Zheng He. They sought to bring South East Asia and countries lining the Indian Ocean

---

4. Wong 1997, pt. 1. But it is important to understand that the notion of "Smithian dynamics" is used as an ideal type. Part 2 then goes on to explore the importance of political economy, in other words of institutional factors, in shaping the early modern Chinese economy. This is an aspect of the analysis that Pomeranz 2000 fails to give due weight in his further development of the basic concept.

5. Deng 1999: 13–16, 193–99 for some brief remarks. On Rome, see Bang 2004 and 2006.

6. Yü 1986.

7. Fairbank, ed. 1968; Wills 1984; Sahlins 1989; Hevia 1995.

within the orbit of the Chinese tributary system and returned triumphantly laden with professions of submission by foreign rulers and precious objects, rarities, curiosities, and marvels to reflect the wide reach of the emperor's mighty sway.[8] The Roman government never acted on its tributary instincts to conceive a similarly grandiose trading policy. But on a smaller scale, it did avail itself of several strategies that we also find employed, though probably in a more systematic fashion, by the Han Chinese court.[9] These included attempts to control the movement of men and goods in frontier regions for taxation purposes, the manipulation of bordering tribes by granting or withholding the privilege to trade on imperial territory. In like fashion, prohibitions were issued on export of goods of strategic value such as iron, flint, wheat grain, and salt. The Roman emperor also prided himself on receiving at court the chieftains of client tribes and kingdoms that submitted tribute. In return, they were generously showered with presents and, frequently, also received the privilege of taking with them goods for their own personal use, however defined, free of export duty.[10]

Tributary empire was a way of controlling and distributing wealth. It aimed to expand the level, range, and diversity of resources available to the ruling class, group, or people. When singing the praises of Rome, ancient authors regularly congratulated themselves on the vast riches and abundance of goods flowing to the capital, the center of human civilization. The power to command and consume the world in all its great variety was publicly celebrated and proclaimed in grand triumphal ovations that followed military victory. Listen to Josephus describing the triumph of Vespasian and his son Titus after the fall of Jerusalem: "It is impossible adequately to describe the multitude of those marvels and their magnificence under every imaginable aspect whether in works of art or diversity of riches or rarities of nature; for almost all the objects which men who have ever been blessed with fortune have acquired one by one—the wonderful and precious productions of various nations—were gathered on this day in massed formation to demonstrate the grandeur of Rome."[11] Gone was the "Golden Age," the era of Saturn, when nature had readily yielded its products and man had been free from toil. But empire held out the promise, to the privileged victors, of enjoying another age of plenty and prosperity.[12] Tributary empire, like markets, embodied an economic strategy. It enabled the victors to pool and command a wide selection of regionally diverse specialities and riches. It was coercion

---

8. Dreyer 2007.

9. Yü 1967, chs. 3 and 5.

10. *Digest* 39.4.11 (Paul, *Sententiae*, book 5); Cassius Dio 72.11.3 (the emperor denies to grant a barbarian tribe the right to trade for fear of barbarians building up supplies). See Whittaker 1994 for a treatment of Roman frontiers informed by a reading of Chinese history.

11. Josephus, *Jewish War* 7.132–33 (trans. modified from Thackeray).

12. In the Golden Age, as observed by Ovid, *Metamorphoses* 5.101, the land yielded its products without being subject to tribute (*immunis*). The imposition and consolidation of empire proclaimed a new golden age; cf. Horace, *Carmen Saeculare*.

leading to consumption. In the remainder of this chapter, I will sketch out three economic dimensions of the workings of agrarian empire: (1) empire as a tributary enterprise; (2) tribute extraction and commercialization; and (3) as a brief conclusion, imperial culture of consumption.

2. EMPIRE AS A TRIBUTARY ENTERPRISE

The celebration of the wide range of rare and wonderful products made available through the acquisition of empire responded to the experience of a world characterized by small, localized communities. It was a world where most products never left their place of origin and consumption was heavily determined by what the local geology, climate, and ecology allowed to be grown or extracted. Peasant agriculture reigned supreme, and the potential for growth was narrowly circumscribed. It was the world of small, near autarkic communities known from Plato's *Republic;* and, as the Greek philosopher candidly explained, if people desired to have access to more than the limited choice available to them, the community had to pursue a strategy of war and imperialism.[13] Only successful conquest would bring more territories into their possession. These were a necessary requirement to obtain control over a greater variety and a larger amount of resources. In Eisenstadt's felicitous expression, imperialism aimed at creating "free-floating resources."[14] By imposing tribute, empire forced resources out of the semiclosed cells of local economies and brought them into a wider sphere of circulation.

Extensive empires such as Rome or Han China drew some of their particular characteristics from their ability to cream off the limited production surpluses of numerous small communities and concentrate consumption of the accumulated wealth to a restricted number of privileged persons and places. The result was, for instance, to turn capital cities such as Rome, Constantinople, Chang'an, and Luoyang into preindustrial giant conurbations. With population numbers running well into six figures, they represented urbanization of an entirely different order of magnitude from what had come before or accompanied it and offered an equally wider palette of consumption opportunities.[15] In Rome, all the world, almost literally, came together. She was "the great whore" of the *Revelation* as well as the "center of the universe" of her panegyrists, a place that received the best and the worst from everywhere. Empires like the Roman and the Han can therefore be described in economic terms as tribute-producing enterprises.

The main cost of the imperial enterprise was the army. Universal empires have a well-earned reputation for lavish expenditure. The Romans were no exception

---

13. Plato, *Republic* 2.372d–74d.
14. Eisenstadt 1963: 26–28.
15. On Rome, see Morley 1996; Edwards and Woolf, eds. 2003. On Luoyang, see Bielenstein 1986: 262–64, and on Chang'an, see Nishijima 1986: 574–76.

to this rule. "Bread and circuses," temples, huge public baths, palatial complexes, and the omnipresent pomp and circumstance were major items of expenditure in the imperial budget.[16] Chinese history has its own tale to tell of conspicuous imperial consumption. It is manifest in the stupendous scale of the recently uncovered mausoleum of the Qin emperor with its thousands of terracotta soldiers, the imposing and magnificent grandeur of the "Forbidden City" in Beijing, and the delicate but lost marvel of the Summer Palace, torched and looted by a Western expeditionary force during the Opium Wars. But however impressive such displays of wealth may appear, historically war was an even more expensive activity. There was nothing like military operations to drain away imperial revenue and thus threaten the creation of the desired surplus. Wudi, the conqueror among the Han emperors, was also the ruler behind one of the most extensive attempts to raise the level of taxation. The costs of his ambitious expansionist policies on the inner Asian frontier stretched existing imperial finances beyond their means: "The late Emperor...caused forts and serried signal stations to be built where garrisons were held ready against the nomads. When the revenue for the defence of the frontier fell short, the salt and iron monopoly was established, the liquor excise and the system of equable marketing introduced; goods were multiplied and wealth increased so as to furnish the frontier expenses."[17]

This kind of expensive military activism did not go down well in all circles of the imperial elite. Echoes of criticism have been preserved in a small first century B.C.E. dialogue pretending to record a debate during the reign of Wudi's successor concerning the merits and faults of his new revenue-raising measures. Confucian literati are here presented admonishing the monarch to curb his military ambitions. The emperor and his ministers should rather "cultivate benevolence and righteousness, to set an example to the people, and extend wide their virtuous conduct to gain the people's confidence. Then will nearby folk lovingly flock to them and distant peoples joyfully submit to their authority. Therefore *the master conqueror does not fight, the expert warrior needs no soldiers; the truly great commander requires not to set his troops in battle array....* The Prince who practices benevolent administration should be matchless in the world; for him, what use is expenditure?"[18] The imperial army was too costly an instrument, in this view, to be employed in all manner of vainglorious projects.

This was advice that no successful empire, no matter how bent on military glory, could afford to ignore in the long term. An imperial army was to be used with caution; it was a scarce resource, not to be wasted indiscriminately. It sounds paradoxical, but even that paragon of militarism, the Roman government,

---

16. The classic analysis would be Veyne 1976. See Duncan-Jones 1994: 45–46 for an estimate of the composition of the Roman imperial budget.

17. *Discourses on Salt and Iron* Id (Gale 1931: 4).

18. Gale 1931: 4–5 (ch. 1f.).

generally only employed its vast military might with circumspection. Failure to recognize this general principle has misled modern commentators on a number of occasions, most notably when they erected an elaborate theory of defensive Roman imperialism in the second century B.C.E. After the victory at Pydna in 168 B.C.E., having definitively defeated the kingdom of Macedon, Rome was reluctant to annex the territory of the conquered foe. Instead, the existing political entity was dismantled and replaced by four self-governing republics. These, however, were left with an obligation to submit an annual tribute to the Roman victor, only, it is true, at half the rate of the old royal tax. But then again, Rome had no intention of garrisoning the former Macedonian territory. Policing and defence against bordering tribes were the responsibility of the newly created polities. On top of this, mines (some of them closed for a brief spell as a result of the rivalries of Roman domestic politics) and probably also the old royal estates were confiscated. This was not reluctant or defensive imperialism; it was an attempt to enjoy empire on the cheap and collect tribute with the least possible effort and expense.[19]

Tribute obtained through a minimum of effort remained a key principle of Roman imperialism for centuries. It may be worthwhile to dwell on the Macedonian example a little longer. It suggests that one of the secrets behind the success of the Romans was the achievement of economies of scale. The Macedonian army was almost wholly dismantled without triggering a similar increase in the number of troops on the Roman side. Gibbon already commented on the relatively small number of soldiers that the imperial state maintained to ensure control of the greater Mediterranean world.[20] On occasion, though often to the accompaniment of hostile sneers from the imperial elite, emperors even preferred to buy off hostile barbarian tribes on the imperial frontiers that were eager for plunder instead of waging an unremunerative war. Such tribes could also be exploited as a cheap source of recruits for the army. In late antiquity, Roman emperors increasingly came to rely on Germanic federate troops to fight their wars and stave off invaders. This meant that the government did not have to divert valuable provincial subjects from taxpaying agricultural activities to army duty.[21] Successive Chinese dynasties cultivated the art of managing loosely organised "barbarian" tribes on the imperial frontier to perfection. Confucian opinion was in general more favorably inclined toward such policies of accommodation than a Roman aristocracy cherishing the memory of its proud republican past. The relationship between the sedentarized agricultural core and the nomadic steppe frontier is a key theme in Chinese history and found its classic

---

19. As Cato was thought to have declared, the Macedonians should be left free "because they could not be protected," *Historia Augusta, Life of Hadrian* 5.3. See Scullard 1980: 282–83 for a brief statement of the facts. More extensive discussion in Gruen 1984, though uncomprehending of the economic mechanisms at work.
20. Gibbon 1993: 23–24.
21. Cassius Dio 72.11–12; Ammianus Marcellinus 31.4.4; Shaw 1999.

exposition in the work of Owen Lattimore.[22] Bestowing rich gifts of grain and silk on nomadic chieftains in return for a token tribute, nominal recognition of Chinese supremacy, and peace were much less expensive than the waging of wars with no end in sight and little prospect of plunder and gain capable of financing the efforts against a mobile enemy that remained hard to control. Equally, such tribes could be usefully employed in war against other nomadic groups that threatened imperial territory.

To be sure, the potential drawbacks of such policies were far from negligible, as the western Roman emperors discovered in the fifth century c.e. Bought peace was frequently unstable. Often the power of tributary chieftains was insufficiently consolidated to guarantee a lasting arrangement. There was also a risk that access to the wealth of the imperial government did not satisfy demand but rather whetted the appetite of barbarian leaders and their warrior retinues for more. This could pose a serious threat if the initial alliance with the empire had helped strengthen the social and military organization of the tribal band. Imperial power and barbarian tribes existed in an uneasy equilibrium. Nonetheless, from the imperial perspective, the financial rewards of these policies frequently outweighed the risks. These, after all, could normally be handled. By contrast, the costs of waging war against the barbarians on the frontier dwarfed the expense of buying them off with gifts and military service. The sources rarely enable us to make precise calculations. But it is sometimes possible to form a rough impression. Chinese figures, for instance, seem to suggest that a set of punitive campaigns against one group of barbarian nomads in the decade from 107–118 c.e. cost the imperial government five to six times the entire amount spent on barbarian appeasement.[23] In the long term, Chinese emperors understandably chose uneasy accommodation over costly mobilization.

The impulse to save on the number of soldiers was irresistible. In this area, extensive empires such as Rome and Han China enjoyed one advantage: they drew their resources from a very broad base. Even at low levels of mobilization, they were still able to field impressive numbers. The difficulties experienced by Roman emperors in waging simultaneous full-scale wars on the Germanic and Persian frontiers have often enough been mentioned as one of the weaknesses of the empire. Yet it ought to have been possible temporarily to expand the size of the army. At some twenty-five to thirty legions, the imperial army was bigger than the peace-time force retained by the republican government in the late 60s b.c.e. to guard its much less extensive territories, but smaller than the peak numbers reached during the following decades of conquest and revolutionary struggles. The imperial army, furthermore, increasingly drew its recruits from all over the empire while the brunt of the burden of fielding the vast armies of the

22. Lattimore 1940.
23. Yü 1967: 61.

late republic had fallen on the Italian population. Mobilization levels, therefore, were considerably lower than they had been.[24] However, the pressure to expand numbers was not strong enough. The emperor was already in possession of the biggest military force by far anywhere in western Eurasia. He could forego the extreme levels of military recruitment that the Italian population had had to sustain even during the most peaceful times of the late republic without losing the ability to command, on a regular basis, a larger number of soldiers. In other words, he had come to depend on the benefits of economies of scale.

This ability to save on manpower resources and achieve economies of scale in army organization may provide an important part of the explanation for the frequent longevity of tributary empires such as Rome and the successive Chinese empires. History, of course, cannot be reduced to economics. When first established, inertia and cowardice, for instance, would also have been forces favoring the persistence of empire. On the other hand, much spoke against their lasting success. With their vast territories they almost seem to violate the limits of the possible. Low speed of transport and communication made tight control of all areas impossible. One might have expected the imperial state to splinter at any time. Yet these empires survived for surprisingly long periods, probably because they were able to maintain hegemony at relatively low costs. The Chinese experience, with its long history of reining in the army, seems to confirm the plausibility of such an interpretation.[25]

Tribute extracted with a minimum of effort also entailed keeping administrative costs at a low. The imperial state, and Rome rather more so than Han China, was spread very thin on the taxpaying ground of provincial societies. During the Antonine era, the Roman Empire with its population of perhaps sixty million people was partitioned into some forty provinces, each with a governor, a financial officer (sometimes two), a few assistants, and imperial slaves plus a small secretariat. "Government without bureaucracy," the label coined by Peter Garnsey and Richard Saller, is not an exaggeration. In the fourth and fifth centuries, provincial administration expanded.[26] This brought the number of administrators

---

24. The Roman imperial army counted some twenty-five to twenty-eight legions during most of the Principate. This was rather more than the numbers maintained by the Republic at the peace-time low of the late 60s B.C.E., but less than the thirty-five legions on record for 44 B.C. or the peak of fifty to sixty during the following years of renewed civil war. Each legion would ideally have been staffed by five to six thousand men. The number of legionaries can thus be estimated to somewhere between 125,000 and 168,000 under the emperors. To this must be added a considerable number of auxiliary troops drawn from subject populations. They are customarily thought to have been approximately of the same size. The army would thus have stood between 250,000–330,000. Such numbers were almost matched on the basis of Italian recruits during the peak periods of revolutionary struggles and surpassed if regular recruits and auxiliaries drawn from provinces and client kingdoms are counted in. Military recruitment was thus much more evenly distributed during the empire than the extreme levels under the Republic. Hopkins 1978, ch. 1, and Scheidel 2007a: 325 fig. 1, for the levels of recruitment during the republic. See also Keppie 1996.

25. Wong 1997: 90, 131–35 makes the point in general. The ability to concentrate resources drawn from vast territories enabled imperial governments to burden individual communities relatively lightly.

26. Garnsey and Saller 1987, ch. 2; Garnsey and Humfress 2001, ch. 2; Saller 1982, chs. 3 and 5.

closer to that of Han China, whose administration penetrated to the county level. In 140 C.E., the government comprised at its lowest level some 1,179 counties, each headed by a state magistrate assisted by one or two commandants and a few bureaus. On average, this miniscule administrative set-up would have been responsible for overseeing law, order, tax collection, maintenance of the census records as well as other governmental tasks for a population of some forty to fifty thousand.[27] With such lean bureaucracies, the administration of both Han China and Rome had to depend on the active collaboration of groups that exercised a commanding influence in rural societies: primarily local landowning aristocrats and the wealthiest segments of the peasantry. But nothing ever comes for free. Here is a letter from the Roman province of Egypt in 288 C.E.: "The accounts have themselves proved that a number of persons wishing to swallow up the estates of the treasury have devised for themselves various titles, such as administrators, secretaries, or superintendents, by which means they secure no advantage for the treasury, but swallow up its surplus."[28] Wastage was an endemic and even an institutionalized feature of the tributary system. The imperial administration could only aspire to limit the number of recipients who benefited from its resources. But it could not evade the problem; it depended on local supporters to have its taxes collected.[29]

The imperial government had to accept that local gentry and aristocracy retained and acquired control of a sizeable part of the agricultural surplus in return for presiding over the process of tax collection. The rate of imperial taxation could not easily be increased. Most of the time, taxes were kept at a stable and relatively low level in both the Roman Empire and Han China.[30] Both the establishment of the Han dynasty and its restoration under the later Han were followed by tax reductions.[31] Augustus, in his own account of his reign, boasted that he had subsidized the treasury out of his own funds rather than, it is implied, burdened the population with further taxes.[32] Emperors who attempted to increase or introduce new taxation frequently encountered tough opposition. New taxes were the product of bad husbandry on the part of the monarch: this

27. See the analysis of Bielenstein 1986: 508–9.

28. *The Oxyrhynchus Papyri* 58, lines 4–10 (translated by the editor).

29. Huang 1974 provides a fascinating insight into these processes. Elvin 1973: 90–91 sees low taxation as specific to late imperial China, whereas Han is presented as a much heavier burden on society. However, this impression is more likely a reflection of the much sparser documentary record of the early periods of Chinese history where we depend much more on normative statements than administrative records. There is little reason to credit Han government with greater extractive capacity than the more developed administration of Ming and Qing.

30. Roman taxation: Garnsey and Saller 1987: 20–21 and passim; MacMullen 1980: 41–44; and Hopkins 1980. Han taxation: see the observations by Loewe, Nishijima, and Ebrey in Twitchett and Loewe, eds. 1986: 487, 595–600, 619–22; and Hsu 1980: 72–77. A low level of overall taxation does not preclude that some groups felt the burden more heavily. Very low land-tax rates in Han China were compensated by a higher poll tax. This meant that landowners came off lightly in comparison to peasants.

31. Swann 1950: 146–50 (*Hanshu* 24a: 7b–8b: lowering of oppressive Qin taxes by the Han), 179–83 (*Hanshu* 24a:14b–15b: critique of heavy Qin tax regime and call for abandonment of taxes).

32. Augustus, *Res Gestae* 17–18.

was a tenet on which Greco-Roman and Han elites would generally have been able to agree.[33] It was, in any case, one thing to issue a demand for taxes, quite another to receive payment. Tax arrears, in the Roman world, were allowed to build up for decades and the tax base suffered constant erosion as local people attempted to have their lands exempted from official tax records, either through grants of imperial privilege or by silent evasion.[34] One way to interpret the drop in the number of households recorded by the two best-known Chinese census figures, dating respectively from the turn of our era and the middle of the second century C.E., would be to see them as a barometer of the difficulties experienced by the later Han in rebuilding and holding on to the tax base of the former period.[35]

Aristocracies and the wealthier segments of the peasant population consequently benefited from their collaboration with the imperial power. It enabled them to expand the acreage under their control. This process took different forms. In some areas, clan- and kinship-based types of land control dominated; in others, land markets were more important. It is possible that the buying and selling of land played a bigger role in the Roman world, with its clear definition of property rights promoted by imperial law. On the other hand, patronage and other social ties were far from insignificant there, just as markets in land property also played a role in Han China. Whatever the precise articulation of land tenure, the result was a gradual but steady growth of larger estates and an increase in aristocratic wealth. These developments characterize both Roman and Han history and acquire critical importance in their later phases as aristocratic holdings reached a size where they began to squeeze the imperial state out of the agricultural economy.[36] Peasants who fell under the control and protection of big landowners and were thus lost to imperial tax collectors are a common concern of the later histories of both empires. But before competition over the control of the

33. Cf. Swann 1950: 135–36 (*Hanshu* 24a: 6a: neglect of the ruler's own fields leads to taxation), 157–62 (*Hanshu* 24a: 10a–11a), 170–72 (*Hanshu* 24a: 13b: remission and lowering of taxes as an expression of virtuous rule). For Rome, see the edict by Severus Alexander remitting his crown gold (Oliver 1989: no. 275) and the coinage issued by Hadrian celebrating his gigantic remission of taxes, Mattingly and Sydenham 1926: 416 (Hadrian no. 590); *Inscriptiones Latinae Selectae* 309; *Historia Augusta, Life of Hadrian* 7.4.6. Cassius Dio 74.5–6 contrasts the economy of Pertinax with the destructive spending habits of Commodus, which forced him to lay his hands on aristocratic wealth.

34. Some examples of privileged aristocrats using their position to escape some of their local obligations: Augustus, *Cyrene Edict* 3 (Oliver 1989: 8–12, lines 55–62) and Aelius Aristides, *Oration* 50.

35. Cf. the analysis by Nishijima 1986: 596–97 of Han census information (the later figure may have been unusually depressed due to temporary disturbances, but that does not explain most of the discrepancy. Indeed, other less well-attested figures for the intervening period seem to show a government struggling to rebuild its tax base). Hsu 1980: 210–11 provides translations of passages from the chronicles of the later Han, the *Hou Hanshu*, describing the strong resistance and intense conflict that was spawned by the attempt of the emperor to have a census taken in 39 C.E.

36. Elvin 1973: 32–34 for the comparison between ancient Rome and China. See Nishijima 1986: 557–59 and Ebrey 1986: 617–27 on the growth of large estates in Han China. See De Ste Croix 1981, pts. III and IV on Greco-Roman forms of rural dependency and exploitation, and Sarris 2006a and Wickham 2005 for two recent discussions of aristocratic landholdings and the late antique Roman state.

agricultural surplus intensified between imperial state and landed aristocracies, mutual benefits had accrued for a long time. This process is much more clearly visible in the Roman Empire because Greco-Roman elites chose to build with marble and fired brick rather than perishable materials. During the first two centuries C.E., the accumulation of aristocratic riches was accompanied by a spate of building activities and conspicuous consumption that forever transformed the landscape of the Mediterranean and beyond. Throughout the Roman Empire, aristocrats proudly proclaimed their wealth and strength by adorning their cities with monumental buildings and works of art. Ever since, the copious remains of this activity have commanded the attention of crowds of travellers and tourists, who continue to flock to museums and excavation sites to admire the accomplishments of a long-gone past. The imposition of a tributary empire increased consumption and the flow of resources both locally and empire-wide.

So far, the tribute-producing enterprise has been sketched as an instrument of pure exploitation. This was how it looked to Finley, for instance. Certainly, lofty notions of a "Rechtstaat" underpinning an imperial peace that enabled enterprising subjects to prosper under the free spirit of the market seem distinctly misplaced.[37] The backbone of the imperial economies, in Rome as well as in Han China, was not provided by capitalist entrepreneurs; it consisted of peasants, very large numbers of them. Roman moralists and Confucian literati never tired of ramming home this message: "The fundamental way of governing the people is to make them settle on the land."[38] But the prevalence of peasant agriculture need not have made the imperial economy a zero-sum game. It is well known how throughout history the production of most peasants has not been directed toward making a profit on the market. Rather, peasants generally geared their activities to satisfying the consumption needs of their household first. It was when these needs were met that peasants stopped working, and not when further activity would have been unable to generate a profit in the market place. As a result, the peasant household often had unused labor reserves.[39] In favorable circumstances, markets might induce peasants to mobilize these resources in pursuit of profit. But markets also posed risks to the peasant. Markets increased his dependence on unpredictable price fluctuations. Production primarily for the market was a dangerous strategy: it could only be complementary.[40] By contrast, demands imposed on the peasant by the imperial state and aristocratic landlords were not optional. Historically, the combination of imperial tribute and aristocratic rents has been able to claim a very sizeable share of peasant production.

37. Drexhage, Kohnen, and Ruffing 2002: 24–25 for a recent attempt to resurrect this idea.

38. Swann 1950: 116.

39. Classic formulations of the production logic of the peasant household are contained in Chayanov 1986 and Thorner 1965. For Rome: Garnsey 1988, chs. 4–5; for China: Deng 1999.

40. Erdkamp 2005: 98–104. Hsu 1980: 80 lists similar market imperfections for early imperial China. Markets, therefore, were a treacherous ally, only to be used as a complement.

They forced the peasant to increase his surplus production to a considerable extent.[41]

The mutual alliance of empire and local elites may thus be hypothesized to have strengthened their position in relation to peasant producers and enabled them to mobilize the untapped labor reserves of society.[42] This happened in very direct form when peasants were conscripted to perform corvée labor on the maintenance or construction of canals, dykes, irrigation works, roads, and other such things in the agricultural off-peak seasons. Corvée labor was an important element in the set of obligations the Han government imposed on its subjects. It was less conspicuous in the Roman Empire, at least outside the province of Egypt with its irrigation agriculture, but nevertheless far from insignificant.[43] The formation of a tributary empire, in other words, did not merely serve to bring more resources into circulation and concentrate consumption, it may also have had the added effect of producing a modest increase in per capita production by forcing producers to work harder. This cannot be proven. But in the Mediterranean, the huge surge in chattel slavery sparked off by the Roman conquests may be indicative of the existence of such a process.

3. Tribute and Commercialization: The Market as Transformer

The reception of tribute, however, entailed a practical problem. Most taxpayers were grain-producing peasants. But the needs of the imperial government were far more diverse. Roman authorities partly attempted to get around this problem by regularly monopolizing access to strategic goods or stipulating their delivery as part of the tribute. The range was wide, stretching from ox hides delivered by barbarian tribes to the silver mines of Spain and the quarries of red porphyry and grey granodiorite in the Egyptian desert.[44] The Han imperial court received parts of its tribute in the form of diverse local products. But such arrangements did not remove the basic problem: tribute delivered in kind would not necessarily have corresponded to the consumption needs of the government. Roman and Han power also required the assistance of market institutions to mobilize the tributary surplus to the fullest and transform it into a flexible and freely disposable resource. Market trade supplied a number of services. It enabled the state to sell products in excess of its current needs, buy

41. Hsu 1980: 79 shows the need imposed by imperial taxes on peasants to increase production. In general, see Bang 2007.

42. For further studies of this process, Finley 1976 and Foxhall 1990.

43. On Han corvée, see Hsu 1980: 163–64; Hulsewé 1986: 536–37. Roman examples: Johnston 1936: no. 6 (corvée labor on canals in Egypt); *Digest* 50.4.1 (lists various *munera*, "burdens" that could be imposed, such as transport service or road maintenance).

44. Tacitus, *Annals* 4.72 (Frisians paying tribute in ox hides); Domergue 1990; Delbrueck 1932; Peacock and Maxfield 1997–2001.

those it lacked, and obtain a more convenient form of storing and saving by converting goods into cash.

These functions were performed at a number of levels. At the top, the Roman government availed itself of contractors, individually and in groups, to exploit mines, handle some of the tax collection, organize transport, and so on. This promoted strong groups of financiers, typically with solid land possessions to back them up but also with commercial interests. Their strength culminated during the late Republic, whereas the emperors subsequently curtailed their power.[45] Comparable groups are known from Han history. Here the government attempted to tap into commercial profits by monopolizing the production and sale of salt and iron, not least of the important iron farming tools. The administration of the government monopolies was left in the hands of some big businessmen, who accumulated vast riches, including large land holdings. But, as already indicated, these revenue policies were controversial. Under the later Han dynasty, the monopolies were more or less abandoned, only to be partially revived much later in Chinese history.[46]

The process of commercial mobilization of the surplus was, however, not solely articulated in the periodic emergence of a limited layer of wealthy state contractors. Even more important were the activities taking place at a much more basic level of agricultural society. Under the emperors, the Roman state, as suggested by the late Keith Hopkins, may have attempted to shift most of its taxes from delivery in kind to payment in cash.[47] In that, it would have resembled the Han authorities. The latter compensated for a very low land tax rate by claiming a rather more substantial poll tax, which was supposed to be paid in coin. It is equally difficult to determine, in the two cases, just to what extent such a shift actually succeeded.[48] The sparse evidence, which survives, suggests that the picture is an uneven one. Monetary defrayment of taxes continued to exist side-by-side delivery in kind throughout both empires. What is certain, however, is that neither the Roman nor the Han state could easily have found useful ways to consume most of its taxes in kind.[49] Even when by the late third century c.e. the Roman state, struggling to increase its income, seems to have introduced an elaborate system of detailed taxation in kind, commercial commutation of obligations was intrinsic to its successful functioning.[50] In Rome, furthermore, where the emperors operated a public grain dole, installments of the Egyptian grain tribute were moved into the market by private agents. Medicinal herbs, grown

---

45. Badian 1972 is the classic analysis. See Love 1991, ch. 5 for an excellent theoretical discussion.
46. Nishijima 1986: 602–7. *Hanshu* 24b 11a–12a (Swann 1950: 271–72, 275–78).
47. Hopkins 1980.
48. For discussions of the mode of Han taxation, see Hulsewé 1986: 536–37; Nishijima 1986: 598–601. Garnsey and Saller 1987, ch. 5 on the mixed modes of surplus consumption employed by the Roman state. See also below, ch. 7, sec. 9.
49. See Hopkins 1995/96 for a forceful deductive formulation of the argument.
50. Cerati 1975.

on the emperor's Cretan estates and collected in excess of the court's requirements, also found an outlet on the open market through a number of grocers.[51] Commercialization of the tributary surplus is bound to have happened in one way or other.

As in the last two cases, some of this would have been channelled to commercial agents by the state itself. Peasants living near market towns would not infrequently have been able to market their own products. In other regions, marketing might have happened through the agency of large landowners who would have collected taxes and rents from their tenants and then shipped the produce to urban markets.[52] This process would also have given rise to groups of commercial middlemen investing in the local collection of taxes. A set of fourth century C.E. papyri enables us to observe such persons in action. They report the activities of two brothers who specialized in tax collection. We find them speculating in the price of gold in order to convert the many small individual tax payments of peasants made with the hugely devalued silver *follis* into the gold coins required by the Roman state. They can also be seen borrowing money to pay the taxes of villages in advance and then afterward proceeding to collect those taxes, obviously in the hope of making a profit.[53] The process of tributary extraction would have spawned a complex process of commercialization. It involved several levels of activity and different groups of middlemen.[54] But it is also important to stress that this process would have been uneven and varied considerably both in intensity and in character depending on prevailing local conditions.

This brings us back to the beginning of this chapter and the relationship between tribute and trade. In spite of aristocratic prejudice toward commercial activities and hostility against "the middleman," market trade was an integral and in some respects valued part of the tributary process. Pliny the Elder, a prominent aristocrat in the emperor's service, included among his praise of Roman power this observation: "For now that the world has been united under the majesty of the Roman Empire, who would not think that life has benefited from the exchange of things and the partnership in blessed peace and that even all those things which were previously hidden have now been made widely available."[55] As has also become increasingly clear in recent Chinese scholarship, markets were crucial instruments to grease the wheels of the agricultural economy and mobilize the peasant production surplus of the tributary system.[56] But it was in precisely that capacity they were needed. Hence the Chinese imperial authorities had

51. Galen 14.9 ("On the Medicinal Herbs"), Camodeca 1999: nos. 45, 46, 51, 52, 79 (on Alexandrian wheat used for commercial speculation in Puteoli).

52. Nishijima 1986: 600–1.

53. *The Oxyrhynchus Papyri* 48.3384–3429.

54. *Hanshu* 24b: 9b (Swann 1950: 264–65) for some Chinese examples.

55. Pliny the Elder, *Natural History* 14.2 (author's translation).

56. Skinner 1964–1965.

little inclination to promote traders and merchants as such through the grant of monopolies and privileges in the fashion of European mercantilist policies.[57]

The parameters of the Chinese position can be mapped out from debates that occurred during the Han period among Confucian literati and imperial ministers concerning the various government monopolies on salt, iron, and equitable marketing.[58] The view taken by the ministers was that while commercial and artisanal pursuits could be suspected of diverting energies from the agricultural sector, they were nevertheless necessary. For

> the ancient founders of the commonwealth made open the ways of both fundamental [agricultural] and branch industries and facilitated equitable distribution of goods. Markets and courts were provided to harmonize various demands; there people of all classes gathered together and all goods collected, so that farmer, merchant, and worker could each obtain what he desired.... Thus without artisans, the farmers will be deprived of the use of implements; without merchants, all prized commodities will be cut off. The former would lead to stoppage of grain production, the latter to exhaustion of wealth.

By intervening in this process the government would be able to curtail commercial profits of dubious social value and divert them to public benefit. So it was asserted: "it is clear that the iron and salt monopoly and equable marketing are really intended for the circulation of amassed wealth and the regulation of the consumption according to the urgency of the need."[59] The result would be a prosperous agricultural economy.

The hard-line Confucian view, however, rejected this position. Through these various measures, the dissenters held, the government competed with the population for profits and had raised taxes. Far from succeeding in turning people to agriculture, the state monopolies had only made this branch of economic activity less profitable. Instead, the government should forego the profits from its monopolies and reduce its level of spending. Nothing would be more efficient in promoting agriculture than such a show of imperial frugality that taught the people modest living. Good government knew that the wealth of the empire was best left with the subjects and did not get deeply involved in the pursuit of money: "merchants are for the purpose of draining stagnation and the artisans for providing tools; they should not become the principal concern of the government."[60] In other words, the circulation of goods was important, but it was important in that it was subservient to the tributary process. Both sides of the

57. Wong 1997, ch. 6.

58. Translations of these debates are available in Gale 1931 and Swann 1950.

59. *Discourses on Salt and Iron* (transl. Gale 1931: 6), chap. 1 i.

60. *Discourses on Salt and Iron* (transl. Gale 1931: 7), chap. 1 j. Compare ch. 5b (Gale 1931: 31) on the monarch who keeps away from the wealth of his subjects.

debate were interested in expanding the frontier of agriculture, not in capturing and retaining markets.

The observation about Greco-Roman colonization that Montesquieu made long ago could equally well be extended to the Chinese case. Unlike the Europeans of the early modern period, they did not treat new or subject territories as commercial opportunities by monopolizing trade between mother country and outlying region.[61] Provinces, in other words, were not managed as colonies and retained in a division of labor controlled by the metropolitan regions, such as in the European Atlantic system. From the perspective of the imperial state, it mattered more to serve the expansion of more self-sufficient forms of agriculture. That would guarantee the creation of many more new peasant households that were sufficiently prosperous to pay the imperial taxes. After an initial start-up phase, newly opened territories on the agricultural frontier would normally have been able to become more or less economically independent of the more "developed" parts of the country. Imports from the old core region diminished and were gradually replaced by local products. This, for instance, is a process that has been delineated for the much better-known history of China in the eighteenth and nineteenth centuries. For some of its food grains, raw cotton, and timber, the wealthy and densely populated Yangzi delta had come to depend on imports from farther up river and from northern China. These imports were paid for by exporting cloth in return. However, as the population grew and the regions supplying primary products began to fill up, the development of this trade was arrested. Instead of further increasing specialization and regional interdependence, the peasant population in the Middle Yangzi region and northern China responded by diverting some of its labor into handicraft and protoindustrial cloth production, thus substituting the need for imports with products of their own. The Chinese imperial economy, shaped in part by long held Confucian ideals, developed more by reproducing itself in small identical agricultural cells than by intensifying regional specialization and exchange.[62]

Incidentally, that path of economic development has been one of the most intensely debated problems of Roman economic history. Rostovtzeff ascribed a key role to the phenomenon of import substitution in his classic study of the rise and fall of the imperial economy. From the late second century B.C.E., sizable exports of Italian wine, later followed by red slip ceramic tableware, had developed, particularly in the Western Mediterranean. Under the reign of the emperors, however, this flow was reversed. As the western provinces became more Romanized, they freed themselves from the need for Italian imports. Instead, local production of red slip pottery, wine, and many other goods developed in Gaul, Spain, and Africa, even to the extent of exporting these products to Rome

---

61. Montesquieu, *L'Esprit des Lois*, bk. 21, ch. 21.
62. Wong 1997: 138–39 and Pomeranz 2000: 242–53.

and Italy. For Rostovtzeff and many of his later followers, this produced an economic crisis, first in Italy and then in the empire. The Roman economy had been trapped in a process of decreasing specialization of labor.[63] This, however, is not a helpful way of approaching these developments. The reduction in Italian exports was more than offset by increased and more diverse agricultural and artisanal production in the provinces. While imperial Italy was far from reduced to penury, agriculture and manufacturing reached a level of intensity in the western provinces that remained unmatched for centuries after the fall of the empire.[64] The Chinese comparison teaches us that what really took place was simply the reproduction and expansion of "civilized" agricultural production. Aggregate production and the disposable surplus had increased.

4. Imperial Styles of Consumption

With the formation of extensive dominion and the concentration of wealth through tributary extraction, new forms and styles of consumption in food, dress, entertainment, building, burial, public ceremony, and religious ritual developed in the worlds of Rome and Han. As the rulers of "all the world," the emperors set the pace and tone for the imperial aristocracy and the groups of local elites across the two empires. They promoted an urban style of consumption that sought to emphasize the ability of its practitioners to command, in imperial fashion, large concentrations of wealth and a great variety of rare products from far away. The cities provided the scene for symbolic aristocratic displays of power. There, large followings and groups of spectators and service people were maintained by the expenditure of elite incomes. Bulk trade in various agricultural products expanded to provision these groups.

But aristocratic excellence was not only expressed in an ability to assemble great numbers of people. The cities also afforded members of the elite a convenient stage on which to compete and distinguish themselves through the possession of rare and expensive products. More intense socializing and frequent interaction among the aristocracy brought with it the emergence of a civilization of refinement; it was a culture of luxury consumption and connoisseurship where "the special qualities and savour of a great range of local producing units across the whole of Eurasia, stretching out into Africa..., were preserved and cherished for their difference," as emphasized by Chris Bayly. As he goes on to explain,

> therefore [it] differed from modern capitalist consumption in that they emphasised the special products and qualities of distant realms. Whereas

---

63. Rostovtzeff 1957; Carandini 1988; von Freyberg 1989.
64. Woolf 2001.

modern complexity demands the uniformity of Levis and trainers, the archaic simplicity of everyday life demanded that great men prized difference in goods, learned servants, women and animals and sought to capture their qualities. Modern 'positional' goods are self-referential to themselves and to the markets that create demand for them; the charismatic goods of archaic globalization were embedded in ideologies which transcended them. In one sense archaic lords and rural leaders were collectors rather than consumers. What they did, however, was more than merely to collect because the people, objects, foods, garments and styles of deportment thus assembled changed the substance of the collector.[65]

This capacity to change the substance of the consumer, however, also generated anxieties. In both empires, moral discourses developed about the proper appropriation of luxury. Change, after all, could signify either enhancement of personal qualities or moral corruption. It was crucial not to become a slave of one's desires, as Dio Chrysostomus urged at the beginning of this chapter. Had he or other Greco-Roman moralists been known to Confucian literati, they would have garnered much sympathy. Han moralists can be found to complain in a similar vein about the craze for luxuries, the enormous riches wasted on dinners and adorning womenfolk, and the consequent drain on the empire's wealth: "Beautiful jades and corals come from mount K'un. Pearls, rhinoceros horns and elephant tusks are produced in Kuei Lin. These places are more than ten thousand li distant from Han. Calculating the labour for farming and silk raising and the costs in material and capital, it will be found that one article of foreign imports costs a price one hundred times its value.... As the rulers treasure the goods from distant lands, wealth flows outward. Therefore, a true King does not value useless things."[66]

Such statements of disapproval, however, did nothing effectively to counter the new luxurious styles of consumption. Rather, they served to police the boundaries of elite society and reinforce the mystique and cultural allure of aristocratic consumption. Money that might buy the emblems of elite status, they insisted, was not enough to ensure its proper use. In both societies, the nouveau riche outsiders, such as wealthy merchants or aristocratic freedmen, who sought to establish themselves in upper-class society were stigmatized and satirized for their alleged vulgarity and lack of discernment. The *Satyricon* of the Roman writer Petronius is a famous example of this genre that has become a part of world literature. No amount of riches, as the novel teaches through its most colorful character Trimalchio, could prevent the newcomer from becoming the laughing stock of polite society. To avoid humiliation, one had to be immersed in

65. Bayly 2002: 51–52.
66. Gale 1931: 15–16 (ch. 2d). In general, see the analysis of Ebrey 1986: 609–12.

established elite culture. The true aristocrat knew how to avoid the vulgar excess of the merely rich but also how not to appear mean, stingy, and common: "In ancient times, reasonable limits were set to the style of palaces and houses, chariots and liveries. Plain rafters and straw thatch were not part of the system of the ancient Emperors. The true gentleman, while checking extravagance, would disapprove of parsimoniousness because over-thriftiness tends to narrowness."[67]

Mere acquisition, in other words, was far from sufficient to guarantee successful appropriation of the trappings of aristocratic culture. Elite ideology required them to be difficult to handle. Mastery was reserved for the exclusive group in command of the complex codes of literary and philosophic aristocratic civilization.[68] Of course, the prevalence of prejudices like these did not stop rich outsiders and the socially ambitious from staking out whatever claim to distinction they could by emulating the style of the governing classes. But these notions did serve to assert the cultural hegemony of the latter and consolidate their ability to set the tone in the world of consumption. Imperial styles of consumption developed under the leadership of the court and the governing classes. At each end of the Eurasian landmass, they sponsored an exquisite but regionally distinct culture of delicate, refined agricultural and artisan production. Fine silks, lacquerwork, vintage wine, glass, sculpture, the list could easily go on. Roman archaeology has shown that the material culture of the empire was both more diverse and extensive than that of the periods before and after.[69]

But aristocratic styles of consumption did not merely increase demand for internally produced goods; they also generated an upsurge in long-distance trade.[70] Merchants traveled for years to bring back the rare and refined substances and products of faraway regions for the rituals of power and religion in which the consuming upper classes put their wealth on display. In this period, trade between the Mediterranean and Arabia and India expanded enormously. Merchants brought back from the East rich cargoes of incense, ivory, precious stones, rare spices, medicinal substances, and delicate clothes. Among these were Chinese silks, which can still be seen on display in surprising quantities in the National Museum of Syria in Damascus, brought to the Roman world from India by the caravans of the desert-city of Palmyra.[71] At the same time,

---

67. Gale 1931: 22: (ch. 3e).

68. Restriction of access to goods in order to keep social status stable was thus less a matter of taboos or legal regulation (though that was occasionally attempted) than a question of controlling fashion/style; cf. Appadurai, ed. 1986: 25. Such consumerism may provide a basis on which modern middle-class consumerism can develop, but there is no reason to see any automatic link between the two phenomena, as Pomeranz 2000, ch. 3 attempts. A rising market in luxuries was not peculiar to the early modern period. The tensions of this process were already familiar to the societies of Han China and Rome.

69. Dalby 2001 provides a convenient literary survey of the celebration of refined luxury in the Roman world but is disappointing in terms of analysis. Ebrey 1986 provides an overview of the elite-led styles of consumption in Han China.

70. Young 2001; Yü 1967.

71. Schmidt-Colinet 2000.

Chinese demand spawned trading contacts with South-East Asia and even India to obtain exotic luxuries. Around the first century C.E., the contours of a Eurasian world trade emerged with Alexandria and the Middle East on one end, India (and Indonesia) as a midway station, and China at the other end. This system would gradually develop and expand over the following centuries. The scale of activity and the number of participants were always limited.[72] At the same time, the cargoes of this trade represented enormous values.[73] Eventually, they would tempt the Portuguese, followed later by merchants from the northwestern parts of Europe, to break into this system to capture some of its profits by circumnavigating Africa. The early modern period produced a new conjuncture in the old pattern of world trade for which the rising demand of imperial elites in Rome and Han China had laid the foundations.

These developments provide the real background to the enigmatic entry in the *Hou Hanshu* that "in the ninth *yanxi* year [166 C.E.], during the reign of Emperor Huan, the king of Da Qin [i.e., the Roman Empire], Andun [i.e., Marcus Aurelius Antoninus?], sent envoys from beyond the frontiers through Rinan [i.e., a commandery on the central Vietnamese coast], to offer elephant tusks, rhinoceros horn, and turtle shell. This was the very first time there was [direct] communication [between the two countries]."[74] The imperial chronicler, however, did not put much faith in this information. He thought the list of gifts too inconspicuous. Certainly, it seems quite unlikely that Marcus Aurelius, if he was indeed the ruler hiding behind "Andun," should have sent an embassy to the Han Court. One plausible hypothesis, therefore, is that a group of merchants from the Roman Empire in search of rare products managed to make their way across the trade routes of Eurasia to reach China's center of power and consumption. Such incidents, however, were few and far between. The emerging pattern of long-distance trade did not join the Eurasian cores of civilization tightly together. This trade was organized in stages. The two world empires remained hidden to each other in a twilight realm of fable and myth.[75] Han China and imperial Rome represent two separate cultural traditions. But they do seem to have had much in common and even to have shared some products at the level of luxury trade. They were comparable worlds.

---

72. Raschke 1978 provides a solid antidote against much of the loose speculation and wishful thinking that has thrived in this field.

73. One papyrus documents a cargo valued at several times the minimum fortune of a Roman senator: see Rathbone 2001.

74. *Hou Hanshu* 88, following the most recent translation by Hill 2003. Cf. also Leslie and Gardiner 1996: 155.

75. Chinese descriptions of Da Qin, the term that used to be thought to refer to the Oriental parts of the Roman Empire, thus owe much to Daoist utopian thought and have little idea of the Roman world (cf. Raschke 1978: nn. 849–50). Likewise, the far eastern sections of Ptolemy's geography are given to speculation and fantasy; cf. Humbach and Ziegler 1998, who warn against the temptation to make close identifications of real places on the basis of the text. See also above, in the introduction to this volume.

6

Gift Circulation and Charity in the Han and Roman Empires

Mark Edward Lewis

T HE giving of gifts and charitable relief was a fundamental aspect of both political and social authority in Han China as well as the Roman Empire. However, while the Roman case has been the object of considerable study, the Han case, despite an abundance of references to the topic, has been largely ignored.[1] In this chapter I will sketch the range of references to gifts and charity by the emperor, the imperial elite, and local elites of Han China and suggest a few of the major differences from the Roman case.

1. CHINESE PRACTICES

Gift giving as a mode of authority had a considerable history in preimperial China. Most importantly, the bronzes that are our key written source for the Western Zhou dynasty (c.1045–771 B.C.E.) are devoted largely to recording royal gifts to the nobility, which served as permanent charters for noble status and privilege. The fundamental political role of such gifts is theorized in several passages in the fourth century B.C.E. *Zuozhuan*. In the Spring and Autumn period (771–481 B.C.E.), the political power of the hegemon, the militarily dominant state ruler who in name remained subordinate to the Zhou king, was also strongly identified with a beneficent mode of action, the restoration or preservation of perishing states. While this was not explicitly charity or gift, from early times it came to be described as a form of *de*, which by the middle of the Warring States period was glossed as actions of generosity or the giving of life by the ruler who gained the support or loyalty of the people. Even more explicit is the relation between masters and clients (*ke*) that came to be fundamental to political and social status in the Warring States and remained so throughout the period of the Han dynasty. In this relation the master provided food and lodging for his

---

1. For significant works on Rome, see Veyne 1976; Millar 1977, chs. 4, 8; Saller 1982; DeSilva 2000, chs. 3–4; Bowditch 2001; Flaig 2003. Cf. now also Zuiderhoek 2006 and 2007.

guest-retainers, who served him in a variety of ways such as entertainment, debt collection, and assassination. Finally, political power was theorized in several traditions as the pairing of "punishment (*xing*)" and "life-giving" or "generosity (*de*)," and this model informed the calendars of royal activity that were included in several major works of the period. The *de* described in this literature ranged from the granting of life through acts of deliberate mercy to material payments and gifts from the ruler to his allies and subordinates.[2]

In the imperial period gift giving became definitive of the Chinese emperor's role, as is clearly shown in the "Fundamental Chronicles (*benji*)" of the dynastic histories. These chronicles of court activities focus on the emperor's acts and decrees, and gift giving in all its forms is the single most frequently noted type of action. Imperial gifts and charity included at least the following eight types.

First, the emperor bestowed ranks in a seventeen- or twenty-rank hierarchy (the number shifted across time) that established the hierarchical positions of all free males in the empire. These ranks had originated in the Warring States period as rewards for military service or for providing grain for the army, and they had become the structuring principle of the Qin state from the middle of the fourth century B.C.E. They were closely linked to the emperor's right to make appointments, and the higher ranks in the hierarchy were calqued onto the hierarchy of bureaucratic offices. They were carried forward into the early empires and remained a major structuring principle of the state at least into the beginning of the Eastern Han in the early first century C.E. In the Qin period such ranks entailed the right to own specified amounts of land and command the services of a specified number of servile laborers (probably convicts or captives). In the Han period the primary benefit of rank holding, apart from status in the local community, was privileged treatment in law, as certain punishments could be redeemed through the surrender of ranks. Posthumously awarded ranks could also be transferred to descendants, who would similarly benefit from them.[3]

As military service became less important under the Han, with the concentration of fighting at the frontiers where peasant levies were of no use, the ranks were primarily awarded on happy occasions in the "family" life of the emperor, such as the birth of a son or the establishment of an heir, so they became a form of largesse that united the emperor with his people in shared celebration.[4] Many occasions on which ranks were granted included the distribution of wine and meat to local communities for purposes of the celebration, with the quantities given to each individual determined by rank, as is indicated in a math primer that gave problems in dividing up meat depending on the ranks of those present.

2. Hsu and Linduff 1988: 153–58, 177–79, 185–88, 206, 245–46, 249–57; *Chunqiu Zuozhuanzhu*, annotated by Yang Bojun (Beijing 1981): 71–72, 194, 200, 264–73, 814–15, 860–61, 1318–20; 1475–77; 1535–42; Lewis 1990: 67–68, 73–94; Lewis 2006: 82–84, 215–27; Major 1987.

3. Lewis 1990: 60–63; Nishijima 1961.

4. Lewis 2000.

This shift from rewards for military service to periodic "universal" awards is conventionally treated as a decline from the original purpose of encouraging military service, but the development actually made it more explicitly a ranking of the entire society through imperial gifts that flowed to all adult males. Moreover, since at this time ranks were largely universally awarded for empire-wide events, rather than bestowed on individuals for their specific achievements, the rankings in the Han came to closely coincide with age. Consequently, the system reinforced the Han policy of honoring the aged and the general emphasis on age as a basis of status and authority in the village community. Other gifts that were specifically targeted to the aged as elements of this policy will be discussed below.[5]

This was the closest that Han China had to a distinctive public realm that included a significant percentage of the population, as opposed to the narrowly defined "public" realm consisting of the ruler, his family, and those employed by the state. Through these ranks, which were regularly issued, included in all the records that the state kept of its subjects, marked status in recurrent local celebrations, and bestowed clear legal privileges, the emperor's beneficence was made visible at the local level, and his role as patron or protector of the common people was given manifest institutional expression. The hierarchy constituted through these ranks was also intended to dictate the terms in which people were to be graded and judged. This vision of the social order was articulated in a memorial by Chao Cuo, who posited a radical tension between an ideal but unrealized "public" order marked by the law and ranks and a subversive order constituted through private wealth and official corruption that pervaded actual customs and values:

> Now the laws debase merchants, but merchants have become rich and honored. The laws honor peasants, but peasants have become poor and base. Thus what is honored by current custom (*su*) is treated by the ruler as base, while those who are scorned by the minor officials are honored by the law. With proper hierarchy thus inverted, and standards of good and bad perverted, it is impossible for the state to be prosperous and laws enforced.
>
> The most important task at the moment is simply to cause the people to devote themselves to agriculture. To achieve this, grain must be made more valuable. The way to make grain valuable is to allow the people to use it to secure rewards and redemptions from punishments. If you call on the people of the empire to present grain to the local officials, and thereby to be given ranks and also to redeem crimes [which was a function of ranks], then rich people will have ranks, peasants will have money, and

5. Bodde 1975: 341–48, 361–80.

grain can be dispensed [to the needy]. Those who are able to submit grain to receive ranks are those with surpluses. If one takes grain from those with surpluses to contribute it to the emperor's use, then exactions on the poor can be reduced. This is what is called taking away from those with surplus to supplement those in need.[6]

This complicated argument posits a complete opposition between the mores of the time and the conduct of subordinate officials, on the one hand, and the proper order posited by law and the emperor's gifts, on the other. It presents a method of modifying the practice or awarding gifts—both the grant of titles and the redemption of punishments, which was the primary mode of using titles—so that they could become valuable in the marketplace, which Chao Cuo recognized as the true locus of popular values and judgment. A similar combination of imperial gifts—in the form of pardons for capital crimes, redemption from penal servitude, and the award and sale of titles—and the manipulation of people's desire for wealth was suggested by Chao Cuo as a method for attracting population to settle on the frontiers to provide for defense against the Xiongnu.[7]

The reference to pardons for capital crimes leads to the second major form of imperial gift, which was precisely the ruler's power to issue pardons to those condemned to death or penal servitude. Such pardons were a regular feature of imperial policy, with empire-wide pardons—that included all people in the empire awaiting execution, except for those convicted for treason—being issued on average every three years over the course of the Han dynasty. The treatment of those pardoned varied, but in general those sentenced to death had their sentence commuted to servile labor or service in the army (see below), while those sentenced to servile labor had the physical marks of their conditions—iron collars, red clothing, shaved beards and heads—removed but continued to perform labor for the government for the period of the sentence. So-called "great" acts of grace led to the actual release of servile laborers, and some of these acts were extended even to those condemned for treason. Fugitives were in general freed from any future prosecution and thus able to return home. Interestingly, many of these pardons were accompanied by the issuing of ranks to free people, as well as gifts of grain or cloth to paupers, widows, and other impoverished categories. The practice of regular universal pardons seems to have been an innovation of

6. *Hanshu* 24a (Beijing 1962, p. 1133).
7. *Hanshu* 49 (pp. 2284, 2286). "In all cases people will fight to the death and not surrender due to calculations. It is because attacking or defending lead to obtaining ranks, and the storming of towns produces booty to enrich their households.... First set up houses and agricultural implements [at the borders] and then recruit convicts and those who have been pardoned from capital punishment to dwell there. If this is insufficient, recruit adult slaves, men and women, who will be allowed to redeem their punishments, and those who desire to receive ranks. If this is not enough, recruit free people who desire to go, bestow high ranks on them, and excuse their families from corvee labor.... Commoners on the registers of the districts and commanderies can purchase high titles [at the frontier] that will make them the equals of high officials."

the early imperial period, although this may simply reflect the lack of solid documentation from the Warring States period.

In addition to universal pardons, there were also more specific pardons restricted to a specified region or category of the population. Yet a third type of pardon was the policy of "inspection of cases" in which special agents of the emperor toured the local administrative cities to verify that punishments were correct and to overrule any cases of perceived injustice or excessive severity. In the later Han this became a ritual performed as one element of attempts to relieve drought in which the emperor personally visited prisons and bestowed free acts of grace on those being held on suspicion of relatively light crimes. A version of this clemency restricted to members of the elite was the regular practice of the emperor granting officials the right to kill themselves—involving a ritual presentation of a sword to cut one's throat and bowl to catch the blood—rather than suffer the humiliation of public execution or a punishment of physical mutilation such as castration.[8]

The reasons for this policy of routine pardons are not entirely clear and may have varied across time. All recorded cases justified the acts as responses either to happy events—capping of an heir, establishment of a capital city, naming of an empress, marvelous events that indicated celestial approval—or to misfortunes—floods, droughts, marvelous events that indicated celestial condemnation. However, there are many records of such events that do not elicit a pardon, so it seems that all of these were possible occasions for an act of grace but not a sufficient motive. Several recorded parts of decrees suggest that the acts were intended to reduce popular discontent, which could manifest itself "magically" in inauspicious events or more realistically in banditry and rebellion. It is notable that pardons were invariably given in the spring or summer, the seasons of growth and life that in the ritual calendars of the period were to be devoted to the life-giving aspects of the emperor's role.

Another significant point is that several of the decrees, as well as the aforementioned policy of "inspection of cases," indicate suspicion that local officials manipulated the law to their own benefit. This same suspicion of officials acting at odds with the law and the emperor's will was articulated above in Chao Cuo's memorial. Finally, in the Eastern Han, when the bestowal of great acts of grace became routine, these pardons became a regular source of manpower for the frontier armies, which were continually restocked with men pardoned for capital offences.[9] In conclusion, it seems that the Han emperors clearly recognized the need to balance the severity of their legal administration, which was the physical foundation of their state, with regular manifestations of beneficence

8. McKnight 1981: ch. 2. Hulsewé 1955: 209–14, 225–50. On the "gift" of allowing suicide as a privilege for officials, see, for example, *Hanshu* 48 (p. 2254).
9. Lewis 2000: 53–57.

in the form of pardons, grants of titles, poor relief, and related acts of manifest generosity. Such acts were also one aspect of the policy of assimilating the status of the emperor to that of Heaven, which over the course of the year balanced the bestowing of life and vitality in the spring and summer with the killing of living things in the autumn and winter.[10]

The practice of poor relief was the third major aspect of Han imperial gift giving. The above discussion touched on the combination of pardons with gifts to stipulated categories of the poor, and records of such gifts of food or clothing appear frequently in the chronicles. The gifts of wine and meat for public celebrations in association with the granting of titles were a related activity. The aforementioned policy of honoring the aged was supposed to include providing foods of varying quantities for those above certain ages, although memorials indicate that this policy soon fell into abeyance as local officials replaced grain with chaff. The famous institution of the "Ever-Normal Granaries" that bought up grain in times of abundance to release it at lower prices in times of scarcity was also in theory a means of benefiting the poor.[11] However, probably the single most important form of poor relief, and the one that consumed the greatest amount of the government's wealth, was the policy of providing assistance to regions afflicted with flood or drought. This included tax relief, the issuing of grain, moving populations to unaffected areas, and the distribution of money to victims so that they could purchase grain in the regions to which they temporarily moved.[12]

A fourth form of gift giving to the peasants was the distribution of land. This activity is particularly notable in debates over the problem of imperial hunting parks and state pasturelands for army horses, both of which were constantly targets of calls that they be pared away through distribution to needy peasants. Equally significant was the distribution to peasants of land that had been confiscated from high officials, nobles, and the kin of eunuchs who had fallen afoul of the law or a political purge. Rather than having the land worked by convicts or state slaves, which seems to have been inefficient, the state rapidly divided such land into small plots and awarded it to peasants from overcrowded regions. Gifts of land, grain, and livestock, as well as cash payments, were also frequently offered to colonists who were willing to settle at the frontiers. As a correlate of this policy, the Western Han state repeatedly attempted to restrict the scale of landholdings by the wealthy, although this policy was generally ineffective and was abandoned in the Eastern Han. Nobles and officials, who were presumed to

---

10. The fundamental importance to the Han state of the exploitation of servile labor provided by convicts is discussed in Lewis 2007: 248–52.

11. Swann 1950: 195–56; Hsu 1980: 79–80.

12. *Hanshu* 4 (pp. 113, 117, 124, 125, 131), 5 (p. 143), 6 (pp. 156, 174, 178, 180, 193, 195, 196, 198, 207 [2]), 7 (pp. 221, 225, 232), 8 (pp. 239, 242, 245, 248, 254, 255, 257, 259 [2], 263, 267, 269), and so on throughout the "Chronicles."

be acting on the model provided by the emperor, were also recorded distributing some of their lands to needy neighbors.[13]

A fifth and final mode of gift giving to peasants was the regular gifts that were not mentioned in the "Chronicles" since they were routine. The most distinctive of these were the presentations to the aged, which included giving dove-staffs to anyone who had reached the age of seventy, as well as a staff and arm rest to individuals who were no longer required to attend court. (The choice of doves in the decoration of the staffs is explained in several ways, the most persuasive of which is that they were a bird associated with spring and the rejuvenation of life.) The dove-staffs would have been yet another distinctive and visible sign of the imperial presence in the village community, for even relatively small villages would have had a few individuals who reached the age of seventy and hence were entitled to carry the staff. Like all objects associated with the emperor, these staffs would have been charged with a numinous power and prestige. This is clearly shown in a legal case recorded on some writing strips discovered in a Han tomb. An official struck an old man, thus causing him to drop his staff, which broke when it fell to the ground. Since the object was a gift of the emperor, the official was executed for having broken it.[14]

In addition to these five modes of distributing honors and goods to commoners, the emperor also showed conspicuous generosity to officials and nobles. Apart from bestowing additional ranks on his officials, just as he did to the commoners, and to paying their salaries, which was also a form of imperial generosity, the emperor also gave frequent gifts to all officials or to chosen individuals. These gifts were most commonly cash, as was presumably their salaries, which were formally measured in quantities of grain, but not infrequently the emperor also gave specified amounts of precious metals, especially gold. This practice dated back to the Warring States period, when precious metals were used as special gifts awarded to officials whom the ruler wished to honor. In addition to gifts cited in the "Chronicles," some biographies of officials also describe receiving such gifts from the emperor, usually when the official retired. As will be discussed below, these gifts were sometimes in turn distributed by the official to his family or neighbors, so that the official acted as a conduit that directed imperial charity downward to the common people.[15]

The range of the emperor's gifts also extended to the non-Chinese peoples at the frontiers of the Han state. These gifts included the *heqin* offerings of gold,

13. Hsu 1980: 22–24, 27–34, 164–66, 172–83, 186, 204, 210–13.

14. Lewis 2006: 173–74.

15. For cases of gifts to officials, nobles, and imperial kin in the "Chronicles," see *Hanshu* 4 (pp. 110, 126, 132), 6 (p. 179), 7 (pp. 218, 220, 221, 223, 224, 228, 229), 8 (pp. 239, 245, 249, 254, 257, 259, 264, 272), and so on throughout the subsequent chronicles. On gifts of precious metals in the Warring States, see Lewis 1999a: 606–7. For an example from a biography of a Han official who receives a retirement of precious metal, see *Hanshu* 71 (p. 3040). See also below, ch. 7.

silk, and imperial princesses to the Xiongnu; the presents (largely silk) sent to the rulers of the oasis states of Central Asia (modern Xinjiang) that accepted titular Han sovereignty; money and silk given to surrendered barbarians who agreed to be resettled inside China; and bounties for the heads of Xiongnu paid to tribes-man allied to the Han. Thus, any non-Chinese peoples who entered into relations with China—whether as enemies negotiating temporarily peaceful relations, independent states recognizing Han overlordship, or tribes that maintained de facto autonomy while providing military service for the Han—had their position instantiated through the acceptance of some gift from the Han emperor. That these payments were explicitly regarded as gifts is demonstrated by the fact that the Han invariably gave far more than they received in "tribute" payments from the non-Chinese.[16] Such routine imbalance would indicate only stupidity if the purpose of these exchanges were economic, as has been posited by many modern scholars. However, in a gift relationship such an imbalance creates a hierarchical relationship in which the one who gives the greater amount places the other in his debt and thereby marks his or her own status as a patron and a superior.

The eighth and final form of the emperor's gift giving was sacrifices. While one might argue that it is not analytically useful to conflate offerings to spirits with gifts to humans, the fact remains that the foods and material objects presented to deities—as well as human ancestors—were a noncoerced presentation that served to constitute permanent ties between the two parties. Furthermore, it is notable that in China political/social authority was always identified with the right to offer sacrifice: the head of a household, the leader of a region, the ruler of the state, and any other person in charge of a social grouping always served as the chief sacrificer for that group. Thus, the emperor's power was always justified in part through his unique ability to make offerings to the highest and most powerful deities. In the course of the Han dynasty, the spirit of Heaven was established as the highest god, and the great periurban sacrifice to Heaven became the ultimate religious ritual performed in the Chinese Empire throughout the rest of imperial history.[17]

More important is the sense that imperial sacrifices are done for the sake of the common good (unlike other forms of sacrifice, which benefited the specific groups who made them), and the proper offerings to Heaven would in theory elicit the bestowal of Heaven's blessings on the people of the empire in the form of timely rain and abundant harvests. The Han emperor's sacrifices were thus a form of euergetism in the sense defined by Veyne. It is also worth noting that writers in early imperial Rome explicitly spoke of sacrifice as a form of gift circulation including the ruler, the gods, and the people, for whom the peace of the

---

16. Yü 1967 and 1986; Lewis 2000: 58–61.

17. On the protracted development of cults to differing high gods in the Han, culminating in the establishment of the cult to Heaven, see Lewis 1999a; Bujard 2000; Puett 2002, ch. 7 ("The Sacrifices that Order the World").

Principate was a divine gift, and that the description of offerings to the gods as "gifts" (*dona*) was a conventional usage.[18]

In addition to all these forms of concrete or institutional gifts, one must also examine the rhetoric of the period. Thus, a request to retire would be described as asking the emperor for the "gift of one's skeleton," since the emperor controlled the persons of his officials and had to give them back to their families before they would be allowed to depart from the court. Similarly a reply from the emperor to a memorial from an official was also described as the bestowal of a gift.[19] Such phrases are to a certain extent rhetorical, but they are also aspects of the phenomenon noted by Veyne in which the Roman ruler's very existence and every act that he performed could be treated as an act of benevolence or generosity.[20]

As noted in the above list, several of the forms of imperial gift giving, such as the distribution of land to peasants, were imitated on a smaller scale or lower level by members of the imperial family or the court. In addition, locally powerful families also engaged in forms of gift giving or charity as an element of their status and power. One recipient of such gifts was the emperor, who received the tribute of goods and people from the different regions of his realm. Another form was the gathering of "guest-retainers (*ke*)," who continued to be a major element of locally eminent households (as well as urban gangs) in Han China. Particularly in the Eastern Han the practice of local charity and poor relief also figures prominently in the biographic accounts, stone inscriptions, and philosophical essays of the Han great families. The primary recipients of such charitable actions were more distant kinsmen and fellow villagers, but at certain periods they spread more broadly to include whole commanderies. The importance of such activities to the organization and the activities of the Han local elite is one of the major themes of the Han sources from the period, including the stone inscriptions that members of the great families commissioned for their own kin and that thus demonstrate how these people understood the bases of their own eminence.[21]

Such charity took several forms. First, wealthy men often entertained kin and neighbors in great banquets. In several cases, the wealth for such activities is explicitly described as coming from prior gifts by the emperor or members of the imperial family. One of the most interesting is the case of Shu Guang, who had received a quantity of gold from the emperor as a retirement gift and who used it to feast all his neighbors. When members of his family had the village elders remonstrate that he was wasting too much of his family's newfound wealth, Shu Guang replied:

---

18. Bowditch 2001: ch. 2 ("Tragic History and the Gift of Sacrifice"). On *dona* to the gods, see ibid. 65–68. See also DeSilva 2000: 100–2.

19. Lewis 2006: 309–10; *Hanshu* 49 (p. 2283).

20. Veyne 1976: 658–60.

21. Lewis 2006: 218, 220, 223–27.

How could I be so old and muddleheaded as not to think of my descendants? I have my old fields and shacks, and if my descendants work diligently these are sufficient to provide food and clothing as good as those of ordinary people. If I should increase them in order to have a surplus, I would just cause my descendants to become lazy. For the worthy man, having much wealth diminishes his ambition. For the stupid man, having much wealth augments his faults. Moreover, wealth is what is hated and resented by the masses. Since I am unable to morally transform my descendants, I do not desire to augment their faults and produce resentment against them. Moreover, the money I am spending is what was granted by the sage ruler to nourish his old servant. Therefore I am happy to enjoy what he has given me together with my fellow villagers and members of my patriline, and thus live out my remaining days.[22]

This is of interest in that it explicitly cites the emperor's gift giving as the source and pattern for that of Shu Guang, who claims to only be fulfilling the sage ruler's will. However, this and a handful of related passages are also notable for articulating a theory of gift giving that almost anticipates the model articulated in James Scott's *The Moral Economy of the Peasant*.[23] Money that is hoarded undermines the character of those who hold it and attracts the resentment of neighbors, whereas money that is distributed in banquets and assistance to the poor secures loyalty and support. This pattern in which wealth at the village level was to a certain degree redistributed through sponsorship of banquets, often in association with local cults, or through helping neighbors in times of emergency, has remained a feature of rural Chinese society down to the present day.

Such feasting also was a part of Han local cults sponsored by powerful landed families and merchants, although such practices are noted only in a few cases where local officials undertook to suppress the cult, which consequently was cited in imperial records.[24] In another form of "routine" beneficence, wealthy families adopted orphans or other more distant kin. Closely related, although analytically distinguishable, was the importance of gift giving to high officials, which became in practice little more than bribes, in the attempts of locally important families to secure access to or the support of eminent figures at court.[25] Toward the end of the Han local families also became very active in the building of roads, reservoirs, and other facilities for more general use, an activity that was recorded in several

---

22. *Hanshu* 71 (p. 3040). See also *Dongguan Hanji jiaozhu* 15 (pp. 598–99): "Much accumulation increases losses and is a burden to one's descendants"; and *Hou Hanshu* (Beijing 1965) 82a (pp. 2720–21).

23. Scott 1976: ch. 6 ("Reciprocity and Subsistence as Justice").

24. A detailed account of a cult that had initially been sponsored by the state in one town but that spread across all of what is now Shandong and that entailed large-scale public feasts sponsored in rotation by local merchants is described in the late Eastern Han *Fengsu tongyi jiaoshi* (Tianjin 1980), 333–34. Less detailed references to the cult also appear in *Hou Han shu* 11 (pp. 479–80); *Dongguan Hanji jiaozhu* 21 (p. 863).

25. *Hou Hanshu* 27 (pp. 945–46), 41 (pp. 1398–99), 43 (p. 1458), 91 (p. 3690).

funerary inscriptions. Finally, local families increasingly provided famine and flood relief, as well as defense against bandits.

The exact relationship between the emperor's gift giving and that of the powerful families is not entirely clear and probably shifted across time. On the one hand, many of the charitable actions of the families seem to have been directly patterned on those of the emperor. As noted above, they even claim to be extending or carrying out imperial benefactions, as in the cases of distribution of land to peasants or Shu Guang's use of an imperial gift to provide banquets for poorer neighbors. However, the emphasis in late Han stories on public works, local military defense, and relief from flood or famine indicates that the locally influential families were directly taking charge of the roles that the imperial state—due to impoverishment and the consequences of military reforms—was no longer capable of handling. This was on the one hand a mode of upholding the court, but it would also have been perceived as a form of usurpation. The links of local gift giving to unsanctioned cults also suggest ways in which the beneficence of the great families was a direct challenge to the imperial order.

2. COMPARISONS

Many of the activities described above are not dissimilar to the gift giving or charitable activities of the Roman emperor or the imperial elite. (Due to the easy accessibility of accounts of these activities, I will not recapitulate the major elements.[26]) However, there are a few differences that clearly relate to the varying structures of the two empires and the defining hallmarks of political authority.

First, public benevolence and charity in the Roman Empire, like that in the Greek world that formed its eastern half, was defined by its urban frame. Veyne's "euergetism" was inseparable from the city, which was the basic unit of the political order. The same emphasis on the ultimate urban focus of this conduct also figures in Saller's account of patronage in the early empire.[27] The primary forms of public benevolence, both for the ruler and members of the elite, were the construction of new buildings for public use (theaters, gymnasia, baths, arenas for games), the sponsorship of games, and the maintenance of aqueducts and roads. All of these, and additional charities such as the feeding of the specified number of the Roman plebs or charity for poor children provided by interest on loans to farmers, were focused on the cities. They assured the provision of the basic requisites of an existence that was "civilized" in the etymological sense of being urban.

In Han China, on the other hand, the bulk of imperial gift giving and virtually all private offerings went to the countryside. This difference reflects the

---

26. See above, n. 1. The following observations focus on the monarchical period of Roman history.
27. Veyne 1976: 103–4, 110–15; Saller 1982: ch. 5.

political distinction between the Roman Empire, which was structured as a multiplicity of urban centers—both old established ones and new ones built to a standard model—and the Chinese Empire, where the political power of the ruler and his agents derived directly from the registration, mobilization, and taxation of rural households.[28] The pattern of Roman euergetism carried on the Greek precedent of local regimes formed through groupings of urban notables who demonstrated a devotion to the public good. In contrast, imperial gift giving in the Han dynasty was directed toward the elements of the population who provided the fiscal and military foundations of the state, which is to say the peasantry and the officials whose families and life patterns remained rooted in the rural world (see below).

The differential pattern of gift giving also reflects a difference between the uses of the rural bases of the Roman elite and the Han Chinese. For the former, large estates worked by servile or contract labor and managed by local agents were primarily sources of income that enabled the eminent man to pursue his career in the cities. For the Chinese elite, on the other hand, estates remained relatively small through the process of division among heirs, and the primary source of local influence was the forming of extended social networks on the basis of kin ties, marriage with other leading families, and the patronage offered to poorer neighbors. This required a much more regular presence in the countryside and made the gift giving relations with peasant neighbors described above a crucial element of the great families' authority.[29] As imperial power declined and the great families became responsible for an ever wider range of local governmental functions, this rural focus intensified.

Second, Veyne makes a clear distinction between simple charity to the poor, as exemplified by later Christian practice, and Greek or Roman euergetism, which consisted of making a contribution to a *public* good shared by all citizens. This depended on the existence of a clearly defined public space that was distinct from government offices, palaces, and temples, a public space that was fashioned and maintained by the elite as the necessary setting for the cultivation and display of their authority.[30] Such a public space did not exist in Han China, and there is no evidence at all in the period of specifically urban charity. This would develop only with the rise of Buddhism, with private foundations of temples open to the public, and at roughly the same time with the development of private gardens that similarly evolved into early public parks. Only with the emergence of such new spaces in the fifth and sixth centuries do we begin to find a Chinese version of a distinctive urban public realm.[31]

28. Lewis 1990: ch. 2 and passim.
29. Lewis 2006: 212–13.
30. Veyne 1976: chs. 2, 5, 11.
31. Lewis forthcoming: ch. 4.

The absence of nongovernmental public spaces in Han China was also linked to an absence of monumental building in stone. For reasons that are not entirely clear, whether a scarcity of raw material or simply a choice to build in perishable materials that could readily be rebuilt in the latest style at regular intervals, the Chinese never developed a tradition of building in stone.[32] Given the emphasis on private or imperial donations to the public good, much euergetism in the Mediterranean consisted in the building of great stone structures inscribed with the name and purposes of the donor. It is for this reason that we possess the masses of stone inscriptions from which one can reconstruct so much of Roman and Greek social history, including the history of donations to the public good. The absence of such structures in China, and their associated records of public-spirited conduct, meant that prestige and influence could not be generated through the sponsorship of such buildings and that no honor could be gained by being recorded on them. This led both to radically different modes of experiencing a cityscape and to the development of clearly divergent modes of transforming material wealth into symbolic capital through the agency of benefactions.

Third, the other great form of imperial public benevolence, the sponsorship of games, also entailed a mode of political behavior in Rome that would have been unthinkable in China. Specifically, one of the key aspects of the games sponsored by the emperor was that the ruler himself would have appeared in public and shared the games with the urban populace. This physical presence, as Veyne points out, was essential to the role of the games; the emperor made a gift of his person as much as of the entertainment in the arena proper.[33] In Qin and Han China, in contrast, the ruler did not display himself in public. Power was generated not through the public adulation of the people, but through a policy of sequestration and hiding away. Sealed up behind layer after layer of walls, the emperor rewarded only his closest followers with the supreme honor of letting them come into his presence. This power of the inside over the outside, and of the hidden over the visible, became a longstanding principle of the spatial construction of power in imperial China.[34]

A related difference was that the Roman emperor, as discussed by Fergus Millar, would often provide gifts to humble people with whom he came into contact in the course of his duties, just as he could receive petitions from such people and adjudicate cases on their behalf.[35] Again, such contact for the Chinese ruler would have taken place only with his own officials and hence, as noted above, they—and the chieftains of surrendered barbarians who were ceremonially allowed into the imperial presence—were the only people who would have

---

32. Lewis 2006: 188.
33. Veyne 1976: 701–6.
34. Lewis 2006: 114–18, 155–57.
35. Millar 1977: ch. 8.

received gifts from the emperor as a consequence of coming into his presence. The Han emperor's gifts, like his decrees and punishments, were distributed outward solely through the agency of his servants.

A fourth, and final, distinction between the Roman and Chinese cases is the distinctive preimperial history of gift giving as a mode of elite action. As the layout of Veyne's book demonstrates, imperial euergetism was established on the basis of centuries in which public charity and private patronage had together served to generate and define elite status. Leaders in Greek cities, Hellenistic monarchs, and the Roman senate and order of *equites* had all in various forms contributed to public liturgies, made conspicuous gifts to the urban populace, or gathered networks of clients. The forms of beneficence practiced by the Roman emperor were in many ways extensions or elaborations of existing models, so that Augustus could map out many elements of the radically new imperial role through adopting established forms by which leading political figures had distinguished themselves.

The converse of this, as Egon Flaig has demonstrated, was that the emperor was both inextricably enmeshed in a society defined by patterns of *beneficia* and *gratia* but at the same time of necessity beyond claims of reciprocity. This was to a degree theorized by Seneca, who posited a society constituted through gift and obligation but asserted the new monarchy as an innovation in which a single, superior giver "inundated all groups and persons in the empire with *beneficia* to such a degree that they were all in *gratia*, obligated to gratitude to him." Given the emperor's unique contribution to a new world order, loyalty and service to him were absolute duties that could not command any reciprocal obligations on his part. Gifts flowed in both directions, notably the bequests to the emperor in wills, but the obligations entailed in such gifts moved in one direction only.[36]

To the extent that is not a product of the biases of our sources, the evidence for the Chinese case suggests a model of imperial generosity that evolved not from any prior form of euergetism or any elite self-constitution through conspicuous giving, but rather from the mode of state formation in the Warring States period. The rulers of these emerging states, who provided the pattern for the later imperial role, distinguished themselves from their rivals through the steady incorporation of ever greater numbers of peasants into military service and their structures of taxation. The *quid pro quo* for such service, as theorized in the political manuals of the period and practiced by the states, was the granting of titles and land.[37] The primary gifts of the Han emperors—titles, land, tax relief, or monetary presentations in times of crisis—were the later forms of the earlier Warring States' awards to the peasantry.

To the extent that there was an ideological pattern for such beneficence, it was conventional to claim as a model not any earlier form of public service or

36. Flaig 2003: esp. 53–61.
37. Lewis 1990: ch. 2.

giving by a noble elite, but rather the action of a beneficent Heaven that freely bestowed life on all beneath it, without requiring any service in return. (Certain similar themes appear in early imperial Roman literature, where accounts of the Golden Age in which nature freely yielded up her wealth without the necessity of human labor were invoked as a precedent for the new imperial order.[38]) As a matter of policy, the Han emperor's gifts were also part of a larger aim of preserving a small-holding, free peasantry that was the foundation of the state. This contrast in the origins of standard imperial gifts in the two systems once again draws our attention back to the urban bias of the Roman case and the rural focus of the Chinese.[39]

3. CONCLUSION

"Gift," as many scholars have noted, is not always an analytically useful term. It is necessary to distinguish various types of gift circulation or charity, because the types of goods that are conventionally given and the roles that are defined in their giving and receiving will mark the difference between two cultures. Thus, as noted above, Veyne emphasizes the contrast between Christian charity, which would become the standard model of giving in late antiquity, and classic euergetism. The latter is defined as gifts to a public realm that would be potentially received by all members of that realm. Indeed, the collective gifts of the elite to the common good are in some sense constitutive of the public realm, as a cluster of constructed spaces that would not otherwise exist, as a set of distinctive virtues ("public spirit"), and as a series of personal relationships defined on the model of patron and client. In this way we can see how in the ancient Mediterranean world particular modes of distributing wealth, distinct from market transactions, defined first the city-state and later the empire as distinctive public forms, and how these would be replaced by yet another form in the Christianized world.

In the Han Chinese case the public realm was not clearly distinguished from the political, so that participation in a *res publica* meant to be in the service of the ruler. (The same sort of pun/homophone gloss by which Cicero defined the "republic" could also be done in Chinese, where what was "public" [*gong*] was what pertained to the "lord" [*gong*].) Thus, it was above all the gift of titles by which the ruler brought all free men into his service and granted them corresponding legal privileges that constituted a broader "public" space. The other associated gifts, as noted above, were primarily extensions of policies aimed at preserving this political space defined by the participation of a free-holding peasantry.

38. Bowditch 2001: ch. 3 ("The Gifts of the Golden Age: Land, Debt, and Aesthetic Surplus").
39. Attempts to support small holders were confined to the Republican period of Roman history and ceased with the creation of a monarchical regime.

The clear emergence of a realm in which local rural order was defined and maintained through the conspicuous charity and public-spirited actions of powerful families was to a certain degree the reflection of the breakdown of the earlier "imperial" model. This breakdown was marked by the parallel abandonment of universal military service and of all attempts to restrict the concentration of land ownership at the beginning of the Eastern Han and followed shortly by the eclipse of the old system of public ranking through the emperor's gift of titles. This shift from the imperial realm defined by the emperor's bestowal of ranks to one based on flow of gifts through circles of local charity indicated the replacement of a military-bureaucratic model of the state by a state-family union, in which the state order was transmitted and preserved through powerful local families. This shift toward a semipublic realm defined by an uneasy joining of a reduced political state with an extended kin and village hybrid defined the shift from the early imperial (Qin-Han) era to the centuries of the Northern and Southern Dynasties.

7

The Monetary Systems of the Han and Roman Empires

Walter Scheidel

1. INTRODUCTION

Beginning in the third century B.C.E., the imperial unification of both East Asia and the Mediterranean gave rise to increasingly standardized currency systems that sought to establish stable means of payment. In both cases, the eventual monopolization of minting tied the success of these currencies to the fortunes of the state. Yet despite these basic similarities, substantial differences prevailed. While silver and later gold dominated the monetary economy of the Roman Empire, the victorious Chinese regimes operated a system of bronze coinages supplemented by uncoined precious-metal bullion. This raises a series of questions. How did these differences arise, and why did they persist well beyond antiquity? How did the use of different metals affect the relationship between the nominal and intrinsic value of monetary objects? Did the minting of precious metals in the West and China's reliance on copper determine overall levels of monetization? To the best of my knowledge, none of these issues has ever been addressed from a comparative perspective. The failure to do so has made it harder to appreciate the specific properties of each of these two monetary systems. Explicit comparison brings the constituent elements of each tradition into sharper relief: by defamiliarizing the familiar, it invites us to question established interpretations and reconsider the nature of putative causal relationships.

Because this survey is the first of its kind, much of it is taken up by a parallel exposition of monetary histories that provides a basis for the comparative analysis of specific features. The format of this exposition is in large part determined by the historiography of the subject. It is not an exaggeration to say that the existing body of research scholarship on Roman coins, money, and the monetary economy greatly exceeds corresponding scholarship on early Chinese money in terms of both volume and sophistication. As a consequence, while the physical characteristics of Roman coins and their distribution have already been studied in very considerable detail and much attention has been paid to their relevance to broader questions of economic history, our knowledge of ancient Chinese money and its uses remains much more limited and fragile, and many important questions have barely been addressed at all. Taking account of this massive imbalance, I discuss the Chinese evidence at some length (sections 2–5) but limit myself to a skeletal outline of conditions in the Roman world (section 6). Each survey is followed by a brief summary of what I consider to be the principal trends and patterns (sections 5 and 6.2).

These parallel surveys prepare the ground for more systematic comparative analysis. In section 7, I explore the causes of the dominant monetary position of different metals in eastern and western Eurasia in antiquity and argue for a combination of geological and culturally contingent factors. In section 8, I challenge the conventional "nominalistic" understanding of early Chinese money by documenting the crucial significance of its intrinsic (metal) value. I argue that the emergence of monopolistic superstates in both eastern and western Eurasia favored the creation of hybrid currency systems in which the lack of competition relaxed "metallistic" constraints without removing them altogether, and that coin users in both systems retained a substantial degree of sensitivity to the intrinsic value of their currencies. The final section seeks to quantify the metal money stocks of the Han and Roman empires at the peak of their powers. My findings lead me to the conclusion that in real terms, the Roman imperial economy was probably considerably more monetized than that of the Han state.

It is important to clarify the scope of this study. "Money" is a notoriously elusive concept. In historical societies, "all-purpose" money that simultaneously served as a medium of exchange, a store of wealth, and a unit of account represented merely a subset of all monetary objects and instruments: while coinage often—though not always—met all three criteria, weighed bullion, tokens, "near-money" (such as bills of exchange), foodstuffs, textiles, real estate, livestock, slaves, or cowrie shells were all similarly capable of performing one or more of these functions. Under the right circumstances, they could all "count" as "money." In the following sections, I concentrate primarily on coined or otherwise normed metal money. This focus owes more to necessity than to choice: the nature of the evidence forestalls a meaningful comparative assessment of credit money in the Han and Roman economies, and the actual scale of monetary use of normed textile fabrics in the former is impossible to gauge. Moreover, constraints of space compel me to forego comparative consideration of monetary thought and the invocation of money in literary discourse, a fascinating topic that would readily support a book-length study.[1] Finally, it is worth noting that as far as the physical nature of coined money is concerned, conditions in

---

1. Matters of monetary policy enjoy greater prominence in the ancient Chinese tradition than in Roman sources: for texts and discussion, see esp. Swann 1950 and Hu 1988: chs. 1–12 (China), and compare Nicolet 1971 and 1984 and most recently Wolters 1999: 350–71 (Rome).

Ptolemaic and Roman Egypt—where bronze and much-debased billon issues played a central role—bore a much closer resemblance to early Chinese practices than those in most other parts of the Roman Empire.[2] These similarities likewise warrant comparative investigation in the future.

2. PREIMPERIAL COINAGE IN ANCIENT CHINA

With regard to the mythical and semimythical distant past, later textual sources ascribe monetary uses to a variety of objects such as tortoise shells, cowrie shells, pearls, skins, teeth, horns, wheat, textiles, and stone tools.[3] Archaeological evidence confirms the use of cowrie shells (*bei*) since the Shang period (*c.*1600–1045 B.C.E.) and especially during the Western Zhou Dynasty (*c.*1045–771 B.C.E.). Assembled on strings of ten (*peng*), cowries gradually came to serve as a standard of value.[4] It is less clear, however, whether cowries ever fulfilled the additional monetary function of a medium of exchange: they may primarily have been used as gifts and prestige items comparable to jade objects and are mostly discovered in mortuary settings.[5] Imitation cowries made of bone and later bronze already appeared in the late Shang period, although production did not peak until the Eastern Zhou period (770–256 B.C.E.).[6] Cowrie use was particularly widespread in Yunnan in the far south: 260,000 of them have been unearthed from tombs dating from before the Qin-Han period. Their presence strongly diminished under later Han rule but increased again afterward; they did not disappear from that region until the final imposition of imperial control in the seventeenth century.[7]

Miniaturized tools that served as a store of value date back to the late second millennium B.C.E., but most finds have been made in Western and early Eastern Zhou tombs.[8] Spade blades that kept shrinking in size and weight were the most prevalent type. From the seventh century B.C.E. these spades came to bear inscriptions (mostly the cowrie symbol *peng* and numbers): it is only from that point onward that monetary usage can safely be inferred. Spade money was produced in a number of distinctive shapes that may cast light on chronology and provenance but requires further study. In the late Spring and Autumn period, spades with square corners represented the most common type, usually 7–10

2. E.g., Maresch 1996; von Reden 2007.

3. Thierry 2003b: 25.

4. For examples, see Thierry 2001b: 118–19. However, Li 2006 argues that cowries did not become a standard of value until the middle Western Zhou period. Peng and Zhu 1995: 9–12 discuss the geographical spread of cowrie shells: use peaked in the Yellow River valley from the Shang into the early Spring and Autumn periods, waned in the Central Plain during the Warring States period, and ended under Qin and Han.

5. Thus Li 2006: 7, 11, 17–18.

6. Thierry 1997: 46–48, referring to over 27,000 specimens found in tombs of that period.

7. Yang 2004: 305–12.

8. Wang 1951; Thierry 1997: 49–65, 89–102; Peng 2000: 33–117.

centimeters long and weighing 20–30 grams, whereas smaller specimens weighing around 5–7 grams were typical of the Warring States period.[9] Knife-shaped money developed in the northern and northeastern reaches of China.

Monetization expanded in the increasingly competitive and dynamic environment of the Warring States period (480–221 B.C.E.). The main contenders for overall supremacy—Qi, Qin, and Chu—developed closed monetary systems, whereas the "Three Jin" states of Zhao, Wei, and Han experienced less governmental centralization and thus more local autonomy in money production. In Han and Wei, spade money was produced to a set weight standard (of 7, 14, 28 g). Knives continued to be common in the northeastern states of Yan and Qi. Qi, Qin, and Chu all developed state-specific currency systems.[10]

Judging by the archaeological record, round coins appeared in the fourth century B.C.E. in the states of the central Great Plain and subsequently came to be used in all major states except Chu in the south. Presumably modeled on earlier circular jade disks (*bi*) with small holes in the center, these coins were cast according to regional weight standards and often inscribed with their denomination or the name of the issuing city.[11] The state of Qin followed the *liang* standard, casting *banliang* (i.e., half-*liang*) coins with a target weight of approximately 8 grams, the weight being inscribed on the face of the coins. Later texts claimed that Qin Shihuangdi created this coin in 221 B.C.E., an erroneous conflation of the later imperial predominance of this type of coin with the circumstances of its creation. *Banliang* coins have been found in strata dating from the mid-fourth century B.C.E., more than a century prior to Qin's imperial unification. They were introduced in a period of profound state-sponsored changes, and it is possible that a state monopoly was established or at least claimed in connection with the sweeping legalist reforms of Shang Yang in the 340s and 330s B.C.E.[12]

A divergent monetary system developed in the southern state of Chu, based on bronze cowries and coin-sized thin square plates of gold bearing punch marks denoting the name of the currency (*yuan*) and the name of the Chu capital.[13] The archaeological record suggests that both currencies circulated only within

9. See the catalog in Thierry 1997: 194–97, 202–37. The bulk of Warring States cash was made up of small spade coins: ibid. 89.

10. Peng 2000: 183–207.

11. Thierry 1997: 83–88. Jade disks as model: Wang 2004: 11; and cf. Thierry 1997: 84. (The National Museum of China in Beijing displays numerous *bi* that are barely larger than large bronze coins.) The early coins of Wei, Han, and Zhao preserved the round hole characteristic of the jade disks whereas Yan, Qi, and Qin opted for square holes.

12. Thierry 1997: 165–75. In 336 B.C.E., the Zhou congratulated the Qin on issuing coins; but it is a modern presumption that this marks the *first* issue of such coins at Qin: Peng 1994: 76, n. 2; Thierry 1997: 173. For Shang Yang's reforms, see Li 1977. Thierry 1997: 173–75 distinguishes among seven types of Qin *banliang* coins. The oldest *banliang* coins (*c.*370s–340s B.C.E.?) are large and heavy (usually in excess of 10g) and feature more "archaic" round holes. The most regular issues (7–10g) may date from the Shang Yang period. Underweight specimens from the late Warring States period dominate the archaeological record.

13. See below, section 4.1. Thierry 1997: 143 stresses the different character of this system.

Chu. While the use of imitation cowries continued older local traditions,[14] the circulation of gold in a quasi-coin format remained exceptional in China (although it also occurred farther south in Vietnam and may represent a regional and ultimately "foreign" custom). I discuss this evidence in more detail below (section 4.1).

Who issued these coins? The literary tradition conveys the impression that rulers (i.e., the state) made decisions concerning the issuing of money. Thus, it was possible to imagine that in 524 B.C.E., King Jing of Zhou replaced "light" coins with "heavy" coins, thereby somehow allegedly depriving his subjects of their property.[15] The *Guanzi*, a series of dialogues set in the seventh century B.C.E. but believed to be composed at the Jixia Academy in Qi in the fourth and third centuries B.C.E. and collated in their final form in the first century B.C.E., emphasizes the desirability of state control over the money supply. This position is normally envisioned as the ruler's control over the circulation of an existing stock of money rather than as policy-making regarding the manufacturing of money per se. For instance, in order to establish desired price levels, the ruler was meant to manipulate the money supply and hence prices by hoarding or spending cash rather than by issuing or demonetizing coin.[16] It has been argued that at least early on, merchants manufactured coins, employing regional weight standards. However, circumstantial evidence suggests that by about 300 B.C.E., Qin and Qi had established state control over coin production. The situation in the other states remains obscure, although high levels of uniformity within each polity may speak in favor of significant government involvement throughout the region.[17] In textual sources covering the preimperial period, cash is rarely mentioned in elite contexts, and no state salaries in cash are recorded.[18] This interpretation is supported by the fact that for much of the first 80 years of the Han Dynasty, private individuals were permitted to make coins, and that the state only gradually entered this market (see below).

Under these circumstances, given both the likely involvement or perhaps even predominance of private coin manufacturers, and the initial political fragmentation of the region later encompassed by the Qin and Han empires, a wide variety of currencies and denominations must have been in circulation during the Warring States period, and coins would not always—indeed not normally—meet

14. Wei and Fang 1997 argue that the local miniature version of imitation cowries, known as "ant-nose" money and found in large quantities, served as the main currency of Chu but maintain that it did not become common until the late Warring States period, and that use of genuine cowries had still predominated up to that point. Peng 2000: 150 also dates these *yibi* coins to c.330–223 B.C.E. See also Thierry 1997: 143–46.

15. *Hanshu* 24B: 2a–b in Swann 1950: 225–28; cf. Peng 1994: 91–92.

16. *Guanzi* 74 "Shanguogui" 3.71, in von Glahn 1996: 33. See also the passage cited in the previous note, and more generally Hu 1988: 133–38.

17. Peng 2000: 155–61. Thierry 1997: 172 notes that the spread of *banliang* coins matched the expansion of the Qin state. However, even in Qin coin issues by vassals and members of the ruling family were permitted: Thierry 2003a: 24.

18. Peng 1994: 87; and Lewis 1999: 374–75, n. 53 for salaries in grain.

nominal target weight standards. We have no information about the metal prices of the constituent elements of these coins (such as copper and tin) or about the relationship between their intrinsic value and their face value. The fact that coins were repeatedly cast in keeping with prevailing regional weight standards and even marked as such indicates that their face value was at least in theory meant to represent their metal value, always allowing for a degree of seigniorage to defray production costs and latent vulnerability to weight debasement driven by public and private profit seeking.

Legal provisions of the Qin state dating from before 242 B.C.E. that were discovered in a tomb at Yunmeng in 1975 shed light on this issue.[19] The pertinent section of this text (the *Jinbulu*) holds that round coins (i.e., presumably the *banliang* coins of that period) were to be accepted regardless of whether they were "fine" or "bad" (i.e., heavy or light), and that it was illegal to sort coins according to size and weight: "When commoners in their deals use cash, fine and bad (pieces) are to be used together; one should not venture to differentiate between them."[20] This text demonstrates three things: that coins deviated from conventional weight standards (which is amply confirmed by archaeological data); that people valued and hence exchanged coin according to its weight as a proxy of its metal value; and that the Qin state, a mere generation prior to its final victory, sought to reduce transaction costs by upholding the preeminence of the face value of coin vis-à-vis its intrinsic value. The Qin state may well have attempted to define its coins as fiduciary money whose exchange value was meant to be divorced from its metal content.

However, it is naive to maintain that this establishes the fiduciary character of this monetary system:[21] the very existence of this law points to the contrary aspirations of money users who accorded greater significance to intrinsic value. This reading receives support from Jia Yi's memorial of 175 B.C.E. and other evidence that will be presented in the following sections. At the same time, this should not be taken to imply that the state was completely unsuccessful in imposing the principle of freely interchangeable mixed-quality coins of uniform face value: textual references to a unit called *pen*—1,000 coins in a large basket or pot—have been validated by the discovery, in Shaanxi Province, of a pot that contained exactly 1,000 coins of various weights and sizes. Of them, 997 were *banliang* coins of Qin: about one-fifth of them weighed around 6 grams or more (up to 10 g) while the others weighed in at less than 5 grams, and in 6 percent of all cases at less than 3 grams.[22] Another jar with 1,000 *banliang* coins has since been found in Gansu province.[23] The *Jinbulu* (§65) states that it was

---

19. Translation and commentary of the Shuihudi texts in Hulsewé 1985a. See also Hulsewé 1985b: 227–29; Thierry 1993: 3–4, 1997: 168–70.
20. Hulsewé 1985a: 52.
21. *Contra* Thierry 1983; 2001b: 126–33.
22. Thierry 1997: 170 and 2001b: 129–30.
23. Thierry 1997: 171.

the state authorities who mixed 1,000 "beautiful and ugly" coins in a container and then sealed it, but also that these containers were to be opened if the government needed to use their contents: hence, coins reentered circulation not in opaque packages but as individual objects, and intermittent random "baggings" were hardly sufficient to curtail more discriminate money use in market transactions. The very fact that most coins in the Shaanxi pot—and more generally in the archaeological record[24]—are significantly underweight casts doubt on the notion that they could readily have circulated at their nominal value. Given the continuing persistence of coin weighing (see below, section 3.1), the most likely scenario may be one of an uneasy mix of state-enforced rules and private preferences that ultimately depended on the willingness and ability of the state to enforce fiduciary exchange practices. In this regard, late Qin, with its powerful and ambitious state apparatus and strong legalist tradition, may well have occupied an unusual position within the Chinese state system.[25] Later (albeit admittedly much more extravagant) attempts of the Han state to dissociate face value from metal value invariably yielded disastrous results (see below, sections 3.2–3), thereby highlighting the limits of the coercive capabilities of the imperial state. I return to this problem farther below in a more general discussion of the limits of fiduciary money in the Chinese and Roman economies (section 8).

3. The Bronze Currency of the Qin-Han Period

3.1. Monetary Developments under the Qin and the Early Western Han

Upon the completion of the Qin takeover in 221 b.c.e., the *banliang* coins of Qin were meant to be the only legal tender other than gold (which was, however, not cast in coin form: see below, section 4.2). Inevitably, coins of different size and weight continued to circulate, and even the *banliang* coins themselves varied in these respects, usually by falling short of the target weight.[26] This may well reflect the inevitably huge financial exertions of the Qin state in taking over its rivals in the third century b.c.e.: from a comparative perspective, it would be truly remarkable if the kind of depreciation that commonly ensued in other historical societies that faced massive military challenges could somehow have been avoided by the late Qin kingdom. More research is required to shed light on this process.[27] If some greatly underweight *banliang* issues were indeed associated with Qin Shihuangdi's short-lived

---

24. Cf. Tierry 1997: 172 for a find of 645 *banliang* coins in Shanxi, 5 percent of which were regular, 14 percent heavy, and 81 percent underweight.
25. Bodde 1986; cf. Fu 1996.
26. Swann 1950: 228, n. 386.
27. See now Peng 2000: 175–79.

successor,[28] this would document the first of several crisis-driven debasements of the imperial period.

When the Han seized power, the gold-bronze system was maintained. In general, we observe strong continuity from the Qin into the early Han periods.[29] Since Qin money was considered "heavy" (i.e., scarce) and "difficult for practical purposes" (whatever that means), the first Han emperor allowed—or in any case was not in a position to deny this right to—his subjects to cast their own coins.[30] Down to the 110s B.C.E., a large number of mints existed side by side: the imperial palace, individual princes, vassal kings, and private operatives all contributed to the overall coin supply. Given the wide spread of coin weights at the time (and in light of the episode of 175 B.C.E. discussed below), the weighing of coins (and thus usage according to metal value) may be presumed to have been common. It is possible that the price inflation recorded for this period was due not so much to hoarding[31] as to the inflationary consequences of issuing underweight coinage at (much?) higher face value. This association is repeatedly established in later texts.

The historiographical tradition as represented by the *Shiji* and the *Hanshu* ascribes a whole series of monetary measures to early Han rulers. Resultant attempts to match the archaeological record to these reports have confined numismatic study of this period to a literature-centered interpretive framework that has made it difficult to analyze the material evidence on its own terms.[32] More than anything else, the dispersed nature of coin production militates against overly schematizing categorization.

Thus, when the sources claim that in 186 B.C.E., an 8-*zhu* coin (*bazhu banliang*, theoretically *c*.5.2g) bearing the customary *banliang* inscription (signaling a—notional—weight of 12 *zhu*) was issued, this need not indicate a significant break from existing practice: after all, many *banliang* coins of the Qin period de facto already conformed to a similar weight standard.[33] Four years later, we are told, a *wufen* coin (i.e., 5 *fen* or 1.18 cm in diameter) was introduced.[34] Since a "former" prohibition of private coining is alluded to in an episode set in 175 B.C.E., it is possible that these reforms were accompanied by such a decree.[35] If true, this might have constituted an attempt to stem the inflationary slide of coin weights by imposing tighter state control or, conceivably, to secure seigniorage on the scale of one-third by compelling users to accept an 8-*zhu* coin at a 12-*zhu* face value.

28. Thus He 1996.
29. Thierry 2003a: 21.
30. *Hanshu* 24B: 3a, for "elm-pod" coins set at 3 *zhu* (*c*.1.95g); cf. Peng 1994: 102.
31. As alleged in *Hanshu* 24B: 3a.
32. Thierry 2003a: 21, 27 stresses this problem.
33. Swann 1950: 378; Peng 1994: 102. See Thierry 2003a: 28 for continuity.
34. See Thierry 2003a: 28–29.
35. Peng 1994: 102.

In 175 B.C.E., the emperor Wendi introduced a 4-*zhu* coin (*sizhu banliang*) while lifting the prohibition on private coining.[36] These coins likewise bore the legend *banliang*, implying a face value three times as high as their metal value. Thus, over the first thirty years of the Han period, we observe a gradual official depreciation of coinage that presumably aimed to catch up with the de facto decline of actual coin weights. The *banliang* coin was retariffed from an original (but already largely illusory) Qin target weight of 12 *zhu* that had only occasionally been approximated by state authorities to more realistic standards of 8 *zhu* and then 4 *zhu*.[37] In analogy to similar events in the Roman Empire from the third century C.E. onward (see below, section 6.1), these reforms might best be understood as attempts to catch up with inflationary price increases caused by underweight coinage by adjusting official weight standards downward as well.

For the same year, 175 B.C.E., the *Hanshu* preserves a memorial presented to the court by Jia Yi, arguing for the reimposition of a state monopoly on coinage.[38] This text provides invaluable context for our understanding of the workings of the monetary system of the early Han period. It notes the existence of moderately severe penalties (face tattoos) for individuals who debased coins by adulterating the prescribed bronze alloy with lead and iron but points out that some measure of debasement was required to motivate private individuals to manufacture coins in the first place. As a result of the resuscitation of private coining, this offense had supposedly greatly proliferated, and private coin production had been boosted to the extent that many people abandoned other professions to make coins.[39] Yet the lack of a state monopoly was considered undesirable for another reason also: "Coins which the people are using vary from province to province, and from county to county. In some places the coins used are [so] light that to every one hundred of them must be added a certain number. In other places those used are [so] heavy that it is impossible to balance them equitably." Official weight standards were ignored, and officials could not simply impose arbitrary exchange rates that—as the author points out—they could not hope to enforce. This text, which purports to refer to actual conditions instead of simply reporting official pronouncements, flatly contradicts the notion that users habitually accepted coins at their face value: rather, the actual exchange value of money was determined by its weight—that is, its (presumed) metal value (barring adulterations)—and money users exchanged coins of different quality by adjusting their face value according to weight. This created persistent discrepancies between nominal values and prices and "real" exchange values.

---

36. *Hanshu* 24B: 3b. Thierry 2003a: 29 refers to a find of 100 coins of 2.7–3.3g in a tomb dating to 167 B.C.E. that may reflect this new standard.

37. Note that the 33 *banliang* coins dating from 179 to 118 B.C.E. catalogued by Thierry 2003a: 163–71 average 2.6g or exactly 4 *zhu*.

38. *Hanshu* 24B: 3b–5b, in Swann 1950: 233–39.

39. This is a common and no doubt largely fantastic claim of the *Hanshu*.

A modern observer might expect this problem to have been alleviated in the long term by the effect of Gresham's Law: light coins ought to have driven heavy ones out of circulation, allowing the latter to be profitably recast according to lower standards. Jia Yi, however, seems more concerned with the distress arising from the necessity to punish so many counterfeiters than with the money supply per se. In the first century B.C.E. *Yantielun*, an interlocutor links variations in coin weight to the inexperience of peasants who "have faith in the old and suspect the new" and "do not know the false from the genuine," and are consequently cheated by merchants who "barter the bad [cash] for the good; for half make an exchange for double the amount."[40] This points to serious equity issues arising from the circulation of debased coinage, especially in the context of a regionally fragmented monetary system that would eventually rely on the massive coin production levels of the first century B.C.E. to achieve some measure of empire-wide coherence and uniformity, and of a gradual expansion of money use into the agricultural sphere driven by the monetization of taxation. In this scenario, knowledgeable intermediaries were in an excellent position to manipulate money exchanges to their own advantage. Jia Yi's proposed solution to this problem was extreme (and duly rejected)—a state monopoly not merely on coin production but on the possession of copper as well. A mere monopoly on coining without cutting off the copper supply to prevent counterfeiting was considered insufficient because it would lead to a scarcity of (legal) coin that would in turn increase the benefits of (illegal) private coin production: "Upon promulgation of the law to prohibit the casting of money, then coins would surely be heavy [i.e., scarce]. When [coins are] heavy, then the [counterfeiters'] profits are excessive. Thieving counterfeiters thereupon will arise like clouds. Even execution in the market-place will not in itself be enough to prevent it." From his early Han vantage point, Jia Yi was unable or unwilling to consider alternative options, such as a huge increase in the public money supply to avoid deflation and the introduction of technical features such as precise coin standardization that would raise the cost of effective counterfeiting—or, in other words, the solutions that eventually came to be adopted from the 110s B.C.E. onward.

Greater state control over the money supply was thought to entail a variety of benefits, such as the ruler's supposed ability to adjust prices by increasing or reducing the money supply,[41] as well as increased levels of trust in this medium of exchange: "if the coinage is unified, the people will not serve two masters; if the coinage proceeds from above, then those below will not be in doubt."[42]

---

40. Gale 1931: 29; Peng 1994: 176. In this context, this point is made to argue against a state monopoly on coin-making (that allows fraudulent mint officials to manipulate the quality of coins?); but it is clear that it applies even more so to the context of private coining, despite the author's strange contention that people were "happy" in the good old days when many different coins were in circulation.

41. At *Hanshu* 24B: 5b, going back to the *Guanzi* tradition (cited above).

42. *Yantielun*, in Gale 1931: 28–29; Peng 1994: 176.

Political aspects also deserve attention. "To allow the people to make coins is to have the ruler share his authority with them: this cannot be done for long."[43] That this was more than just an abstract concern is made clear by the report that in the second quarter of the second century B.C.E., the client king of Wu "went to [local] mountains [for copper] and cast coins. His wealth rivaled that of the Son of Heaven. Later, eventually, being disobedient, he revolted."[44] This curt comment refers to the so-called "Revolt of the Seven Feudatories" in 154 B.C.E. that temporarily threatened to pit a coalition of powerful vassal states encompassing the south-eastern half of the Han Empire against the central government.[45] Yet despite the potentially subversive features of private coining, the custom continued into the reign of emperor Wudi (140–87 B.C.E.).

3.2. The Monetary Reforms of the 110s B.C.E. and the Late Western Han Period

For four years following his accession, from 140 to 136 B.C.E., Wudi promoted an even lower 3-*zhu* standard that was, for the first time, explicitly advertised on the face of the coins before returning to the 4-*zhu banliang* coin of 175 B.C.E.[46] The circumstances surrounding this measure are obscure. A much later source (dating from the thirteenth century) claims that these 3-*zhu* coins were used more than the coins cast on the restored 4-*zhu* standard,[47] an observation that is consistent with Gresham's Law, assuming uniform face value. Substantial reforms were implemented in the 110s B.C.E. in the face of massive war-related expenses. Wudi's switch to an aggressive military strategy to defeat the Xiongnu boosted governmental need for revenue.[48] In 119 B.C.E., the 4-*zhu banliang* coin was abolished and melted down and was replaced by a 3-*zhu* coin, to be cast by the central government, which lasted for between one and five years. The likely motive was further depreciation of the intrinsic value relative to the face value.[49] However, in 118 B.C.E., Wudi introduced a 5-*zhu* standard (*wuzhu*, at 3.2–3.3 g), inviting governors and vassals to cast coins (the *junguo wuzhu*) according to this new and elevated standard. What would have been their incentive to do so is an open question, especially if lighter coins continued to circulate or even be produced. Unfortunately, owing to somewhat divergent accounts in the pertinent sources, the precise chronology of some of these changes remains uncertain.

Even so, it seems very likely that one way or another, the reforms of 119/118 B.C.E. aimed to increase government revenue for warfare by manipulating the

---

43. *Hanshu* "Biography of Jia Shan," in Peng 1994: 177.
44. *Hanshu* 24B: 5b–6.a.
45. Emmerich 2002.
46. Thierry 2003a: 29.
47. Swann 1950: 379.
48. For context, see Barfield 1989: 54–59; Di Cosmo 2002: 206–52; Chang 2007: 67–134; and cf. Lelièvre 2001 for Wudi's reign in general.
49. Cf. Peng 1994: 103, n. 3.

monetary system. This interpretation is supported by the fact that at the same time the state also introduced novel forms of nonbronze token money known as "white metal" and "hide money," reportedly to reduce the state deficit.[50] The latter variety appears to have been a fairly straightforward money-spinning scheme designed to increase the government's share of the surplus appropriated by the empire's ruling class. Made of the hides of white deer kept in the emperor's park, a square-foot piece of hide was priced at 400,000 cash and handed out as gifts to nobles visiting the court who were expected to return the favor with gifts of genuine value. As such, "hide money" cannot have had any significant impact on the general monetary system. "White metal" (*baijin*) was the term used for what was—supposedly—China's earliest coined silver money. Made of an alloy of silver and tin, it came in three denominations, the round "dragon" coin weighing 8 *liang* (*c*.125g) and valued at 3,000 cash (i.e., 3,000 4-*zhu* coins), the square "horse" coin for 500 cash, and the oval "tortoise" coin for 300 cash. However, far from containing any significant amount of silver at all, round "dragon" coins that have appeared in the archaeological record are either made of bronze or of lead and tin.[51] This shows these types were conceived of as pure token issues. This is consistent with—necessarily exaggerated—reports that as a result, counterfeiting of the new coins took off on a dramatic scale: "several hundred thousand" people were supposedly condemned to death for counterfeiting, and "over a million" others were cleared or pardoned, while "the law breakers had become so numerous that the authorities had been unable to inflict punishment upon them all."[52] Be that as it may, "white metal" was consequently abolished soon after its inception, in 117, 115, or 113 B.C.E.[53] Even allowing for rampant hyperbole, this story probably contains a kernel of truth: the introduction of token coinage would have created massive incentives for counterfeiting. Nevertheless, it is perhaps more likely that the detrimental effects of "white metal," while negligible, were grossly exaggerated in the more general context of the failure of other forms of token money that had been introduced at roughly the same time, such as the greatly overvalued "red-rim" bronze coin.[54]

As was to be expected, the new 5-*zhu* coin was undermined by underweight versions "criminally counterfeited" by "the people."[55] In response, in 115 B.C.E.

---

50. Peng 1994: 105–6, 152; Thierry 2003a: 31–32.

51. Thierry 2003a: 31 references a find of 1 round coin with a dragon motif, 3 square "horse coins" and 1 oval "turtle" coin in Changxingzhen in Shaanxi in 1990. Their weights of 118.5g to 21g to 15g are very roughly proportional to their nominal value, with a silver content of a mere 6 percent, compared to 40 percent lead and 38 percent tin. Moreover, some 300 round bronzes with dragon motifs (ranging in weight from 105 to 142g) have been found in other settings. Their design may have been borrowed from Greco-Bactrian issues (ibid. 32).

52. *Hanshu* 24B: 13a; Peng 1994: 153.

53. The date is unclear: Swann 1950: 384; Peng 1994: 153, n. 5.

54. Sima Qian, the *Hanshu*'s main source for the reign of Wudi, had been castrated under this ruler, which is known to have affected his judgment of Wudi's actions and their consequences. For Sima Qian's methods, see in general Durrant 1995 and Hardy 1999.

55. *Hanshu* 24B: 14a.

the central government launched its own version of the 5-*zhu* coin, valued at 5 cash or 5 times the previous (provincial) *junguo wuzhu* and known as the "red-rim" coin (*chice wuzhu*). While the exact meaning of this term is obscure,[56] the context shows that it must refer to some kind of safety feature that was supposed to protect these token coins from counterfeiting. The authorities apparently appreciated that the creation of a token coin would greatly increase the incentives for counterfeiting and sought to prevent this from happening. Moreover, the underlying objective—to replace existing metal coins by more heavily overvalued token coins to shore up the imperial budget—can hardly be in doubt: as only these coins were to be "allowed to circulate for payment of taxes and official use" and only the government was meant to be able to manufacture them, existing full metal coins would have to be handed over to the authorities (for remelting and reissuing at a much higher face value) in exchange for the new token coins. However, "two years later the red-rim coins became worthless, the people having ingeniously [evaded] the law. Their use was of no advantage, and so they were demonetized."[57] We can only suspect that the people's "ingenious" subversion techniques either involved some way of manufacturing credible copies of these token coins or their continuing insistence on exchanging coins according to their metal value.

In the meantime, the new salt and iron monopoly of the central government set up in 117 B.C.E. may have increased revenues sufficiently to permit the state to abort its failed experimentation with token coinage.[58] In or around 113 B.C.E., coin production by the provinces and fiefs was outlawed. By 112 B.C.E., a government monopoly on coining had finally been established. Henceforth, all legal tender was to be cast by the central mint in the capital, Chang'an, or its subsidiaries, and all earlier coin was—at least in theory—demonetized. From that point onward, the monetary system stabilized, and counterfeiting reportedly fell to much lower levels. A convergence of several factors accounted for this development: the abolition of overt token coinage reduced incentives for counterfeiters; central minting curbed fraud and raised faith in the official currency; and technological advances further diminished the appeal of counterfeiting by raising production costs for criminals. Bronze molds were used to produce large numbers of identical clay molds used to cast highly uniform coins that were now endowed with raised rims and perfectly smooth rims.[59] Once large numbers of these coins had been put into circulation, poorly crafted fakes were more likely to face rejection while the production of credible copies became difficult and costly.

56. Cf. Peng 1994: 106; Thierry 2003a: 34–35.
57. *Hanshu* 24B: 14a.
58. Wagner 2001; cf. Peng 1994: 153–54.
59. Peng 1994: 117; Thierry 2003b: 56. The filing of rims commenced in 115 B.C.E.: Thierry 2003a: 36–37.

Whereas complete withdrawal of existing coins must have been hard to achieve, the central government eventually succeeded in imposing a uniform standard by raising coin output to enormous levels. Between 112 B.C.E. and the opening years of the first century C.E., over 28 billion *wuzhu* coins were said to have been produced by the state,[60] for a mean output of 230 million (or 750 tons of metal) per year or 7 to 8 coins per second.[61] It was in that period that the Han achieved monetary unification across much of their far-flung territory. Although usable data are scarce, price stability appears to have maintained for much of the first century B.C.E. This system required fiscal discipline at the central mint and was therefore sensitive to changes in revenue requirements: thanks to the return to the tribute system to appease the Xiongnu after Wudi's reign, dramatic spikes in funding demands were absent, and the temptation to devalue (and thus trigger counterfeiting and inflation) was curtailed: although mean coin weights steadily decreased during this period, they did so only very slowly and gradually.[62] Thus, despite (ideologically driven) Confucian complaints about malfeasance and incompetence at the central mint—"officials and artisans alike steal from the profits of the mint; moreover, they fail to ensure that coins are made to exact standards"[63]—this arrangement ensured stability for as long as the imperial budget was reasonably well balanced.

3.3. The Monetary Reforms of Wang Mang

This equilibrium was upset during the usurpation of Wang Mang (6/9–23 C.E.), who sought to establish his own new dynasty, Xin, to replace the Han.[64] Internal resistance and renewed external conflict increased fiscal needs while unrest interfered with revenue collection. This led to a whole series of bewilderingly complex currency reforms that were compressed into a short period from 7 to 14 C.E. All of them revolved around the introduction of new token coins at varying degrees of overvaluation.[65]

The first reform, during Wang Mang's regency in 7 C.E., created three new denominations: the *daqian*, a 12-*zhu*-weight coin valued at 50 times the face value of the Han *wuzhu* coin (i.e., overvalued 21 times), and knife-shaped coins (a deliberate revival of a pre-Han format) weighing either 16–17g and valued at 500 Han *wuzhu* (i.e., overvalued c.100 times) or 28–29g and valued at 5,000

---

60. *Hanshu* 24B: 19b.

61. These rates, albeit very high, are consistent with an annual output of 327 million coins in the Tang period and dwarfed by the scale of coin bronze production under the Northern Song: see below, section 9.1. Han bronze coins were also minted at other locations, including a site in southwestern China in close proximity to rich copper mines: Jiang 1999. For the debate over the precise location of the main mint in Chang'an, see the references gathered in *China Archaeology and Art Digest* 4.2–3, 2001: 287–88.

62. See below, section 8 and esp. fig. 4.

63. *Yantielun* 4, in van Glahn 1996: 36.

64. For Wang Mang's career in general, see Thomsen 1988.

65. For detailed discussions, see Dubs 1955: 507–18; Thomsen 1988: 88–90, 117–24; Peng 1994: 110–14, 157–59; Ehrend 2000; Thierry 2003a: 41–47.

(i.e., overvalued *c*.560 times not counting the minuscule amount of gold inlay in the inscription).[66] This array coexisted with the Han *wuzhu* coin valued at 1 cash. Private ownership of gold was outlawed, and subjects were to submit their holdings to the treasury in exchange for cash. It may be that the new large-denomination token coins were designed to absorb private gold at low cost. One wonders to what extent this regulation could be enforced; however, reports of huge stocks of gold at the end of Wang Mang's reign (see below, section 4.2) seem to suggest that the government was not entirely unsuccessful in this endeavor, although compulsion may well have been a more important factor than faith in the new token currency. In any case, we are told that the creation of token coins was immediately followed by a surge in counterfeiting.[67]

Upon his accession to the throne in 9 C.E., Wang Mang abolished the *wuzhu* coin as well as his own knife coins. The former was replaced by a 1-*zhu* coin valued at 1 cash (i.e., equivalent in face value to the now demonetized Han *wuzhu* coin and thus overvalued 5 times). The *daqian* continued to circulate. This reform removed the vastly overvalued knife coins once they had accomplished whatever they could do to draw cheap bullion into the treasury,[68] shifting instead to a low-denomination token coin of far greater potential for widespread use that consequently promised new streams of revenue.[69] In order to curtail counterfeiting, private possession of copper or charcoal was prohibited,[70] a patently impracticable injunction that the state could hardly hope to enforce. The new 1-*zhu* coins met with a predictable response: owing to the minimal intrinsic value of the new denomination, the population continued to use the Han *wuzhu* coins that must have been available in abundance.[71] In consequence, the new coins "finally did not circulate."[72] Hoarders of Han coins were to be deported to the frontiers, and large numbers of counterfeiters received harsh penalties.[73]

In 10 C.E., massive war preparations against the Xiongnu prompted a new round of monetary reforms. By creating an extraordinarily complex new system comprised of 28 different denominations of generally extremely overvalued coins, the state appears to have sought to boost revenue in the run-up to the campaign. The new system featured gold and silver ingots, tortoise shells and cowrie shells of paired value, and 16 different kinds of bronze coins (six of them round and ten spade-type). As in the previous year, the basic unit was a 1-cash

---

66. The gold inlay did little to mitigate overvaluation: even if the entire coin had been made of solid gold, it would have had to be between two and four times as heavy as it actually was to be worth its weight in Han *wuzhu* coins (cf. below, section 4.2, for the probable cash value of gold).

67. *Hanshu* 99A: 30a.

68. Cf. Peng 1994: 158.

69. Cf. Thomsen 1988: 119.

70. *Hanshu* 99B: 7b.

71. *Hanshu* 99B: 9a.

72. *Hanshu* 99B: 14b.

73. *Hanshu* 99B: 9a.

piece weighing 1 *zhu* but equivalent in value to the discontinued *wuzhu* coin. The degree of overvaluation of higher denomination pieces rose with their face value: from 1,567 percent for the 10 round cash coin weighing 3 *zhu* to a staggering 20,733 percent for the 1,000 cash spade coin weighing 24 *zhu*.[74] It is telling that the top-valued spade coin (equivalent to 1,000 cash) survives in far greater numbers than the other nine denominations in that format, either because the government put particular emphasis on the most overvalued denomination or because counterfeiters did.

The success of this reform is unclear. On the one hand, later Han sources aver that private users rejected most of these new currencies and counterfeiting was rife. This account entails a paradox: the new token coins could not have been widely rejected *and* have brought profit to counterfeiters at the same time. More importantly, the former claim is inconsistent with the large numbers of spade coins that have been recovered not merely all over eastern China but even in Korea.[75] In reality, for a few years the 1,000-cash spade coins, the 5-cash *daqian*, the 1-cash *xiaoquian*, and the Han *wuzhu* circulated side by side. (Nevertheless, the sheer amount of *wuzhu* coins put into circulation during the previous century leaves little doubt that Han currency dominated the economy throughout the short-lived Xin period.) Later on, the *Hanshu* painted a gory picture of the draconian measures that were needed to impel acceptance of the new coin issues: not only was a counterfeiter's family to be executed but five neighboring families were to be enslaved as well.[76] Travelers were supposedly required to carry spade money and were checked at roadblocks. Court officials all had to have them on them when they entered the palace. It would seem that a currency system in need of such bizarre means of compulsion was clearly doomed to failure. However, it is well known that the historiographical tradition under the restored Han was hostile to Wang Mang's regime, and we must therefore surely allow for a large degree of hyperbolic distortion.[77] Moreover, even if regulations such as these had indeed been passed, it is unclear to what extent they could ever have been enforced. Nevertheless, even if we discount the more lurid details of Ban Gu's account, the extreme levels of overvaluation inherent in the new currencies suggest a priori that these reforms had scant prospect of success. The rapid pace of change must have further undermined trust in new denominations.

Soon thereafter, Wang Mang, allegedly aware that "the common people hated [his arrangements]," temporarily suspended most of the newly introduced

74. Dubs 1955: 491.

75. Thierry 2003a: 44. Cf. also Wang 2004: 28 for the presence of (round, though never spade) issues of the Wang Mang period in eastern Central Asia.

76. *Hanshu* 99B: 15a.

77. Historians of China have commonly insisted on the veracity of the historiographical tradition regarding Wang Mang (see the survey in Thomsen 1988: 9–14), despite the fact that these accounts were composed under the restored Han dynasty—hardly *sine studio*. Thierry 2003a: 42 rightly urges skepticism.

denominations and retained only the 1-cash and 50-cash coins for circulation.[78] We can only speculate that his subjects would subsequently alienate overvalued coins to pay their taxes (at their nominal value) while government officials who received half of their salary in cash would feel the pinch when the coins they received failed to be accepted at face value in private transactions. In 14 C.E. these two token coins were abolished as well and replaced by the *huoquan* weighing 5 *zhu* and worth 1 cash (i.e., essentially the old Han *wuzhu* coin) and a fiduciary spade coin (*huobu*) of 25 *zhu* valued at 25 cash, and thus overvalued by a factor of five. The existing 1-*zhu* coin simply ceased to count as legal tender, whereas the 12-*zhu* 50-cash *daqian* was to circulate for another six years at a reduced value of 1 cash. The latter provision was particularly odd given that it undervalued the coin relative to the others in terms of metal value. As a result, both denominations were likely to be melted down and recast to manufacture counterfeit 25-cash spade coins. As the impractical ban on private ownership of copper and charcoal had already been rescinded in 13 C.E. and penalties for counterfeiting were significantly reduced in 14 C.E., illicit production of the new spade coins presumably continued for as long as this denomination was in circulation. In response, penalties were raised again, providing for the enslavement (to the mint in Chang'an) of any culprit's five neighboring families.[79]

Since we lack price data for this period, it is impossible to determine whether successive waves of token coins drove up market prices, although extremely high (albeit possibly symbolic and/or deliberately inflated) prices for rice and grains are reported for the latter years of Wang Mang's reign.[80] Enough Han coins may have been available to maintain pre-Xin price levels. In that case, 1-*zhu* coins valued at 1 cash could have been used as de facto fractional coinage, at five to a *wuzhu* coin, and larger denominations avoided. However, in as much as new coins with higher face values were in use and the government was able to enforce acceptance of fiduciary coins, their presence ought to have had an inflationary effect. Specimens of Wang Mang's currencies survived in greater numbers than Wudi's elusive "white metal" issues and cannot have been completely sidelined by money users even during their very short period of circulation. The consequences of successive demonetizations must have been particularly severe for members of the elite who had come to hold high-denomination token coins that subsequently lost their value. The resultant fallout need not have been entirely unintentional, as Wang Mang sought to accumulate precious metal stocks in exchange for token bronze coins and more generally aimed to undermine the existing aristocracy in order to benefit his own supporters.[81] Just as in the early

---

78. *Hanshu* 24B: 21b. This statement is particularly hard to reconcile with the survival of numerous spade-coins.

79. *Hanshu* 24B: 25b.

80. Peng 1994: 159.

81. Cf. Thomsen 1988: 90, 105–8.

110s B.C.E., experimentation with token coins had failed to produce lasting benefits for the treasury and had met with widespread rejection in the general population and increased counterfeiting. At the same time, short-term financial and political gains may indeed have accrued to the new regime. Even so, long-term monetary stability was predicated on a return to the far more "metallistic" coinage system of the late Western Han.

3.4. Conditions under the Eastern Han

After 25 C.E., the restorer of the Han Dynasty, Liu Xiu, continued to use the 5-*zhu huoquan* that was functionally equivalent to the former Han *wuzhu* denomination.[82] Production of *wuzhu* coins finally resumed in 40 C.E. under the control of the superintendent of agriculture.[83] No output figures are available for the Eastern Han period. A return to low grain prices by the mid-first century C.E. signals monetary stability.[84] In the second century C.E., intense warfare against the western Qiang created extraordinary military expenses: 14 years of campaigning in the early second century C.E. absorbed 24 billion cash, almost equivalent to total cash output during the last 120 years of the Western Han, followed by another 8 billion from 140 to 145 C.E. and 4.4 billion in the late 160s C.E.[85] Once again, military needs prompted calls for debasement via "large coins," but on this occasion, in the reign of Huandi (147–168 C.E.), the government resisted such schemes.[86] Instead, the authorities developed the so-called "reduced-hundred" system based on units of 100 cash that entailed the use of fewer than 100 actual coins.[87] This accounting fudge became more common in later periods of Chinese history.[88] Local issues eventually reappeared under emperor Lingdi (168–189 C.E.). This process, together with the growing erosion of central state power, precipitated significant weight loss.[89]

3.5. Epilogue: Later Monetary Developments

Although the *wuzhu* tradition was reportedly maintained in the northern successor state of Wei (221–280 C.E.) after the collapse of the unified empire, no actual specimens have been safely identified.[90] Conversely, the other two kingdoms,

---

82. This coin type is common in finds up to the mid-first century C.E.: Thierry 2003a: 44. A sample of 53 of these coins (ibid. 194–98) averages 2.63g, light by Western Han standards but fairly close to the moderately underweight Eastern Han *wuzhu* of c.2.8–2.9g: see below, table 1.
83. Thierry 2003a: 49–54.
84. Peng 1994: 160.
85. Peng 1994: 161. For context, see de Crespigny 1984: 76–172.
86. *Hou Hanshu* 87 in Peng 1994: 179; cf. 161, n. 9.
87. Peng 1994: 161 cites a contract from 184 C.E. referring to "a thousand cash lacking fifty."
88. Von Glahn 1996: 52, 70.
89. Thierry 2003a: 62–64. During the terminal phase of the Han Dynasty, the central government reportedly melted down *wuzhu* coins and recast them into small cash coins of unknown face value. However, circulation was probably limited to the Luoyang area: Peng 1994: 162–64. Small cash was abolished in 208 C.E.
90. Thierry 2003a: 65.

Han-Shu and Wu, experienced a rapid deterioration of their respective monetary systems. In 236 C.E., Wu issued *daquan* valued at 500 cash (*daquan wubai*), followed by a 1,000-cash issue (*daquan dangqian*) two years later. Even more overvalued token coins of 2,000 cash and 5,000 cash followed in the 240s C.E.[91] We can only conjecture that accelerating inflation and unmet fiscal demands lay behind this increase in face value. In 246 C.E., the state suspended coin production altogether and demonetized the top-valued denominations.[92] These developments once again illustrate the unfeasibility of a pure token coinage. According to textual sources, in the territory of the later Han-Shu state, token coins valued at 100 cash were cast as early as 214 C.E. However, it has proven difficult to relate surviving specimens to this tradition, although it has been claimed that the weight of regional issues gradually declined.[93] Scarcity of new coin characterized the Jin period (280–317 CE): hoards of the period predominantly contain Han coins supplemented by Xin and Han-Shu issues.[94] Silk and other textiles as well as grain served as the primary media of exchange and stores of value during the fourth and fifth centuries C.E., while Han *wuzhu* continued to circulate. Occasional experimentation with token coinage failed as usual.[95] Stable coinage returned only temporarily under the early Tang dynasty with the introduction of the *kaiyuan tongbao* in 621 C.E. At 10 coins per (Tang) *liang* (41g), it restored the Han tradition of issues that were based on a clearly defined weight standard. However, deprecatory pressures soon resumed: in 732 C.E., a law had to reimpose the original 4.1g standard in the face of intervening weight loss. For the first time, the coin alloy was officially set at a fixed configuration with an 83.5 percent copper component (see below, section 8). In the following centuries, the weight and composition of coin issues continued to vary depending on the state of public finances and copper production.[96]

4. MONETARY USES OF GOLD AND SILVER IN ANCIENT CHINA

4.1. Preimperial Practices

All known tool coins and round coins were made of copper, bronze, or occasionally iron. Given the prevalence of precious metal coins in all other monetary systems of the ancient world, from Celtic Britain to Gupta India, this raises questions about the uses of gold and silver within the Chinese sphere of exchange.

91. Thierry 2003a: 69. Specimens have been found at various locations.
92. Peng 1994: 173.
93. Thierry 2003: 65–66. Decline: Peng 1994: 171–73.
94. Thierry 2003a: 71–73.
95. Thierry 2003a: 92–93 (media), 94 (tokens).
96. See Wang *et al.*, eds. 2005 for a broad overview.

In traditions about the past, gold occupies a prominent position. Sima Qian lumps together "tortoise and cowrie shells, gold and bronze coin, knife-shaped and spade-shaped money" as the means of exchange that were created as commerce developed.[97] The same line-up is featured in a debate set in 81 B.C.E. where primordial barter arrangements are considered to have been replaced by the use of "tortoise and cowrie shells, gold, and bronze coins as the media of exchange."[98] The *Guanzi* establishes a hierarchy of different types of money. Thus, the Zhou kings were thought to have "made pearls and jade their superior currency and gold their second currency, while knife-shaped and spade-shaped bronzes were relegated to the position of inferior currencies."[99] While pearls and jade never served as money per se, they were certainly exchanged in the top echelons of society within an elite transactional order that excluded commoners (see below, section 7.3). It appears that both pearls and jade could even be imagined to be imbued with quasi-magical properties.[100] Gold, by contrast, was considered to be more widely available and used: "The five grains are the Sovereigns of Destiny to the people. Gold and knife-shaped specie serve as their common currency."[101] In numerous other passages, "gold and knife-shaped and spade-shaped specie" are referred to as "the common currency of the people."[102] In some contexts, gold could even be singled out as the anchor of the whole monetary system: "Gold is the standard of expenditures. The prince who discerns the fundamental laws of gold will understand the dangers of parsimony and prodigality."[103] The context suggests that it was rulers (rather than ordinary money users) who appear to have viewed gold as the key standard for expenditures and that the value of gold fluctuated according to the ratio of the gold supply to the supply of (other) commodities,[104] one of several invocations of the quantity theory of money in the *Guanzi* tradition and beyond.[105]

In the preimperial period, how were precious metals used in actual transactions? The "Treatise on Food and Money" in the *Hanshu* imagines that in the early Zhou period the state did not only issue round coins on the *zhu* standard—which is clearly wrong—but also circulated "actual gold" in units of one Zhou square inch (c.2.3 cm²) and 1 *jin* (c.250g).[106] In this scenario, gold served as "the

97. *Shiji* 30: 1442.
98. *Yantielun* in von Glahn 1996: 27.
99. *Guanzi* 77 "Dishu," 3.84.
100. Peng 1994: 69.
101. *Guanzi* 73 "Guoxu," 3: 66.
102. Von Glahn 1996: 31.
103. *Guanzi* 4 "Shengma," 1.18.
104. Von Glahn 1996: 32.
105. Von Glahn 1996: 33; see esp. *Guanzi* 74 "Shanguogi," 3.71; also *Guanzi* 76 "Shanzhishu," 3.81–82; plus the references in von Glahn 1996: 267, n. 44. On monetary thinking in *Guanzi*, see also Hu 1988: 131–38.
106. *Hanshu* 24B: 1a; Swann 1950: 220–21. It is difficult to determine the weight of the *jin* (or of its constituent unit, the *zhu*) with precision: modern scholarship variously reckons with a *zhu* of 0.64–0.66g and a *jin* of 244–256g. Compare Wang 2005: 287–91 for metrological analysis based on Chu, Qin, and Han weights and bullion. In the following, I use *c.*250g as a rough approximation of 1 *jin*.

most precious medium of exchange" while "the most convenient one was the knife-money, [and] the one which flowed [like water from a spring] was coins."[107] While there is currently no sign of these tiny gold ingots in the archaeological record,[108] the fact that the other denominations did in fact circulate in later periods raises the possibility that at least as far as *jin*-sized gold is concerned, this claim reflects conditions at a later stage, most likely in the Han period.[109]

Gilded cowries and imitation cowries made entirely of gold have been unearthed at early sites.[110] Given the monetary use of bronze cowries in the Zhou period (see above, section 2), we may wonder if these objects also served a monetary purpose, but nothing further is known. In addition, excavations have repeatedly yielded spade-shaped silver bars from as early as the Spring and Autumn Period.[111] Their function is unknown and they do not appear in the textual tradition.

Textual records pertaining to the Warring States period frequently mention certain numbers of *jin*, a term that can mean "gold" but also refers to other metals, and likewise to the gold value of other—that is, bronze—denominations.[112] References to *huangjin*, or "yellow gold," invite a literal reading as units of actual gold,[113] but even in those cases the context sometimes suggests that this need not necessarily have been the intended meaning (see below). The value of a *jin* of gold relative to bronze coins or other commodities would fluctuate: according to the *Guanzi*, if grain prices stood at a certain level, the price of (1) *jin* was 4,000 (cash).[114]

Gold use is commonly situated in elite settings: "With but 40 *yi* [*c*.12.5kg] of gold, six pairs of white jade pendants, I dare not face Your Grace."[115] Rulers and other elite members could be portrayed as handing out gold.[116] The *yi* (*c*.310g) often occurs as a unit of gold. Peng lists a large number of references, often associated with regal actions on an appropriately grand scale: the most commonly mentioned amounts are 1,000 *jin* or *yi* of gold (i.e., *c*.250–310kg) (16 times) and 100 *jin* or *yi* (i.e., *c*.25–31kg) (12 times); the highest ones 11,000 *jin* (i.e., *c*.2.75 tons) (once) and 10,000 *jin* or *yi* (i.e., *c*.2.5–3.1 tons) (4 times); tallies below 100 units are rare.[117]

107. *Hanshu* 24B: 1a.

108. Thierry 2001b: 131.

109. The imaginary Zhou gold squares may have been derived from the gold squares produced in Chu: see below.

110. Peng 1994: 69.

111. Yao and Wang 2003: 22. However, 18 silver spades found in a village in Henan province may not date from the preimperial period at all, as they were mixed with items from the Warring States and early Han periods: Peng 2000: 169–70.

112. Peng 1994: 70, and see below.

113. Swann 1950: 220, n. 362.

114. Peng 1994: 70. See below, section 4.2.

115. *Dialogues of the States*, "Dialogues of Jin" 2, in Peng 1994: 71, n. 16.

116. References in Peng 1994: 70–71, nn. 15, 17–18.

117. Peng 1994: 71–72, n. 21.

Official salaries were usually paid in foodstuffs, whereas gold was reserved for special gifts and rewards.[118] If the literary tradition is to be trusted, governmental use of bronze cash appears to have been correspondingly rare: taxes were due (mostly) in grain and cloth and labor services rather than coin, and elite documents rarely mention coin, except with reference to merchants and small payments.[119] We might speculate that in this context, (unminted) gold would stand out as a high-value prestige good reserved for large-scale state business, representing a socially elevated transactional sphere that may have been poorly integrated with the bronze currency system of the commoner population (see further below, section 7.3). This notion, however, is hard to reconcile with conventional assertions that gold as well as the various categories of bronze coins served as the "common currencies" of "the people" (see above). Unfortunately, evidence for the use of gold in nonelite contexts appears to be very rare in the textual record. One decidedly nonelite story is related in the *Liezi*: "Formerly there was a man of Qi who desired gold. One bright morning, he donned his clothes and hat and went to the market, where he encountered a gold-seller's booth, from which he snatched some gold and fled. The clerk stopped him and asked: 'Why did you snatch the gold with people standing all around?' The man replied: 'When I took the gold, I did not see the people, I only saw the gold.'"[120] That gold would have been available for sale is clear from its widespread use in the production of jewelry and ornaments.[121] However, its monetary function at subelite levels remains unclear.

Information pertinent to this issue is limited to the southern state of Chu that provides the main exception to the bronze-based currency systems of the preimperial period.[122] The local rivers were an important source of gold, and Chu enjoyed a reputation as a gold-rich region.[123] All gold bullion finds from the Warring States period originate from the territory of this state.[124] Gold was cast in large flat sheets stamped with a number of (ideally) rectangular seal marks; these rectangles could be broken off for separate use. Each rectangle bore an incised inscription with the term *yuan* (the name of the money) and the name of the current capital city of Chu (first Ying, then Cheng).[125] Individual sheets could consist of 16, 20, or

---

118. Peng 1994: 87.

119. Peng 1994. See however Peng 2000: 171–72 for the use of coins as tax payments alongside grain and cloth. Two passages in *Guanzi* merely recommended that state officials be paid in cash rather than in kind (ibid. 171). For evidence suggestive of coin among peasants, see ibid. 173–75.

120. *Liezi*, "On tallies" 8, in Peng 1994: 70, n. 14.

121. Cf. Andersson 1935.

122. Thierry 1997: 146–52; 2003b: 49–50. For the gold plates, see Ivotchkina 1993; Lu and Wu 1997; Peng 2000: 209–12. On Chu in general, cf. Blakeley 1985–87; Lawton 1991; Cook and Major 1999. For bronze plates, cf. Thierry 1997: 152–57.

123. References in Peng 1994: 72–73, nn. 23–25, and Peng 2000: 211–12. Cf. also Bunker 1993: 47 for gold finds in the adjacent southwestern kingdom of Dian.

124. Peng 2000: 209. Ran 1997 concludes that gold and silver objects were relatively rare in the pre-Han period and mostly concentrated in Chu. For early finds of gold objects, see Bunker 1993: 29–35.

125. Peng 1994: 73–74; Thierry 1997: 148; 2003b: 50. Issues commenced in the fifth century B.C.E.

24 rectangles. Many surviving units are far from square or rectangular: corners or larger bits are missing, sometimes fragmented squares are joined together, and so forth. As a consequence, individual units must always have been weighed to determine their actual exchange value.[126] Peng lists the weights of 36 items, ranging from 4 incomplete squares weighing 66 grams to fragments as light as 4 grams. Twelve reasonably complete and regular squares range from 10 to 20 grams, with a mean of 15 grams. Individual squares in another sample of 35 items weigh between 12 and 17 grams.[127] This puts them somewhat above the usual weight of western gold coins, equivalent to 1.2–2.5 Augustan *aurei* or 2.2–4.5 Constantinian *solidi*, rendering them functionally equivalent to large gold coins.

The volume of gold rectangles in circulation is necessarily unknown. Even so, it is probably significant that specimens have been found across the Chu territory except in the south and mostly in hoards (reflecting their monetary function) rather than tombs. Moreover, more than 100 excavated Chu tombs contain scales and exceptionally tiny weights that appear to have been designed for the weighing of gold.[128] All this suggests that this type of currency was not particularly rare: an observer from the Song period reports that "very many people" had found specimens in the soil and in rivers.[129] For these reasons, and given their moderate weight, these units may well have performed genuine monetary functions even beyond narrow elite circles.

Was this type of gold money an indigenous development? There are no known parallels in other parts of China, but similar items were also in use farther south, all the way to Vietnam. The closest parallel is provided by the square silver plates of northwestern India in the fourth century B.C.E., which likewise bore seal marks and could be broken into pieces.[130] We would need to know more about the relative chronology of the Indian and Chu coinages to assess the probability of eastward diffusion. Chu gold plates continued to be hoarded (though not necessarily circulated) until the Eastern Han period.[131] A possible parallel to Chu gold money may conceivably be provided by gold ornaments with inscribed weights found at Yanxiadu, the capital of the northeastern Yan state from 311 to 222 B.C.E.[132] However, the monetary properties of these items remain unknown.

4.2. Gold and Silver in the Qin-Han Period

The first Qin emperor imposed a bimetallic system of gold and copper: "Actual gold which weighed a *yi* [20 *liang*, or *c*.310 g] was given the name of 'currency

126. Peng 1994: 73–74.
127. Peng 1994: 73–74, n. 27. This weight range centers on the *liang* of 15.26 g: see below, n. 134. Peng 2000: 169 refers to a find of 170 specimens, but no weights are given. Cf. also Thierry 1997: 147.
128. Thierry 1997: 149–51 with map 10.
129. Peng 1994: 73, n. 26.
130. Göbl 1978: 111; cf. Peng 1994: 75.
131. Peng 2000: 210.
132. Bunker 1993: 45–46.

of the first class,' and while the copper coins were the same as the Zhou cash on the reverse surface, their inscription read *banliang*, and their weight accorded with the legend."[133] However, while gold may have been measured in *yi*, there is currently no evidence of *yi*-sized standardized gold ingots or other forms of money: two gold ingots found in Shaanxi bear the legend "*yi*" but weigh 253.5 and 260 grams, broadly equivalent to the subsequent Han gold unit of 1 *jin* or *c*.250 grams.[134] The following observations that "pearls, jade, tortoise [shell], cowries, silver, and tin were used in or for vessels or ornaments, but they were not [used as] money," and that "each of them according to demand and supply fluctuated [in price] from time to time, never being [of] constant [monetary value],"[135] might be taken to suggest that gold and copper did in fact possess fixed monetary value, which would imply that the two metals were to be exchanged at a fixed ratio as well. This is consistent with the fact that the Qin regulations on the Shuihudi bamboo strips from the mid-third century B.C.E. stipulate that "if one pays and receives coins in terms of gold or cloth money, he must follow the official rates."[136] It is unknown if this fixed rate was obeyed, if it remained stable over time, and especially if it survived into the Han period.

Under the Han, the unit of gold measurement was the *jin* (16 *liang* or *c*.250 g). Finds from that period include rounded gold biscuits as well as the so-called "horse-hoof" and "deer-hoof" pieces, the latter types having been introduced in the reign of emperor Wudi.[137] Recent surveys list 29 sites in 14 provinces across the country where a total of 1,047 Han gold ingots were found.[138] The two largest known hoards consist of 197 Han gold pieces discovered alongside 170 Chu gold plates and 18 silver spades at Gucheng village in Henan province in 1974 and of 219 Han pieces with a total weight of 54 kilograms that were unearthed in the Chang'an area in 1999.[139] Only some of the Han gold ingots bore markings specifying their weight. A recent analysis of 54 unmarked pieces yields an average weight of 251.2 grams, compared to a mean of 247.3 grams in the Chang'an sample of 219 (as yet unpublished) pieces.[140] These data strongly indicate that unmarked gold pieces were expected to conform to a uniform weight standard of 1 *jin*. This impression is reinforced by the fact that most unmarked pieces did not stray far from this target (fig. 7.1).

---

133. *Hanshu* 24B: 3a.
134. Li 1997: 52. Wang 2005: 274 refers to three different pre-Han gold pieces found at the Qin capital of Xianyang with weights from 249 to 265 grams. Hou 1996 argues that *yi* and *liang* had already been used as units of gold measurement in Chu. See also Wang 2005: 287–88, 294. If Qin had adopted Chu gold standards, this would further confirm Chu's standing as the principal gold user in this period (see above, section 4.1).
135. *Hanshu* 24B: 3a.
136. Peng 2000: 208.
137. For discussions of the different shapes, see Li 1997: 52–53 and Wang 2005: 267.
138. Li 1997 (26 sites) and Wang 2005: 270–71 (3 more recent sites). Of them, 344 have been identified as "horse-hoof" and 90 as "deer-hoof" pieces, but not all the reports provide detailed classification. Even so, it is clear that biscuits dominate the record (Li 1997: 53).
139. Zhu 1992: 168; Peng 2000: 169; Wang 2005: 270.
140. Wang 2005: 290–91, table 6. (I have excluded item no.43, which does in fact bear markings.)

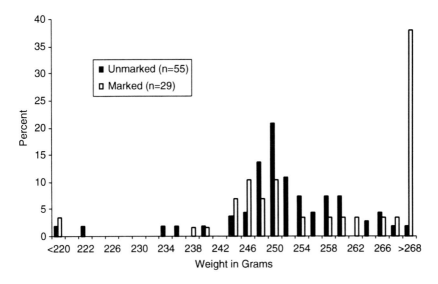

FIGURE 7.1. *Weight distribution of marked and unmarked Han gold biscuits*
Source: Wang 2005.

By contrast, marked pieces did not fall into a similarly narrow range: only one-third of a smaller sample of 29 marked items range from 244 to 250 grams, whereas almost half of them exceed 1 *jin* by anywhere from 6 to 85 percent.[141] This suggests that markings were applied primarily in order to specify deviations from an otherwise normative weight standard. The notion of a *jin*-based weight standard is likewise consistent with the observed weight of a number of fractional pieces. Individual quarter pieces have weighed in at 60.9 grams (twice), 62 grams, 63.66 grams (the mean for 9 pieces), and 64.6 grams, thereby indicating a mean target weight of 252.7 grams for the underlying complete "deer-hoof" disks.[142] Moreover, 29 small gold pieces found in the royal tomb at Mancheng average 15.1 grams or approximately one Han ounce (*liang*).[143] Fineness was consistently high: an analysis of more than 200 Han "deer-" and "horse-hoof" gold pieces found that most of them fell in a range from 97 to 99 percent purity, with only a few outliers as low as 77 percent.[144]

The question of how the value of these objects was expressed in terms of the dominant bronze currency is very difficult to answer. In 9 C.E., Wang Mang valued 1 *jin* of gold at 10,000 cash while 1 *liu* (*c.*125g) of particularly pure silver

141. Wang 2005: 282–83, table 3. The heaviest reported item weighed 462g.
142. Zhu 1992: 168–71. Cf. also Peng 1994: 144, n. 68.
143. Zhu 1992: 162–63 (Tomb II). Forty gold biscuits from Tomb I average 18g.
144. Wang 2005: 273, summarizing Zhang 1985.

was valued at 1,580 cash and a *liu* of all other kinds of silver was deemed worth 1,000 cash.[145] This passage raises several serious problems. First of all, it is not clear how these state-imposed ratios compared to actual market rates. Secondly, the implied gold/silver ratios of 5 to 1 for ordinary silver and $3^1/_6$ to 1 for high-grade silver appear very low by comparative standards.[146] And thirdly, we cannot even be sure what kind of cash is referred to. The common assumption that this passage somehow supports the notion of an exchange rate of 10,000 *wuzhu* coins for 1 *jin* of gold cannot readily be reconciled with the fact that Wang Mang's official valuation of gold and silver coincided with the demonetization of the Han *wuzhu* and its replacement by a 1-*zhu* coin valued at 1 cash in the same year.[147] The latter translates to an extraordinarily low gold/bronze ratio of 64 to 1 and silver/bronze ratios of 5–8 to 1, which mark out the new bronze issues as pure token coins.[148]

Contrary to the tenor of modern scholarship, there is nothing to suggest that 1 *jin* of gold was either officially or de facto valued at 10,000 (*wuzhu*) cash at any time during the Han period.[149] In fact, there is no evidence to support the assumption that there was an officially determined exchange rate at all.[150] The

145. *Hanshu* 24B: 20b.

146. Under the Northern Song, the gold/silver ratio stood at 6.25 to 1, similar to the putative 5 to 1 ratio 1,000 years earlier, but rose considerably in the course of the second millennium: to (perhaps) 8 to 1 around 1100; 13 to 1 by 1134, and 12–13 to 1 around 1200; then dropped back down to *c*.10 to 1 in the first half of the fourteenth century, followed by a reduction to between 4 and 6 (but mostly 5) to 1 in the late fourteenth and the first half of the fifteenth centuries; and gradually trended from about 7 to 1 in the late fifteenth century to about 13–14 to 1 in the late seventeenth century. See von Glahn 1996: 61. Chinese rates differ consistently from exchange rates in ancient western Eurasia: for gold/silver, 8–12 to 1 in late third century B.C.E. Rome; 9.6–11.7 to 1 *c*.80 B.C.E.; 8.6 to 1 in 50 B.C.E.; 11.5 to 1 in the 40s B.C.E.; and 11.75 to 1 under Augustus. The general impression that gold was cheaper and/or silver dearer in the East than in the West is corroborated by gold/silver ratios of 8.5 to 1 in Umayyad and early Abbasid Iraq and Syria, 6 to 1 in early thirteenth-century Iraq, and 6 to 1 in Abbayyid Egypt (Ashtor 1976: 84, 257, 292), as well as 5–6 to 1 in medieval India and Malaya (Peng 1994: 208, 282). The relatively low value of gold in the early medieval Near East was a function of large imports from Nubia and especially the Senegal/Niger region, and its price soared as these inflows abated: Ashtor 1976: 80–81. Gold/silver ratios rose to 12 to 1 in late thirteenth-century Iraq and 13.4 to 1 in early Mamluk Egypt (ibid. 257, 292). This shows that the relative availability of bullion was the crucial variable.

147. Modern observers tend to accept the valuation of 1 *jin* of gold at 10,000 cash as a customary and thus more generally "representative" rate (e.g., Swann 1950: 253, n. 453; Dubs 1955: 510; Peng 1994: passim, but cf. 143, where he denies the existence of a stable exchange rate).

148. Rightly emphasized by Li 1997: 55. For the relative valuation of gold and bronze, see below, section 8.

149. Thus Peng 1994: 143 and Li 1997: 55. For a survey of documentary evidence from the Juyan garrison site, see Wang 2004: 52, table 8. The valuation of 4 *liang* of gold at 2,500 cash for the purpose of payment of a fine recorded on a bamboo strip from Juyan reflects a ratio of 10,000 cash per 1 *jin* but almost certainly dates from the Wang Mang period itself: Gansu sheng, etc., 1990: 337 (EPT 57:1; cf. the reign year in EPT 57:8). Two further texts report fines of 4 *liang* each (but without cash conversions) and two others refer to fines of 2,500 and 5,000 cash, respectively (but without corresponding gold valuations). In this context, the latter two references (Xie, Li, and Shu 1987: 379 (231: 115A, B) imply a conversion rate of 10,000 cash per *jin* but likewise appear to date from the Wang Mang period (cf. 231: 106). A reference to 2 *liang* valued at "more than 1,000 cash" (Xie, Li, and Shu 1987: 366 (227: 13) dates from 44 B.C.E. but is too unspecific to be of much help.

150. I am unable to follow Swann's reasoning that the monetary reform of 14 C.E. that equated 5 *zhu* of bronze with 1 unit of cash (i.e., restoring the previous Han standard) "fixes, it seems [sic], the Han cash value of actual gold, of the weight of 244 g. or 7.84 oz. troy to have been 10,000 coins of the legal copper coins in use at the time of exchange" (Swann 1950: 351, n. 726): there is nothing in the text to support this interpretation. Instead, the

available sources fail to create a coherent picture. A valuation of 1 *jin* at 4,000 (cash) in the Warring States period may envision cash in the form of Qi knives (weighing 40–50 g) or small spades of much lower weight and cannot be applied to the Han currency. At first sight, several other textual references might be taken to suggest that a ratio of 1 to 10,000 approximates the right order of magnitude. The *Jiuzhang suanshu*, a mathematical exercise from the Western Han period, on one occasion puts the value of 1 *jin* of gold at 6,250 cash but in another problem equates 1 *jin* with 9,800 cash.[151] In other examples, the same text prices heads of cattle at 1.619 *liang* of gold and at 1,200 and 1,818 cash; if the first amount were priced at 10,000 cash per *jin* or 625 cash per *liang*, it would equal 1,012 cash and therefore resemble the other two. The same is true for sheep prices, variously given as 0.952 *liang* (or 595 cash at 10,000 cash per *jin*) and from 150 to 500 cash.[152] At the same time, however, these prices appear generally very low by contemporary standards: bamboo strips from the northern frontier dating from the first centuries B.C.E. and C.E. convey the impression that an ox cost 2,500–3,500 cash and a sheep 900–1,000 cash.[153] Thus, we have to allow for the possibility that the *Jiuzhang suanshu* may preserve price levels of an earlier period when heavier bronze coin enjoyed greater purchasing power—in relation to livestock as well as bullion. This reading is consistent with the fact that four bamboo strips from the frontier suggest a much higher average gold price of about 20,900 cash per *jin*.[154] The discrepancy between this ratio and the much lower official ratio of 9 C.E. may arguably have been caused by Wang Mang's policy of promoting overvalued token coinage and discouraging private ownership of bullion through nominal depreciation.[155] Notwithstanding the introduction of normed gold pieces under emperor Wudi, there can be no doubt that gold was always valued according to

---

preceding text vaguely alludes to government orders "concerning [the use of] gold, silver, tortoise [shell], and cowries as media of exchange, to some extent increasing and decreasing former values." This passage seems to support the view that the exchange ratios imposed in 9 C.E. were to some extent arbitrary and may not in fact coincide with customary market rates. It is true that according to the *Hanshu* 99A: 10a, court officials claimed in 3 C.E. that according to "ancient practices, an empress was betrothed [with a gift of] 20,000 *jin* of actual gold, which would be 200 million cash" (Dubs 1955: 162). However, several other references to this custom merely mention 20,000 *jin* of gold: Dubs 1955: 162, n. 9.9). This suggests that Ban Gu's aside may have been prompted by Wang Mang's subsequent gold tariffing.

151. *Jiuzhang suanshu* 6.15 and 7.5 in Vogel 1968: 63 and 72. The lower figure might conceivably refer to higher pre-*wuzhu* weight standards: at 12 *zhu* per cash, the gold/copper ratio would be 200 to 1; at 8 *zhu*, 134 to 1, i.e., essentially the same as the 131 to 1 ratio for 5-*zhu* cash.

152. *Jiuzhang suanshu* 8.7 in Vogel 1968: 84 (gold prices); 8.8, 8.11 (cattle) and 7.6, 8.8, 8.17 (sheep).

153. Wang 2004: 63, table 17. Hsu 1980: 76 uses a valuation of 3,000 cash for an ox for his hypothetical model of a family farm in central Han China.

154. Xie, Li, and Zhu 1987: 604 (504: 13, 81 B.C.E.: 3.5 *liang* = 4,714 cash), 605 (505: 20, 81 B.C.E.: 58 *liang* = 79,714 cash), 609 (506: 11, 12 B.C.E.: 8 *liang* = 10,776 cash), 611 (506: 27, 12 B.C.E.: 1 *liang* = 1,327 cash, although in this case this equation is merely a conjecture). The overall mean is 1,369.23 per *liang* (and not 1,347 as stated by Li 1997: 56, which is however the precise valuation in two of these slips), equivalent to 21,908 per *jin*. None of these texts specifically mention "gold" but only that substance was sufficiently valuable to correspond to these cash amounts: see also Li 1997: 56.

155. See above, section 3.3.

its weight and not per unit.[156] Under these circumstances, an official gold price was not required to sustain that metal's monetary function: I am inclined to agree with Li Zude's assessment that this metal was valued like any other commodity and that its price floated in response to supply and demand.[157]

Our understanding of the extent of gold use in the Han period suffers from persistent uncertainties regarding the actual meaning of the term *jin* in contemporaneous sources. *Jin* was repeatedly employed to denote wealth without necessarily referring to gold per se.[158] While some reports of imperial largesse mention *jin*, others speak of "yellow" *jin*, and although it is tempting to interpret the latter as references to transfers of certain amounts of actual bullion (rather than cash of equivalent value), it is troubling that in parallel accounts of the same gifts in the *Shiji* and the *Hanshu*, one source sometimes refers to *jin* while the other specifies "yellow" *jin*. On a maximalist reading, these terms may have been considered interchangeable because—at least in certain contexts—both of them were thought to describe actual gold.[159] Conversely, a minimalist reading might suggest that cash value mattered more than the actual medium of exchange.[160] As it is, certainty is only possible in those cases where amounts of gold and cash are mentioned side by side as elements of the same transaction: for example, in 76 B.C.E., a vassal king was granted 200 *jin* of "yellow metal" and 20 million in coin.[161]

Transfers of *jin*—whether "yellow" or not—that may or may not refer to actual gold are frequently reported in elite contexts: foremost, for royal gifts to high-ranking recipients.[162] Gold's cachet may also be reflected in the marking "*shang*" ("higher") that repeatedly appears on gold biscuits.[163] Government reserves partly consisted of gold (and silver), and gold was used in international transactions beyond the Han currency zone. Golden or gilded plaques with Chinese characters denoting their weight that have been excavated in Xiongnu territory may have been manufactured for use in trade with the northern nomads or as part of tribute payments.[164] A special tax, the "wine-toast for gold," was

156. Weight variation even among unmarked "deer-" and "horse-hoof" pieces was too large to allow their valuation "al marco": cf. above, fig. 1.

157. Li 1997: 56.

158. Peng 1994: 134, n. 1.

159. However, a maximalist reading needs to confront the problem of how the court acquired large quantities of actual gold to give away, given that we do not know of any taxes that were paid in gold except for the relatively small-scale "wine toast" tax (see below) and, perhaps, some fines (see above, n. 149). Cf. already Li 1997: 58.

160. *Hanshu* 99A: 9b, stating that when Wang Mang rejected 20,000 *jin* of gold (valued at 200 million cash) he was given 40 million cash instead does not mean, *contra* Peng 1994: 136, that "the term yellow metal is explicitly used here, but actual payment was made in copper cash," since the two transactions are not the same.

161. *Hanshu* 7: 9b.

162. Peng 1994: 135–38; Wang 2005: 294–95. Emperor Wudi observed that gold was "for bestowing favors on the various dukes and kings." Li 1997: 59 notes that in Han literary texts, amounts of gold are commonly stated in a vague fashion, with a strong preference for stereotypical round numbers (such as 10, 100, 1,000 etc).

163. Thus Li 1997: 54.

164. Bunker 1993: 45, 47.

imposed on aristocrats (see below). More mundanely, fines and bribes were often expressed (though not necessarily paid) in gold.[165]

Peng tallies up all references to imperial grants of *jin* recorded in the *Hanshu* to arrive at a grand total of (at least) 900,000 *jin*, 90 percent of them disbursed in the long reign of Wudi.[166] This is consistent with the report that under this ruler, gold was cast in deer- and horse-hoof shapes and distributed "among the vassal kings as grants to them."[167] Unfortunately, it remains unclear how many of these transfers actually entailed gold: only 30 percent of all references explicitly mention "yellow" *jin*,[168] and as noted above, even these are not above suspicion. In theory, if all these payments had been made in gold, their cumulative weight would have amounted to 225 tons. Nevertheless, we need to allow for the possibility of a (much?) smaller actual total.

Unequivocal evidence for large bullion holdings is provided for the imperial treasury. In 23 C.E., the inner apartments of Wang Mang's Weiyang palace were said to contain sixty chests, each of which was filled with 10,000 *jin* of gold, whereas other offices housed "several" additional chests.[169] The veracity of this claim is hard to determine. Dubs, while conceding that "sixty" is a suspiciously round number and that some chests may not have been completely full, defends the credibility of this passage.[170] Even discounting the contents of the "several' additional chests, 600,000 *jin* of gold amount to 150 tons, equivalent to 6 billion cash according to the conventional conversion ratio of this period and perhaps to twice that amount in market prices (see above). In specie, this quantity resembles total American gold exports to Spain from 1503 to 1660, of 180 tons,[171] and (in weight) equals 19 million Augustan *aurei* worth 1.9 billion sesterces, more than the annual Roman imperial budget. It closely resembles the tally for the public gold reserve of the Eastern Roman Empire in 527 C.E., of 129 tons of (actual?) gold.[172] In cash terms, this amount is not very different from the 8.3 billion in cash reserves reportedly held by the Han treasury in the 40s/30s B.C.E.[173] At the same time, it compares very favorably with the 20–30,000 *jin* of

---

165. References in Peng 1994: 134, nn. 2–6. For fines in the Juyan documents, see above, n. 149.

166. Peng 1994: 135–36. According to the *Shiji*, the bulk of this expenditure was associated with two campaigns in Wudi's reign in 123 and 119 B.C.E.: Qi 1999b: 81.

167. *Hanshu* 6: 35b.

168. Peng 1994: 136.

169. *Hanshu* 99C: 25a–b, with Dubs 1942.

170. Dubs 1942: 36, n. 2. I should add that due to the high specific weight of gold, 10,000 *jin* or 2.5 tons of this metal, cast in solid bars, would fit into a chest of moderate size (e.g., 80cm by 40cm by 40cm): this aspect of the tradition is not inherently incredible.

171. Dubs 1942: 38, n. 6.

172. Harl 1996: 176: government stocks had risen from 32 tons in 450/57 C.E. to 103 tons by 518 C.E. and 129 tons in 527 C.E. The values are expressed in *centenaria*, or units of 100 Roman pounds of gold. It is, however, uncertain, if all these treasures consisted of gold: in 468 C.E., the same state covered one-third of the costs of a massive campaign by spending some 226 tons of silver (ibid.).

173. Nishijima 1986: 593–94.

gold and 80–90,000 *jin* of silver held by the treasury in the late second century C.E.[174] However, if a single vassal could be endowed with 7,000 *jin* (*c*.1.75 tons) of gold alongside 60 million in cash and 17,000 households,[175] the existence of much larger governmental gold stocks might well be regarded as credible. As usual, it is impossible to tell if the 200,000 "yellow" *jin* that the emperor Wudi had spent, from *c*.135 to 123 B.C.E., on rewarding his troops were in their entirety composed of actual gold:[176] only in that case could this figure lend some measure of support to the tally for 23 C.E. In short, the reported gold accumulation under Wang Mang appears extraordinarily—though not impossibly—large.[177]

The "wine toast" tax instituted by the emperor Wendi (180–157 B.C.E.) required fiefholders of a certain standing to submit, once a year, 4 *liang* (*c*.62g) of gold per 1,000 population under their control.[178] Given a fief population total of 6.38 million, this would amount to no more than 400kg of gold. (At this rate, it would have taken 375 years to accumulate Wang Mang's gold stocks of 600,000 *jin*.) Even so, this tax was taken seriously enough to prompt the dismissal of officials who failed to surrender the correct amount.[179]

Gold use in subelite settings may be inferred from the existence of relatively small gold ingots (see above). The Mancheng ingots of 6.2–21.5 grams equaled 0.4–1.4 *liang*. In one text, remission of a death sentence is priced at 2½ *jin*, equivalent to tens of thousands cash.[180] This must have exceeded the capacities of most commoners, as the wealth of a medial family could be set at 10 *jin*.[181] Yet these figures also suggest that even individuals of moderate means could, however, on occasion make good use of small gold ingots of 0.025–0.0875 *jin*. It is true that, at 20,000 cash/*jin*, the value of any one of these specimens would exceed the Han poll tax of between 80 and 120 cash for adults aged 15 to 60[182] by anywhere from 300 to 2,100 percent. Yet the margins are such that gold use need not have been completely out of reach for rare big-ticket transactions. If higher reported tax rates for merchants are anything to go by,[183] members of that profession would have more frequently been involved in "gold-sized" transactions. Whether gold was in fact regularly exchanged in such contexts remains, of course, an open

174. *Hou Hanshu* 102 "Biography of Dong Zhuo," in Peng 1994: 134, n. 5. It also far exceeds the 1.2 million *liang* or 45 tons of gold reportedly captured by the Jurchen when they seized the Song capital of Kaifeng in 1127: see von Glahn 2004: 169 and n. 20.

175. Nishijima 1986: 593.

176. *Shiji* 30.11; Dubs 1942: 37.

177. If this tradition is genuine or at any rate not wide off the mark, the gold withdrawal scheme of 7 C.E. must have met with considerable success (see above).

178. Thus Nishijima 1986: 592–93. According to Peng 1994: 134, n. 2, the *Hou Hanshu* "Monograph on Ceremonials" holds that lords of fiefs from 500 to 1,000 people were liable to the same payments.

179. Peng 1994: 134, n. 2 for references.

180. *Hanshu* 44, "Biographies of the Kings of Huainan, Hengshan, and Jipei," in Peng 1994: 137.

181. Swann 1950: 384. This estimate is, of course, highly uncertain.

182. Nishijima 1986: 598.

183. Nishijima 1986: 599.

question. The archaeological record merely suggests that this cannot have been completely unheard of. In subelite circles, gold may have been used primarily as a means of storing wealth. In the event of a crisis, "the common people" were seen "selling gold, silver, pearls, jade, and precious objects."[184] Moreover, gold may not have been directly usable for purchases: in a story about the Eastern Han period, a "poor and sickly scholar" carries 10 *jin* of gold under his belt, one of which then gets sold to meet the expenses for his funeral.[185] On the other hand, one of the mathematical exercises in the *Jiuzhang suanshu* gives prices in *liang* of gold for two groups of seven cattle and sheep each, whereas cash is consistently used in a large number of other cases: each head of cattle is valued at 1.619 *liang* (or *c.*25g), and one sheep costs 0.952 *liang* (or *c.*14g).[186] Given the persistently down-to-earth character of the contexts provided for the mathematical problems, this scenario may well have been considered plausible: at the very least, there is no indication that the use of small units of measurement such as *liang* ounces served some specific mathematical purpose.[187] One of the exercises mentioned above envisions a group of 33 men who pool their resources to buy gold. Another one talks about "a man carrying 12 *jin* of gold beyond the frontier. The frontier tax is one part in ten. Now at the frontier two *jin* of gold are taken, and change of 5,000 cash is given in return."[188] In all these cases, gold use is located in nonaristocratic contexts, and bullion is portrayed as a commodity to be purchased with or exchanged for bronze cash.

According to Peng's survey,[189] the sources for the Eastern Han convey the impression that far fewer imperial gifts were made in gold than during the first half of the Han period. Thus, the *Hou Hanshu* records a total of 21,740 *jin* (or 5.4 tons) of (putative) gold, compared to over 40 times as much in the Western Han period. However, looked at more closely, this difference is almost entirely a function of the absence of very large grants in the later centuries: almost eight-ninths of the much larger Western Han tally is made up of three huge donations. The relative distribution of gold (or "gold") gifts remained the same: we hear of 85+ gifts of 2–1,000 *jin* and 13 gifts in excess of 1,000 *jin* in the first period and of 8+ gifts of 10–1,000 *jin* and just one in excess of 1,000 *jin* in the second. At the same time, the overall incidence of records differed dramatically: 9 gold gifts and

184. *Record of the Three Kingdoms* 5, in Peng 1994: 135, n. 7.
185. *Hou Hanshu* 111, in Peng 1994: 135, n. 7.
186. *Jiuzhang suanshu* 8.7, in Vogel 1968: 84. Priced in cash at around 10,000 per *jin* (but see also in the text above), the corresponding valuations of 1,012 and 595 would be broadly consistent with analogous prices in other problems: cattle are variously priced from 1,200 to 1,818 (*Jiuzhang suanshu* 8.8, 8.11) and sheep from 150 to 500 (ibid. 7.6, 8.8, 8.17). It merits notice that commodity prices vary considerably between different problems but always fluctuate within a particular range that may have appeared plausible. Stated price ratios, e.g. between different kinds of farm animals, also seem to aim for verisimilitude.
187. Cf. *Jiuzhang suanshu* 8.8 for a very similar problem with the same animals and cash prices.
188. Ibid. 7.5 and 6.3, in Vogel 1968: 72, 63.
189. Peng 1994: 137–38.

64 cash gifts in the second period compare poorly with *c*.100 gold gifts and *c*.50 cash gifts in the first one. We are left wondering if this shift signifies mere literary fashion (that gave greater prominence to cash valuations as opposed to the earlier—*perhaps*—often nominal gold valuations) or whether it reflects genuine changes in money use at the imperial court.

Later Chinese sources marveled at the supposed abundance of gold in the (Western) Han period that contrasted with later scarcity.[190] A Tang commentary on the *Hanshu* noted that "nowadays people frequently get 'horse-hoof' gold from the earth. The gold is extremely pure, and artfully shaped." Plowing could turn up an entire jar full of these precious objects.[191] Various explanations for the late and post-Han decline in gold use have been mooted, such as the immobilization of bullion in gilded Buddha statues following the spread of Buddhism; the appropriation of gold stocks under Wang Mang and its subsequent retention by the restored Han clan;[192] and the outflow of specie to Central Asia in order to pay off hostile neighbors and to acquire horses and other imports.[193] Increased use of gold for ornamentation is another candidate: while court society (both in the center and among the vassal rulers) had always absorbed considerable quantities of gold for adornment,[194] in the Eastern Han period, gold (and silver) objects became much more common in graves than they had been in previous centuries, a trend that further strengthened during the Jin period.[195] At the end of the Han period, the plundering of a single princely tumulus tomb allegedly yielded tens of thousands of *jin* of gold.

Concurrently with the apparent decline of the monetary use of gold in the Eastern Han period, silver assumed greater significance in the sources. Following Wudi's short-lived experiment with "white metal" coinage (see above, section 3.2), Wang Mang was the first officially to recognize silver (measured in half-*jin* units called *liu* and graded according to purity) as a monetary means of exchange, a reversal of Qin Shihuangdi's regulation that silver was not to be used in that capacity (see above). From the first century C.E. onward, references to stocks and grants of silver measured in *jin* appear in the record: in 111 C.E., a group of Qiang was rewarded with 100 *jin* of gold and 200 *jin* of silver; and as already mentioned above, in the late second century C.E., Dong Zhuo hoarded 20–30,000 *jin* of gold

190. Peng 1994: 135, n. 9 for references.

191. Peng 1994: 144, nn. 69–70.

192. The younger brother of the empress of Guangwudi, the first emperor of the restored Han Dynasty (25–57 C.E.), reportedly "accumulated gold to the amount of several hundred million, had over four hundred servants, and used gold for utensils. The sounds of his smelters resounded in the capital suburbs," and "was granted gold, coin, fine and ordinary silks in incomparable abundance" (Wang Jia, *Record of Anecdotes Missed by History* 6, and *Hou Hanshu*, "Annals of Empress Guo," in Peng 1994: 141, n. 53).

193. Peng 1994: 138–41.

194. Peng 1994: 142–43, n. 59.

195. Peng 1994: 143. On late Han money-trees, see Erickson 1994.

and 80–90,000 *jin* of silver.[196] Rectangular and boat-shaped silver ingots have occasionally come to light: Peng cites four inscribed specimens weighing 125, 205, 356, and 403 grams that date from the years 57 and 148 C.E.[197] After a protracted hiatus, these items resumed the tradition of casting silver ingots that is first documented for the Spring and Autumn Period (see above, section 4.1).

Monetary use of gold and silver greatly increased under the Western Jin. Gold may well have increased in value relative to copper, and prices began to be expressed in silver. Coin-shaped gold and silver entered circulation, as did cakes and ingots.[198] The restorationist Tang regime returned to cash pricing. Gold and silver were used largely as a store of value while silver ingots were increasingly employed in international transactions.[199]

5. PATTERNS OF MONETARY DEVELOPMENT IN ANCIENT CHINA

It is possible to distinguish between four principal stages in the monetary history of ancient China. In phase 1 (from very roughly 1000 to *c*.220 B.C.E.), individual polities—or private individuals within them—supplemented and gradually replaced cowries by casting bronze money in the form of miniaturized tools and (from the fourth century B.C.E.) also in the form of round coins. While the most urbanized states in the central Great Plain used both their own issues and those from neighboring states, more peripheral polities developed closed and putatively state-controlled currency systems. The southern state of Chu followed a separate trajectory, combining bronze imitation cowries with small punch-marked gold plates. In the other states, gold and silver reportedly circulated as bullion but remained rare in the archaeological record. The two distinctive Chu currencies were discontinued upon conquest by Qin, and no further coin-sized gold units were issued in the unified empire. In phase 2 (*c*.220–112 B.C.E.), the imperial center formally imposed a bronze currency composed of coins of varying (but gradually lowered) weight standards. Periods of (nominal) state monopoly on coining alternated with those in which private individuals were permitted to contribute to the money supply. Gold circulated in the form of bullion but officially counted as money. In phase 3 (112 B.C.E.–*c*.170 C.E.), the imperial government upheld a state monopoly on coin production and for most of the time maintained a single fixed weight standard. Experimentation with token money between 7 and 14 C.E. proved short lived and unsuccessful. Gold bullion

196. Peng 1994: 145.
197. Peng 1994: 145–46.
198. Peng 1994: 203 (but see below, n. 238), 206. The production of normed silver ingots commenced in the Sui period: Bunker 1994: 73.
199. Peng 1994: 276–78.

may increasingly have circulated in the form of standardized ingots. In the first and second centuries C.E., silver bullion may have increased in importance relative to gold, but the evidence is ambiguous. Phase 4 (*c.*170–*c.*250 C.E.) witnessed the partial collapse of the standardized bronze coin currency and inflationary debasement, followed by a prolonged slump in coin production and reliance on existing issues in combination with payments in kind, most notably in the fourth and fifth centuries C.E.

6. PATTERNS OF MONETARY DEVELOPMENT IN THE ROMAN EMPIRE

6.1. *From Bronze to Silver to Gold*

The monetary systems of ancient Italy and ancient China shared a feature that was lacking from other historical societies: when coinage appeared for the first time, it was manufactured of cast bronze.[200] In Italy, unlike in China, Romans, Etruscans, and Samnites issued relatively large and heavy bronze denominations, functionally equivalent to the small metal bars that had previously been in use (such as *aes rude* in Rome and "ramo secco" copper bars in Etruria). The earliest Roman coins were cast on the libral weight standard (1 *as* at *c.*323g), with 1 *uncia* (one-twelfth of an *as*, or 27g) providing the smallest fractional issue. Other Italian polities employed different standards: *c.*200g in Etruria and Umbria, *c.*350–400g in Ariminum and Hatria. As in Eastern Zhou, Qin, and early Han China, debasement was achieved by reducing weight standards, a process that was primarily driven by fiscal exigencies caused by military pressure: during the First Punic War (264–241 B.C.E.), the intrinsic value of the *as* was lowered by one-sixth to 10 *unciae* while retaining its nominal value. Debasement accelerated greatly during the Second Punic War (218–202 B.C.E.): between 218 and 213 B.C.E., target weights for an *as* dropped from 268g to 133g to 83g to 69g to 40.5g, reducing the (putative) metal value to one-eighth of the original standard. In the later years of the war, the uncial standard became the norm (1 "*as*" = 27g, or one-twelfth of the original weight). These smaller coins came to be issued in large quantities during the first half of the second century B.C.E.

In contrast to China, however, the Roman-Italian monetary system was embedded in a much larger and older international currency system based on coined silver. As a result of intensifying military engagement with this sphere, the Roman state gradually adopted a bimetallic system that paired traditional bronze with "Greek-style" silver: from the late fourth century B.C.E. onward, the Campanian stater (falling, between *c.*310 and 240 B.C.E., from 7.3 to 6.6g gross and

---

200. The following survey is primarily based on Harl 1996: 21–206, which despite its strongly "metallistic" perspective (see below, section 8) and various inadequacies provides a convenient summary of existing scholarship.

from 6.8 to 6.4g silver weight) was used alongside the *as* and its fractions. The subsequent silver *quadrigatus/denarius* was debased in the opening years of the Second Punic War (from 6.4 to 6g silver, or from 97 to 91 percent fineness), and around 216/14 B.C.E. the state cast bronze *multipla* (such as the 10-*as decussis*) to mitigate the war-induced scarcity of silver. Silver coinage survived in the form of the devalued *denarius* of *c.*213/12 B.C.E., minted at 1/72 pound (*c.*4.5g) at 96 percent fineness. In the final years of the war, standards continued to slide, from *c.*1/72 to *c.*1/76–80 pound per *denarius*. In 187 B.C.E., the *denarius* was reset at 1/84 pound (3.85g) but—thanks to continuing Roman successes and improved access to mines—remained stable for the following 250 years.

Although large numbers of bronze coins were turned out in the first half of the second century B.C.E., production does not appear to have kept up with rising demand caused by the gradual monetization of the Roman economy: silver *denarii* were often cut in half or quarters to compensate for the scarcity of fractional coinage. It did not help that the Italian allies cast *asses* at different standards (at 18 to 32 to the Roman pound) and that Roman bronze coining was sharply curtailed in the second half of the second century B.C.E. As a result, older *asses* continued to circulate in an increasingly worn state, often losing as much as a third of their original weight. Moneychangers discounted these underweight *asses* and silver/bronze exchange rates fluctuated accordingly. In 141 B.C.E., the *denarius* was retariffed at 16 *asses*. Instead of *as* coins, the state produced mostly smaller fractional denominations (*semis, triens, quadrans*).

Gold had been temporarily coined during the emergency of the Second Punic War (a process paralleled by short-lived gold issues in Athens in the final years of the Peloponnesian War, or at Syracuse during the Athenian invasion). In the second century B.C.E., Macedonian gold coins captured in the wars of 200/197 and 171/67 B.C.E. circulated in significant numbers (perhaps in sealed bags). Large purchases were settled in ingots of gold and silver, cast in multiples of the pound and certified by official stamps.

Thanks to state's access to large quantities of silver, the weight of the silver *denarius* remained stable while its fineness fluctuated only mildly even in times of crisis: from 97.5 percent at the beginning of the first century B.C.E. to 95 percent during the Social War (91–89 B.C.E.), back to 96 percent by the mid 80s and 98 percent in the late 80s; down to 95–96 percent at the beginning of civil war in 49 B.C.E. and again in 44/42 B.C.E. During the second triumviral period, Octavian's issues in the west exhibited low fineness of 95 percent down to 36 B.C.E., thereafter improving to 97 percent, whereas Antony started out with 98.5 percent in the east in 41–38 B.C.E. but eventually debased to 92 percent. As a consequence, Antony's later issues, struck in large quantities, continued to circulate for generations in keeping with "Gresham's Law" that bad money drives out good.

Gold coins reappeared under Sulla's dictatorship (struck at 30 to the pound) to provide donatives to the military, and again in 49 B.C.E. The gold/silver ratio had been as low as 8 to 1 during the 210s B.C.E.; but as silver inflows increased, these coins were melted down to take advantage of a market ratio of closer to 10–12 to 1. By 50 B.C.E., Caesar's conquests in Gaul had lowered the market price of gold to 750 *denarii* per pound, for an 8.6 to 1 ratio. The nominal standard for gold and silver coins set in 46 B.C.E. was 1 *aureus* = 25 *denarii*, or 1 pound of gold = 1,000 *denarii*, for a gold/silver ratio of 11.5 to 1. Under Augustus, the *aureus* was issued in virtually pure gold at 40 to the pound, whereas the *denarius* continued to be struck at 1/84 pound, its silver content restored to 97.5–98 percent. Pent-up demand for fractional coinage was met by the brass *sestertius* (valued at ¼ *denarius* or 4 *asses*) accompanied by the copper *as*, *semis* (½ *as*), and *quadrans* (¼ *as*).

Roman expansion precipitated progressive unification of the Mediterranean monetary system(s). In the west, local coinages gradually disappeared from the market: Greek and Punic gold and silver on Sicily and Sardinia by the 210s B.C.E.; Celtic gold in northern Italy by c.200 B.C.E.; all Carthaginian coins by 146 B.C.E.; Iberian coins in the first century B.C.E.; precious metal coins in Gaul in the 50s B.C.E., and later hybrids by the 10s B.C.E.; Celtic coins in Britain in the first century C.E. In the east, increasing quantities of gold and silver coins issued by the Hellenistic kingdoms were absorbed by the Roman state and transferred to Italy for recoining. From 189 to 176 B.C.E., for instance, Rome received c.370 tons of silver coins as war reparations from the Seleucid Empire, enough to mint 100 million *denarii* (and to undermine the Seleucid silver currency). In the Aegean, the Attalid *cistophori* silver coins continued to be minted under Roman rule, and various generals would on occasion produce tetradrachms. Unprecedented depredations under Sulla and in the second triumviral period caused the demise of many local (urban) silver currencies and the suspension or debasement of surviving coinages. By the time Augustus restored the *cistophorus* in Asia Minor and the Syrian tetradrachm, Roman *denarii* had already made major inroads into the monetary sphere of the Hellenistic east, as documented by hoards of the period.

The huge drain on eastern bullion encouraged a shift to local bronze issues, now pegged to the Roman *denarius*. Continuing local bronze coin production guaranteed the availability of small-denomination units that were vital to market transactions in traditionally monetized communities. In the west, by contrast, most communities had ceased production of local bronzes by the 30s C.E. It appears that centralized production of the Roman mint (first in Lugudunum [Lyons], then in Rome itself) was capable of providing the (arguably significantly less monetized) western half of the empire with at least somewhat adequate amounts of small-denomination coins.

As a result of monetary unification, the central government increasingly gained the ability to control and manipulate weight and purity standards across its far-flung realm, either directly through imperial issues or indirectly via local systems that were formally or de facto pegged to the central currency system.

Thus, once the center decided on debasement, local issuers had to follow suit to maintain circulation. From the mid-first century C.E. onward, the imperial silver coinage underwent a gradually accelerating process of debasement and concurrent nominal overvaluation. Gold and base metal denominations were also affected to varying degrees. In 64 C.E., Nero reduced the weight of the *aureus* to 1/45 pound (from 1/40) and that of the *denarius* to 1/96 pound (from 1/84), while the latter's fineness dropped from 98 to 93 percent. Debasement of the silver standard proceeded in fits and starts, usually driven by military requirements: down to 80–89 percent under the early Flavians; restored to 98.5 percent in 82 C.E. but down to 93 percent in the following years; down to 89–90 percent under Trajan (98–177 C.E.); and on to 83–84 percent under Antoninus Pius (by 148 C.E.) and to less than 80 percent by 161 C.E. Base metal coins likewise experienced significant debasement in the course of the second century C.E.; the *semis* and *quadrans* formats were discontinued; overall output was reduced; and the *sestertius* began to be made of (cheaper) bronze instead of brass and adulterated with lead.

Provincial currencies were debased or retariffed accordingly. At the same time, a record number of cities produced bronze coins, rising from *c.*150 under Augustus to *c.*375 by 200 C.E. Often consolidated in major workshops, output was huge: some 900 countermarks on civic base metal issues are known. In Egypt, traditionally a separate currency zone, the local silver tetradrachm was gradually debased, from 3g of silver or 23 percent fineness under Claudius to 2.2g of silver or 16–17 percent fineness in 58 C.E., when existing issues were recoined in vast numbers. Local drachms (nominally silver coins) were now issued as bronze coins.

Debasement of the imperial silver currency picked up from the 160s to the 230s C.E., with a drop in fineness from *c.*80 percent to *c.*50 percent, or from 2.7g to 1.5g of silver (while gross weight remained largely stable). Again, this development was driven by rising military expenditure, increasingly due to growing internal instability. An experiment in fiduciary silver money failed: a "double" *denarius* (*antoninianus*), at 1.5 times the weight of the *denarius* but twice its face value, was introduced in 215 C.E. but merely prompted hoarding of single *denarii* of higher intrinsic value and had to be abolished a few years later. In 213 C.E., the *aureus* was reset at 1/50 pound (down from 1/45). Military events necessitated the return of the *antoninianus* in 238 C.E., now even more debased, and as a result the (now intrinsically overvalued) *denarius* soon disappeared from circulation. During the following period of foreign invasions and temporary internal fragmentation, debasement soon reached dramatic levels. Between 238 and 269 C.E., the gross weight of the *antoninianus* double *denarius* was halved, while its fineness fell from about 50 percent to 1.7 percent, or from 2.4g to 0.1g of silver. At that stage, the empire had de facto switched to a bimetallic system based on gold and bronze, especially as users began to extract the thin silver veneer of the new nominal silver coins to sell as bullion. The number of mints kept increasing to raise output in the face of accelerating inflation. The *aureus* also fell in weight, yet to a much lesser extent than silver: from 1/50 to 1/52–54 (235/38 C.E.) to 1/65 (238/44 C.E.) to 1/90 (by 250 C.E.). In the 250s and 260s, putative multiples of reduced fineness (commonly 93–95 percent, but as low as 80 percent) were issued. By 269 C.E., however, standards had been restored to 1/60 pound and 99 percent fineness.

As the silver currency turned into de facto bronze coinage, the nominal bronze fractions had to be debased further, first through weight reductions (in the 230s/240s C.E.) and then through adulteration with lead (at *c.*20–25 percent). Increasingly poorly manufactured pieces were churned out in large quantities, and, from the 250s C.E. onward, large denominations were hoarded as a hedge against silver inflation. This is consistent with a de facto switch to a bronze standard and indicates that coins were ultimately valued due to their metal value. By the 270s C.E., de iure bronze coins had become too expensive to manufacture (compared to largely bronze "silver" coins of higher face value), and production ceased for about a century.

The civic coinages in the provinces were caught in a race to the bottom, suffering debasement in keeping with the trends set by the imperial mints. Heavily debased silver issues finally ceased in the 250s C.E. Production of bronze coins crashed in the late 250s and 260s C.E. due to competition with radically debased imperial "silver" coins and resultant inflation. In the 260s C.E., most local mints were abandoned. In Egypt, by 274 C.E., greatly debased billon tetradrachms had driven out all local bronze coins.

Following imperial reunification, Aurelianus introduced a feebly improved "radiate" *aurelianianus* of 3.9g gross weight and 4.5–5 percent fineness (i.e., *c.*0.2g of silver), tariffed at 5 *denarii communes* or 20 *sestertii*, both of them now reduced to mere units of account. The *aureus*, officially set at 1/50 pound but also struck at 1/70–72, was valued at 100–120 *aurelianiani*. This system remained in place for the next twenty years. Just as before, it was de facto anchored in gold coins that traded against billon (i.e., heavily adulterated silver) coins that were mostly bronze.

A reform in 293 C.E. aimed to restore a functioning silver currency. The weight of the *aureus* was raised from 1/70 to 1/60 pound, and gold was to be accompanied by a new pure silver coin (*argenteus*) struck at 1/96 pound (the Neronian rate) and valued at 25 *denarii communes* (as unit of account). A silver-wash billon coin was valued at 5 *denarii communes*, and a bronze coin at 1 *denarius communis*. This reform was shored up by massive recalls and reminting but failed immediately—and predictably—as the nominally hugely overvalued billon coin rapidly lost real exchange value. Two retariffings (from 600 to 1,200 and then 2,400 *denarii communes* for the *aureus*, and from 25 to 50 to 100 *denarii communes* for the *argenteus*) failed to keep pace with the collapse of the billon coin or *nummus*: once again, fiduciary coinage had proven unworkable, and market valuations according to metal content persisted. In response to the hoarding or remelting of pure silver coins, the imperial mints ceased production of the *argenteus* soon after 305 C.E. while the billon coins continued to circulate at much discounted rates until the 360s C.E. Constantine adjusted the gold "anchor" by switching to the gold *solidus* struck at 1/72 to the pound and at 99.5 percent fineness. Silver continued to be invested into ever increasing numbers of billon coins that went through several cycles of debasement and retariffing of the multiples that subsequently continued this process. From 303 to 348 C.E., the silver content of the billon *nummus* dropped from 1/32 pound to 1/196 pound, or from 10.75g to 1.65g of silver, and from 4 percent to 0.4 percent fineness. Price inflation progressed accordingly: between 323 and 445 C.E., the value of the *solidus* rose from 6,000 *denarii communes* to up to 42 million, or from 240 to 7,000–7,200 actual billon *nummi*.

In 367 C.E., production of billon coins finally ceased, only to be replaced, de iure, by another pure silver coin that underwent heavy debasement and devaluation in the late fourth century, and to be continued, de facto, by various denominations of bronze coins, among which the *centenionalis* (2.45g) became the most important. Developments in the fifth century C.E. further reinforced the gold-bronze currency system that had emerged in the second half of the third century C.E. Despite ongoing losses of bullion to foreign powers, gold expanded its dominance as the only reliable value standard. Gold circulated in *solidus* coins, packed into leather sacks of 100 pounds (*centenarium*) for larger transactions. Despite outflows, the treasury of the eastern empire reportedly managed to amass large quantities of gold: 32 tons by 457 C.E., 103 tons by 518 C.E., and 129 tons by 527 C.E.

By the mid-fifth century C.E., (coined) silver had largely dropped out of circulation. A massive ad hoc emission of over 100 million pure silver coins in 468 C.E. remained a one-off emergency measure. Two currency tiers survived: the gold *solidus* and *tremissis* at the top, and low-value bronze *nummi minimi* at the bottom. The latter continued to be devalued as they were adulterated with lead. Weight reductions were insufficient to keep the weight of bronze coins valued at 1 *solidus* under 25 pounds (8kg), and repeated retariffing was required. By 498 C.E., 1 *solidus* traded for 16,800 *nummi*, instead of 7,000–7,200 as decreed in 445 C.E. A text from Egypt from around 440 C.E. describes how a group of taxpayers met their obligations by handing over 1,522,080 bronze coins weighing 1,705kg and equivalent in value to 211.4 *solidi* (which would have weighed 0.95kg, or about 1,800 times less). Owing to poor production standards, *nummi* were readily counterfeited and commonly appear in hoards of the fifth century C.E. This shows that despite their low intrinsic value, these coins were nevertheless considered sufficiently valuable to be forged out of even cheaper materials than those employed by the authorities, and likewise valuable enough to be hoarded as a store of wealth. This chimes well with the ancient Chinese practice of counterfeiting low-value bronze coins despite comparatively tiny profit margins and the ability of low-value bronze coins to sustain an extensive monetary economy (see below, section 9).

In 498 C.E., small bronze coins were recoined into bronze multiples (*folles*), at 8.5g, with the *nummia* serving as the base standard. The exchange rate was set at 1 *solidus* = 420 *folles* = 16,800 *nummiae*, for a real gold/bronze ratio of 800 to 1 (4.45g gold = 3,570g bronze). In 512 C.E., both the weight and the nominal value of the *follis* were doubled. Due to renewed crises, a further upgrade to 22g (at 180 *folles* per *solidus*) in 538/9 C.E. could not be sustained: by the end of the seventh century C.E., the weight of the *follis* had dropped to 3.5g, and its value to 1/950 of the *solidus* (roughly maintaining the existing gold/bronze ratio). The disastrous wars of the seventh century C.E. spawned huge quantities of various denominations of debased *folles* and chaotic exchange rates that once again wrecked the base metal element of the imperial currency system.

6.2. General Trends

Well into the third century B.C.E., monetary practices in Italy developed at the margins of an expanding international system that originated in the silver coinages of the sixth century B.C.E. Aegean. Greek silver money spread along the main axes of Greek overseas migration, including the western settlements in Sicily (by the mid-sixth century B.C.E.), southern Italy, and the coast of Spain and Provence. From the late sixth century B.C.E., non-Greek populations in the northern Aegean imitated the Greek format. At the end of the fifth century B.C.E., Carthage adopted silver coinage in direct consequence of its intensifying engagement with the western Greeks. In the last third of the third century B.C.E., the conquests of Alexander the Great led to the replication of Greek minting practices all across the former Achaemenid Empire. Northwestern India, which had previously begun to develop an indigenous tradition of square silver coins, also followed suit, and successive waves of foreign dynasties (Greco-Indian, Sakas, Pahlavas, Kusan) extended Greek-style money use across large parts of the Indian subcontinent and into Central Asia to the north.

Initially, in the archaic and early classical Greek world, low-value coins were invariably made of silver, down to impracticably miniscule weights and apparently in very large quantities.[201] Fractional bronze emerged only belatedly, from the late fifth century B.C.E. onward, as increasing levels of monetization raised demand for low-value media of exchange beyond levels that could be satisfied by very small silver issues. Before the Roman period, widespread bronze use was confined in the first instance to the closed currency system of Ptolemaic Egypt. This puts the original Italian currency system in a genuinely unique position within western Eurasia.

201. Kim 2001.

About a century after Carthage had been drawn into the "Aegean" currency universe,[202] Rome followed suit with its Campanian series of silver staters. The shocks of the Second Punic War and subsequent inflows of silver from the Iberian mines and the Hellenistic kingdoms transformed the original bronze-based system into a bimetallic silver-bronze system that soon came to be anchored in silver. On one estimate, in the second century B.C.E., Roman bronze coins accounted for at least half of the amount of coin in circulation but only 10–15 percent of its overall value.[203] Full monetary unification was a protracted process: significant steps included the absorption and recoining of much eastern silver in the first century B.C.E. and the concurrent demise of local coinages in the western regions; massive injections of coined gold from the mid-first century B.C.E. onward that created a uniform empire-wide gold standard; the destruction of provincial coinages in the eastern provinces in the mid-third century C.E.; and repeated reminting programs and standardized empire-wide reissues of new formats from *c*.300 C.E. onward.

Very broadly speaking, the Roman monetary system evolved in six principal phases. In phase 1 (down to *c*.300 B.C.E.), bronze coins circulated in units of 27 to 323 grams. In phase 2 (*c*.300–50 B.C.E.), silver and bronze circulated in coined form, with silver accounting for the bulk of value. In addition, silver and especially gold were stored and exchanged as bullion. Between 200 and 167 B.C.E., Rome captured 38,000 pounds (or 12.3 tons) of gold in war, some of it in the form of Macedonian coins (the *philippei*). In 157 B.C.E., the treasury held 17,410 pounds (or 5.6 tons) of gold, which accounted for more than four-fifths of its total cash reserves (with coined and uncoined silver making up the balance). Transfers running into thousands of pounds of gold are repeatedly reported for the first century B.C.E..[204] If these snapshots are anything to go by, gold bullion must have accounted for an unknowable but significant share of monetary media in the late Republican period. Thus, if bronze really accounted for no more than 10–15 percent of the overall value of Roman coinage, its share in the total amount of monetary media including gold (and silver) bullion must have been smaller still, perhaps well under one-tenth. In phase 3 (*c*.50 B.C.E.–*c*.200 C.E.), coined gold entered the market in very large numbers. Duncan-Jones has estimated that in the 160s C.E., 120 million *aurei* (i.e., 880 tons of coined gold) and some 1.7 billion silver coins (i.e., 5,770 tons of coined silver), perhaps three-quarters of them Roman imperial issues, were in circulation. The probable share of bronze is guessed at no more than 5–10 percent of the total, for up to 5–6 billion low-value coins. In this scenario (which may well inflate actual quantities), gold accounted

---

202. For this concept, see Scheidel 2008b: it refers to all types of coinage that descend from the earliest Lydian and Greek issues in the eastern Aegean in the late seventh century B.C.E.

203. Harl 1996: 47.

204. Howgego 1990: 13–14.

for about 60 percent of overall coin value, compared to 30–35 percent for silver and the remainder for base metal coins.[205] In phase 4 (*c*.200–*c*.270 c.e.), progressive debasement reduced silver denominations to a de facto base metal currency while gold coins maintained much of their value. As a result of the decline of silver coin, bronze coins were largely driven from the market. Phase 5 (*c*.270–*c*.370 c.e.) witnessed several failed attempts to restore full-bodied silver coin. Gold remained the only stable value standard. In phase 6 (*c*.370–*c*.700), soon limited to the eastern Mediterranean, attempts to restore silver were finally abandoned and a gold-bronze system remained in place. Cyclical debasement of the base metal tier drove periodic inflation, underscoring the dominance of gold as the only reliable means of storing wealth.

7. Base-Metal or Precious-Metal Coinage

7.1. Origins

At its earliest stages, the Roman currency system bore greater resemblance to the Chinese system than to any monetary system that existed anywhere between those two regions. Had Rome and Italy developed in a similarly isolated environment as the early Chinese states, would they have continued to rely on coined bronze while silver and gold would have circulated as bullion? At the very least, the Chinese case demonstrates that this kind of trajectory was perfectly feasible and viable even within a world empire that rivaled the mature Roman Empire in terms of both territory and population number. In reality, however, the Italian polities were soon drawn into the Hellenistic monetary system that favored coined silver at the expense of bronze. The Warring States never faced comparably dominant neighbors with centuries-old precious-metal currencies. The coin-sized gold plates of Chu represented the only locally available alternative to the bronze coin system of the Great Plain. As Qin (ultimately largely via the subsequent Han) imposed its *banliang* currency system (again, ultimately in the form of the derivative *wuzhu* standard of the late second century b.c.e.) on all of China, one might wonder what would have happened if Chu had accomplished imperial unification of the Warring States under its leadership or succeeded in overthrowing the Qin regime in the revolt of 209/8 b.c.e. Is it reasonable to suppose that in that case, China would have ended up with a bimetallic currency system of coined (or quasi-coined) gold and coined bronze (round or as imitation cowries)?

7.2. Metal Supply

Both of these counterfactual questions raise an important issue. How did the physical preconditions for the development of a high-volume precious-metal

205. Duncan-Jones 1994: 168–70. But see below, section 9.1.

coinage in western Eurasia compare to those at the opposite end of the continent? In order to address this question, we need to get a better idea of the availability of bullion and the overall size of gold and silver stocks in the Mediterranean and in China to assess the comparative viability of different currency systems.[206]

According to a recent reconstruction, the Roman Empire may have been able to put close to 1,000 tons of coined gold into circulation, as well as six times as much coined silver (see below, section 9.1). As Banaji has argued, gold circulation may have increased even further in late antiquity, from the fourth to the seventh centuries C.E., at least in the eastern remnant of the empire: this notion is supported by textual references to large gold stocks in cities and the treasury, by documentary evidence for increasing use of gold in tax payments even at the village level, and by the discovery of gold-rich late antique coin hoards.[207] Mining output had long been considerable. In the first century C.E., the Baebelo mines in Spain were said to produce 300 pounds of silver per day "for the state" (i.e., presumably as the state's share rather than gross yield), or 35.4 tons per year. The gold mines of northern Spain reportedly netted 20,000 pounds, or 6.5 tons, per year, while Bosnian gold mines produced 50 pounds per day, or 5.9 tons per year. Subsequent operations in Dacia may well have reached a similar scale.[208]

No comparable estimates are available for the Han period. However, we are told that the Tang Empire enjoyed mining yields of 12,000–15,000 ounces of silver per year (or some 500–600kg at 41g per Tang ounce), although one source refers to as many as 25,000 ounces, or one metric ton.[209] These rates are extremely low compared to Roman silver production in Spain. Under the Song, output was boosted to 145,000 ounces in 998 and a record 883,000 ounces in 1022 before dropping to 215,000–220,000 ounces in 1049/78. The most productive prefecture was then credited with 100,000+ ounces per year.[210] These annual output figures range from 6 to 9 tons. Even the peak in 1022, at 36 tons, merely equals Roman production levels in a single province. In the same period, gold was produced at annual levels of c.10,000–15,000 ounces, or 400–600 kilograms, an entire order of magnitude lower than output in any one of the most profitable Roman provinces. If anything, precious metal yields in the Han period must have been lower still: gold was mostly derived from placer deposits while underground mining of gold, in so far as it occurred at all, appears to have been rare: few of the known historical gold mines in China were active in that period.[211] Silver was virtually

206. Elements of this and the following subsection draw on the argument first laid out in the section on "causation" in Scheidel 2008b.

207. Banaji 2001: 39–88, esp. 60–65, 76–84.

208. Pliny the Elder, *Natural History* 33.67 and 33.97, with Harl 1996: 81–82 and the references 408–9. See in general Domergue 1990. These figures imply an aggregate total in excess of the national total for China of 10 tons in 1925: Golas 1999: 15.

209. Peng 1994: 278.

210. Peng 1994: 430. By 1925, annual output had dropped to a single ton: Golas 1999: 15.

211. Golas 1999: 109–23, esp. 119–20, and the key to map 8 (113–18).

unknown in central China prior to the Warring States period.[212] This metal is generally rare in central China and concentrated in the far south, and the earliest evidence for the cupellation of argentiferous sulphide ores comes from the Tang period.[213] In fact, because of supply constraints, China appears to have been incapable of establishing a solid silver-based currency system until massive silver imports from Japan, the Philippines, and the New World between the mid-sixteenth and the mid-seventeenth centuries injected some 7,300 tons of this metal into the Chinese economy.[214]

Considered together, these various reports, estimates, and conjectures suggest that ancient China might not have been capable of sustaining a high-volume precious-metal currency system *even if* the authorities had wished to do so. At the same time, this notion might seem difficult to reconcile with the historical record concerning the scale of gold stocks and disbursements during the Western Han and Xin periods (see above, section 4.2). If Wang Mang had actually managed to accumulate anywhere near 150 tons of gold in his palace, a "bullion scarcity" explanation for the presumed unsustainability of a precious-metal currency system in ancient China would become more difficult to sustain. As noted in section 4.2, this quantity of gold equals 19 million Augustan *aurei* worth 1.9 billion sesterces, more than the annual Roman imperial budget; and it is reminiscent of East Roman government stocks of 129 tons (or less, if silver was also involved) in 527 C.E. In order to maintain that gold was *comparatively* scarce in ancient China—that is, in relation to western Eurasia—we would have to assume that the Xin government was able to concentrate a much larger share of overall gold stocks in its own hands. This is indeed what scholars have been prepared to believe, though for no better reason than a generic (and, to anyone familiar with the standards of criticism applied to Greco-Roman texts, somewhat naive) belief in the overall reliability of the contemporary historiographical tradition—and thus in the powers of the central government to implement a measure as sweeping as the "nationalization" of (a very substantial share of all) privately held gold stocks, within a very short period of time.[215] This is not to say that a model predicated on the notion of a high degree of government hoarding in early imperial China is out of the question: reports from the Northern Song period point in the same direction.[216]

In the end, there are several ways of reconciling the literary tradition about generous Han and Xin gold stocks with the more modest archaeological record

<hr>

212. Bunker 1994: 74. Luxury items made of silver were rare prior to the Tang and Song periods: ibid. 76–77.

213. Golas 1999: 123–36, esp. 132–33. Hardly any known silver mines were operated in the Han period: ibid. 126–32.

214. Von Glahn 1996: 133–41. The margins of error are huge, but the general order of magnitude ought to be correct. Earlier estimates used to be even higher. Incidentally, von Glahn's tally is of the same order of magnitude as the estimated total coined silver stock in the Roman Empire (see above).

215. The estimate of Qi 1999b: 81 that the Han sources refer to close to 2 million *jin* having been used for various purposes does not tell us anything about the scale of overall gold stocks.

216. See Gao 1999: 64 with von Glahn 2004: 171.

and later output figures: the early tallies may be exaggerated; they need not always refer to actual gold; or they may be correct but reflect the successful sequestration of assets by the state. Regardless of which option we prefer, there can be little doubt that gold and especially silver were scarcer in ancient China than in the ancient Mediterranean. Historical comparison shows that the metal supply repeatedly played a critical role in determining the character of different currency systems. The earliest "Aegean" coins were made of electrum found on Mount Tmolos and in the Paktolos River in Lydia. Silver dominated the Greek currency system thanks to the deposits of Attica, Thrace, Siphnos, and Samos. Central Asian and Indian gold supported the Kushan and Gupta dinars. Gold issues by Celtic polities were driven by supply, just as bullion imports from Nubia and the Senegal/Niger region accounted for the temporary shift from silver to gold currencies in the early Islamic Middle East; the opening of new mines in twelfth- and thirteenth-century Europe ended the previous monetary recession; fourteenth-century gold imports from Guinea facilitated the reintroduction of gold coinage in late medieval Italy; the discovery of rich Tyrolean silver mines in the fifteenth century and subsequent massive transfers from the newly acquired Spanish territories of Mexico and Peru sustained the production and eventual dominance of heavy silver coins in western Europe; and Brazilian gold supported the later British gold currency.[217] All this suggests that the relative scarcity of precious metals in ancient China militated against the creation of empire-wide gold or silver currencies.

7.3. Cultural Factors

The impact of supply constraints may have been reinforced by a lack of structural demand for normed high-value low-weight monetary instruments in the form of precious-metal coin. While the reasons for the creation of coinage in western Asia Minor are controversial—and the desire to pay mercenaries may not be the most compelling solution on offer—and while archaic Greek coinage, once adopted, was frequently used in private market exchange (as the growing evidence for small-denomination silver coins very compellingly shows), subsequent imitations often appear to have been triggered by military needs: this is almost certainly true of the Hellenistic kingdoms, imperial Carthage, and Republican Rome, and probably of various Iberian, Celtic, and Iranian polities as well. In the late fourth century B.C.E., the area of coin use in western Eurasia suddenly increased several times by force of arms alone, and this expansion was subsequently sustained by military funding demands.

---

217. I have borrowed this summary from Scheidel forthcoming b. The Boians' switch from gold to silver after their move from Bohemia to Slovakia around 60 B.C.E. is a good example (Göbl 1978: 118). For the early medieval Middle East, see Ashtor 1976: 80–81, and for Europe Williams, ed. 1997: 78, 80, 162, 165, 176.

In the Warring States period, the major powers drew on conscript armies of tens and perhaps hundreds of thousands of peasants; and even in the Qin and Western Han periods, universal conscription propped up the military apparatus of the unified empire. It was not until the Eastern Han period that professionals, convicts, foreign settlers, and mercenaries took over.[218] How were these conscripts provided for? I am not aware of any evidence of regular monetary payments in the pre-Han period.[219] If troops were mostly provisioned in kind, bronze cash would have proved adequate for small additional outlays.[220] It is perhaps not a coincidence that in the same period, at the opposite end of the Eurasian land mass, the Mediterranean power that employed life-cycle conscription of smallholders on an unprecedented scale was also the one that initially disbursed payments in the form of (large) bronze coins and apparently felt no great need for precious metal coinage as long as it primarily faced opponents that employed the same kind of bronze money. It was only when the Roman state became more deeply engaged with Greek or "Hellenized" communities that it added silver coins to its armory.

Even increasing professionalization from the late Western Han period onward need not have caused dramatic changes. The best evidence is provided by excavated coins from Gansu and the border regions to the west. Large finds of Qin and early Western Han *banliang* coins in Gansu document monetary demand created by the novel ambitions of the imperial state at the frontier. *Wuzhu* coins were subsequently locally manufactured in large quantities.[221] In addition, occasional later references to the arrival of additional coin from central China point to the net transfer of tax revenue in cash from the core to the periphery.[222] Farther west in Xinjiang, finds are mostly confined to (imported) *wuzhu* coins from the Eastern Han period whose presence coincides with Han military occupation.[223] The wood slips found at the garrison of Juyan in Inner Mongolia throw some

218. Lewis 2000. Note also that the early Tang Empire (which restored a Han-type bronze currency) relied on the *fubing* system that combined military service with farming, which likewise limited demand for high-value coin (Graff 2002: 189–90).

219. References to cash compensation do not seem to appear on relevant bamboo strips that mention grain and cloth rations. I am indebted to my colleague Mark Lewis for advice on this issue.

220. Stacks of bronze coins were among the personal belongings of a group of hastily buried soldiers in the capital of Yan (Peng 2000: 173). As noted above, "gold or cash" are mentioned as special rewards for soldiers in the mid-third century B.C.E. Shuihudi bamboo strips (ibid. 170).

221. Wang 2004: XII, 27, who notes local finds of coin molds.

222. Wang 2004: 27, 49–50. Tax coin (*fuqian*) was used as (military) salary coin (*fengyongqian*). Two documents (Xie et al. 1987: 597 [498: 8] and 636 [520: 6])—one of them dating from 80 B.C.E.—mention "Henei tax coins," indicating long-distance transfers from central Henan province. Xie et al. 1987: 230 (139: 28) refers to the movement of over 14,300 "tax coins." However, Wang's view that according to the Juyan garrison documents of such transfers were exceptional and local supply was the norm (2004: XIV) is hard to reconcile with her observation that local coin production appears to have been concentrated in the immediate aftermath of the Wang Mang period when no centrally issued coins were available (27 and esp. 49). We would need to know how coin was supplied under "normal" conditions in order to appreciate the overall significance of regular transfers from the state core.

223. However, the subsequent appearance of imitation coins following the Han withdrawal in the second century C.E. points to nonmilitary demand for cash in this region: cf. Wang 2004: XIII, 39–41 on the Qiuci (Kucha) issues.

light on the importance of coin in a military setting during the late Western Han, Wang Mang, and earliest Eastern Han periods.[224] Values were generally expressed in cash terms: more specifically, while military salary entitlements were always quantified in this way, the actual payments could be made either in coin or in kind.[225] It has been argued that cash payments predominated, and Helen Wang notes that the fact that the proposal to resume *wuzhu* production after the restoration of Han rule was reportedly made by Ma Yuan, the governor of Longxi (Gansu) may reflect the demand for cash at the northwestern frontier.[226] However, while these texts leave no doubt that officers and associated civilian officials were at least in part compensated in cash, it is not at all clear whether ordinary soldiers commonly received payments in the form of coin. For instance, the monthly allowance of 3⅓ *shih* of grain frequently issued to regular servicemen—amounting to 66 liters and equivalent to somewhere around 200–400 cash as well as supplemented by salt rations and smaller food allowances for family members—may well have represented the total compensation of privates and (at somewhat lower pay levels) of convicts.[227] In the mature Roman Empire, by contrast, only portions of the nominal salaries of common soldiers were either converted into allocations in kind or retained in personal accounts.[228] Thus, in the Chinese case, initial reliance on conscription, an emphasis on payments in kind, and the absence of competitors operating precious-metal currency systems failed to create strong demand for large quantities of standardized high-to-medium-value and low-weight monetary objects.[229]

The extent to which different elements of the population used precious metal for monetary purposes is also relevant here. A much later observer, Gu Yanwu in his "Record of Daily Knowledge," may have claimed that "during Han gold circulated among both upper and lower classes."[230] However, later reports were ultimately spun out of reports of large amounts of yellow *jin* handed out by Han rulers and need not reflect any genuine knowledge of past conditions. As I have

224. Wang 2004: 47–54 provides the most recent survey in English. Some 31,000 wood slips have been found at that site.

225. One document orders values to be given in cash (*quan*), and accounts that list both money and goods value both in coin: Wang 2004: 48, who also lists numerous cash prices of various goods (59–64, table 17). On military salaries, see ibid. 48 and already Loewe 1967: I 93–98.

226. Wang 2004: 49–51 and 27.

227. Officers: Loewe 1967: I 96; Wang 2004: 49, table 4. Rations: Loewe 1967: I 93–94, II 69–71. For instance, a section commander received as little as 900 per month in cash (Loewe 1967: 96). If soldiers had received substantial amounts of cash on top of their food rations, they would have been as well compensated as junior officers. It would seem more reasonable to consider regular cash payments as a marker of elevated status within the military hierarchy.

228. See Herz 2007: 308–13 for a concise up-to-date summary for the situation in the early monarchical period; and cf. also Rathbone 2007. Compensation in kind gained in importance from the third century C.E. onward as the imperial silver currency declined.

229. For comparative studies of the relationship between patterns of coin denominations and the nature of wage payments, see Lucassen, ed. 2007.

230. Peng 1994: 135, n. 9.

outlined above (sections 4.1–2), gold use was primarily—albeit not exclusively—associated with elite protagonists. If this image reflects reality, it might be helpful to define the imperial monetary system in terms of "transactional orders." This concept, developed by Parry and Bloch and recently applied by Kurke to the study of exchange and monetization in archaic Greece, derives from the observation that "many societies constitute the activities of exchange and economics as two separate but organically articulated transactional orders"—a "long-term transactional order [that] is always positively valued, insofar as it is perceived to perpetuate and reproduce the larger social and cosmic order," and a short-term order in the sphere of individual acquisition that "tends to be morally undetermined since it concerns individual purposes which are largely irrelevant to the long-term order."[231] In the early Greek context, Kurke singles out binaries "opposing the symbolic 'refined gold' of aristocratic *hetairoi* to the 'counterfeit coin' of the excluded *kakoi*, opposing the stable and secure circuit of elite gift exchange to the indiscriminate and promiscuous circulation of money in the public sphere."[232]

The memorial of Chao Cuo, set in 178 B.C.E., might profitably be interpreted within this framework, emphasizing as it does the subversive potential of high-value objects: "Pearls, jade, gold, and silver... are light, small articles, and are easy to hide. Having them in one's grasp [a person] can travel all around within the seas without the hardships of hunger or cold. These cause those in government positions lightly to turn their backs upon their rulers; [these cause] people indifferently to go away from their native townships; [these give] thieves and robbers the incentive [for crimes]; and [these make] fugitives able to have lightweight wealth."[233] By contrast, the text goes on to relate, grain or textiles are too heavy to carry around, yet essential for survival—the implication being that those without access to precious low-weight items are reduced to using these commodities and hence safely pinned down. "For this reason an enlightened ruler esteems the 'five grains,' and despises gold and jade." Although this text does not say in so many words, the physical burden represented by high-value amounts of bronze coins would also have served to constrain undesirable mobility.

Nevertheless, with regard to Han China, transactional constraints may well have been more relaxed in practice: the anecdotes related in section 4.2 suggest that commoners were free to handle gold in as much as they were able to afford to. De facto, however, most people, for most of the time, must have been excluded from the gold economy. At first sight, the situation in the Roman Empire from 367 C.E. onward, and essentially already since the 260s C.E., bears a strong

---

231. Kurke 1999: 14–15. This aspect warrants more detailed investigation: the Chinese annals habitually locate counterfeiting among "the people," whereas gold tends to be portrayed as circulating in more pristine environments.
232. Kurke 2002: 93. See esp. 1999: 41–64, 101–29.
233. *Hanshu* 24A: 11a.

resemblance, in formal terms, to that in Qin-Han China: in both cases, the monetary system was built around a two-tier structure of gold and bronze. Looked at more closely, however, profound differences come to the fore. The late Roman system relied on (coined) gold as an anchor while bronze or copper were periodically abandoned to debasement and devaluation. This modus operandi was conducive to the formation of a corresponding two-tiered economy of privileged recipients and owners of (reliable) gold coin and disadvantaged users of (unreliable) base metal denominations, creating strong structural demand for gold that had no parallel in ancient China. In fact, as the Han bronze coinage remained stable for most of the time, the impetus for a "flight into gold," if it existed at all, would have been much weaker than in the unstable monetary environment of the later Roman Empire. In consequence, gold use would have remained more (socially) limited than in the later Roman Empire.

Conditions in ancient China may have had more in common with those in republican Rome, where gold bullion served as a means of payment, store of wealth, and unit of account. While its overall significance for the late republican economy is difficult to determine, Hollander stresses the casual way in which elite sources (especially Cicero) refer to the use of uncoined gold and silver in monetary transactions: bullion was clearly regarded as a useful and not at all uncommon form of money.[234] On occasion, recipients could even be low class, such as soldiers or even slaves.[235] Overall, however, bullion transactions appear to have been limited in the first instance to the state, the wealthy, and traders. The key difference lies in the relative abundance of silver that could be turned into coin in the West and its near-absence from early China.

However, the existence of a stable bronze-coinage system, the apparent scarcity of gold and especially silver, and low structural demand for precious-metal coin are insufficient to account for the fact that gold and silver did not normally circulate in coined form—*not even in limited quantities.*[236] The stamped gold plates of Chu would have provided a workable template, and later on, the Chinese state encountered "Greek-style" coins in its western protectorate in Xinjiang. Hybrid "western"-type coins that combined Karoshthi (i.e., Indian) and Chinese legends were in fact produced at the intersection of the two monetary spheres,[237] yet were not imitated in China proper where precious metal coins were only issued under foreign domination.[238] Later arrivals of Sasanid and early

234. Hollander 2007: 31–39.
235. Cicero, *For Caelius* 51; Plutarch, *Cato the Elder* 10.4, cited by Hollander 2007: 31–32.
236. In Scheidel 2008b, I draw attention to the fact that even in medieval Japan, where Chinese round coins were imitated from the seventh century C.E. onward, the dominant copper issues were occasionally supplemented by silver (and once also gold) coinage produced in the same format.
237. Thierry 2003b: 73, 76; Wang 2004: XIII, 37–38.
238. Rare well-made silver *wuzhu* coins modeled on Eastern Han *wuzhu* are thought to be later imitations, perhaps in the wake of the Tang silver "Inaugural coin" (Peng 1994: 146). Irregular silver *wuzhu* coins have been excavated from a Six Dynasties tomb in Nanjing, perhaps contemporary counterfeits (ibid.).

Byzantine coins ended up as jewelry items. From the Han perspective, precious metal coins were a feature of strange and distant barbarians such as the Parthians and Romans.[239] The production of massive numbers of low-value bronze coins became a defining characteristic of restorationist dynasties such as the Tang and Song. Even as China moved to a silver-based economy from the Song period onward and imported vast amounts of foreign silver under the late Ming, precious metal continued to circulate as bullion alongside base-metal coins and, intermittently, paper money.[240] Any attempt to explain this long-term resistance to precious-metal coins would require much more extensive consideration of cultural features than is possible here.

Asking the question of why something did *not* happen (and thereby implying that it really ought to have happened) may smack of what has been called the "inventionist fallacy," the assumption that activities (such as advanced premodern levels of monetary exchange) that commonly rely on a particular mechanism (such as precious-metal coinage) could not have been properly performed in the absence of this mechanism. Yet such concerns would be misplaced. The experience of the ancient Near East very clearly shows that elaborate systems of monetary exchange do not require coined money.[241] In a case like that, it would be meaningless to ask why coined cash was not developed or how its absence may have impeded economic performance. Ancient China, however, differed from ancient Egypt or Mesopotamia in a crucial way. Coined money was not only not unknown, but it was in fact produced in huge quantities, running into tens of billions over the course of the Han period. This suggests that the ubiquitous presence of base-metal coin does not necessarily precipitate the concurrent use of precious metals in an analogous format. This simple observation invites us to take a fresh look at the contextual determinants of the creation of electron, gold, and silver coinage in western Asia Minor in the late seventh or early sixth century B.C.E.[242] The complete lack of visual imagery on Chinese coins (beyond the simple elegance of the central hole) likewise merits attention. The contrast between the outcomes of Aegean and Chinese coin creation is rendered all the more striking by the fact that Chinese coins were developed in circumstances that shared putatively important features with the world of the archaic Greek polis: they emerged within a cluster of highly competitive polities (which had been created out of city-states) vying for supremacy that would have had obvious uses for visual

239. *Hanshu* 96A, in Hulsewé 1979: 106, 115, 117: gold and silver coins showing a rider and face in Jibin (Gandhara/Kashmir); coins showing face and rider in Wuyishanli (Arachosia); silver coins showing the king's face in Anxi (Parthia). According to *Hou Hanshu* 88D, in Daqin (the Roman Empire), "they make coins from gold and silver, ten pieces of silver being equal in value to one piece of gold" (trans. Leslie and Gardiner 1996: 50). For discussion, see Leslie and Gardiner 1996: 224–25.
240. Von Glahn 1996.
241. See esp. Le Rider 2001, and forthcoming work by Peter Vargyas.
242. For recent discussion, see von Reden 1995; Kurke 1999; Schaps 2004.

imagery highlighting the origins of coins beyond mere ideographs, and spread at a time of unprecedented social and economic development and mobility.[243] This suggests that existing inquiries into the origins and development of Aegean or Chinese coinage that ignore contextual contrasts and similarities between western and eastern Eurasia are inherently incapable of meaningful causal analysis.[244] Explication of the long-term and ultimately near-global success of the "Aegean" model of precious-metal coinage requires close engagement with the real-life counterfactual provided by the Chinese evidence.

7.4. A Preliminary Explanation

I have identified three factors that may have accounted for the creation and long-term persistence of a monetary system based on coined bronze and uncoined gold and silver in China: the bullion supply, military demand, and cultural preferences. The relative scarcity of gold and silver would have made it difficult to sustain precious-metal currencies. This interpretation is consistent with the fact that the only early state (Chu) that issued what might be called protocoinage in gold was located in the only (comparatively) gold-rich part of central China. Furthermore, the apparent absence of strong demand for low-bulk high-value denominations in the context of military recruitment may have further reduced the appeal of precious metal coinages during the formative stages of the imperial system. However, these factors cannot by themselves explain the state's continuing rejection of silver coins even in the Ming period when huge bullion stocks had finally became available. Once the Qin had (at least in theory) imposed an empire-wide uniform standard of low-value bronze coin and the Han had shored up this regime by disseminating tens of billions of these money objects, later dynasties that sought to link up to the ancient imperial tradition had come to regard this particular currency system as a vital element of "proper" governance and shunned alternative options even when they became feasible. If we want to explain the divergent development of money in western and eastern Eurasia, we need to find ways to assess the relative significance of each of these variables and their interconnectedness.

8. METALLISM AND NOMINALISM

Debates about the nature of money in historical societies revolve around the concepts of "metallism" and "nominalism" (also known as "chartalism"). The former defines money as a commodity whose monetary value is determined in the first instance by the market price of its constituent elements such as gold or silver (plus labor), whereas the latter considers money's value to be

---

243. E.g., Hsu 1965.
244. Comparative approaches have been rare: so far Schaps 2006 and Scheidel 2008b are the only exceptions.

distinct from that of its medium and envisions monetary value as a function of state fiat. Modern scholarship tends to stress the metallistic foundations of the Roman imperial and provincial currencies on the one hand and the fiduciary character of early Chinese coin on the other.[245] However, the implied contrast between these two systems is in large part imaginary:[246] it neglects both the fiduciary dimension of Roman coinage and the physical constraints that governed coin use in China. Despite profound differences in terms of the relative value of the constituent elements of their monetary objects, the two currency systems had much in common. In both cases, the exchange value of coins was determined by a combination of their intrinsic—metal—value and users' willingness to accept them at their nominal value, a willingness that in turn depended on a whole range of factors such as information costs, trust, and choice, all of which were to some extent a function of state power and policies.

The "fiduciary model" of Chinese money suffers from a variety of problems. For example, it needs to account for the fact that Qin coins were explicitly labeled with a weight denomination (*banliang* or "half-ounce") that the state at least initially sought to adhere to.[247] One recent observer notes the "apparent contradiction of having a fiduciary coinage where the coin inscription indicated a precise weight."[248] But this contradiction becomes apparent only in retrospect, in the context of gradual weight loss over time. However, the incontrovertible fact that for much of the third century B.C.E. coin weight trended lower must not be interpreted as a sign that it was somehow irrelevant: competition by underweight local issues and budgetary pressures on the central authorities are among the most obvious alternative explanations. From this perspective, the eventual coexistence of overweight, "regular," and—above all—underweight *banliang* coins was the result of chance, not design.[249] State-manufactured "regular" Qin coins—both of the Shang Yang period and afterward—document a desire to match weight and formal denomination.[250] It was only under the pressure of the

245. Strobel 2002: 91–93 lists references to scholarship on Roman coinage that adopts a metallistic perspective. For China, see esp. Thierry 1993, 2001a, 2001b.

246. See Thierry 2001a: 132–33 for a particularly dichotomous vision: "En Occident, la monnaie…se fonde sur le fait que sa valeur d'échange est fonction de sa valeur intrinsèque….La monnaie chinoise repose sur des bases différentes…à l'inverse de l'Occident, en Chine, c'est la valuer d'échange du signe monétaire qui détermine sa valeur intrinsèque."

247. See above, section 2. It would be unwarranted to regard the introduction of the *banliang* as a break with an earlier fiduciary tradition, as suggested by Thierry 1993: 3. For instance, cowrie shells, by virtue of being scarce goods, would have had an intrinsic value, and we have no way of telling how the metal value of tool money was related to its face value. Moreover, the discovery of lumps of bronze that may have served as precursors of later bronze coin (Dai and Zhou 1998) indicates that metal content may have been the original source of value for monetary objects made of this material.

248. Wang 2004: 12. See likewise Thierry 1993: 4.

249. For this outcome, see above, section 2; Thierry 1997: 173–75.

250. Twenty-eight relevant specimens in Thierry 1997: 247–50 (*banliang* Types II–III) yield an average weight of 7.99g, very close to the nominal target weight of *c*.7.8g.

terminal wars of unification that weight standards kept sliding.[251] What we are observing is the incremental erosion of a system of ideally full-bodied bronze coin that was unable to withstand the stress of continuous large-scale war and consequently spiraling state demands.

I already noted above that the Qin regulation that sought to enforce indiscriminate use of coins of uneven quality hints at the existence of divergent everyday practices in the subject population (see above, section 2). Be that as it may, it is simply incorrect to claim that the "bamboo slips from Yunmeng *prove* that Chinese coins did not have an intrinsic value, but instead functioned as a medium of payment, *agreed upon* by the state and the people" (my italics).[252] These texts "prove" nothing of this kind: the only thing they demonstrate is the state's avowed intention to coerce its subjects into accepting state-issued coin without regard to its precise physical characteristics. They do not and indeed cannot reveal whether this measure met with success or failure, nor do they tell us anything about the ambitions of the state beyond the confines of the late Qin period. Moreover, the fact that this fiduciary premise was unilaterally imposed by the state rather than in any meaningful way "agreed on" by society might be taken to suggest that a genuine token coinage was not a viable option.[253] This impression is reinforced by Jia Yi's memorial of 175 B.C.E. that referred to the people's habit of assessing coins according to their physical properties, a practice that would seem unsurprising and indeed unavoidable if coins were thought to be valuable because of their weight and fineness but unintelligible if unquestioning acceptance of fiat issues had been the norm.

Once state revenues had been put on a more solid basis, the maturing Han state was able to take proper account of metallistic concerns. Thus, while the early Han *banliang* issues had continued the Qin trend toward creeping weight loss, the introduction of the *wuzhu* format in the 110s B.C.E. marked a fundamental shift to long-term consistency and fairly stable intrinsic value. *Wuzhu* coins of the Western Han period in two (partly overlapping) modern samples exhibit a bell-curve-shaped weight distribution that leaves no doubt that state mints aimed for a set target weight that was subject to periodic adjustment (figures 7.2–7.3 and table 7.1).

It catches the eye that the earliest *wuzhu* issues (118–113 B.C.E.) tend to exceed their nominal weight of 5 *zhu* by an average margin of 20 percent (or 1 *zhu*). If metal content mattered to users, this would have been a suitable means of establishing the credibility of the new currency that may, however, not have been

---

251. Strongly underweight Qin coins date from the very late Warring States period in third century B.C.E.: Thierry 1997: 175.

252. Wang 2004: 13, with reference to Hulsewé 1985b, who does not actually support this statement.

253. Even Thierry 1993: 4 must concede that Qin monetary policy was constrained by actual practices in the general population.

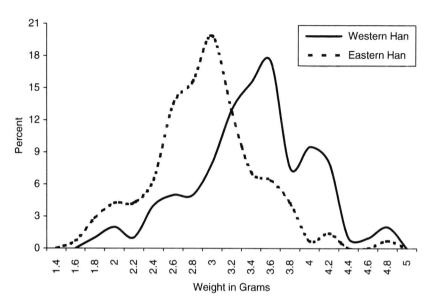

FIGURE 7.2. *Weight distribution of 241* wuzhu *coins (113 B.C.E.–184 C.E.)*
Source: Thierry 2003a.

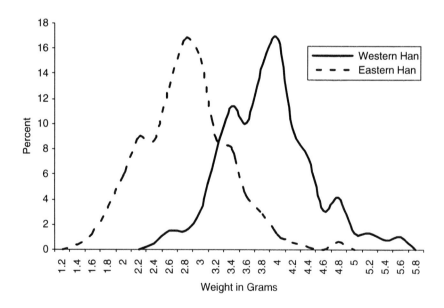

FIGURE 7.3. *Weight distribution of 476* wuzhu *coins in the collection of the Shanghai Museum (118 B.C.E.–184 C.E.)*
Source: Shanghai Bowuguan qingtongqi yanjiubu 1970.

Table 7.1. Mean Weight of *Wuzhu* Coins in Different Periods

Period	Number	Mean Weight in Grams
118–113 B.C.E. (Thierry 2003a)	44	3.90
113 B.C.E.–8 C.E. (Thierry 2003a)	100	3.40
113–49 B.C.E. (Thierry 2003a)	50	3.68
33 B.C.E.–8 C.E. (Thierry 2003a)	29	3.04
23–184 C.E. (Thierry 2003a)	141	2.91
118 B.C.E.–8 C.E. (Shanghai…1970)	193	3.87
23 C.E.–184 C.E. (Shanghai…1970)	283	2.80

viable in the long run.[254] For the remainder of the Western Han period, average coin weights closely approximate the notional target weight.[255]

A more detailed breakdown reveals that these broad averages and overall distribution patterns conceal gradual change over time (fig. 7.4). Until the mid-first century B.C.E., the nominal standard of 5 *zhu* appears to have served as a

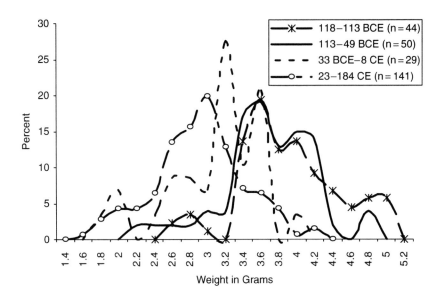

FIGURE 7.4. *Weight distribution of 264* wuzhu *coins (118 B.C.E.–184 C.E.)*
Source: Thierry 2003a.

254. Compare overweight Qin *banliang* pieces in the first half of the fourth century B.C.E.: see above, n. 12. Thierry 2003a: 36 reports that most of the approximately 2,000 early *wuzhu* coins found in a tomb in Mancheng that dates from 113 B.C.E. range from 2.9 to 5.2g. See fig. 4.
255. See table 1, Thierry 2003a sample for 113 B.C.E.–8 C.E. The discrepancies between the Shanghai and Thierry samples in terms of weight distribution and mean weight appear to be due to the preponderance of earlier (and thus heavier) specimens in the Shanghai collection.

lower limit rather than as a genuine target weight, given that a large proportion of specimens exceed 5 *zhu*. It was only in the final decades of the Western Han period that production aimed for an actual target weight of 5 *zhu*. This slide continued in the Eastern Han period, resulting in a reduction of about 25 percent relative to the initial mean weight of the mid 110s B.C.E. It is striking that in both samples, Eastern Han coins were consistently cast according to a target weight of 2.8g to 3g that was approximately 10 percent short of the nominal weight. The bell-curve shape of these distributions indicates that this was mint policy rather than just random slippage. It appears that the state aimed to strike a balance between metallistic stability and the ever-present desire to increase revenue. This cautious approach is inconsistent with the notion that coins were mere tokens and that users were indifferent to its metal content. Instead, it is reminiscent of the Roman imperial policy of very slowly reducing the weight and fineness of its precious-metal coins (see below).

Observable variation in fineness reflects some measure of awareness and appreciation of intrinsic value. Metallurgical analysis of ancient Chinese coins is still in its infancy, and much more work needs to be done to provide us with representative results. Nevertheless, preliminary work in this area has already begun to shed light on general trends. According to a pioneer study, mean copper content averages 74 percent in a very small sample of coins from the unified Qin and early Western Han periods and subsequently rises to 92 percent in specimens dating from the mid-second century B.C.E. to the mid-second century C.E., while the share of lead dropped from 15 to 1.5 percent. During the following 1,000 years, fineness was consistently positively correlated with state strength. By analogy, this suggests that for some three centuries Han finances were in reasonably good shape and that the state was committed to maintaining high coin quality and stable weights.[256] Once again, this pattern is logically consistent with a metallistic tradition of valuing coin but hard to reconcile with the notion of a predominantly fiduciary currency system.

Moreover, the repeated failure of genuine token issues provides an even stronger and potentially decisive argument against the latter. The unsuccessful experiments of Wudi and Wang Mang are a case in point. While it is true that the historiographical tradition was hostile to these two emperors and sought to cast their actions in an unfavorable light, the short-lived nature of their respective token coinages is an objective fact that is supported by the archaeological

---

256. Coins from the late second century C.E. until the end of the Period of Disunion show lower copper (*c.*70–80 percent) and higher lead (*c.*15–20 percent) content. The early Tang period witnessed improved standards (85 percent copper in the seventh century C.E.) followed by drops in the eighth and ninth centuries (mostly 60–80 percent copper). Song coins show a slow slide from 66–77 percent before 1068 to 63–73 percent from 1068 to 1127 and 56–73 percent later on. See the measurements in Bowman, Cowell, and Cribb 2005: 11–19. As Bowman, Cowell, and Cribb 2005: 7, fig. 2 and Cowell et al. 2005: 65, fig.1 show, Han standards of fineness were never reattained in later periods.

record and not merely a facile impression generated by negative spin. Wudi's "white metal," "hide money," and "red-rim" coins as well as Wang Mang's *daqian*, knives, and spades had been introduced in response to surging state demand for revenue and a concurrent desire to discipline entrenched elites.[257] Even if we were to disregard the reasons for their failure proffered by biased sources, we would nevertheless have to conclude that these token issues did not achieve the desired results: if they had been viable, they would not have been abandoned as rapidly as they were. Due to the nature of the evidence, we cannot be sure whether it was public noncompliance and fraud (as intimated by the sources) or sudden price inflation or both that doomed these innovations. In the following centuries, unmet fiscal needs periodically triggered similar token issues that also lacked staying power.[258]

I am not aware of any direct evidence for the intrinsic value of coins from the preimperial or Han periods. In the Tang mints around 750 C.E., the production of 1,000 coins consumed 123 *liang* (then 5.043kg) of a normed alloy composed of approximately 83.5 percent copper, 14.5 percent lead, and 2 percent tin. Allowing for wastage during the production process, the finished coins were supposed to weigh 100 *liang*, or 4.1g each, and it cost the authorities 750 coins to produce a string of 1,000.[259] This implies that the intrinsic value of 123 *liang* of this alloy plus labor costs and other overhead such as fuel added up to 750 cash. While the latter expenses are impossible to quantify, the application of mass manufacturing techniques makes it seem likely that raw materials accounted for most of the overall cost of coin production. A simple thought experiment indicates the limits of the plausible. If there had been no expenses beyond the procurement of metal (which cannot have been the case), the intrinsic value of a finished coin would have equaled 61 percent of its face value. On the other hand, if metal had accounted for not more than two-thirds of total production expenses, the intrinsic value would only have been 41 percent of the nominal value. It therefore seems likely that coins were denominated at approximately twice their metal value.[260]

The average copper content of Han *wuzhu* coins that have undergone metallurgical analysis is around 85 percent, similar to properly normed Tang issues.[261] On the simplifying assumptions that the intrinsic value of a given amount of alloy of a (high-quality) Han or Tang coin equaled close to 90 percent of its weight in copper (given that admixtures such as lead must have been cheaper than copper), and that in the late Western Han period 21,000 *wuzhu*

257. See above, sections 3.2.–3 and 4.2.
258. See above, section 3.5, and cf. Thierry 1993: 7–8.
259. Thierry 2003a: 115, with source references.
260. For modest seigniorage in the subsequent Northern Song period, cf. von Glahn 2004: 168.
261. Bowman, Cowell, and Cribb 2005: 11. However, the actual copper content of Tang coins from the eighth century C.E. tends to fall short of the official standard: ibid. 12.

coins bought 1 *jin* of gold, gold would have been worth roughly 500 times its weight in (uncoined) copper.[262] This ratio is comparatively low but by no means impossible. In China in the second half of the fourteenth century, gold may have been valued at 1,600 times its weight in copper, and in 1908 this ratio stood at 1 to 1,645.[263] However, in neither one of these periods did the currency system depend on mass production of bronze coin that drove up demand for copper. In the Tang and Song periods, by contrast, inelasticities in copper output constrained coin production and monetization: as a consequence, copper prices rose relative to those of other metals. Mass-manufacturing of *wuzhu* coins for much of the Han period would likewise have boosted the relative value of copper.[264]

Later records support this conjecture. In the eleventh century C.E., the minting of cash regularly absorbed some 4,000 tons per year, equivalent to the entire output of the copper mines of the Northern Song Empire.[265] While this tally is a multiple of the 700–850 tons of copper that had been required to produce 230 million Han *wuzhu* coins per year in the late Western Han period, it is likely that mining yields had greatly increased during the intervening 1,100 years.[266] No output figures are available for the Han period. All we know is that the volume of silver production increased between 10 and 15 times between Tang and the Northern Song periods.[267] It is impossible to tell whether copper production grew to a similar extent.[268] However, if annual copper yields had risen only by a few times between the Han and the Northern Song periods—much less than silver output rose from the Tang to the Song periods—the production of *wuzhu* coins would have been sufficient to put a heavy strain on the copper supply of the Han state, driving up the price of this commodity. In fact, comparative evidence from other parts of the world shows that specific configurations of supply and demand were perfectly capable of generating high copper prices. For example, in Alexandria in Egypt around 1400, gold was worth only 490 times as much

262. Gold: see above, n. 154, 21,000 *wuzhu* ~68,250g of alloy ~61,425g of copper times two to account for the higher face value ~250g of gold.

263. Peng 1994: 489–90, 760, 762. In England around 1400, gold was worth 2,400 times as much as copper: Blanshard 2005: 1456 (at *c*.16 grains per gold shilling).

264. In this context, it also merits attention that reported gold prices from the Western Jin period and the Period of Disunion (280–589 C.E.)—when levels of bronze coin production were low—were high, with one (Han) *jin* priced at 100,000 or 150,000 cash (Peng 1994: 202–3, nn. 4–5 with references). However, due to uncertainties regarding the "typical" weight of bronze coin in this period, it is difficult to deduce real gold/bronze ratios (*pace* Peng 1994: 203). If "cash" refers to Han *wuzhu* coins (which continued to circulate in large quantities), this ratio could have been as high as 1,300–1,950; for more light-weight bronze coins, ratios would have been correspondingly lower.

265. Von Glahn 1996: 49.

266. The estimate of 700 tons is based on an annual production of 230 million *wuzhu* coins with an average copper content of 92 percent, whereas the higher figure of 850 tons takes account of the processing losses implied by the Tang regulations mentioned above.

267. Peng 1994: 278, 430.

268. For a surge in copper output *during* the Northern Song period, see Golas 1999: 87–88.

as copper, a ratio that happens to match my estimate for the late Western Han period.[269]

In light of all this information, there is nothing to suggest that the intrinsic value of Han bronze issues was minimal or strictly dissociated from their nominal valuations and therefore of minor importance, let alone irrelevant. Instead, various strands of evidence are consistent with the notion that the market showed awareness of the intrinsic value of coins and priced them accordingly.[270] User discrimination based on the physical properties of coins (as insinuated by the Qin rules of the *Jinbulu* and explicitly reported in Jia Yi's memorial in the *Hanshu*), the state mints' sustained focus on target weights and levels of fineness in times of fiscal stability (as borne out by numismatic material from the Shang Yang, late Western Han, early Eastern Han, and early and mid–Tang periods), the multiple weight adjustments of the Han *wuzhu*, the ratio of intrinsic to nominal coin value prescribed in the mid-eighth century C.E., and the persistent failure of genuine token issues all converge in supporting this conclusion. What is more, these trends continued beyond the Tang period. To the best of its—increasingly limited—abilities, the Song state sought to supply the market with large quantities of full-bodied bronze issues and charged only modest seigniorage. As a result, bronze coin served as a store of value, and hoarding by the wealthy was common.[271] Conversely, both the debasement of existing coin types and the introduction of token coins were known to prompt counterfeiting and price inflation.[272]

Schematic distinctions between a "Western" preference for "full-bodied" coin and the "fiduciary" monetary tradition of China are at best exaggerated and at

269. Blanchard 2005: 1211. One report even puts the gold/copper ratio in Mali in 1353 at 240 to 1: ibid. 1514. However, unlike ancient China, Mali was a gold-rich environment. Comparative evidence from different parts and periods of the ancient Mediterranean points to silver/bronze ratios of 50–120 to 1 (von Reden 2007: 74, n. 53, with references), which imply gold/bronze ratios of the order of 500–1,500 to 1.

270. Cf. also von Glahn 2004: 168. Thierry 2001a errs in consistently foregrounding ideology at the expense of logic and basic economics. Thus, if early China had truly been "profondément attachée à une monnaie idéalement fiduciare" (133), why is it that the assignation of the same nominal value to coins of 3g and 10g "n'est pas admissable par la population, et l'imposer est, dans l'optique confucéenne, un cas exemplaire de rupture du contrat entre l'État et le peuple" (134)? And if this (relatively moderate) imbalance was incompatible with putatively "Confucian" preferences, how can we define the *wuzhu* tradition as a "pratique…donc confucéenne (monnaie fiduciare) avec une apparence légiste (lingot de métal à poids marqué)" (135)? It is likewise naive to explain Wang Mang's budget-boosting reforms purely as an ideological response to the aforementioned hybrid arrangement—"Le régime idéologiquement confucéen et antilégiste de Wang Mang…ne se satisfait pas de cette contradiction" (135). And finally, if fiduciary issues had really been a perennial ideal, why would it have been the case that "l'inscription pondérale '5 *zhu*' posera un grave problème à toutes les dynasties postérieures aux Han qui ne seront que rarement capables d'émettre une monnaie dont les poids correspondent véritablement à l'inscription" (136)? This solipsistically ideational framework is inadequate for a realistic appreciation of monetary processes.

271. Gao 1999: 38, 64; von Glahn 2004: 168, 171. In the Roman Empire in the fifth century C.E., low-grade base-metal coins known as *nummi* were readily counterfeited and commonly appear in hoards of the fifth century C.E. (Harl 1996: 179). This shows that despite their low intrinsic value, these coins were nevertheless considered sufficiently valuable to be forged out of even cheaper materials than those employed by the authorities, and likewise valuable enough to be hoarded as a store of wealth.

272. Miyazawa 1998: 349, 353; von Glahn 2004: 173, 177. This is why convertibility was crucial for the success of early paper money: ibid. 173.

worst seriously misleading. The mature Han currency system accommodated a significant degree of seigniorage due to the basic fact that production costs for base-metal coin are nontrivial relative to the price of the raw materials. Moreover, centralized mass production of carefully normed coins and legal injunctions against private issues raised the cost of counterfeiting. Taken together, these factors supported a relatively high monopoly price of state coinage: under these circumstances, even if the nominal value of a *wuzhu* coin exceeded its metal value by 100 percent, the use of state-manufactured base-metal coin at nominal exchange rates remained the least costly option for the general public. It was only when the state introduced cash that was overvalued by a margin that was high enough to be both conspicuous and render imitations profitable that "Gresham's Law" became operative, price inflation ensued, and counterfeiting proliferated. Multiples of 300, 500, and 3,000 cash under Wudi, of 5, 25, 50, and up to 10,000 under Wang Mang, of 100, 500, and up to 5,000 in the Three Kingdoms, and of 10 under the Song all fall in this category.[273] The system tolerated only a moderate degree of currency manipulation.

This limited elasticity of the ratio of intrinsic value to nominal value was by no means unique to early China.[274] Regarding this relationship, comparison between the currency systems of the Han and Roman empires reveals striking similarities. The target silver content of the Roman *denarius* of one eighty-fourth of a pound (*c*.3.85g) remained unchanged for two centuries from the 180s B.C.E. until the early first century C.E. Instances of exceptionally intense pressure on state finances occasioned only relatively minor and short-lived debasements around 90 B.C.E. and in the 30s B.C.E. (see above, section 6.1). From 64 to 235 C.E.—very slowly at first and at an accelerating rate later—the mean silver content of the *denarius* fell by about 56 percent.[275] It is unknown to what extent prices rose in response to the decreasing intrinsic value of newly minted coinage.[276] Usable serial price data are largely confined to Roman Egypt where the mean silver content of the provincial Alexandrine tetradrachm fell by around 30 percent between the 60s and the 160s C.E. while prices remained stable and by another 50 percent between 170 and 192 C.E. The latter drop coincided with

---

273. See above, sections 3.2–3 and 3.5; Thierry 1993: 7–8; von Glahn 2004: 173.

274. *Contra* Thierry 1993: 10, who invokes "la spécificité chinoise en matière monétaire: la monnaie reste un instrument d'échange dont la valeur repose sur la confiance et la mise en place d'un contrat tacite entre les différents acteurs économiques," this was also true of other currency systems, most notably that of the Roman Empire in the first few centuries C.E. Ultimately, of course, *all* money use rests on confidence.

275. Duncan-Jones 1994: 227.

276. The data surveyed in Duncan-Jones 1994: 25–29 and Rathbone forthcoming cannot tell us about conditions outside Egypt (on which see below). Modern estimates of the increase in legionary base pay between the 80s and the 230s C.E. mostly suggest a rate of 500 percent (e.g., Wolters 1999: 224; Herz 2007: 313; but cf. Rathbone 2007 for the overall degree of uncertainty): given that a 200 percent increase would have matched the concurrent debasement of the imperial silver currency, an aggregate raise on that scale implies a substantial increase in real terms regardless of whether prices tracked coin debasement.

a rapid doubling of prices.[277] This might be taken to suggest that sudden large changes in metal content were more likely to impact prices than slow gradual debasement. Between 238 and 269 C.E., as fiscal demands escalated and precious metal supplies diminished due to incessant military campaigning and temporary internal fragmentation, the silver content of the new imperial silver coin (the "double" *denarius* known as *antoninianus*) fell by 98 percent: gross coin weight was almost halved while fineness was reduced from 50 to 1.7 percent.[278] Once again, the consequences of this precipitous slide remain obscure. Much the same is true of bimetallic exchange rates. The gold content of the imperial *aureus* had gradually been lowered by 55 percent between the early first century and the 240s C.E., tracking but not fully keeping up with the concomitant loss of 75 percent of the silver currency's intrinsic value. In the 250s and 260s C.E., as the development of the *aureus*—whose intrinsic value remained relatively stable—was finally decoupled from the dramatic debasement of silver, nominal exchange rates between gold and silver coins are likely to have come under growing pressure. Unfortunately, the evidence sheds little light on actual outcomes in most parts of the Roman world. In Egypt, prices appear to have remained fairly stable throughout this period but suddenly rose more than tenfold in the mid 270s C.E. when the imperial government officially retariffed the imperial silver coinage in ways that appear to have caused it to be conspicuously overvalued relative to existing standards. A similar link between official retariffing and sudden price inflation has been suggested for 301 C.E. when the state doubled the nominal value of silver and billon coins relative to gold: price controls that were—unsuccessfully—imposed immediately afterward may have been an attempt to curtail an ensuing or anticipated rise in prices.[279]

This suggests a complex reality in which both official valuations and the metal value of coins were of relevance and sudden government intervention was the principal cause of the market's refusal to accept certain types of coin at face value.[280] Just as the Qin state of the third century B.C.E. had sought to assign a uniform value to coins of different weights (see above, section 2), the Roman authorities expected to determine the rates at which state-manufactured coins were to be exchanged regardless of their precise physical properties. Roman jurists repeatedly emphasized the interchangeability of individual coins, the character of any (Roman, though not foreign) coin as the embodiment of a given value or price (*pretium*) and not as a commodity (*merx*), and the expectation that the value of Roman coins was a function of their number as opposed to their actual

---

277. Debasement: Harl 1996: 142. Prices: Rathbone 1997.
278. Harl 1996: 130.
279. See, e.g., Howgego 1995: 131–33; Rathbone 1997; Strobel 2002: 139–44. These measures are only poorly understood and continue to be debated; pertinent scholarship is much more substantial than can be indicated here.
280. Howgego 1995: 115–40 remains the most valuable discussion of the underlying complexities.

weight.[281] Within the empire, the market tolerated slow downward trends in coin weight and fineness in the sense that prices do not appear to have immediately responded to each incremental reduction of intrinsic value. At the same time, the gradual disappearance of the lowest-value denominations of bronze coins from the second century c.e. onward is consistent with the notion of creeping price inflation. Moreover, changes in the composition of Roman coin hoards have been interpreted as a sign that during the accelerating debasement of the silver currency in the first half of the third century c.e., users preferred to hoard coins with a higher intrinsic value and thus attached significance to the growing divergence of nominal and metal value.[282]

The resilience of the imperial currency system may have owed much to the enormous size of the Roman Empire that trapped most coin users within a single system of exchange dominated by state-manufactured coin or its local surrogates. In this monopolistic environment, the lack of competition in the form of alternative monetary media or monetary inflows from the outside tended to stifle market responses to currency debasement. It need not be by coincidence that the structure of Roman coin finds from beyond the borders—in India and later also Germany— seems to reflect greater sensitivity to changes in precious-metal content.[283] The mature Han constituted a similarly self-contained system of currency exchange.

In the final analysis, the Roman currency system was not any more "metallistic" than the Han system was "fiduciary," or vice versa. Both monetary regimes combined an appreciation of intrinsic value with varying degrees of tolerance of long-term debasement. In both empires, known incidents of widespread loss of trust in the official coinage tended to be closely associated with bold measures that dissociated nominal values from prevailing standards: experiments with various kinds of large-denomination token coins in China (see above) and monetary reforms in the late third and early fourth centuries c.e. in Rome. While the state generally benefited from its monopoly status in the monetary sphere that enabled it to increase revenue through gradual debasement without undermining the currency,[284] the sheer scale of its dominance also magnified the consequences of more ambitious state intervention.

---

281. Paulus, *Digest* 18.1.1 is a key text. For discussion of the sources, see esp. Wolters 1999: 356–62; Strobel 2002: 115–18.

282. Wolters 1999: 379–81, but cf. Strobel 2002: 96–111. Critical awareness of government policy is also reflected in a contemporary historian's complaint that the emperor Caracalla had issued debased coin (Cassius Dio 78.14.3–4).

283. See esp. Wolters 1999: 381–94. This may also explain the more overtly "metallistic" character of later European currencies that operated in a competitive market.

284. The numismatic data suggest that both the Roman and the Han economies were capable of accommodating gradual debasement: a weight loss of 25–30 percent for *wuzhu* coins between the early 110s b.c.e. and the second century c.e.; an 18 per cent reduction of the gold content of the *aureus* between the early first century and the 230s c.e.; and the 56 percent debasement of the *denarius* in the same period (see above). It is unfortunate that we do not know whether the rapid debasement of the Roman bronze *as* in the late third century b.c.e.—by 85 percent between 218 and 213 b.c.e. (see above, section 6.1)—was accompanied by corresponding price inflation (cf. Rathbone 1993: 124–25).

9. MONETIZATION

9.1. Money Stocks

Did the preponderance of base-metal coins in Han China result in lower levels of (metal-based) monetization than in the precious-metal-rich Roman Empire?[285] According to the *Hanshu*, the Han state issued more than 28 billion *wuzhu* coins between 112 B.C.E. and the end of the Western Han dynasty, at an average rate of 230 million per year. The credibility of this figure is reinforced by later references to the annual production of 327 million bronze coins at one point in the Tang period and corresponding tallies of 800 million to 1.3 billion in the first century of the Northern Song period.[286]

It is unclear to what extent pre-*wuzhu* issues were still in use at the end of the Western Han period or later: while it seems unlikely that *banliang* issues from the early Han or even Qin periods had completely disappeared from circulation, there is no good reason to believe that they accounted for a large part of the total money stock.[287] Only a detailed analysis of all known coin hoards from the Han period could shed some light on this issue. Moreover, the stock of *wuzhu* coins was exposed to attrition through loss and other forms of wastage. Although the scale of this process defies quantification, the loss of *wuzhu* coins and the continuing use of earlier issues would have pushed the total volume of the money stock in opposite directions, to some unknown degree canceling each other out. A few thought experiments help us demarcate the limits of the plausible. Modern sources report annual rates of loss of 0.7 to 1 percent for low-value base-metal coins (pennies) in early twentieth-century Britain, whereas estimated wastage rates for precious-metal coins in earlier periods vary dramatically from 0.125 to 7.7 (!) percent.[288] At an annual rate of loss of 0.7 percent and schematically assuming constant annual minting rates, one-third of the 28 billion *wuzhu* coins would already have disappeared by the beginning of the first century C.E. If, say, 10 billion Han *banliang* coins had been produced prior to the 110s B.C.E.—at one-half of the subsequent mean annual production rate—two-thirds of them would already have disappeared by the end of the Western Han period if the

---

285. Just as coins are only one form of money (see above, section 1), "monetization" cannot be reduced to changes in the volume or circulation of coin. Unfortunately, I am not aware of a specific term for what might be labeled "metal-based" or "metalliform" monetization, that is, the extent to which coins and bullion were used as money in a given economic system. As before, in this section I focus primarily on the use of coin but also touch briefly on the role of other monetary media. A detailed assessment of the importance of coin use relative to the use of other monetary instruments is well beyond the scope of this survey.

286. *Hanshu* 24B: 19b; von Glahn 1996: 49–50.

287. It is telling that the only first century C.E. hoard that contained monetary objects from the Warring States period reported by Peng 2000: 207–8 was located outside the Han Empire proper. See also Harada 1931: 10–11 for the discovery of 14 fragments of knife money, 5 round coins from the Warring States period (?), 7 *banliang* coins, 3 *wuzhu* coins, and 1 *daqian* coin of Wang Mang at a site in southern Manchuria. Cursory review of Huang 1984, Tang 2001, and http://scholar.ilib.cn/S-C.CK0.html (accessed March 28, 2008) failed to identify Han coin finds with pre-Han admixtures.

288. Duncan-Jones 2004: 204, n. 40 with references.

annual rate of wastage was as high as that, creating a total "hybrid" stock of 22 billion coins. By comparison, if we assume a lower annual loss rate of 0.3 percent and—probably unrealistically—double the size of the pre-*wuzhu* Han money stock, we end up with an early first century C.E. tally of 23 billion *wuzhu* and 12 billion earlier coins, for a total of 35 billion. This suggests that it would be difficult to reckon with a total money stock of either below 20 billion or much over 30 billion bronze coins at the end of the Western Han period. If pre-*wuzhu* coin had been successfully demonetized, our estimate would have to be near the lower end of this range. As noted, the archaeological record favors a low-end tally.

The amount of gold and silver that was used for monetary purposes is, of course, unknown. As discussed above, references to the disbursement of 900,000 *jin*—or *c.*225 tons of gold if all of this did indeed consist of actual gold—in the Western Han period and to Wang Mang's hoard of 600,000 *jin* or *c.*150 tons of gold are of uncertain value and in any case cannot be used to estimate total gold stocks at the time.[289] The relative scarcity of gold hoards from the Han period suggests that in the most general terms, monetary gold stocks were smaller than in the Roman Empire. If we were to speculate that the amount of Han gold money was half as large as that of Roman coined gold, the resultant total of 220–440 tons might have been priced at anywhere from 9 to 37 billion cash.[290] It merits attention that higher estimates of the quantity of gold money would imply that gold rather than bronze dominated the Han currency system, which seems incompatible with the tenor of the sources as well as evidence from later periods of Chinese history. Given the very low profile of silver in the Western Han period, this metal would not have made a significant contribution to the money supply.

These crude conjectures suggest that the aggregate cash value of all gold, silver, and bronze money at the end of the Western Han period could have ranged from 30 to 70 billion cash. Given that both the high-end guesses of the number of bronze coins and the amount of gold money rest on assumptions that are likely to inflate the results, an actual tally of the order of 40 or 50 billion seems more plausible.[291] Converted into grain equivalent, metal money stocks of 30 to 70 billion cash may have corresponded to anywhere from 6 to 28 billion liters of grain, while the conservative estimate of 40 to 50 billion cash would have translated to 8 to 20 billion liters.[292]

289. See above, section 4.2.

290. For Roman totals, see in the text below. Possible gold prices range from 10,000 cash per *jin* (at Wang Mang's official rate) to about 21,000: see above, section 4.2.

291. It is unlikely that pre-*wuzhu* coins accounted for a large share of all coins in circulation and that Chinese gold stocks were as high as 400–500 tons: for the latter, see in the text below. Twenty to 25 billion bronze coins and 200–300 tons of gold at 20,000 cash per *jin* would yield a total of 36 to 49 billion cash. For the use of nonmetallic token money, see below.

292. Han grain prices are poorly known. The conventional conversion rate of 100 cash per *hu* (19.9 liters) of grain (Bielenstein 1980: 126) in the Eastern Han period may refer to elevated prices in the capital. Comparative data from early modern China show that grain prices in outlying regions were only half or two-thirds as high as in

Drawing on estimates of coin output under particular rulers and allowing for wastage, Richard Duncan-Jones sought to extrapolate the total amount of precious metal in circulation in the Roman Empire in the 160s C.E. His conjectural calculations indicate the existence of a coined money stock of approximately 900 tons of gold and 5,800 tons of silver. Adding base-metal issues, the total cash value of all coins would have amounted to roughly 20 billion sesterces.[293] Expressed in grain equivalent, this corresponds to some 45 to 90 billion liters.[294] However, although Duncan-Jones believed that Roman liquidity levels were generally low, comparative evidence shows that the size of the money stock implied by his own estimate is actually very high by historical standards: it approximates the probable annual GDP of the empire as a whole, whereas the money supply of the more economically developed Dutch Republic in the late eighteenth century has been estimated at less than its annual GNP.[295] The numismatic foundations of Duncan-Jones's extrapolations are also liable to criticism.[296] For these reasons we have to allow for the possibility that Roman imperial money stocks were significantly smaller than suggested. At the same time, convergent reports concerning the considerable annual output of gold and silver mints in the Roman period speak against the notion of much more modest overall stocks: in principle, cumulative yields of a dozen tons of gold and several dozen tons of silver per year would have been sufficient to build up large stocks of precious metal on the scale envisioned by Duncan-Jones.[297] Moreover, money stocks that were large in relation to GDP do not necessarily translate to high levels of liquidity as long as hoarding immobilizes a large share of the available assets, which may well have occurred in the Roman Empire. A compromise

central areas: e.g., Wang 1991: 46. Thus, Han grain prices may have ranged from 50 to 100 cash per *hu*. An intermediate figure would seem to provide the most plausible notional average and is consistent with estimates of average grain prices of 30–80 or 70–80 cash per *hu* in the Western Han period (Hsu 1980: 79; Yang 1961: 154, n. 47) and the fact that grain prices of between 67 and 110 cash per *hu* are repeatedly recorded in the Juyan garrison documents (Wang 2004: 59). See also Peng 1994: 164–69.

293. Duncan-Jones 1994: 168–70.

294. Rathbone forthcoming is the most recent survey of grain prices in the Roman world, referring to grain prices of 2–2.25 sesterces per *modius* (8.62 liters) in parts of the eastern Mediterranean in the first and second centuries C.E. Prices were higher in Italy, especially in the city of Rome: see Duncan-Jones 1982: 346, 365; Rathbone 1996: 217–22 and forthcoming. I have chosen a range from 2 to 4 sesterces per *modius* whose upper limit probably overstates *average* grain prices and thereby understates the purchasing power of Roman money (and hence the degree of monetization) in order to make it more difficult to me to make a case that the Roman world was more monetized than Han China. Two to 3 sesterces per *modius* might be a more reasonable mean for the Roman Empire as a whole.

295. Duncan-Jones 1994: 32 ("liquidity was generally low"). For Roman GDP, see Friesen and Scheidel forthcoming. The comparison with the Netherlands was made by Jongman 2003: 187, with reference to De Vries and Van der Woude 1997: 88–91. See also Lo Cascio 2008: 162–63.

296. I am indebted to William Metcalf for information on work in progress. See also Lo Cascio 1997. Some modern estimates for late Roman gold stocks are much lower: see Depeyrot 1991: 212 (59 tons of gold in 310 C.E., 200 tons in 370 C.E., 95 tons in 490 C.E.).

297. See above, section 7.2. These textual claims are consistent with physical evidence in the form of lead deposits in Arctic ice cores that were caused by Roman silver smelting: see most recently de Callataÿ 2005. However, outflows of gold and silver coins would have helped to offset gains from mining: see esp. Turner 1989 and also Wolters 1999: 389–93 for surveys of the monetary dimension of Roman trade with India.

estimate of total money stocks worth between 10 and 20 billion sesterces would
translate to anywhere from 22 to 90 billion liters of grain.

Due to the deficiencies of the evidence, my estimates for size of both the
Han and the Roman money stocks vary by a factor of four or five. However,
despite these very considerable margins of uncertainty, even the broadest range
of guesses for the money stock in Han China of between 6 and 28 billion liters
of grain equivalent barely overlaps with the much higher range from 22 to 90
billion liters proposed for the Roman Empire. More conservative guesses of 8
to 20 billion liters for Han China and of 30 to 40 billion liters for the Roman
Empire would have even less in common.[298] With all due caution, I conclude that
due to the dominance of gold and silver coin in western Eurasia and in light of
the documented valuation of different metals relative to grain in both regions,
the Roman Empire had achieved higher levels of monetization than its Chinese
counterpart.

This conclusion rests on a comparison of metal stocks and their real value
expressed in terms of grain. However, nonmetallic monetary media likewise
require consideration. In the Han Empire, cash and bullion were supplemented
by money in the form of textiles, above all silk. The first known normed unit was
the *bu* of the late preimperial Qin state, a piece of cloth measuring 8 *chi* by 2 *chi*
5 *cun* (or 188 x 58.5 cm) and valued at 11 *banliang* cash. References to fines that
are expressed in multiples of the latter figure—such as 110, 220, 1,100, or 2,200
cash—suggest that these payments may have been collected in cloth rather than
coin.[299] Under the Han dynasty, bolts of 2 *chi* 2 *cun* by 5 *zhang* (51.7 x 1,175 cm)
became the standard size. Silk remained a popular gift throughout that period,
and the monetary use of textiles generally surged during periods of state instability such as the later years of Wang Mang's reign, or later on in the Jin Dynasty,
the Period of Disunion, or the late Tang Dynasty.[300] In addition, payments in the
form of "salary-silk" (*luyongbo*) and "salary-cotton" (*lubu*) are mentioned in
the documents from the Juyan garrison site.[301]

We cannot tell how much the monetary use of textiles contributed to the
overall money supply. However, it is crucial to realize that for cloth money to
close the gap between the money stocks of the Han and Roman empires, it would
have had to be as abundant (in cash terms) as all varieties of metal money combined.[302] The sources certainly do not convey the impression that this was the

298. For the former, see above. The latter estimate reckons with a relatively small money stock worth 10 billion
sesterces and a more realistic empire-wide mean grain price of 2 to 3 sesterces per *modius* (cf. above, n. 294).

299. E.g., Hulsewé 1985b: 227–29; Thierry 1997: 170; Wang 2004: 14.

300. See briefly Wang 2004: 14 with references, and Peng 1994 passim (esp. 209, on the Han period) for more
detail.

301. Wang 2004: 51 with 50, table 6, and cf. 51, table 7 for the issuing of *dahuangbu* or "large yellow cloth" in
11 C.E.

302. The above estimate of Han metal money stocks worth 6 to 28 billion liters of grain would need to be
doubled in order to overlap substantially with the Roman estimate of 22 to 90 billion liters.

case in times of stability such as much of the Western Han period. Thus, while nonmetallic monetary media must have helped to shore up the Chinese money supply, it is highly unlikely that they would have offset the underlying imbalances in metal stocks between eastern and western Eurasia.[303]

Moreover, the Roman money supply was also boosted by nonmetallic means of payment. Recent scholarship has emphasized the considerable role of credit money in the Roman economy, especially for large-scale transactions in elite circles and for long-distance trade.[304] The nature of comparable arrangements in the Han Empire remains obscure. In the Tang and Song periods, shortages of bronze coin caused deflationary price decreases that had to be offset by the introduction of monetary remittances and account notes. These innovations expanded the money supply well beyond monetary metal stocks. However, comparable arrangements are not recorded for any period of Chinese history prior to the Tang dynasty.[305] Money remittances called "flying cash" (*feiqian*) or, later, "convenient exchange" (*bianhuan*) first appeared around 800 C.E.[306] Paper money can be traced back only as far as the tenth century C.E.[307] Thus, in so far as Han merchants and bankers made use of credit money, there is no good reason to assume that they did so on a much grander scale than their Roman counterparts. The use of nonmetallic monetary media does not affect my overall conclusion that levels of monetization—in both gross and per capita terms—in the Roman Empire at its peak significantly exceeded those in the equivalent period of the Han Empire.

9.2. Money Use

As already mentioned, the volume of the money supply does not tell us much about liquidity per se. A better idea of how much coin circulated can be obtained by comparing my above estimates to budgetary requirements. In the case of Han China, surviving documents from an official archive of Donghai Commandery that date from around 10 B.C.E. provide unique insight into the workings of the fiscal system. One of these texts reports the presence of 1.4 million residents in 266,000 households who in a given year had provided the government with

---

303. Although grain was also used as a means of payment in Han China (see, e.g., Bielenstein 1980: 125–31 for the salaries of state officials and Wang 2004: 51 for practices in a frontier context), the information contained in the Donghai Commandery archive suggests that such transactions cannot have accounted for more than a small fraction of government spending (see below). We do not know enough about practices in the private sector.

304. See Mrozek 1985 and now esp. Harris 2006 and 2008.

305. We cannot rule out the possibility that the merchants of the Han period operated private credit systems that have left no trace in the aristocratic (and usually antimerchant) sources, but it seems unlikely that they could have been sufficiently substantial to compensate for the relative scarcity of metal money.

306. Peng 1994: 329–31, esp. 330, n. 3. Cf. De Ligt 2003 for a comparative perspective, and Adshead 2004: 68–100 for the increasing sophistication of the Tang economy. Carlson 2006 compares traditions of money lending in the Roman and Han empires. For a survey of the rudimentary credit institutions of the Han period, see Peng 1994: 183–85. The Juyan texts record deferred payments and debts but no more sophisticated arrangements: Wang 2004: 53–54.

307. Peng 1994: 367–69. Cf. Elvin 1973: 146–63.

an annual revenue of 267 million cash and 507,000 *shih* (10 million liters) of grain.[308] Given that Donghai Commandery accounted for approximately one-fortieth of the imperial population at the time and that it might be considered a reasonable "average" province in the sense that it was neither located in the capital region or the highly developed old core of the central Great Plain nor particularly peripheral either, and therefore arguably not entirely unrepresentative in terms of its overall economic development, a simple extrapolation from the reported revenue points to annual imperial gross income of about 10 to 11 billion cash and 400 million liters of grain worth another 1 or 2 billion cash. As I will argue in greater detail elsewhere, a number of indicators support the notion of an annual imperial budget of this order of magnitude.[309]

Unless conditions in Donghai Commandery were highly anomalous, a large proportion of these funds was remitted in cash rather than in kind.[310] Cash payments of 10 billion per year would have required the mobilization of anywhere from 30 to 50 percent of all existing bronze coins. We cannot tell whether and to what extent gold could be substituted for cash: however, the sources do not report the payment of tax in gold beyond a relatively small levy on top-level aristocrats (see above, section 4.2). Even if (say) one-third of all revenues had been obtained in the form of precious metal, 20 or probably closer to 30 percent of all bronze coins would have had to change hands every year to satisfy state demands. It appears that the circulation of assets between the state and its subjects was a key function of Han coinage.

Two competing models of the monetary system of the Northern Song period help put this estimate into perspective. In the eleventh century c.e., according to Miyazawa Tomoyuki's model of "fiscal circulation," which considers the imperial bronze currency above all as a medium for state savings and payments, each year about one-quarter of the coined money stock was used for tax payments, one-tenth for commercial exchange, and most of the remainder was hoarded by the government. By contrast, Gao Congming's more market-oriented model envisions annual tax payments equivalent to one-sixth of the total money stock, commercial exchange on a much grander scale (closer to one-half), and smaller state savings (perhaps one-seventh).[311] While the latter scenario may be better

---

308. Loewe 2004: 60 (YM6D1). For 1–2 c.e., *Hanshu* 19A: 28b reports 1.56 million people in 358,000 households. I have rounded off all these figures.

309. Scheidel forthcoming b.

310. See above. Payment of the poll tax in kind is portrayed as an emergency relief measure in *Hanshu* 7:7b and 7:10a: see Hsu 1980: 240–41. This also implies that cash payments were considered the norm. Cf. also Loewe 1985: 256, n. 39. We cannot rule out the possibility that some of the "cash" revenue reported in the Donghai document had actually been remitted in the form of gold, silver, or cloth but that the accountants employed "cash" as a universal unit of account for all these pecuniary assets. Compare, however, the report that a fiefholder received 7,000 *jin* of gold, 60 million cash, and 30,000 bolts of silk in the first century c.e. (*Hanshu* 68 cited by Nishijima 1986: 593), which distinguishes among different monetary media.

311. Miyazawa 1998 and Gao 1999 as discussed by von Glahn 2004.

supported for the Song period itself, the Han data place the early imperial monetary system in closer proximity to Miyazawa's reconstruction. Reported government savings of 8.3 billion cash in the second half of the first century B.C.E. would probably have accounted for no more than one-sixth or one-fifth of the overall money stock, including precious metals, or 30 to 40 percent of all coin, implying an intermediate scenario in between Miyazawa's and Gao's more extreme positions.[312] Then again, Wudi's supposed ability to disburse some 200 tons of gold or its cash equivalent in a short period of time and the purported scale of Wang Mang's gold hoard would once again seem to be far better consistent with Miyazawa's perspective (see above, section 4.2). These issues warrant further consideration. What matters here is that these reconstructions show that there is nothing inherently implausible about the notion that the annual tax revenues of the Han state may have represented a very sizeable portion of the total money stock.

Recent estimates of the Roman imperial budget in the middle of the second century C.E. converge on approximately 1 billion sesterces.[313] It is certain that not all of these funds were collected in cash.[314] However, even if we employ the simplifying assumption of an annual revenue stream of 1 billion sesterces in coin, this amount would not have exceeded 10 percent of the coined money stock. Allowing for assessments in kind and/or a coinage volume in excess of 10 billion sesterces (see above)—its actual share was probably smaller still.

In terms of grain equivalent, the annual revenues of the Han Empire in the late first century B.C.E. and the Roman Empire of the mid-second century C.E. appear to have been roughly similar: 2 to 6 billion liters in the former and 2 to 4.5 billion (figures that increased soon thereafter and to which we must add municipal taxes, which lacked a Han equivalent) in the latter. Given similar levels of technological development and similarly sized populations, this match is perfectly plausible. At the same time, unless my above estimates of total metal stocks are very wide of the mark, the Roman Empire was significantly more monetized than the Han state and more coin was therefore available for commercial exchange or hoarding. In view of the dramatic surge of Mediterranean trade and production for a mass market in the Roman period and the growing wealth of the Roman elite that does not seem to have been matched by that of its Han peers, both commerce and elite hoarding may well have been sufficiently important to absorb the larger stock of coinage in the Roman Empire.[315] This raises important questions

312. Nishijima 1986: 594.

313. Compare Duncan-Jones 1994: 33–46, esp. 45 (between 832 and 983 million sesterces *c.* 150 C.E.) and Wolters 1999: 202–34, esp. 223 (implying a total of *c.* 1.1 billion in the same period).

314. Duncan-Jones 1990: 187–98.

315. On the expansion of trade under Roman rule, see most recently Morley 2007: 90–102. In the Han Empire, in the absence of significant maritime trade and the massive north-south canal network that helped shape later periods of Chinese history, the overall volume of supralocal exchange may well have fallen short of Roman levels. In

about the character of the Han and Roman economies that go well beyond the scope of this survey and call for more systematic investigation.[316]

APPENDIX: GLOSSARY OF WEIGHTS AND DENOMINATIONS

argenteus: late Roman silver coin of 1/96 Roman pounds (*c*.3.4g) introduced in 293 C.E.

as: initially (*c*.300 C.E.) a bronze coin weighing 1 Roman pound (*c*.323g), by 211 B.C.E. reduced to 1/6 of the original weight, and since the 20s B.C.E. issued as a copper coin of *c*.11g

aureus: Roman gold coin struck at 1/40 of a Roman pound (*c*.8.1g) from 46 B.C.E. and at 1/45 pounds (*c*.7.2g) from 64 C.E., with further weight reductions in the third century C.E.

banliang: Qin and early Han bronze coin with a target weight of *c*.7.8g created by the Qin state probably in the second quarter of the fourth century C.E.

billon: technical term for an alloy of a precious metal with a majority base-metal content

denarius: Roman silver coin struck at 1/72 of a Roman pound (*c*.4.5g) from 213/12 B.C.E., at 1/84 pounds (*c*.3.8g) from 187 B.C.E., and at 1/96 pounds (*c*.3.4g) from 64 C.E., with further reductions in weight and especially fineness in the late second and third centuries C.E. A double *denarius* known as *antoninianus* was introduced in 215 C.E. As *denarius communis*, the *denarius* continued to be used as a unit of account well beyond the discontinuation of actual issues.

follis: late Roman bronze coin with an initial target weight of 1/36 of a Roman pound (*c*.9g) introduced in 498 C.E.

jin: Han pound of *c*.250g

liang: Han ounce equivalent to 1/16 *jin* or *c*.15.6g

libra: Roman pound of *c*.323g

Han historiography, "100 million cash" served as a proverbial figure denoting a very large fortune. This translates to 20–40 million liters of grain or anywhere from 5 to 18 (or probably rather 14) million sesterces. In second century C.E. Rome, by contrast, an aristocratic fortune of 20 million sesterces would not have placed the owner among the super-rich, as the grandest estates were (imagined to be?) fifteen or twenty times as large: see Duncan-Jones 1982: 17–32, 343–44. See Jongman 2006: 248 for a minimum estimate of aggregate Roman imperial elite wealth of 13 billion sesterces and the likelihood of a much higher actual total, accounting for a very sizeable share of all assets in the empire. Cf. also Friesen and Scheidel forthcoming. Although, as I point out in chapter 1, the ideal-typical contrast between Rome as an empire of property holders and China as an empire of office holders (Wood 2003: 26–37) is overdrawn, it nevertheless contains a kernel of truth.

316. Morris forthcoming constructs a long-term historical index of social development that uses coded data for energy capture, organizational capacity, information processing, and war-making abilities as proxies of overall macroregional development. He finds that in these respects, western Eurasia in the Roman period enjoyed a noticeable lead over eastern Eurasia in the Han period.

I would like to thank Yan Haiying for procuring copies of key Chinese numismatic publications, Michelle Wang for translating or summarizing several of these texts, Hsin-Mei Agnes Hsu and Mei-yu Hsieh for further assistance with Chinese sources and scholarship, David Schaps for advice, Qi Dongfang for presenting me with a copy of his book, and Peng Ke for sending me an article.

liu: Han weight equivalent to ½ jin or c.125g

ounce: see liang and uncia

pound: see jin, libra, and yi

sestertius: Roman fractional silver coin (¼ denarius) intermittently minted from the late third century B.C.E. to the mid-first century B.C.E., and from the 20s B.C.E. issued as a brass alloy coin of c.25g

solidus: late Roman gold coin struck at 1/60 of a Roman pound (c.5.4g) and at 1/72 pounds (c.4.5g) from 309 C.E.

uncia: Roman ounce equivalent to 1/12 libra or c.26.9g

wuzhu: Han bronze coin with a target weight of 5 zhu or c.3.3g introduced in 118 B.C.E.

yi: Qin pound equivalent to 20 liang or c.313g

zhu: Han weight unit of c.0.65g.

Bibliography

Adshead, S. A. M. 2000. *China in World History*. 3rd ed. Basingstoke.

Adshead, S. A. M. 2004. *T'ang China: The Rise of the East in World History*. Basingstoke.

Allen, D. 1999. *The World of Prometheus: The Politics of Punishing in Democratic Athens*. Princeton.

Anderson, M. M. 1990. *Hidden Power: The Palace Eunuchs of Imperial China*. Buffalo.

Andersson, J. G. 1935. "The Goldsmith in Ancient China," *Bulletin of the Museum of Far Eastern Antiquities* 7: 1–38.

Aperghis, G. G. 2004. *The Seleukid Royal Economy: The Finances and Financial Administration of the Seleukid Empire*. Cambridge.

Apparadurai, A., ed. 1986. *The Social Life of Things: Commodities in Cultural Perspective*. Cambridge.

Arbuckle, G. 1995. "Inevitable Treason: Dong Zhongshu's Theory of Historical Cycles and Early Attempts to Invalidate the Han Mandate," *Journal of the American Oriental Society* 115: 585–97.

Arnason, J. P., Eisenstadt, S. N., and Wittrock, B., eds. 2005. *Axial Civilizations and World History*. Leiden.

Ashtor, E. 1976. *A Social and Economic History of the Near East in the Middle Ages*. Berkeley.

Ausbüttel, F. M. 1998. *Die Verwaltung des römischen Kaiserreiches*. Darmstadt.

Badian, E. 1972. *Publicans and Sinners: Private Enterprise in the Service of the Roman Republic*. Oxford.

Balazs, E. 1967. *Chinese Civilization and Bureaucracy: Variations on a Theme*. New Haven.

Banaji, J. 2001. *Agrarian Change in Late Antiquity: Gold, Labour, and Aristocratic Dominance*. Oxford.

Bang, P. F. 2002. "Romans and Mughals: Economic Integration in a Tributary Empire," in L. de Blois and J. Rich, eds., *The Transformation of Economic Life under the Roman Empire*, 1–27. Amsterdam.

Bang, P. F. 2003. "Rome and the Comparative Study of Tributary Empires," *Medieval History Journal* 6: 189–216.

Bang, P. F. 2004. "The Mediterranean: A Corrupting Sea? A Review-Essay on Ecology and History, Anthropology and Synthesis," *Ancient West and East* 3: 385–99.

Bang, P. F. 2006. "Imperial Bazaar: Towards a Comparative Understanding of Markets in the Roman Empire," in Bang, Ikeguchi, and Ziche, eds. 2006: 51–88.

Bang, P. F. 2007. "Trade and Empire: In Search of Organizing Concepts for the Roman Economy," *Past and Present* 195: 3–54.

Bang, P. F. Forthcoming. *Roman Bazaar: A Comparative Study of Trade and Markets in a Tributary Empire*. Cambridge.

Bang, P. F. In progress. *Universal Empire: A Comparative Study of the Roman State and Patrimonial Government*.

Bang, P. F., Ikeguchi, M., and Ziche, H. G., eds. 2006. *Ancient Economies, Modern Methodologies: Archaeology, Comparative History, Models and Institutions*. Bari.

Bang, P. F., and Scheidel, W. Forthcoming. "Comparative Synthesis," in P. F. Bang and W. Scheidel, eds., *The Oxford Handbook of the Ancient State: Near East and Mediterranean*. New York.

Barfield, T. 2001. "The Shadow Empires: Imperial State Formation along the Chinese-Nomad Frontier," in S. Alcock et al., eds., *Empires: Perspectives from Archaeology and History*, 10–41. Cambridge.

Barfield, T. J. 1989. *The Perilous Frontier: Nomadic Empires and China, 221 BC to AD 1757*. Cambridge, MA.

Barrett, A. A. 1996. *Agrippina, Mother of Nero*. London.

Barrett, A. A. 2002. *Livia: First Lady of Imperial Rome*. New Haven.

Bartlett, B. 1994. *Monarchs and Ministers: The Grand Council in Mid-Ch'ing China, 1723–1820*. Berkeley.

Bauman, R. 1996. *Crime and Punishment in Ancient Rome*. London.

Bayly, C. A. 2002. "'Archaic' and 'Modern' Globalization in the Eurasian and African Arena, c.1750–1850," in A. G. Hopkins, ed., *Globalization in World History*, 47–73. London.

Bell, D. A. 2006. *Beyond Liberal Democracy: Political Thinking for an East Asian Context*. Princeton.

Bellah, R. N. 2005. "What's Axial about the Axial Age?" *Archives Européennes de Sociologie* 46: 69–87.

Bielenstein, H. 1980. *The Bureaucracy of Han Times*. Cambridge.

Bielenstein, H. 1986. "The Institutions of Later Han," in Twitchett and Loewe, eds. 1986: 491–519.

Bielenstein, H. 1987. "Chinese Historical Demography A.D. 2–1982," *Bulletin of the Museum of Far Eastern Antiquities* 59: 1–288.

Birley, A. R. 2000. "Hadrian to the Antonines," in Bowman, Garnsey, and Rathbone, eds. 2000: 132–94.

Blakeley, B. B. 1985–87. "Recent Developments in Chu Studies: A Bibliographic and Institutional Overview," *Early China* 11–12: 371–87.

Blanchard, I. 2005. *Mining, Metallurgy and Minting in the Middle Ages, 3: Continuing Afro-European Supremacy, 1250–1450*. Stuttgart.

Bland, R. 1997. "The Changing Pattern of Hoards of Precious-Metal Coins in the Late Empire," *L'Antiquité Tardive* 5: 29–55.

Bodde, D. 1975. *Festivals in Han China*. Princeton.

Bodde, D. 1986. "The State and Empire of Ch'in," in Twitchett and Loewe, eds. 1986: 20–102.

Bonnell, V. E. 1980. "The Uses of Theory, Concepts and Comparison in Historical Sociology," *Comparative Studies in Society and History* 22: 156–73.

Boodberg, P. A. 1938. "Marginalia to the Histories of the Northern Dynasties," *Harvard Journal of Asiatic Studies* 3: 223–53.

Borkowski, A. 1997. *Textbook on Roman Law*. Oxford.

Boulvert, G. 1970. *Esclaves et affranchis impériaux sous le Haut-Empire romain: Rôle politique administratif*. Naples.

Bowditch, P. L. 2001. *Horace and the Gift Economy of Patronage*. Berkeley.

Bowman, A. 2005. "Diocletian and the First Tetrarchy, A.D. 284–305," in Bowman, Garnsey, and Cameron, eds. 2005: 67–109.

Bowman, A., Champlin, E., and Lintott, A. eds. 1996. *The Cambridge Ancient History*, 2nd ed. Vol. 10: *The Augustan Empire, 43 B.C.–A.D. 69*. Cambridge.

Bowman, A., Garnsey, P., and Cameron, A., eds. 2005. *The Cambridge Ancient History*, 2nd ed. Vol. 12: *The Crisis of Empire, A.D. 193–337*. Cambridge.

Bowman, A., Garnsey, P., and Rathbone, D., eds. 2000. *The Cambridge Ancient History*, 2nd ed. Vol. 11: *The High Empire, A.D. 70–192*. Cambridge.

Bowman, S., Cowell, M., and Cribb, J. 2005. "Two Thousand Years of Coinage in China: An Analytical Survey," in Wang et al., eds. 2005: 5–61.

Breuer, S. 1994. "Kulturen der Achsenzeit: Leistung und Grenzen eines geschichtsphilosophischen Konzepts," *Saeculum* 45: 1–33.

Brunt, P. A. 1987. *Italian Manpower 225 B.C.–A.D. 14*. Rev. ed. Oxford.

Bujard, M. 2000. *Le sacrifice au ciel dans la Chine ancienne: théorie et pratique sous les Han occidentaux*. Paris.

Bullough, V. L. 2002. "Eunuchs in History and Society," in Tougher, ed. 2002: 1–17.

Bunker, E. C. 1993. "Gold in the Ancient Chinese World: A Cultural Puzzle," *Artibus Asiae* 53: 27–50.

Bunker, E. C. 1994. "The Enigmatic Role of Silver in China," *Orientations* 25.11: 73–78.

Camodeca, G. 1999. *Tabulae Pompeianae Sulpiciorum (TPSulp): Edizione critica dell' archivio puteolano dei Sulpicii*. 2 vols. Rome.

Campbell, B. 1984. *The Emperor and the Roman Army 31 B.C.–A.D. 325*. Oxford.

Campbell, B. 2005. "The Army," in Bowman, Garnsey, and Cameron, eds. 2005: 110–30.

Carlson, J. L. 2007. "Money-Lending and Society in the Ancient Roman and Chinese Empires," unpubl. paper. Georgetown University.

Carandini, A. 1988. *Schiavi in Italia: Gli strumenti pensanti dei Romani fra tarda Republica e medio Impero* Rome.

Cerati, A. 1975. *Caractère annonaire et assiette de l'impot foncier au Bas-Empire*. Paris.

Chang, Chun-shu 2007. *The Rise of the Chinese Empire*. Vol. I: *Nation, State, and Imperialism in Early China, ca. 1600 B.C.–A.D. 8*. Ann Arbor.

Chaniotis, A. 2005. *War in the Hellenistic World*. Malden.

Chase-Dunn, C., and Hall, T. D. 1997. *Rise and Demise: Comparing World-Systems*. Boulder.

Chayanov, A. V. 1986. *The Theory of Peasant Economy*. Madison.

Chien, Tuan-Sheng 1950. *The Government and Politics of China*. Cambridge, MA.

Ch'ü, T'ung-Tsu 1972. *Han Social Structure*. Ed. J. L. Dull. Seattle.

Clauss, M., ed. 1997. *Die römischen Kaiser*. Munich.

Coedès, G. 1910. *Textes d'auteurs grecs et latins relatifs à l'Extrême Orient (depuis le 4ème siècle avant J.C. jusqu'au 14ème siècle après J.C.)*. Paris.

Cohen, J. E. 1995. *How Many People Can the Earth Support?* New York.

Cook, C. A., and Major, J. S., eds. 1999. *Defining Chu: Image and Reality in Ancient China*. Honolulu.

Cornell, T. J. 1995. *The Beginnings of Rome: Italy and Rome from the Bronze Age to the Punic Wars (c.1000–264 B.C.)*. London.

Cowell, M., Cribb, J., Bowman, S., and Shashoua, Y. 2005. "The Chinese Cash: Composition and Production," in Wang et al., eds. 2005: 63–68.

Csikszntmihalyi, M. 2004. *Material Virtue: Ethics and Body in Early China.* Leiden.

Dai Zhiqiang and Zhou Weirong 1998. "A Study of the Pieces of Bronze Used as Primitive Currency in Ancient China," *Numismatic Metallurgy* 4: 295–303.

Dalby, A. 2001. *Empire of Pleasures: Luxury and Indulgence in the Roman World.* London.

De Callataÿ, F. 2005. "The Graeco-Roman Economy in the Super-Long Run: Lead, Copper, and Shipwrecks," *Journal of Roman Archaeology* 18: 361–72.

De Crespigny, R. 1984. *Northern Frontier: The Policies and Strategy of the Later Han Empire.* Canberra.

De Ligt, L. 2003. "Taxes, Trade, and the Circulation of Coin: The Roman Empire, Mughal India and T'ang China Compared," *Medieval History Journal* 6: 231–48.

De Ste Croix, G. E. M. 1981. *The Class Struggle in the Ancient Greek World from the Archaic Age to the Arab Conquests.* London.

Delbrück, R. 1932. *Antike Porphyrwerke.* Berlin.

Demandt, A. 1989. *Die Spätantike: Römische Geschichte von Diocletian bis Justinian, 284–565 n. Chr.* Munich.

DeMarrais, E. 2005. "A View from the Americas: 'Internal Colonization', Material Culture and Power in the Inka Empire," in H. Hurst and S. Owen, eds., *Ancient Colonizations: Analogy, Similarity and Difference*, 73–96. London.

Demiéville, P. 1986. "Philosophy and Religion from Han to Sui," in Twitchett and Loewe, eds. 1986: 808–72.

Deng, G. 1999. *The Premodern Chinese Economy.* London.

Depeyrot, G. 1991. *Crises et inflation entre antiquité et Moyen Age.* Paris.

De Rachewiltz, I. 1997. "Marco Polo Went to China," *Zentralasiatische Studien* 27: 34–92.

DeSilva, D. A. 2000. *Honor, Patronage, Kinship and Purity: Unlocking New Testament Culture.* Downers Grove.

Dettenhofer, M. H. 2003. "Das Interregnum des Senats des Jahres 41 v. Chr.," in P. Defosse, ed., *Hommages à Carl Deroux III*, 187–99. Bruxelles.

Dettenhofer, M. H. 2006. "Das römische Imperium und das China der Han-Zeit: Ansätze zu einer historischen Komparatistik," *Latomus* 65: 879–98.

De Vries, J., and Van der Woude, A. 1997. *The First Modern Economy: Success, Failure, and Perseverance of the Dutch Economy, 1500–1815.* Cambridge.

Di Cosmo, N. 2002. *Ancient China and Its Enemies: The Rise of Nomadic Power in East Asian History.* Cambridge.

Diamond, J. 2005. *Guns, Germs, and Steel: The Fates of Human Societies.* New ed. New York.

Dien, A. 2001. "Civil Service Examinations: Evidence from the Northwest," in S. Pearce, A. Spiro, and P. Ebrey, eds., *Culture and Power in the Reconstitution of the Chinese Realm, 200–600*, 99–121. Cambridge, MA.

Dihle, A. 1984. "Serer und Chinesen," in A. Dihle, *Antike und Orient: Gesammelte Aufsätze*, ed. V. Pöschl and H. Petersmann, 201–15. Heidelberg.

Domergue, C. 1990. *Les mines de la péninsule ibérique dans l'Antiquité romaine.* Rome.

Doyle, M. W. 1986. *Empires.* Ithaca.

Drexhage, H.-J., Kohnen, H., and Ruffing, K. 2002. *Die Wirtschaft des Römischen Reiches (1.–3. Jahrhundert): Eine Einführung.* Berlin.

Dreyer, Edward L. 2007. *Zheng He: China and the Oceans in the Early Ming Dynasty, 1405–1433*. New York.

Drinkwater, J. 2005. "Maximinus to Diocletian and the 'Crisis,'" in Bowman, Garnsey, and Cameron, eds. 2005: 28–66.

Dubs, H. 1942. "An Ancient Chinese Stock of Gold," *Journal of Economic History* 2: 36–39.

Dubs, H., transl. 1955. *The History of the Former Han Dynasty*. Vol. 3. Baltimore.

Duncan-Jones, R. 1982. *The Economy of the Roman Empire: Quantitative Studies*. 2nd ed. Cambridge.

Duncan-Jones, R. 1990. *Structure and Scale in the Roman Economy*. Cambridge.

Duncan-Jones, R. 1994. *Money and Government in the Roman Empire*. Cambridge.

Dunlop, J. E. 1924. *The Office of the Grand Chamberlain in the Later Roman and Byzantine Empires*. London.

Durrant, S. W. 1995. *The Cloudy Mirror: Tension and Conflict in the Writings of Sima Qian*. Albany.

Duyvendak, J. J. 1928. *The Book of Lord Shang*. Chicago.

Dworkin, R. 1986. *Law's Empire*. Cambridge, MA.

Eberhard, W. 1965. *Conquerors and Rulers: Social Forces in Medieval China*. 2nd ed. Leiden.

Eberhard, W. 1971. *Geschichte Chinas*. 3rd ed. Stuttgart.

Ebrey, P. 1986. "The Economic and Social History of Later Han," in Twitchett and Loewe, eds. 1986: 608–48.

Eck, W. 1995. *Agrippina, die Stadtgründerin Kölns*. Cologne.

Eck, W. 2000a "The Growth of Administrative Posts," in Bowman, Garnsey, and Rathbone, eds. 2000: 238–65.

Eck, W. 2000b "Provincial Administration and Finance," in Bowman, Garnsey, and Rathbone, eds. 2000: 266–92.

Eckstein, A. M. 2006. *Mediterranean Anarchy, Interstate War, and the Rise of Rome*. Berkeley.

Edwards, C., and Woolf, G., eds. 2003. *Rome the Cosmopolis*. Cambridge.

Ehrend, H. 2000. *Wang Mang und seine Münzen—The Coins of Wang Mang*. Speyer.

Eich, A., and Eich, P. 2005. "War and State-Building in Roman Republican Times," *Scripta Classica Israelica* 24: 1–33.

Eich, P. 2005. *Zur Metamorphose des politischen Systems in der römischen Kaiserzeit: Die Entstehung einer "personalen Bürokratie" im langen dritten Jahrhundert*. Berlin.

Eisenstadt, S. N. 1963. *The Political Systems of Empire*. London.

Eisenstadt, S. N., ed. 1986. *The Origins and Diversity of Axial Age Civilizations*. Albany.

Elvin, M. 1973. *The Pattern of the Chinese Past: A Social and Economic Interpretation*. Stanford.

Emmerich, R. 2002. "Die Rebellion der Sieben Könige, 154 v. Chr.," in id. et al., eds., *Und folge nun dem, was mein Herz begehrt: Festschrift für Ulrich Unger zum 70. Geburtstag, II*, 397–497. Hamburg.

Erdkamp, P. 2005. *The Roman Grain Market*. Cambridge.

Erickson, S. N. 1994. "Money Trees of the Eastern Han Dynasty," *Bulletin of the Museum of Far Eastern Antiquities* 66: 5–115.

Ertman, T. 1997. *Birth of the Leviathan: Building States and Regimes in Medieval and Early Modern Europe*. Cambridge.

Fairbank, J. K., ed. 1968. *The Chinese World Order: Traditional China's Foreign Relations.* Cambridge, MA.

Ferguson, J. 1978. "China and Rome," in H. Temporini, ed., *Aufstieg und Niedergang der Römischen Welt* II.9.2, 581–603. Berlin.

Finer, S. E. 1997. *The History of Government.* 3 vols. Cambridge.

Finley, M. I. 1976. "Private Farm Tenancy in Italy before Diocletian," in Finley, ed., *Studies in Roman Property*, 103–22. Cambridge.

Finley, M. I. 1985. *The Ancient Economy.* 2nd ed. London.

Finley, M. I. 1986. *The Use and Abuse of History.* London.

Flaig, F. 2003. "Is Loyalty a Favor? Or: Why Gifts Cannot Oblige an Emperor," G. Algazi, V. Gröbner, and B. Jussen, eds., *Negotiating the Gift: Pre-Modern Figurations of Exchange*, 29–61.

Forsythe, G. 2005. *A Critical History of Early Rome.* Berkeley.

Foucault, M. 1990. *The History of Sexuality, 1.* New York.

Foxhall, L. 1990. "The Dependent Tenant: Landleasing and Labour in Italy and Greece," *Journal of Roman Studies* 80: 97–114.

Frank, J. 1973. *Courts on Trial: Myth and Reality in American Justice.* Repr. Princeton.

Friedländer, L. 1922. *Darstellungen aus der Sittengeschichte Roms: In der Zeit von Augustus bis zum Ausgang der Antonine, I.* 10ᵗʰ ed. Leipzig.

Friesen, S., and Scheidel, W. Forthcoming. "Economic Inequality in the Early Roman Empire: Poverty, Middle Classes, and GDP."

Fu, Zhengyuan. 1996. *China's Legalists: The Earliest Totalitarians and Their Art of Ruling.* Armonk.

Gale, E. M. 1931. *Discourses on Salt and Iron: A Debate on State Control of Commerce and Industry in Ancient China.* Leiden.

Gansu sheng wenwu kaogu yanjiuso et al., eds. 1990. *Juyan xinjian: Jiaqu houguan yu disi sui.* Beijing.

Gao Congming 1999. *Songdai huobi yu huobi liutong yanjiu.* Baoding.

Garnsey, P. 1968. "Why Penalties Become Harsher: The Roman Case, Late Republic to Fourth Century Empire," *Natural Law Forum* 13: 141–61.

Garnsey, P. 1970. *Social Status and Legal Privilege in the Roman Empire.* Oxford.

Garnsey, P. 1988. *Famine and Food-Supply in the Graeco-Roman World: Responses to Risk and Crisis.* Cambridge.

Garnsey, P., and Humfress, C. 2001. *The Evolution of Late Antiquity.* Cambridge.

Garnsey, P., and Saller, R. 1987. *The Roman Empire: Economy, Society and Culture.* London.

Gibbon, E. 1993. *The Decline and Fall of the Roman Empire I.* London.

Gizewski, C. 1994. "Römische und alte chinesische Geschichte im Vergleich: Zur Möglichkeit eines gemeinsamen Altertumsbegriffs," *Klio* 76: 271–302.

Göbl, R. 1978. *Antike Numismatik I.* Munich.

Goffart, W. 2006. *Barbarian Tides: The Migration Age and the Later Roman Empire.* Philadelphia.

Golas, P. J. 1999. *Science and Civilization in China.* Vol. 5: *Chemistry and Chemical Technology. Part XIII: Mining.* Cambridge.

Goldstone, J. A. 1991. *Revolution and Rebellion in the Early Modern World.* Berkeley.

Graff, D. A. 2002. *Medieval Chinese Warfare, 300–900.* London.

Graff, D. A. In progress. *The Eurasian Way of War.* London.

Gruen, E. S. 1984. *The Hellenistic World and the Coming of Rome.* Berkeley.

Gustafson, M. 1994. "Condemnation to the Mines in the Later Roman Empire," *Harvard Theological Review* 87: 421–34.

Guyot, P. 1980. *Eunuchen als Sklaven und Freigelassene in der griechisch-römischen Antike.* Stuttgart.

Hahn, J. 1997. "Arcadius," in Clauss, ed. 1997: 374–80.

Haldon, J. F. 1997. *Byzantium in the Seventh Century: The Transformation of a Culture.* Rev. ed. Cambridge.

Hall, D. L., and Ames, R. T. 1995. *Anticipating China: Thinking through the Narratives of Chinese and Western Culture.* Albany.

Hall, D. L., and Ames, R. T. 1998. *Thinking from the Han: Self, Truth, and Transcendence in Chinese and Western Culture.* Albany.

Hall, J. A., and Schroeder, R., eds. 2006. *An Anatomy of Power: The Social Theory of Michael Mann.* Cambridge.

Hansen, M. H., ed. 2000. *A Comparative Study of Thirty City-State Cultures: An Investigation Conducted by the Copenhagen Polis Center.* Copenhagen.

Hansen, M. H., ed. 2002. *A Comparative Study of Six City-State Cultures: An Investigation Conducted by the Copenhagen Polis Center.* Copenhagen.

Harada, Y. 1931. "Mu-Yang-Ch'êng: Han and Pre-Han Sites at the Foot of Mount Lao-T'ieh in South Manchuria: An English Résumé of the Japanese Text," in Y. Harada and K. Komai, *Bokuyojo: Minami Manshu Rotetsu sanroku Kan oyobi Kan izen iseki,* I–XII, 1–37. Tokyo.

Hardy, G. 1999. *Worlds of Bronze and Bamboo: Sima Qian's Conquest of History.* New York.

Harl, K. W. 1996. *Coinage in the Roman Economy, 300 B.C. to A.D. 700.* Baltimore.

Harries, J. 1988. "The Roman Imperial Quaestor from Constantine to Theodosius II," *Journal of Roman Studies* 78: 148–72.

Harries, J. 1999. *Law and Empire in Late Antiquity.* Cambridge.

Harries, J. 2007. *Law and Crime in the Roman World.* Cambridge.

Harris, W. V. 1979. *War and Imperialism in Republican Rome 327–70 B.C.* Oxford.

Harris, W. V. 2006. "A Revisionist View of Roman Money," *Journal of Roman Studies* 96: 1–24.

Harris, W. V. 2008. "The Nature of Roman Money," in Harris, ed. 2008: 174–207.

Harris, W. V., ed. 2008. *The Monetary Systems of the Greeks and Romans.* Oxford.

Hart, H. L. A. 1961. *The Concept of Law.* Oxford.

Haw, S. G. 2005. *Marco Polo's China: A Venetian in the Realm of Khubilai Khan.* London.

He, Weifang 1990. "Zhongguo gudai sifa panjue de fengge yu jingshen—Yi Songdai panjue wei yiju jiben yiju jian yu Yingguo bijiao," *Zhongguo shehui kexue* 1990, no. 6 (transl. as "The Style and Spirit of Traditional Chinese Judicial Decisions—Based Mainly on Song Dynasty Cases, and Compared to Court Decisions in England," *Social Sciences in China* 3, 1991: 74–95).

Heather, P. 2005. *The Fall of the Roman Empire: A New History.* London.

Herz, P. 2007. "Finances and Costs of the Roman Army," in P. Erdkamp, ed., *A Companion to the Roman Army,* 306–22. Malden.

Hevia, J. L. 1995. *Cherishing Men from Afar: Qing Guest Ritual and the Macartney Embassy.* Durham.

Hill, J. E. 2003. "The Western Regions according to the *Hou Hanshu*: The *Xiyu juan* 'Chapter on the Western Regions' from *Hou Hanshu* 88. Second edition," at *Silk Road*

Narratives: A Collection of Historical Texts, http://depts.washington.edu/silkroad/texts/hhshu/hou_han_shu.html.

Hinsch, B. 1990. *Passions of the Cut Sleeve: The Male Homosexual Tradition in China*. Berkeley.

Hirth, F. 1885. *China and the Roman Orient*. Shanghai.

Hollander, D. B. 2007. *Money in the Late Roman Republic*. Leiden.

Honoré, T. 1993. "Some Quaestors of the Reign of Theodosius II," in J. Harries and I. Wood, eds., *The Theodosian Code*, 68–96. Ithaca.

Honoré, T. 1998. *Law in the Crisis of Empire 379–455 A.D.: The Theodosian Dynasty and Its Quaestors*. Oxford.

Hopkins, K. 1978. *Conquerors and Slaves*. Cambridge.

Hopkins, K. 1980. "Taxes and Trade in the Roman Empire (200 BC–AD 400)," *Journal of Roman Studies* 70: 101–25.

Hopkins, K. 1995/6. "Rome, Taxes, Rents and Trade," *Kodai* 6/7: 41–75 (repr. in Scheidel and von Reden, eds. 2002: 190–230).

Hou, D. 1996. "Guanyu Chuguo huangjin huobi chengliang de buchong yanjiu: cong Chu mu chutu de sanzu you ming qingtong kema tanqi," *Zhongguo qianbi* 1996, 1: 10–12.

Howgego, C. 1995. *Ancient History from Coins*. London.

Howgego, C. J. 1990. "Why Did Ancient States Strike Coins?" *Numismatic Chronicle* 150: 1–25.

Hsing I-tien 1980. "Rome and China: The Role of the Armies in the Imperial Succession: A Comparative Study." PhD thesis, University of Hawaii at Manoa.

Hsu Cho-yun 1965. *Ancient China in Transition: An Analysis of Social Mobility, 722–222 B.C.* Stanford.

Hsu Cho-yun 1980. *Han Agriculture: The Formation of Early Chinese Agrarian Economy (206 B.C.–A.D. 220)*. Seattle.

Hsu Cho-yun and Linduff, K. 1988. *Western Zhou Civilization*. New Haven.

Hu, Jichuang 1988. *A Concise History of Chinese Economic Thought*. Beijing.

Huang, R. 1974. *Taxation and Governmental Finance in Sixteenth-Century Ming China*. Cambridge.

Huang, R. 1997. *China: A Macro History*. Armonk.

Huang Zhanyue 1984. *Xin Zhongguo de kaogu faxian he yanjin*. Beijing.

Hui, V. T. 2005. *War and State Formation in Ancient China and Early Modern Europe*. Cambridge.

Hui, V. T. Forthcoming. "China's Rise in Comparative-Historical Perspective: *tianxia datong* or *tianxia daluan?*"

Hulsewé, A. F. P. 1955. *Remnants of Han Law*. Leiden.

Hulsewé, A. F. P. 1979. *China in Central Asia: The Early Stage, 125 B.C.–A.D. 23*. Leiden.

Hulsewé, A. F. P. 1985a *Remnants of Ch'in Law: An Annotated Translation of the Ch'in Legal and Administrative Rules of the 3rd Century B.C., Discovered in Yün-meng Prefecture, Hu-pei Province, in 1975*. Leiden.

Hulsewé, A. F. P. 1985b "The Influence of the 'Legalist' Government of Qin on the Economy as Reflected in the Texts Discovered in Yunmeng County," in Schram, ed. 1985: 211–35.

Hulsewé, A. F. P. 1986. "Ch'in and Han Law," in Twitchett and Loewe, eds. 1986: 520–44.

Humbach, H., and Ziegler, S. 1998. *Ptolemy, Geography, Book 6: Middle East, Central and North Asia, China*. 2 vols. Wiesbaden.

Ivotchkina, N. V. 1993. "The Early Chinese Chu Gold Plates, 5th–3rd Cent. B.C.," in *Actes 11th International Congress of Numismatics, III.* Louvain-la-Neuve: 329–32.

Jensen, J. 1997. "The World's Most Diligent Observer," *Asiatische Studien* 51: 719–26.

Jiang Xianjie 1999. "Xichang Dongping yizhi ye tongzhu bi yuanyin chutan," *Sichuan wenwu* 1999, 4: 46–50.

Jingfa 1980. *Jingfa: Mawangdui Hanmuboshu.* Beijing.

Johnston, A. C. 1936. *Roman Egypt.* Baltimore.

Jones, A. H. M. 1964. *The Later Roman Empire 284–602: A Social, Economic, and Administrative Survey.* Oxford.

Jongman, W. 2003. "A Golden Age: Death, Money Supply and Social Succession in the Roman Empire," in E. Lo Cascio, ed., *Credito e moneta nel mondo romano,* 181–96. Bari.

Jongman, W. 2006. "The Rise and Fall of the Roman Economy: Population, Rents and Entitlement," in Bang, Ikeguchi, and Ziche, eds. 2006: 237–54.

Jugel, U. 1976. *Politische Funktion und soziale Stellung der Eunuchen zur späteren Hanzeit (25–220 n. Chr.).* Wiesbaden.

Kaser, M. 2003. *Römisches Privatrecht.* 12th ed. Munich.

Kautsky, J. H. 1982. *The Politics of Aristocratic Empires.* Chapel Hill.

Kelly, C. 2004. *Ruling the Later Roman Empire.* Cambridge, MA.

Kennedy, H. 2001. *The Armies of the Caliphs: Military and Society in the Early Islamic State.* London.

Keppie, L. 1996. "The Army and the Navy," in Bowman, Champlin, and Lintott, eds. 1996: 371–96.

Kern, M. 2000. *The Stele Inscriptions of Ch'in Shih-huang: Text and Ritual in Early Chinese Imperial Representation.* Honolulu.

Kim H. J. 2007. "Ethnicity and Foreigners in Ancient Greece and China: A Comparative Analysis of the *Histories* of Herodotus and the *Shiji* of Sima Qian." D.Phil. thesis, Oxford University.

Kim H. J. Forthcoming. *Ethnicity and Foreigners in Ancient Greece and China.* London.

Kim, H. S. 2002. "Small Change and the Moneyed Economy," in P. Cartledge, E. E. Cohen, and L. Foxhall, eds., *Money, Labour and Land: Approaches to the Economies of Ancient Greece,* 44–51. London.

Kiser, E., and Cai, Y. 2003. "War and Bureaucratization in Qin China: Exploring an Anomalous Case," *American Sociological Review* 68: 511–39.

Klein, R. 1997. "Galerius," in Clauss, ed. 1997: 276–82.

Knoblock, J. 1988–90. *Xunzi: A Translation and Study of the Complete Works.* 2 vols. Stanford.

Knoblock, J., and Riegel, J. 2000. *The Annals of Lu Buwei.* Stanford.

Konrad, N. I. 1967. "Polybius and Ssu-ma Ch'ien," *Soviet Sociology* 5.4: 37–58.

Kunkel, W. 1966. *An Introduction to Roman Legal and Constitutional History.* Trans. J. M. Kelly. Oxford.

Kuriyama, S. 1994. "The Imagination of Winds and the Development of the Chinese Conception of the Body," in A. Zito and T. E. Barlow, eds., *Body, Subject and Power in China,* 23–41. Chicago.

Kuriyama, S. 1999. *The Expressiveness of the Body and the Divergence of Greek and Chinese Medicine.* New York.

Kurke, L. 1999. *Coins, Bodies, Games, and Gold: The Politics of Meaning in Archaic Greece.* Princeton.

Kurke, L. 2002. "Money and Mythic History: The Contestation of Transactional Orders in the Fifth Century BC," in Scheidel and von Reden, eds. 2002: 87–113.

Kyle, D. 1998. *Spectacles of Death in Ancient Rome.* London.

Langhammer, W. 1973. *Die rechtliche und soziale Stellung der Magistratus municipales und der Decuriones in der Übergangsphase der Städte von sich selbstverwaltenden Gemeinden zu Vollzugsorganen des spätantiken Zwangsstaates (2.–4. Jh. der römischen Kaiserzeit).* Wiesbaden.

Lattimore, O. 1940. *Inner Asian Frontiers of China.* New York.

Lau, U. 2002. "Die Rekonstruktion des Strafprozesses und die Prinzipien der Strafzumessung zu Beginn der Han-Zeit im Lichte des *Zhouyanshu*," in R. Emmerich et al., eds., *Und folge nun dem, was mein Herz begehrt: Festschrift für Ulrich Unger zum 70. Geburtstag, II*, 343–95.

Lawton, T., ed. 1991. *New Perspectives on Chu Culture during the Eastern Zhou Period.* Washington.

Le Rider, J. 2001. *La naissance de la monnaie: pratiques monétaires de l'Orient ancien.* Paris.

Lelièvre, D. 2001. *La grande époque de Wudi: une Chine en evolution (IIe–Ie s. av. J.C.).* Paris.

Leslie, D. D., and Gardiner, K. H. J. 1996. *The Roman Empire in Chinese Sources.* Rome.

Levick, B. 1990. *Claudius.* London.

Lewis, M. E. 1990. *Sanctioned Violence in Early China.* Albany.

Lewis, M. E. 1999. *Writing and Authority in Early China.* Albany.

Lewis, M. E. 1999a, "The *feng* and *shan* sacrifices of Emperor Wu of the Han," in J. P. McDermott, ed., *State and Court Ritual in China*, 50–80. Cambridge.

Lewis, M. E. 1999b "Warring States Political History," in M. Loewe and E. Shaughnessy, eds., *The Cambridge History of Ancient China: From the Origins of Civilization to 221 B.C.*, 587–650. Cambridge.

Lewis, M. E. 2000. "The Han Abolition of Universal Military Service," in H. van de Ven, ed., *Warfare in Chinese History*, 33–75. Leiden.

Lewis, M. E. 2006. *The Construction of Space in Early China.* Albany.

Lewis, M. E. 2007. *The Early Chinese Empires: Qin and Han.* Cambridge, MA.

Lewis, M. E. Forthcoming. *China between Empires: The Northern and Southern Dynasties.* Cambridge, MA.

Li Xueqin and Xing Wen 2001. "New Light on the Early-Han Code: A Reappraisal of the Zhangjiashan Bamboo-Slip Legal Texts," *Asia Major* 14: 125–46.

Li Yung-ti 2006. "On the Function of Cowries in Shang and Western Zhou China," *Journal of East Asian Archaeology* 5: 1–26.

Li Yu-ning, ed. 1977. *Shang Yang's Reforms and State Control in China.* White Plains.

Li Zude 1997. "Shilun Qin Han de huangjin huobi," *Zhongguo shi yanjin* 1: 52–61.

Liang Zhiping 1989. "Explicating 'Law': A Comparative Perspective of Chinese and Western Legal Culture," *Journal of Chinese Law* 3: 55–91.

Liebermann, S. 1957. "Who Were Pliny's Blue-Eyed Chinese?" *Classical Philology* 52: 174–77.

Lieven, D. 2000. *Empire: The Russian Empire and Its Rivals.* New Haven.

Little, L. K., ed. 2007. *Plague and the End of Antiquity: The Pandemic of 541–750.* Cambridge.

Liu Xinru 1988. *Ancient India and Ancient China: Trade and Religious Exchanges AD 1–600.* New Delhi.

Llewellyn-Jones, L. 2002. "Eunuchs and the Royal Harem in Achaemenid Persia," in Tougher, ed. 2002: 19–50.

Lloyd, G. E. R. 1996. *Adversaries and Authorities: Investigations into Ancient Greek and Chinese Science.* Cambridge.

Lloyd, G. E. R. 2003. *The Ambitions of Curiosity: Understanding the World in Ancient Greece and China.* Cambridge.

Lloyd, G. E. R. 2004. *Ancient Worlds, Modern Reflections: Philosophical Perspectives on Greek and Chinese Science and Culture.* Oxford.

Lloyd, G. E. R. 2005. *The Delusions of Invulnerability: Wisdom and Morality in Ancient Greece, China and Today.* London.

Lloyd, G. E. R. 2006. *Principles and Practices in Ancient Greek and Chinese Science.* Aldershot.

Lloyd, G. E. R., and Sivin, N. 2002. *The Way and the Word: Science and Medicine in Early China and Greece.* New Haven.

Lo Cascio, E. 1997. "Produzione monetaria, finanza pubblica ed economia nel principato," *Rivista Storica Italiana* 109: 650–77.

Lo Cascio, E. 1999. "The Population of Roman Italy in Town and Country," in J. Bintliff and K. Sbonias, eds., *Reconstructing Past Population Trends in Mediterranean Europe (3000 BC–AD 1800)*, 161–71. Oxford.

Lo Cascio, E. 2005. "The New State of Diocletian and Constantine: From the Tetrarchy to the Reunification of the Empire," in Bowman, Garnsey, and Cameron, eds. 2005: 170–83.

Lo Cascio, E. 2008. "The Function of Gold Coinage in the Monetary Economy of the Roman Empire," in Harris, ed. 2008: 160–73.

Loewe, M. 1967. *Records of Han Administration.* 2 vols. Cambridge.

Loewe, M. 1985. "Attempts at Economic Co-ordination during the Western Han Dynasty," in Schram, ed. 1985: 237–67.

Loewe, M. 1986. "The Structure and Practice of Government," in Twitchett and Loewe 1986: 463–90.

Loewe, M. 2004. *The Men Who Governed Han China: Companion to* A Biographical Dictionary of the Qin, Former Han and Xin Periods. Leiden.

Loewe, M., and Shaughnessy, E. L., eds. 1999. *The Cambridge History of Ancient China from the Origins of Civilization to 221 B.C.* Cambridge.

Lorenz, G. 1990. "Das Imperium Romanum und das China der Han-Dynastie: Gedanken und Materialien zu einem Vergleich," *Informationen für Geschichtslehrer* 12: 9–60.

Love, J. R. 1991. *Antiquity and Capitalism: Max Weber and the Sociological Foundations of the Roman Civilization.* London.

Lu Xing 1998. *Rhetoric in Ancient China, Fifth to Third century B.C.E.: A Comparison with Classical Greek Rhetoric.* Columbia.

Lu Depei and Wu Yuqing 1997. "Hubeisheng chutu de Chuguo jinbi," *Zhongguo qianbi* 1997, 1: 38.

Lucassen, J., ed. 2007. *Wages and Currency: Global Comparisons from Antiquity to the Twentieth Century.* Bern.

Luttwak, E. 1976. *The Grand Strategy of the Roman Empire: From the First Century A.D. to the Third.* Baltimore.

MacCormack, G. 2001. "The Rule of Law in Pre-T'ang China," in *Studi in Onore di Mario Talamanca*, 95–117. Naples.

MacCormack, G. 2004. "The Transmission of Penal Law (*lu*) from the Han to the T'ang: A Contribution to the Study of the Early History of Codification in China," *Revue Internationale des Droits de L'Antiquité*, 47–83.

MacMullen, R. 1980. *Corruption and the Decline of Rome*. New Haven.

MacMullen, R. 1990. *Changes in the Roman Empire: Essays in the Ordinary*. Princeton.

Maine, H. 1888. *Ancient Law*. New York.

Major, J. S. 1987. "The Meaning of *Hsing-te* [*Xing de*]," in C. LeBlanc and S. Blader, eds., *Chinese Ideas about Nature and Society*, 281–291. Hong Kong.

Mann, M. 1986. *The Sources of Social Power, I: A History of Power from the Beginning to A.D. 1760*. Cambridge.

Mansvelt Beck, B. J. 1990. *The Treatises of Later Han: Their Author, Sources, Contents and Place in Chinese Historiography*. Leiden.

Maresch, K. 1996. *Bronze und Silber: Papyrologische Beiträge zur Geschichte der Währung im ptolemäischen und römischen Ägypten bis zum 2. Jahrhundert n. Chr.* Cologne.

Matthews, J. F. 1989. *The Roman Empire of Ammianus*. Baltimore.

Mattingly, H., and Sydenham, E. A. 1926, *Roman Imperial Coinage, II*. London.

McKnight, B. 1981. *The Quality of Mercy: Amnesties and Traditional Chinese Justice*. Honolulu.

Millar, F. 1977. *The Emperor in the Roman World*. London.

Millar, F. 1984. "Condemnation to Hard Labor in the Roman Empire from the Julio-Claudians to Constantine," *Papers of the British School at Rome* 52: 124–47.

Mitamura, T. 1970. *Chinese Eunuchs: The Structure of Intimate Politics*. Boston.

Miyazawa, T. 1998. *Sodai Chugoku no kokka to keizai*. Tokyo.

Molho, A., Raaflaub, K., and Emlen, J., eds. 1991. *City States in Classical Antiquity and Medieval Italy*. Ann Arbor.

Mommsen, T. 1996. *A History of Rome under the Emperors*. Ed. T. Wiedemann. London.

Morley, N. 1996. *Metropolis and Hinterland: The City of Rome and the Italian Economy 200 B.C.–A.D. 200*. Cambridge.

Morley, N. 2007. *Trade in Classical Antiquity*. Cambridge.

Morris, I. Forthcoming. *Why the West Rules…—For Now*. New York.

Motomura, R. 1991. "An Approach towards a Comparative Study of the Roman Empire and the Ch'in and Han Empires," *Kodai* 2: 61–69.

Mrozek, S. 1985. "Zum Kreditgeld in der frühen römischen Kaiserzeit," *Historia* 34: 310–23.

Mutschler, F.-H. 1997. "Vergleichende Beobachtungen zur griechisch-römischen und altchinesischen Geschichtsschreibung," *Saeculum* 48: 213–53.

Mutschler, F.-H. 2003. "Zu Sinnhorizont und Funktion griechischer, römischer und altchinesischer Geschichtsschreibung," in *Sinn (in) der Antike*, 33–54. Mainz.

Mutschler, F.-H. 2006. "Tacitus und Sima Qian: Eine Annäherung," *Philologus* 150: 115–35.

Mutschler, F.-H. 2007. "Tacitus und Sima Qian: Persönliche Erfahrung und historiographische Perspektive," *Philologus* 151: 127–52.

Mutschler, F.-H., and Mittag, A. 2005. "Conceiving the 'Empire': Ancient China and Rome—An Intercultural Comparison in Dialogue," International Conference Essen (Germany), April 20–23, 2005.

Mutschler, F.-H., and Mittag, A., eds. Forthcoming. *Conceiving the Empire: China and Rome Compared*. Oxford.

Nanda, S. 1998. *Neither Man nor Woman—The Hijras of India.* Wadsworth.

Nicolet, C. 1971. "Les variations des prix et la 'théorie quantitative de la monnaie' à Rome, de Cicéron à Pline l'Ancien," *Annales* 26: 1203–27.

Nicolet, C. 1980. *The World of the Citizen in Republican Rome.* Berkeley.

Nicolet, C. 1984. "Pline, Paul et la théorie de la monnaie," *Athenaeum* 62: 105–35.

Nishijima, S. 1961. *Chūgoku kodai teikoku no keisei to kōzō—nijū tō shakusei no kenkyū.* Tokyo.

Nishijima, S. 1986. "The Economic and Social History of Former Han," in Twitchett and Loewe, eds. 1986: 545–607.

Nock, A. D. 1988. "Eunuchs in Ancient Religion," in A. K. Siems, ed., *Sexualität und Erotik in der Antike.* Darmstadt.

Oliver, J. H. 1989. *Greek Constitutions of Early Roman Emperors from Inscriptions and Papyri.* Philadelphia.

Oost, S. I. 1958. "The Career of M. Antonius Pallas," *American Journal of Philology* 79: 113–39.

Peacock, D. P. S., and Maxfield, V. 1997–2001. *Mons Claudianus Survey and Excavation.* 2 vols. Cairo.

Pearce, S. A. 1987. "The Yü-Wen Regime in Sixth-Century China." PhD thesis, Princeton University.

Peerenboom, R. P. 1993. *Law and Morality in Ancient China.* Albany.

Peng Ke 2000. "Coinage and Commercial Development in Eastern Zhou China." PhD thesis, University of Chicago.

Peng Ke and Zhu Yanshi 1995. "New Research on the Origins of Cowries Used in Ancient China," *Sino-Platonic Papers* 68. Philadelphia.

Peng Xinwei 1994. *A Monetary History of China, I.* Bellingham.

Perkounig, C.-M. 1995. *Livia Drusilla—Iulia Augusta.* Vienna.

Pomeranz, K. 2000. *The Great Divergence: China, Europe, and the Making of the Modern World Economy.* Princeton.

Poo Mo-chou 2005. *Enemies of Civilization: Attitudes toward Foreigners in Ancient Mesopotamia, Egypt, and China.* Albany.

Puett, M. 2001. *The Ambivalence of Creation: Debates Concerning Innovation and Artifice in Early China.* Stanford.

Puett, M. J. 2002. *To Become a God: Cosmology, Sacrifice, and Self-Divinization in Early China.* Cambridge, MA.

Qi Dongfang 1999a *Research on Tang Gold and Silver.* Beijing (in Chinese).

Qi Dongfang 1999b "Zhongguo zaoqi jinyinqi yanjiu," *Huaxia kaogu* 4: 68–85.

Quaritch Wales, H. G. 1965. *Angkor and Rome: A Historical Comparison.* London.

Raaflaub, K. 2005. "From Protection and Defense to Offense and Participation: Stage in the Conflict of the Orders," in K. Raaflaub, ed., *Social Struggles in Archaic Rome: New Perspectives on the Conflict of the Orders.* 2nd ed., 185–222. Malden.

Raaflaub, K., ed. 2007. *War and Peace in the Ancient World.* Malden.

Raaflaub, K., and Rosenstein, N., eds. 1999. *War and Society in the Ancient and Medieval Worlds: Asia, the Mediterranean, Europe, and Mesoamerica.* Washington, D.C.

Raaflaub, K., and Talbert, R., eds. Forthcoming. *Geography, Ethnography, and Perceptions of the World from Antiquity to the Renaissance.* Malden.

Raaflaub, K., and Toher, M., eds. 1990. *Between Republic and Empire: Interpretations of Augustus and His Principate.* Berkeley.

Ragin, C. C. 1987. *The Comparative Method: Moving Beyond Qualitative and Quantitative Strategies.* Berkeley.

Ran Wanli 1997. "Cong kaogu faxian kan Chunqiu Zhanguo shiqi de jinyin zhizhao ye," *Xibei Daxue xuebao* 2: 96–100.

Raphals, L. 1992. *Knowing Words: Wisdom and Cunning in the Classical Tradition of China and Greece.* Ithaca.

Raphals, L. 1994. "Skeptical Strategies in the *Zhuangzi* and *Theaetetus*," *Philosophy East and West* 44: 501–26.

Raphals, L. A. 2002. "Gender and Virtue in Greece and China," *Journal of Chinese Philosophy* 29: 415–26.

Raschke, M. G. 1978. "New Studies in Roman Commerce with the East," in H. Temporini, ed., *Aufstieg und Niedergang der römischen Welt* II.9.2, 604–1361. Berlin.

Rathbone, D. W. 1993. "The Census Qualifications of the *Assidui* and the *Prima Classis*," in H. Sancisi-Weerdenburg et al., eds., *De Agricultura: In Memoriam Pieter Willem de Neeve (1945–1990)*, 121–52. Amsterdam.

Rathbone, D. W. 1997. "Prices and Price Formation in Roman Egypt," in J. Andreau, P. Briant, and R. Descat, eds., *Prix et formation des prix dans les économies antiques*, 183–244. Saint-Bertrand-de-Comminges.

Rathbone, D. W. 2001. "The 'Muziris' Papyrus (SB XVIII 13167): Financing Roman Trade with India," *Bulletin de la Société Archéologique d'Alexandrie* 46: 39–50.

Rathbone, D. W. 2007. "Military Finance and Supply," in P. Sabin, H. van Wees, and M. Whitby, eds., *The Cambridge History of Greek and Roman Warfare, II: Rome from the Republic to the Late Empire*, 158–75. Cambridge.

Rathbone, D. W. Forthcoming. "Living Standards and the Economy of the Roman Empire (I–III AD)."

Ray, H. P. 2003. *The Archaeology of Seafaring in Ancient South Asia.* Cambridge.

Reding, J.-P. 2004. *Comparative Essays in Early Greek and Chinese Rational Thinking.* Aldershot.

Rickett, W. A. 1985. *Guanzi: Political, Economic, and Philosophical Essays from Early China.* Vol. 1. Princeton.

Ringrose, K. M. 2003. *Eunuchs and the Social Construction of Gender in Byzantium.* Chicago.

Robinson, O. F. 2007. *Penal Practice and Penal Policy in Ancient Rome.* London.

Rosen, W. 2007. *Justinian's Flea: Plague, Empire, and the Birth of Europe.* New York.

Rosenstein, N. 1990. *Imperatores Victi: Military Defeat and Aristocratic Competition in the Middle and Late Republic.* Berkeley.

Rosenstein, N. 2007. "Military Command, Political Power, and the Republican Elite," in P. Erdkamp, ed., *A Companion to the Roman Army*, 132–47. Malden.

Rostovtzeff, M. I. 1957. *The Social and Economic History of the Roman Empire.* 2nd ed. Oxford.

Sahlins, M. 1989. "Cosmologies of Capitalism: The Trans-Pacific Sector of the World System," *Proceedings of the British Academy* 74: 1–51.

Saller, R. 1982. *Personal Patronage under the Early Empire.* Cambridge.

Salmon, E. T. 1969. *Roman Colonization under the Republic.* London.

Sanft, C. 2005. "Six of One, Two Dozen of the Other: The Abatement of the Mutilating Punishments under the Han Emperor Wen," *Asia Major* 18: 79–100.

Sargent, T. J., and Velde, F. R. 2002. *The Big Problem of Small Change.* Princeton.

Sarris, P. 2006a *Economy and Society in the Age of Justinian.* Cambridge.

Sarris, P. 2006b "Continuity and Discontinuity in the Post-Roman Economy," *Journal of Agrarian Change* 6: 400–13.

Schaberg, D. 1999. "Travel, Geography, and the Imperial Imagination in Fifth-Century Athens and Han China," *Comparative Literature* 51: 152–91.

Schaps, D. M. 2004. *The Invention of Coinage and the Monetization of Ancient Greece.* Ann Arbor.

Schaps, D. M. 2006. "The Invention of Coinage in Lydia, in India, and in China," Paper presented at the XIV International Economic History Congress, Helsinki, Finland, August 21–25, 2006.

Scheidel, W. 1997. "Continuity and Change in Classical Scholarship: A Quantitative Survey, 1924 to 1992," *Ancient Society* 28: 265–89.

Scheidel, W. 2007a "A Model of Real Income Growth in Roman Italy," *Historia* 56: 322–46.

Scheidel, W. 2007b "Demography," in W. Scheidel, I. Morris, and R. P. Saller, eds., *The Cambridge Economic History of the Greco-Roman World*, 38–86. Cambridge.

Scheidel, W. 2008a "Sex and Empire: A Darwinian Perspective," in I. Morris and W. Scheidel, eds., *The Dynamics of Ancient Empires: State Power from Assyria to Byzantium.* New York.

Scheidel, W. 2008b "The Divergent Evolution of Coinage in Eastern and Western Eurasia," in Harris, ed. 2008: 267–86.

Scheidel, W. 2008c "The Comparative Economics of Slavery in the Greco-Roman World," in C. Katsari and E. Dal Lago, eds., *Slave Systems, Ancient and Modern*, 105–26. Cambridge.

Scheidel, W. Forthcoming a. "Fiscal Regimes and the 'First Great Divergence between Eastern and Western Eurasia," in P. Bang and C. Bayly, eds., *Empires in Contention: Sociology, History and Cultural Difference.*

Scheidel, W. Forthcoming b. "The Budgets of the Han and Roman Empires," in Scheidel, ed. Forthcoming.

Scheidel, W. Forthcoming c. "Comparative History as Comparative Advantage: China's Potential Contribution to the Study of Ancient Mediterranean History," in Huang Yang, ed., *Proceedings of the Third International Conference on Ancient History.*

Scheidel, W., ed. Forthcoming. *State Power and Social Control in Ancient China and Rome.*

Scheidel, W. In progress a. *The Wolf and the Dragon: State Power in Ancient Rome and China.*

Scheidel, W. In progress b. *Explaining Empire: Models for Ancient History.* New York.

Scheidel, W., and von Reden, S., eds. 2002. *The Ancient Economy.* Edinburgh.

Schlinkert, D. 1994. "Der Hofeunuch der Spätantike: Ein gefährlicher Außenseiter?" *Hermes* 122: 342–59.

Schmidt-Colinet, A. 2000. *Die Textilien aus Palmyra.* Mainz.

Scholten, H. 1995. *Der Eunuch in Kaisernähe: Zur politischen und sozialen Bedeutung des praepositus sacri cubiculi im 4. und 5. Jh. n. Chr.* Bern.

Scholz, P. O. 2001. *Eunuchs and Castrati: A Cultural History.* Princeton.

Schram, S. R., ed. 1985. *The Scope of State Power in China.* London.

Schulz, R. 1997. *Herrschaft und Regierung: Roms Regiment in den Provinzen in der Zeit der Republik.* Paderborn.

Scott, J. C. 1976. *The Moral Economy of the Peasant: Rebellion and Subsistence in Southeast Asia*. New Haven.

Scullard, H. H. 1980. *A History of the Roman World 753 to 146 B.C.* 4th ed. London.

Seager, R. 1986. *Ammianus Marcellinus: Seven Studies in His Language and Thought*. Columbia.

Seipel, W., ed. 2003. *Geld aus China*. Vienna.

Shanghai Bowuguan qingtongqi yanjiubu 1970. *Shanghai Bowuguan cang qianbi: Qin Han qianbi*. Shanghai.

Shankman, S., and Durrant, S. W. 2000. *The Siren and the Sage: Knowledge and Wisdom in Ancient Greece and China*. Albany.

Shankman, S., and Durrant, S. W., eds. 2002. *Early China/Ancient Greece: Thinking through Comparisons*. Albany.

Shaw, B. D. 1999. "War and Violence," in G. W. Bowersock, P. Brown, and O. Grabar, eds., *Late Antiquity: A Guide to the Postclassical World*, 130–69. Cambridge, MA.

Shen Yuanyuan 2000. "Conceptions and Receptions of Legality: Understanding the Complexity of Law Reform in Modern China," in K. Turner, J. Feinerman, and R. K. Guy, eds., *The Limits of the Rule of Law in China*, 20–44. Seattle.

Sim, M. 2007. *Remastering Morals with Aristotle and Confucius*. Cambridge.

Sivin, N. 1995. "State, Cosmos and Body in the Last Three Centuries B.C.," *Harvard Journal of Asiatic Studies* 55: 5–37.

Skinner, G. W. 1964–65. "Marketing and Social Structure in Rural China," *Journal of Asian Studies* 24: 3–43, 195–228, 363–99.

Skocpol, T., and Somers, M. 1980. "The Uses of Comparative History in Macrosocial Inquiry," *Comparative Studies in Society and History* 22: 174–97.

Smith, A. 1976. *An Inquiry into the Nature and Causes of the Wealth of Nations*. Eds. R. H. Campbell, A. S. Skinner, and W. B. Todd. Oxford.

Spence, J. 1988. *Emperor of China: Self-Portrait of K'ang-hsi*. New York.

Spruyt, H. 1994. *The Sovereign State and Its Competitors: An Analysis of Systems Change*. Princeton.

Stanford 2005. "Institutions of Empire: Comparative Perspectives on Ancient Chinese and Mediterranean History," International Conference, Stanford University, May 13–14, 2005.

Stanford 2008a "State Power and Social Control in Ancient China and Rome," International Conference, Stanford University, March 17–19, 2008.

Stanford 2008b "The First Great Divergence: Europe and China, 300–800 CE," International Conference, Stanford University, April 6–7, 2008.

Stanford 2009 "The Great Divergences: Europe and China," International Conference, Stanford University, 2009.

Stent, G. C. 1877. "Chinese Eunuchs," *Journal of the North-China Branch of the Royal Asiatic Society* 9: 143–84.

Stevenson, W. 2002. "Eunuchs and Early Christianity," in Tougher, ed. 2002: 123–42.

Strobel, K. 2002. "Geldwesen und Währungsgeschichte des Imperium Romanum im Spiegel der Entwicklung des 3. Jahrhunderts n. Chr.—Wirtschaftsgeschichte im Widerstreit von Metallismus und Nominalismus," in K. Strobel, ed., *Die Ökonomie des Imperium Romanum: Strukturen, Modelle und Wertungen im Spannungsfeld von Modernismus und Neoprimitivismus*, 86–168. St Katharinen.

Stuurman, S. 2008. "Herodotus and Sima Qian: History and the Anthropological Turn in Ancient Greece and Han China," *Journal of World History* 19: 1–40.

Swann, N. L. 1950. *Food and Money in Ancient China: The Earliest Economic History of China to* A.D. *25. Han Shu 24 with Related Texts, Han Shu 91 and Shih-chi 129.* Princeton (repr. New York 1974).

Tang Changru 1990. "Clients and Bound Retainers in the Six Dynasties Period," in A. E. Dien, ed., *State and Society in Early Medieval China*, 111–38. Stanford.

Tang Shifu, ed. 2001. *Zhongguo gu qianbi.* Shanghai.

Teggart, F. 1939. *Rome and China: A Study of Correlations in Historical Events.* Berkeley.

Thierry, F. 1993. "De la nature fiduciaire de la monnaie chinoise," *Bulletin du Cercle d'Études Numismatiques* 30: 1–12.

Thierry, F. 1997. *Monnaies chinoises, I: L'antiquité préimpériale.* Paris.

Thierry, F. 2001a "La fiduciarité idéale à l'épreuve des coûts de production: quelques éléments sur la contradiction fondamentale de la monnaie en Chine," *Revue Numismatique* 157: 131–52.

Thierry, F. 2001b "Sur les spécifités fondamentales de la monnaie chinoise," in A. Testart, ed., *Aux origines de la monnaie*, 109–44. Paris.

Thierry, F. 2003a *Monnaies chinoises, II: Des Qin aux Cinq Dynasties.* Paris.

Thierry, F. 2003b "Die Geschichte des chinesischen Geldes von den Ursprüngen bis zum Beginn des 20. Jahrhunderts," in Seipel, ed. 2003: 25–89.

Thomsen, R. 1988. *Ambition and Confucianism: A Biography of Wang Mang.* Aarhus.

Thorner, D. 1965. "Peasant Economy as a Category in Economic History," in *Deuxième Conference Internationale d'Histoire Économique, Aix-en-Provence, 1962*, 287–300. Paris.

Tienchi, M.-L. 1984. *Frauenerziehung im Alten China: Eine Analyse der Frauenbücher.* Bochum.

Tilly, C. 1984. *Big Structures, Large Processes, Huge Comparisons.* New York.

Tilly, C. 1992. *Coercion, Capital, and European States,* AD *990–1992.* Cambridge, MA.

Tougher, S. F. 1997. "Byzantine Eunuchs: An Overview with Special Reference to their Creation and Origin," in L. James, ed., *Women, Men and Eunuchs: Gender in Byzantium*, 168–85. London.

Tougher, S., ed. 2002. *Eunuchs in Antiquity and Beyond.* London.

Tsai, S. H. 2002. "Eunuch Power in Imperial China," in Tougher, ed. 2002: 221–33.

Turner, K. 1990. "Sage Kings and Laws in the Chinese and Greek Traditions," in P. Ropp, ed., *Heritage of China*, 86–111. Berkeley.

Turner, K. 1992. "Rule of Law Ideals in Early China?" *Journal of Chinese Law* 6: 1–44.

Turner, K. 1999. "The Criminal Body and the Body Politic: Punishments in Early Imperial China," *Cultural Dynamics* 11: 237–54.

Turner Gottschang, K. 1983. "Chinese Despotism Reconsidered: Monarchy and Its Critics in Early Imperial China." PhD thesis, University of Michigan.

Turner, P. J. 1989. *Roman Coins from India.* London.

Twitchett, D., and Loewe, M., eds. 1986. *The Cambridge History of China, I: The Ch'in and Han Empires, 221* B.C.–A.D. *200.* Cambridge.

Van Gulik, R. 2003. *Sexual Life in Ancient China: A Preliminary Survey of Chinese Sex and Society from ca. 1500* B.C. *till 1644* A.D. Leiden.

Veyne, P. 1976. *Le pain et le cirque: Sociologie historique d'un pluralisme politique.* Paris.

Vogel, K. 1968. *Neun Bücher arithmetischer Technik: Ein chinesisches Rechenbuch für den praktischen Gebrauch aus der frühen Hanzeit (220 v. Chr. bis 9 n. Chr.).* Braunschweig.

Von Freyberg, H.-U. 1989. *Kapitalverkehr und Handel im römischen Kaiserreich (27 v. Chr.—235 n. Chr.).* Freiburg.

Von Glahn, R. 1996. *Fountain of Fortune: Money and Monetary Policy in China, 1000–1700.* Berkeley.

Von Glahn, R. 2004. "Revisiting the Song Monetary Revolution: A Review Essay," *International Journal of Asian Studies* 1: 159–78.

Von Reden, S. 1995. *Exchange in Ancient Greece.* London.

Von Reden, S. 2007. *Money in Ptolemaic Egypt: From the Macedonian Conquest to the End of the Third Century* BC. Cambridge.

Vorberg, G. 1932. *Glossarium Eroticum.* Stuttgart.

Wagner, D. B. 2001. *The State and the Iron Industry in Han China.* Copenhagen.

Wallace-Hadrill, A. 1996. "The Imperial Court," in Bowman, Champlin, and Lintott, eds. 1996: 69, 283–308.

Wang, H. 2004. *Money on the Silk Road: The Evidence from Eastern Central Asia to* c. AD 800. London.

Wang, H., Cowell, M, Cribb, J., and Bowman, S., eds. 2005. *Metallurgical Analysis of Chinese Coins at the British Museum.* London.

Wang Yü-ch'üan 1951. *Early Chinese Coinage.* New York.

Wang Yeh-chien 1991. "Secular Trends of Rice Prices in the Yangzi Delta, 1638–1935," in T. G. Rawski and L. M. Li, eds., *Chinese History in Economic Perspective*, 35–68. Berkeley.

Wang Yongbo 2005. "Handai huangjin zhubi jiliang biaoji yanjiu," *Gudai wenming* 4: 263–301.

Watson, B. 1993. *Records of the Grand Historian: Han Dynasty I.* Rev. ed. New York.

Weber, M. 1980. *Wirtschaft und Gesellschaft.* 5th ed. Ed. J. Winckelmann. Tübingen.

Weber, M. 1991. *Die Wirtschaftsethik der Weltreligionen: Konfuzianismus und Taoismus.* Ed. H. Schmidt-Glintzer. Tübingen.

Wei Hangkeng and Fang Qing 1997. English abstract of "A Study of the Shell-Shaped Coin of the Chu State," *China Archaeology and Art Digest* 2.1–2: 148–9.

Weiß, A. 2004. *Sklave der Stadt: Untersuchungen zur öffentlichen Sklaverei in den Städten des Römischen Reiches.* Stuttgart.

Weld, S. 1999. "Chu Law in Action: Legal Documents from Tomb 2 at Baoshan," in Cook and Major, eds. 1999: 77–97.

Whittaker, C. R. 1994. *Frontiers of the Roman Empire: A Social and Economic Study.* Baltimore.

Wickham, C. 2001. "Society," in R. McKitterick, ed., *The Early Middle Ages*, 59–94. Oxford.

Wickham, C. 2005. *Framing the Early Middle Ages: Europe and the Mediterranean 400–800.* Oxford.

Wiemer, H.-U. 1997. "Julian," in Clauss, ed. 1997: 334–41.

Wilbur, M. 1943. *Slavery in China during the Former Han Dynasty.* New York.

Williams, J., ed. 1997. *Money: A History.* London.

Wills, J. E. 1984. *Embassies and Illusions: Dutch and Portuguese Envoys to Kang-his, 1666–1687.* Cambridge, MA.

Wittfogel, K. A. 1957. *Oriental Despotism: A Comparative Study of Total Power.* New Haven.

Wolff, H. J. 1951. *Roman Law: An Historical Introduction*. Norman.

Wolfram, H. 1997. *The Roman Empire and Its Germanic Peoples*. Berkeley.

Wolkow, N. 1995. *La secte russe des castrats*. Paris.

Wolters, R. 1999. *Nummi Signati: Untersuchungen zur römischen Münzprägung und Geldwirtschaft*. Munich.

Wong, R. B. 1997. *China Transformed: Historical Change and the Limits of European Experience*. Ithaca.

Wood, E. M. 2003. *Empire of Capital*. London.

Wood, F. 1995. *Did Marco Polo Go to China?* London.

Woolf, G. 2001. "Regional Productions in Early Roman Gaul," in D. J. Mattingly and J. Salmon, eds., *Economies beyond Agriculture in the Classical World*, 49–65. London.

Wooyeal, P., and Bell, D. A. 2004. "Citizenship and State-Sponsored Physical Education: Ancient Greece and Ancient China," *Review of Politics* 66: 7–34.

Wyke, M., and Hopkins, A. 2005. *Roman Bodies*. London.

Xie Guihua, Li Junming, and Zhu Guozhao 1987. *Juyan Hanjian shiwen hexiao*. Beijing.

Yang Bin 2004. "Horses, Silver, and Cowries: Yunnan in Global Perspective," *Journal of World History* 15: 281–322.

Yang Lien-sheng 1961. *Studies in Chinese Institutional History*. Cambridge, MA.

Yao Shumin and Wang Dan 2003. "Das Chinese Numismatische Museum zu Gast in Wien," in Seipel, ed. 2003: 11–24.

Yates, R. 1999. "Early China," in K. Raaflaub and N. Rosenstein, eds, *War and Society in the Ancient and Medieval Worlds: Asia, the Mediterranean, Europe, and Mesoamerica*, 7–46. Cambridge, MA.

Yates, R. D. S. 1987. "Social Status in the Ch'in: Evidence from the Yun-meng Legal Documents. Part One: Commoners," *Harvard Journal of Asiatic Studies* 47: 197–237.

Yates, R. D. S. 1994. "Boundary Creation and Control Mechanisms in Early China," in J. Hay, ed., *Boundaries in China,* 56–80. London.

Young, G. K. 2001. *Rome's Eastern Trade: International Commerce and Imperial Policy, 31 BC–AD 305*. London.

Yü Ying-shih 1967. *Trade and Expansion in Han China: A Study in the Structure of Sino-Barbarian Economic Relations*. Berkeley.

Yü Ying-shih 1986. "Han Foreign Relations," in Twitchett and Loewe, eds., 1986: 377–462.

Zhang Xiande 1985. "Ji gedu chutude yuanxing jinbing—jianlun Handai lintijin, matijin," *Wenwu* 1985, 12.

Zhangjiashan 2001. *Zhangjiashan 247 hao Hanmu zhujian zhengliu xiazu*. Beijing.

Zhao Dingxin 2006. *Dong Zhou zhanzheng yu rufa guojia de xingcheng*. Shanghai.

Zhou Yiqun 2004. "Kin and Companions: Gender and Sociability in Ancient China and Greece." PhD thesis, University of Chicago.

Zhu Huo 1992. *Guqian xindian*. Xian.

Zuiderhoek, A. 2007. "The Ambiguity of Munificence," *Historia* 56: 196–213.

Zuiderhoek, A. J. 2006. "Citizens, Elites and Benefactors: The Politics of Public Generosity in Roman Asia Minor." PhD thesis, University of Groningen.

Index

currency, 156, 180. *See also* coinage; money
  circulation of, 204
  overvaluation of, 150, 152, 153, 163, 196
  reforms by Wang Mang Emperor, 150–54,
    193, 196
  standardized, 15, 137
currency system, metal supply and, 181

Daoism, 21, 54, 60
death penalty, 67, 68, 71
  odium and, 69–70
decadence, 96
deceit, in warfare, 41
decentralization, of political/military
    power, 22
defense, 45
denarius, coinage, 171, 172, 173, 206
despotism, 59, 67
Dettenhofer, Maria, 7, 8
dichotomy, formal, 4
dictatorship, 35
Dio Chrysostomus, 100, 102, 118
Diocletian, Emperor, 47
districts
  administrative, 11, 26
  conscription, 16
  organization into, 15
divergence, 11
  great, 8, 12, 15
  in state-formation, 28–29
Domitian, Emperor, 86
Dong Zhongshu, 68–69, 73
dowager empress, 88, 90–91, 92
Duncan-Jones, Richard, 201
Dynastic Histories, 88
dynasty(ies)
  annihilation of, 29
  Han, 45
  immigrant, 49
  Liu, 56, 62, 71
  Tang, 14, 62, 179
  Xin, 150

Eastern Han empire, 44
ecology, 12
economy, 8, 17, 37
  of agrarian empire, 100, 101–2
  agricultural, 114, 115
  crisis in, 117
  peasants as backbone of, 111
  punishment and, 77–79
  of scale, 106, 108
  warfare and, 27–28
  wealth of elite and, 22

education, 4, 37, 75
  vs. force, 68
Eisenstadt, Shmuel, 7, 53, 104
election, 28
  to magistracies, 38
elite(s), 4, 9, 16, 53
  autonomy from, 22
  breaking power of, 15
  economy and wealth of, 22
  established, 118–19
  estates of, 132
  gifts from, 132, 134, 135
  gifts to, 127
  local, 13, 14, 19, 28
  punishments and, 52, 73, 75
  resources controlled by, 22
  rights of, 58
  synthesis of foreign/local, 20
  treason and, 70
Elvin, Mark, 101
emperor(s)
  Arcadius, 97
  Augustus, 35–36, 39, 47, 57, 93
  as benefactor, 123
  as chief of military, 40, 42
  Claudius, 93, 94, 95, 96
  coemperors and, 47
  Constantine, 78
  Constantius II, 97
  Diocletian, 47
  Domitian, 86
  exalted status of, 47
  First, 15, 57, 90
  Gaozu, 56, 90
  Jingdi, 80
  Julian, 97, 98
  law and, 61–64, 66
  Maximus, 97
  power of, 22, 53, 132
  public appearance of, 133
  seclusion of, 47
  Theodosius, 63, 65, 97
  Valentinian I, 64–65
  Wang Mang, 16, 150–54, 161, 165, 168, 193,
    196, 200
  Wendi, 63, 69, 71, 72, 73–75, 145
  Wudi, 43, 44, 62, 65, 76, 88, 105, 147, 165,
    193, 196
  Xuandi, 80
  Yuandi, 80
empire(s). *See also* Roman empire; tributary
    empire; *specific empire*
  Achaemenid, 6n9
  Eastern Han, 44

CPSIA information can be obtained at www.ICGtesting.com
Printed in the USA
LVOW110725031112

305700LV00002B/17/P

9 780199 758357